This *Handbook*, along with the National Trust's website at **nationaltrust.org.uk**, provides the complete guide for members and visitors to 534 places to visit in England, Wales and Northern Ireland in 2016.

D0608826

Welcome to your 2016 *Handbook*

You'll find more than 500 places in this *Handbook*. Each one features a brief description of the stories and scenery that make it special. Plus some handy information to help you make the most of your visits. Here's what it all means…

This table shows you when places are open

Example place		M	T	W	T	F	S	S
House								
11 Feb–4 Nov	11–5	M	T	W	T	F	S	S
5 Nov–28 Nov	11–5	M	T	W	T	F	S	S
1 Dec–9 Dec	10:30–4:30	M	T	W	T	F	S	

Last entry to house and tea-room 20 minutes before closing.

These are seasonal opening times.
A letter means the place or facility is **open** on this day.
A grey dot means it's **closed**.
Any special notes about opening times are also shown down here.

These symbols tell you a bit about the place. You'll find them above its description

1939	Acquisition date
	Historic house
	Castle/fort
	Church/chapel
	Watermill
	Windmill
	Other buildings
	Public house
	Archaeological site
	Farm/farm animals
	Garden
	Countryside/park
	Coast
	Nature reserve
	Places to stay
	Campsite
	Licensed for weddings
	Available for functions

These symbols tell you about accessibility. You'll find them towards the bottom of each listing

	Designated parking
	Drop-off point
	Transfer available
	Accessible toilet
	Catering accessible
	Shop accessible
	Induction loop
	Photograph album
	Virtual tour
	Seats/seating available
	Braille (guide or menu)
	Large print (guide or menu)
	Steps/uneven terrain
	Ramped access or slopes
	Level access/terrain, paths
	Lifts
	Stairclimber
	Stairlift
	Narrow corridors
	Wheelchairs available
	Accessible route and/or map available
	Powered mobility vehicle

How to get there

At the start of each section, there's a simple map of the most popular places in that area. Each listing includes the place's address. You'll also see Sat Nav details for those out-of-the-way places where postcodes can be a bit misleading.

The postcodes listed under Sat Nav will take you near to a place, but not necessarily to it, so please look out for signs and be prepared to use road maps.

If you would like more comprehensive directions for all these places, along with detailed maps like those found in previous *Handbooks*, please order our free *Getting Here* guide. You can request your copy by calling 0344 800 1895 or visiting **nationaltrust.org.uk/gettinghere2016**

Alternatively, here are some useful resources to help you plan your journey:

By car: rac.co.uk/route-planner

By bike: sustrans.org.uk or 0117 926 8893

By train: nationalrail.co.uk or 03457 484950

By taxi (from a station): traintaxi.co.uk

By public transport (England, Wales and Scotland): traveline.info or 0871 200 2233

By public transport (Northern Ireland): translink.co.uk or 028 9066 6630

By public transport (London): tfl.gov.uk or 0343 222 1234

Please note

To give you time to enjoy your visit, last entry is **30 minutes before the closing times** shown in the opening arrangements tables, unless stated otherwise. Due to special events and adverse conditions, opening times sometimes change at short notice, so please **always check the online property page** before you leave, ideally on the day of your visit.

Everything you need to plan your visit

Handbook
Discover more than 500 places we look after

Website
Take a closer look by visiting **nationaltrust.org.uk**

Getting Here **guide**
Want printed directions and maps? Request your free copy on 0344 800 1895 or visit **nationaltrust.org.uk/gettinghere2016**

app
500+ places in your pocket. Just search 'National Trust' in your app store

Land Map
This interactive map shows when and how places came into our care. It also tells the story behind 300+ war memorials. Visit **ntlandmap.org.uk**

Social Media
Ask questions, share your experiences or just say 'hi'

Need help? Call us on 0344 800 1895 (9 to 5:30 weekdays, 9 to 4 weekends)

3

Make more of your membership

Your membership card gives you free, unlimited access to most of the places we look after during normal opening hours. Just bring it along with you every time you visit.

By displaying the sticker from the front of this *Handbook*, you're also entitled to free car parking (just make sure you've got your membership card with you too).

And that's not all you get from being a member…

Visit special places abroad

We are part of the International National Trusts Organisation (INTO), a global network of charities and foundations which look after heritage sites of natural and historical importance. This means your current membership card may entitle you to free or discounted entry to other places looked after by INTO members.

For a full list of participating nations, visit **nationaltrust.org.uk/overseas-visitors/ overseas-organisations**

Entry to places owned by us but maintained by English Heritage or Cadw is also free to our members. If this is the case, it will be stated in the entry's Important Note.

Carers go free

Carers and essential companions of disabled visitors also enjoy free entry to all places on request.

To make things easier, you can order an annual Admit One Card by calling 0344 800 1895 or emailing **enquiries@nationaltrust.org.uk**

Bring your dog too

We offer a warm welcome to all visitors, whether they've got two legs or four. To make sure your dog enjoys their visit as much as you, we provide water bowls, exercise areas and shady spaces at many of the places we look after.

If you are bringing your dog, please help us protect the local wildlife and livestock by looking out for Rangers' notices in car parks. Please also keep dogs on a lead when crossing fields between 1 March and 31 July, or any time grazing animals are nearby.

Get snap happy

You are very welcome to take photographs during your visits. If you are a keen photographer, you can even arrange to take interior photographs of many places outside normal opening hours. Simply put the request in writing to the property, giving your address (a fee may apply).

Please note that during normal opening hours, we kindly ask that you respect other visitors and refrain from using a flash or tripod indoors. Prior permission may also be required to photograph items that are on loan to us.

Finally, please be aware that, for safety reasons, amateur drone flying is not permitted at any of the places we look after.

Access

The symbols on page 2 indicate the access and facilities at each place.

Please ring before your visit in case a particular provision needs to be booked.

Other ways to support the National Trust

As a charity, we rely on membership fees to look after special places for ever, for everyone. So from everyone who loves these places, and everyone who ever will, thank you. If you'd like to do more, here are some other ways you can support the places that matter to you.

Events
From live music and open-air theatre to organised sports and conservation walks, we have a busy programme of events. Find out what's happening near you at **nationaltrust.org.uk/visit/whats-on/events**

Volunteering
We wouldn't exist without the passion and hard work of thousands of volunteers. If you'd like to learn some new skills, share your experience, and find rewarding work, please visit **nationaltrust.org.uk/get-involved/volunteer**

Donations
Every penny helps us look after places of natural beauty and historic importance. From supporting an appeal to leaving a gift in your Will, see how you can help at **nationaltrust. org.uk/get-involved/donate**

Supporter groups
Our supporter groups find enjoyable ways to raise funds. From group talks to group walks, enjoying days out to organising social events, find out more at **nationaltrust. org.uk/get-involved/volunteer/ways- to-volunteer/supporter-groups**

Heritage Lottery Fund
Using money raised through the National Lottery, the Heritage Lottery Fund (HLF) has awarded grants totalling £100 million to the National Trust in the last 20 years. Through these donations, it has supported many of our most important projects, including Tyntesfield, the Giant's Causeway, Knole and Castle Drogo.

If you would like to know more please visit **hlf.org.uk**

The Royal Oak Foundation
Through the generous support of its members and donors across the USA, Royal Oak makes grants to the National Trust. Royal Oak members enjoy free access to National Trust places as well as lectures and tours in the USA.

For more information please visit **royal-oak.org**

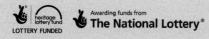

heritage lottery fund
LOTTERY FUNDED

Awarding funds from
The National Lottery

Have your say

Annual General Meeting
Our Annual General Meeting (AGM) each autumn is an opportunity for you to meet our Trustees and staff, ask questions and contribute to debates. Most importantly, you can exercise your right to vote on both resolutions and elections to our Council.

You can also vote online and watch the live AGM webcast. There will be more details in the autumn magazine and on our website **nationaltrust.org.uk/agm**

Governance
A guide to the Trust's governance arrangements is available on our website **nationaltrust.org.uk/about-us** and on request from The Secretary.

Our Annual Report and Financial Statements are available online at **nationaltrust.org. uk/annualreport** and on request from **annualreport@nationaltrust.org.uk**

Privacy policy

The National Trust makes every effort to comply with the principles of the Data Protection Act 1998. The National Trust's Privacy Policy sets out the ways in which we process personal data. The full Privacy Policy is available on our website **nationaltrust.org.uk**

Use of personal information
Personal information provided to the National Trust via our website, membership forms, fundraising responses, emails and telephone calls will be used for the purposes outlined at the time of collection or registration in accordance with the preferences you express.

By providing personal data to the National Trust you consent to the processing of such data by the National Trust as described in the full Privacy Policy. You can alter your preferences as explained in the following paragraph.

Verifying, updating and amending your personal information
If, at any time, you want to verify, update or amend your personal data or preferences please write to:

National Trust, Supporter Services Centre, PO Box 574, Manvers, Rotherham, S63 3FH

Verification, updating or amendment of your personal data will take place within 28 days of receipt of your request.

If subsequently you make data protection instruction to the National Trust which contradicts a previous instruction (or instructions), then the Trust will follow your most recent instructions.

Subject access requests
You have the right to ask us, in writing, for a copy of all the personal data held about you (a 'subject access request').

There's a payment fee of £10. To access your personal data held by the National Trust, please apply in writing to:

The Data Protection Officer, National Trust, Heelis, Kemble Drive, Swindon, Wiltshire, SN2 2NA.

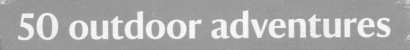

50
**THINGS TO DO
BEFORE YOU'RE**
11¾

50 outdoor adventures

With help from kids all over the country, we've put together a list of great challenges for you; the ultimate 50 things to do before you're 11¾, and we're making it as easy as mud pie for you to do them.

Visit the website to join in the fun for free

nationaltrust.org.uk/50things

Flying a kite, no. 7 of 50 things to do before you're 11¾, at Bateman's, East Sussex.

Cornwall

Botallack, Cornwall

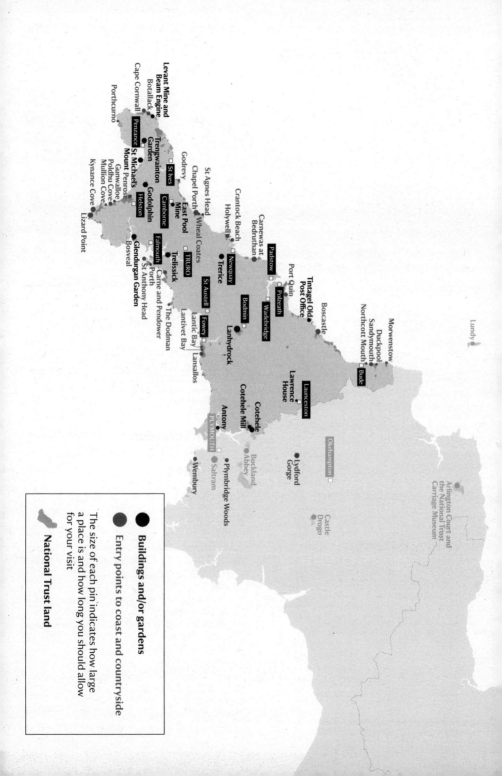

Levant Mine and
Beam Engine
Botallack
Cape Cornwall
Porthcurno

Penzance
Trengwainton
Garden
St Michael's
Mount

St Ives

Godrevy
Chapel Porth
St Agnes Head

Carnewas at
Bedruthan
Holywell
Crantock Beach

Camborne
Godolphin
Helston

East Pool
Mine
Wheal Coates

Newquay

Padstow

Port Quin
Polzeath

Tintagel Old
Post Office

Boscastle

Morwenstow
Northcot Mouth
Sandymouth
Duckpool

Lundy

Gunwalloe
Poldhu Cove
Mullion Cove
Kynance Cove
Lizard Point

Penrose

Glendurgan Garden
Bosveal

Falmouth
Trelissick
St Anthony Head
Carne and Pendower
Porth
The Dodman
Lantic Bay
Lantivet Bay
Lansallos

TRURO

St Austell

Trerice

Bodmin
Wadebridge

Lanhydrock

Fowey

Lawrence
House
Launceston

Bude

Cotehele
Cotehele Mill

Antony

PLYMOUTH

Wembury

Saltram

Plymbridge Woods

Buckland
Abbey

Castle
Drogo

Lydford
Gorge

Okehampton

Arlington Court and
the National Trust
Carriage Museum

Buildings and/or gardens

Entry points to coast and countryside

The size of each pin indicates how large
a place is and how long you should allow
for your visit

National Trust land

Exploring the magical garden at Antony, where there are sculptures, as well as a knot garden and topiary, to discover

Antony

Torpoint, Cornwall PL11 2QA

🏠 ⚙ 🎫 **1961**

Still the family home of the Carew Poles after hundreds of years, this beautiful early 18th-century house has fine collections of paintings, furniture and textiles. The landscape garden offers sweeping views to the River Lynher and includes a formal garden with topiary, a knot garden and sculptures. **Note**: members admitted free to Woodland Garden (not National Trust) only when house is open.

Eating and shopping: self-service tea-room offering light lunches and afternoon tea. Picnics welcome in the grounds. Gift shop with souvenirs, plants and local produce. Small second-hand bookshop.

Making the most of your day: Indoors Quizzes and trails. **Outdoors** Garden and family events. Modern sculpture throughout garden and Woodland Garden. Games and croquet on lawn. Quizzes and trails. **Dogs**: assistance dogs only.

Access: 🅿️🚪🏛️♿🛗🎥📷📶
House 🏠♿ **Grounds** 🏠➡️♿
Parking: 250 yards.

Finding out more: 01752 812191 or antony@nationaltrust.org.uk

Antony		M	T	W	T	F	S	S
Garden, shop and tea-room								
29 Mar–31 May	12–5*		·	T	W	T	·	·
1 Jun–31 Aug	12–5*		·	T	W	T	·	S
1 Sep–27 Oct	12–5*		·	T	W	T	·	·
Woodland Garden (not National Trust)								
1 Mar–30 Oct	11–5:30		·	T	W	T	·	S	S

*House opens at 1. Timed ticket entry to house. Also open Good Friday and Easter Sunday, Sundays 1 and 29 May and Bank Holiday Mondays.

Boscastle

North Cornwall coast, near Camelford

🎫🏛️🛏️ **1955**

There has been a fishing and trading port here for centuries and you can still watch boats come and go between the high cliffs that guard the snaking harbour entrance. Much of Boscastle can be discovered on foot, with footpaths leading in all directions. You can walk in the footsteps of the young Thomas Hardy through the wildlife-rich ancient woodland in the Valency Valley, or explore the rare medieval field system known as 'the Forrabury Stitches' high above the village. Nearby is the striking lookout building on Willapark headland, and the historic churches of Minster and Forrabury. **Note**: toilet by main car park (not National Trust).

Eating and shopping: harbourside café with courtyard seating. Large shop and visitor centre offering a wide range of gifts (many locally produced) plus a wealth of guides and information about local history including a short film about the 2004 flood. Free wi-fi throughout.

Making the most of your day: children's quiz/trail. Coasteering available nearby. Holiday cottages. Combine with a visit to Tintagel Old Post Office, just a few miles along the coast. **Dogs**: welcome on walks and in café courtyard.

Access: 🚾 ♿ 🅿 Grounds 🦽
Sat Nav: use PL35 0HD. **Parking**: 100 yards, pay and display, not National Trust (charge including members).

Finding out more: 01840 250010 or boscastle@nationaltrust.org.uk

Boscastle
Shop, café and visitor centre
Open every day all year*

*Opening times vary throughout year, ranging from 10:30 to 4 in winter to 10 to 5:30 in high summer. Closed 25 and 26 December.

The twisting natural inlet at Boscastle, with the harbour village sheltering at its far end

Bosveal

near Mawnan Smith, Falmouth, Cornwall

🏛 ♿ 🅿 ⌂ | 1980 |

Many walks help you discover woodland valleys, secluded coves and the sheltered shores of the Helford River and Falmouth Bay. **Note**: toilets and other facilities at nearby Glendurgan Garden. For Sat Nav use TR11 5JR.

Finding out more: 01326 252020 or bosveal@nationaltrust.org.uk

Botallack

on the Tin Coast, near St Just, Cornwall

🏕 🍴 🏛 ♿ 🅿 ⌂ 🔔 ☕ | 1995 |

On a wild Atlantic coast transformed by tin and copper mining, the famed Crowns engine houses cling to the foot of the cliffs. Once a busy industrial landscape, it's now part of the Cornish Mining World Heritage Site and the Tin Coast. Recent location for mining scenes in BBC's *Poldark*. **Note**: numerous mine shafts and mining remains – please keep to paths and tracks.

Making the most of your day: plenty of mining remains to explore and dramatic coastal views. Geocaches. Easy walk along the clifftop to Levant Mine and steaming Cornish beam engine. Displays in Botallack workshop. **Dogs**: welcome everywhere on short leads. Drinking bowl and water available.

Access: 🅿 🅿 🚾 ♿
Sat Nav: use TR19 7QQ. Beware, some Sat Navs misdirect. Keep to the B3306 until you reach Botallack village. **Parking**: just beyond Botallack Count House.

Finding out more: 01736 791543 or botallack@nationaltrust.org.uk

Cape Cornwall

on the Tin Coast, near St Just, Cornwall

🏛 🏖 ⛰ 🛏 1987

The distinctive hump of Cape Cornwall on the Tin Coast

Known as the connoisseur's Land's End, the distinctive headland of Cape Cornwall is part of a wild and rugged landscape, rich in tin-mining history and part of the Cornish Mining World Heritage Site. Views to Longships Lighthouse and Isles of Scilly. Seabirds, including puffins, nest on the Brisons rocks. **Note**: narrow lanes, unsuitable for caravans. Seasonal toilets at Cape Cornwall.

Eating and shopping: from Easter to end October, mobile snack van in Cape Cornwall car park offering tea, coffee, sandwiches and amazing homemade cakes and scones. Nearby St Just has several shops, stores, pubs and a post office (none National Trust).

Making the most of your day: perfect beach for rock-pooling and wild swimming. Local crab and lobster fishermen still use Priest's Cove. Coast path goes by Ballowall Barrow and the Coastwatch hut. **Dogs**: welcome, but under control near livestock.

Access: 🏛

Sat Nav: use TR19 7NN for Cape Cornwall car park. **Parking**: at Cape Cornwall, Porth Nanven (Cot Valley) and Ballowall.

Finding out more: 01736 791543 or capecornwall@nationaltrust.org.uk

Carne and Pendower

near Veryan, Cornwall

🏛 🏖 ⛰ 🛏 1961

Two of the best beaches on the Roseland peninsula: fine stretches of sand and rock pools, popular with families. Walks along the coast and inland reveal the area's wildlife – great for butterflies in summer and birds in winter. Lots of history to discover nearby, from Bronze Age to Cold War. **Note**: seasonal toilets in both car parks.

Eating and shopping: Tea by the Sea van at Carne (concession) serves tea, cake and tempting treats. Nearby is the Hidden Hut at Porthcurnick Beach (tenant-run) and the Thirstea Company van at Porth (concession) – all are seasonal with outdoor seating.

Making the most of your day: the beaches are ideal for swimming and rock-pooling. A path leads inland to Carne Beacon, one of Britain's largest Bronze Age barrows. Downloadable walking trails cover the wider area. **Dogs**: seasonal dog restrictions on beaches (please keep under control near livestock).

Access: 🦽

Sat Nav: for Carne use TR2 5PF; Pendower TR2 5PF (turn right at sign for Pendower Beach). **Parking**: car parks at both Carne and Pendower.

Finding out more: 01872 580553 or carne@nationaltrust.org.uk

Pendower Beach on the Roseland peninsula, with the backdrop of Nare Head

Carnewas at Bedruthan

near Padstow, Cornwall

1930

Since Victorian times this has been one of the most popular destinations on the Cornish coast, known for its spectacular clifftop views of giant rock stacks striding across Bedruthan Beach (not National Trust). Those with a head for heights can climb down the cliff staircase to the beach (closed during the winter) but beware of being cut off by the tide. For a longer walk, follow the coast path to Park Head and the sheltered cove of Porth Mear beyond. Carpets of spring and autumn squill bedeck these clifftops and birds nesting from March include linnets, stonechats and skylarks.
Note: unsafe to enter the sea here at any time. Toilet not always available.

Eating and shopping: shop offering a range of gifts, many locally sourced and produced, and popular tea-room (concession) with adjoining clifftop tea-garden. Picnic area.

Making the most of your day: children's quiz, walks leaflet and information panel. Simple play area. Bunkhouse and holiday cottages at Park Head. Why not combine with a visit to Trerice (approximately 9 miles away)?
Dogs: welcome under control.

Access: **Car park and cliff top**
Sat Nav: use PL27 7UW. **Parking**: on site.

Finding out more: 01637 860563 or carnewas@nationaltrust.org.uk

Carnewas at Bedruthan		M	T	W	T	F	S	S
Tea-room*								
13 Feb-24 Mar	11-4	M	T	W	T	F	S	S
25 Mar-30 Oct	10:30-5	M	T	W	T	F	S	S
27 Dec-31 Dec	11-4	·	T	W	T	F	S	·
Shop								
13 Feb-21 Feb	11-4	M	T	W	T	F	S	S
27 Feb-6 Mar	11-4	·	·	·	·	·	S	S
12 Mar-18 Mar	11-4	M	T	W	T	F	S	S
19 Mar-30 Oct	10:30-5	M	T	W	T	F	S	S

Cliff staircase closed from 31 October to mid-February.
*Telephone 01637 860701 to confirm opening times in winter.

Looking across Bedruthan Steps towards Park Head: these spectacular clifftop views have drawn visitors since Victorian times

For information about getting to National Trust places, please see page 3

Chapel Porth Beach, near St Agnes,
loved by families and surfers of all ages

Chapel Porth

near St Agnes, Cornwall

🏖️ 📶 1956

Nestled at the foot of a steep valley between high heathery cliffs, which turn a dazzling purple and yellow in late summer, Chapel Porth Beach is just a shingle strip at high tide but transforms into a huge expanse of sand at low tide. Now a popular family and surfing beach, Chapel Porth is steeped in mining history, with the remains of tin-processing buildings to be seen in the car park. Just up the valley you can discover what's left of Charlotte United Mine. Children love to splash in the stream and all ages love the famous hedgehog ice-cream. **Note**: seasonal toilets. Take care not to get cut off by incoming tide. Seasonal lifeguards.

Eating and shopping: Chapel Porth Beach café open daily in summer and most winter weekends (01872 552487). Picnics welcome. Pubs, cafés and shops nearby in St Agnes (none National Trust).

Making the most of your day: this is great walking country – footpaths link you with Porthtowan and St Agnes Head and the World Heritage Site mine buildings at Charlotte United, Wheal Coates and Trevellas. **Dogs**: seasonal dog ban on the beach (Easter Sunday to 30 September inclusive).

Access: 🅿️ 👶 🐕 💺 🚶
Sat Nav: use TR5 0NS. **Parking**: car park (very busy in summer).

Finding out more: 01872 552412 or chapelporth@nationaltrust.org.uk

Cotehele

St Dominick, near Saltash, Cornwall PL12 6TA

🏠✝🏛❀🌿🛏🍴 1947

The Edgcumbes built their rambling granite and slate-stone home high above the River Tamar, and it remained in their family for nearly 600 years. Time has stood still here. The Hall, with its ancient timber roof and displays of weaponry, and the warren of tapestry-clad rooms beyond have changed little since Tudor times. The 5-hectare (12-acre) garden features historic daffodils, terraces, ponds and orchards with 150 local apple varieties. The Valley Garden, with medieval stewpond and dovecote, leads to Cotehele Quay – thriving in Victorian times – where you'll find 1899 Tamar sailing barge *Shamrock*, lime kilns and the Discovery Centre. **Note**: the house has no electricity, so feel free to bring a torch.

Two views of ancient Cotehele, near Saltash

Eating and shopping: restaurant near house serving hot lunches and cakes. Tea-room on quay offering light lunches, cakes and cream teas. Gift shop and plant centre. Art and craft gallery featuring West Country artists. Second-hand bookshop. Nine holiday cottages. Picnic area.

Making the most of your day: **Indoors** Just hanging? Discover the secret life of tapestries in our self-guided tour for 2016–17. First World War exhibition featuring local memories. **Outdoors** Play area. Year-round events and walks. **Dogs**: welcome throughout estate. Assistance dogs only in formal garden.

Access: 🅿♿👶♿👜🎒📷📠📿📹🅰️
Building 🚶🏛♿ **Grounds** 🚶🏛➡
Sat Nav: ignore from Tavistock, follow brown signs. **Parking**: at house and on quay.

Finding out more: 01579 351346. 01579 352711 (Barn restaurant). 01579 352713 (shop) or cotehele@nationaltrust.org.uk

Cotehele		M	T	W	T	F	S	S
House								
12 Mar–30 Oct	11–4	M	T	W	T	F	S	S
31 Oct–31 Dec*	11–4	M	T	W	T	F	S	S
Garden and estate								
Open all year	Dawn–dusk	M	T	W	T	F	S	S
Restaurant, tea-room, shop, plant sales, gallery**								
13 Feb–11 Mar	11–4	M	T	W	T	F	S	S
12 Mar–30 Oct	11–5	M	T	W	T	F	S	S
31 Oct–31 Dec	11–4	M	T	W	T	F	S	S

*Hall of house and Christmas garland only. Everything closed 25 and 26 December, except garden and estate.
**Tea-room on quay opens daily from 9 January. Restaurant opens 10:30 during main season.

Cotehele Mill

St Dominick, near Saltash, Cornwall PL12 6TA

⬛⬛⬛ 1947

A peaceful walk alongside the Morden stream from Cotehele Quay takes you to the restored 19th-century Cotehele Mill (above). On Thursdays and Sundays you can watch corn being ground into flour. Traditional woodworker and potter on site, as well as re-created wheelwright's, saddler's and blacksmith's workshops. Look out for baking days. **Note**: nearest toilets and parking at Cotehele Quay.

Eating and shopping: Cotehele flour, gifts and ice-cream for sale. The Edgcumbe tea-room at nearby Cotehele Quay serves light lunches and cream teas. Pasties available from the kiosk on the quay. Picnics welcome in meadow.

Making the most of your day: **Indoors** Events, including milling and bakery demonstrations plus dress-up days. Opportunity to mill grain at the hand quern. Interpretation boards. **Outdoors** Family trails. Two holiday cottages. **Dogs**: welcome, but assistance dogs only in bakery and mill.

Access: ⬛⬛⬛⬛⬛ Building ⬛ Grounds ⬛
Parking: by arrangement only. Shuttlebus from Cotehele house.

Finding out more: 01579 350606 (mill). 01579 351346 (Cotehele) or cotehele@nationaltrust.org.uk

Cotehele Mill		M	T	W	T	F	S	S
12 Mar–30 Sep	11–5	M	T	W	T	F	S	S
1 Oct–30 Oct	11–4:30	M	T	W	T	F	S	S

Crantock Beach

near Newquay, Cornwall

⬛ 1956

Close to Newquay, this feels like a different Cornwall: Crantock Beach is an expanse of golden sand, great for sandcastles and surfing. Wonderful walking country – through the dunes on Rushy Green, alongside the gentle waters of the Gannel Estuary, or around the headland of West Pentire, carpeted with wild flowers. **Note**: toilets at Crantock Beach open seasonally.

Eating and shopping: refreshments available at Crantock village and West Pentire. Fern Pit café (not National Trust), across the Gannel Estuary from Crantock Beach, is accessible by ferryboat at high tide during the main season or by footbridge at low tide.

Making the most of your day: surf school and board hire. Spot seals from the coast path. There are vibrant displays of summer wild flowers to discover in the fields above nearby Polly Joke Beach. **Dogs**: welcome under control everywhere, including the beach.

Access: ⬛⬛
Sat Nav: use TR8 5RN for Crantock Beach and TR8 5QS for Treago Mill. **Parking**: on site (height restriction barrier when unmanned) and at Treago Mill for Polly Joke Beach (also known as Porth Joke).

Finding out more: 01208 863046 or crantockbeach@nationaltrust.org.uk

Golden sand at glorious Crantock Beach, near Newquay

The Dodman

Penare, near Gorran Haven, Cornwall

🏛🏖🎢🚌 1919

The highest headland on Cornwall's south coast, with massive Iron Age ramparts. Great walking, wildlife and beaches on either side. **Note**: car park at Penare. For Sat Nav use PL26 6NY. Sorry no toilet.

Finding out more: 01872 580553 or thedodman@nationaltrust.org.uk

Duckpool

near Bude, Cornwall

🏖🎢 1960

Remote beach with rock pools at the mouth of the wooded Coombe Valley, overlooked by cliffs carpeted with wild flowers. **Note**: toilets open seasonally. For Sat Nav use EX23 9JN.

Finding out more: 01208 863046 or duckpool@nationaltrust.org.uk

East Pool Mine

Pool, near Redruth, Cornwall TR15 3NP

🏭🏛 1967

East Pool celebrates the extraordinary lives of the people who worked at the very heart of the Cornish Mining World Heritage Site. With two giant beam engines, preserved in their towering engine houses, this is a great place for all the family to discover the dramatic story of Cornish mining.

Eating and shopping: small shop selling gifts, including local minerals, mining and Cornish history books, and hot drinks.

Making the most of your day: hands-on exhibits and working models. Family activities and trails. Free guided tours. Trevithick Cottage, home of the celebrated Cornish engineer Richard Trevithick, is nearby at Penponds. **Dogs**: welcome in outdoor areas.

Access: 🅿🅳🦽🦽🦽🐕🚼 Taylor's Engine House 🦽 Michell's Engine House 🦽🚶 Grounds ▶ **Sat Nav**: use TR15 3ED; for Trevithick Cottage use TR14 0QG. **Parking**: parking in Morrisons superstore (far end). Also at Michell's Engine House, off A3047.

Finding out more: 01209 315027 or eastpool@nationaltrust.org.uk Trevithick Road, Pool, Cornwall TR15 3NP

East Pool Mine		M	T	W	T	F	S	S
East Pool Mine and Taylor's Engine House								
22 Mar–29 Oct	10:30–5		T	W	T	F	S	
Michell's Engine House								
22 Mar–29 Oct	12–4		T	W	T	F	S	

Open Bank Holiday Mondays and Bank Holiday Sundays (March to October), and for booked visits November to February. Trevithick Cottage opening hours vary.

Inside the winding engine house at East Pool Mine

Glendurgan Garden

Mawnan Smith, near Falmouth,
Cornwall TR11 5JZ

⬛❄🏵🏠📷 1962

Glendurgan Garden was described by its creators, the Quakers Alfred and Sarah Fox, as a 'small peace [sic] of heaven on earth'. Visitors can find out why it proved to be just this for the Foxes and their 12 children by exploring Glendurgan's three valleys, running down to the sheltered beach at Durgan on the Helford River. There's a puzzling maze, created by Alfred and Sarah to entertain the family. You can enjoy camellias, magnolias and primroses in early spring, then rhododendrons and bluebells in May, followed by the exotic greens of summer and dramatic autumn colour in the trees. **Note**: steep paths, steps, uneven terrain.

Eating and shopping: tea-house (concession) serving homemade cakes, soups, sandwiches, jacket potatoes, salads and daily changing specials. Ice-cream on sale at the beach in good weather. Shop and plant centre.

Making the most of your day: Durgan Beach on Helford River. Durgan Fish Cellar provides local information and children's activities (open in good weather). **Dogs**: assistance dogs only in garden. Walks in surrounding countryside (details available at Glendurgan).

Access: 🅿🚼♿📷🖼 Garden entrance ♿♿
Parking: on site.

Finding out more: 01326 252020 or glendurgan@nationaltrust.org.uk

Glendurgan Garden	M	T	W	T	F	S	S
13 Feb–31 Jul	10:30–5:30	·	T	W	T	F	S	S
1 Aug–4 Sep	10:30–5:30	M	T	W	T	F	S	S
6 Sep–30 Oct	10:30–5:30	·	T	W	T	F	S	S

Garden closes dusk if earlier. Open Bank Holiday Mondays.

Godolphin

Godolphin Cross, Helston, Cornwall TR13 9RE

🏠🏛🚻❄🏵🏠 2000

Glendurgan Garden (left); Godolphin farm buildings (above)

Hidden in shaded woodland, Godolphin escaped modernisation and contemporary fashions. The granite-faced terraces and sunken lawns of the Side Garden have seen little change since the 16th century, and Victorian farm buildings tell the story of Godolphin as a tenant farm. The estate, once busy with prosperous tin mines, is now part of the Cornish Mining World Heritage Site and is wonderful walking country, rich in archaeology, rare plants and wildlife. There are panoramic views from the top of Godolphin Hill. The historic house is a holiday home, where you can stay and experience the splendour that mining riches bought. **Note**: house is open to public on limited dates between holiday lets (check before visiting).

Eating and shopping: small tea-room in the Piggery serving tea, coffee, sandwiches, cakes and ice-cream. Range of local gifts and souvenirs. Picnic benches in the grassed farmyard, and blankets available to borrow from the Piggery for picnics in the orchard, garden or estate.

Making the most of your day: gardener's potting shed has information on flora and fauna. Visit the newly conserved cider house. Free guided tours, walks booklet and events. Barefoot trail Easter to October. Trengwainton Garden nearby. **Dogs**: welcome outdoors on short leads.

Access: [symbols]
House [symbols] **Garden** [symbols]
Parking: 300 yards.

Finding out more: 01736 763194 or godolphin@nationaltrust.org.uk

Godolphin		M	T	W	T	F	S	S
Garden and outbuildings								
1 Jan–30 Oct	10–5	M	T	W	T	F	S	S
31 Oct–31 Dec*	10–4	M	T	W	T	F	S	S
Estate								
Open all year	Dawn–dusk	M	T	W	T	F	S	S

*Closed 24 and 25 December. House: open first Saturday to Thursday of every month, February to October (excluding August). Also weekends 26 November to 11 December.

Exploring the Side Garden at Godolphin, near Helston

Godrevy

near Hayle, Cornwall

[symbols] 1939

Long sandy beaches on St Ives Bay with wildlife-rich cliffs and walks. Godrevy café in dunes (concession) open most days. **Note**: unstable cliffs and incoming tides. Toilets open main season only. Parking limited in wet weather and busy times. For Sat Nav use TR27 5ED.

Finding out more: 01872 552412 or godrevy@nationaltrust.org.uk

Gunwalloe

near Helston, Cornwall

[symbols] 1974

Two family-friendly sandy beaches and reedbeds rich in wildlife. Between the two coves, a medieval church shelters behind Castle Mound. **Note**: lifeguards patrol Church Cove in summer. Seasonal toilets. Dogs welcome all year at Dollar Cove, council-enforced ban at Church Cove (Easter to 1 October).

Finding out more: 01326 558423 (Rangers) or gunwalloe@nationaltrust.org.uk

Holywell

North Cornwall coast, near Newquay, Cornwall

[symbols] 1951

A classic north Cornish beach with a sweep of golden sand and a towering dune system. There's lots of history to explore, including the remains of an Iron Age castle on Kelsey Head, a Bronze Age barrow on Cubert Common and the holy well in a cave on the beach.

Surf's up at Holywell: a classic north Cornish beach

Eating and shopping: seasonal refreshments, traditional seaside shopping and pubs at Holywell and a convenience store and café year round at Cubert, 2 miles (none National Trust).

Making the most of your day: surf schools and board hire. Beach great for rock-pooling and building sandcastles. Seals can be seen from Kelsey Head. Wildlife-rich grasslands and coastline. **Dogs**: welcome everywhere, including the beach, but under close control, especially around livestock.

Access: [P] [WC] Coast [symbol]
Sat Nav: use TR8 5PF. **Parking**: on site.

Finding out more: 01208 863046 or holywell@nationaltrust.org.uk

Kynance Cove

on the Lizard peninsula, Cornwall

[symbols] 1935

One of the world's most spectacular beaches, for centuries Kynance (right) has been a magnet for adventurous tourists. The unusual geology in this part of the Lizard creates a rolling landscape of rare heathland, while on the beach – hidden among towering cliffs – are stacks, arches and islands of serpentine rock rising from white sand and turquoise water.

The caves, accessible at low tide, offer a chance to get close to the colourful serpentine. The walk down to the cove takes you through a small section of Lizard heathland that's home to some of the rarest plants and creatures in this country. **Note**: level terrain/access route applies to viewpoint only. Toilets in car park closed through winter.

Eating and shopping: café in cove (concession), with outdoor seating, open from Easter to November, serving crab sandwiches, pasties and cream teas.

Making the most of your day: try to visit at low tide when there's plenty of beach to enjoy, for building sandcastles or taking a dip in the clean turquoise water. This beach is not lifeguarded. **Dogs**: council-enforced ban on beach (7 to7, Easter to 1 October). Welcome on coast path.

Access: [P] [WC] Cove [symbol] Viewpoint [symbols]
Sat Nav: use TR12 7PJ. **Parking**: car park on cliffs above Kynance Cove.

Finding out more: 01326 561407 or kynancecove@nationaltrust.org.uk

Lanhydrock

Bodmin, Cornwall PL30 5AD

🏠 ✝ ❄ ⛵ 🍴 Ⓣ 1953

The home of the Victorian Agar-Robartes family, the house appears as if they have just popped out for tea. There are more than 50 rooms to explore and it's easy to see the contrasts between the servants' life 'downstairs' and the elegant family rooms. The extensive garden is full of colour all year and there is plenty to discover across the estate, from ancient woodlands to tranquil riverside paths. There are off-road cycle trails, with special trails for families and novice riders, and you can even hire a bike from us.

Eating and shopping: Victorian Servants' Hall restaurant, the Stables snack bar and the Park café. Shop selling local foods and gifts. Second-hand bookshop, plant centre and cycle hire.

A corner of the kitchen at Lanhydrock

Making the most of your day: **Indoors** There is a remarkable ceiling in the Long Gallery, Victorian servants' quarters and extensive kitchens to explore. **Outdoors** Garden tours, walks through the woodland, park and riverside paths, as well as a magnificent collection of magnolias, which flower all through spring. Children will love the adventure playground and family-friendly off-road cycle trails (map available).
Dogs: dog-friendly walks throughout estate (assistance dogs only in garden).

Cycling on the popular off-road trails

Access: [icons]
House [icons] Grounds [icons]
Sat Nav: use PL30 4AB (1 Double Lodges).
Parking: 600 yards.

Finding out more: 01208 265950 or
lanhydrock@nationaltrust.org.uk

Lanhydrock		M	T	W	T	F	S	S
House								
1 Mar–31 Oct	11–5:30	M	T	W	T	F	S	S
5 Nov–27 Nov*	11–4	·	·	·	·	·	S	S
1 Dec–31 Dec*	11–4	M	T	W	T	F	S	S
Garden and shop								
14 Feb–31 Dec**	10–5:30	M	T	W	T	F	S	S
Estate and cycle trails								
Open all year	Dawn–dusk	M	T	W	T	F	S	S
Refreshments and cycle hire								
1 Jan–29 Feb	10–4	M	T	W	T	F	S	S
1 Mar–31 Oct	9:30–5	M	T	W	T	F	S	S
1 Nov–31 Dec	10–4	M	T	W	T	F	S	S

*Selected rooms only. **Shop opens at 11; shop and garden
close at 4 in February, November and December. House
and shop close at 5 in March and October. Plant centre and
second-hand bookshop open daily 1 March to 31 October.
Everything closed 25 December.

The 17th-century gatehouse with the house
behind (top) and spring colour (left)

Lansallos

between Polperro and Polruan, Cornwall

🏛 🏖 ⛱ 🚻 🅰 1936

Unspoilt Lansallos, near Polperro

East of the Fowey Estuary is a long stretch of unspoilt coast loved by walkers, with abundant wild flowers and birds. Near Lansallos car park is lovely Highertown Farm Campsite for simple outdoor living, and from Lansallos church a path ambles down the valley to a west-facing sandy beach. **Note**: nearest toilets at Lantivet Bay car park.

Eating and shopping: this is a remote and undeveloped coast, perfect for picnics. Nearest shops and pubs in Polruan, Pelynt, Bodinnick and Polperro (none National Trust).

Making the most of your day: downloadable walking trails. Play trails alongside the valley path at Lansallos (and in Lantic Bay car park). Great coast for kite-flying, paddling and bathing. Trust-run campsite and holiday cottages nearby. **Dogs**: welcome, under close control around livestock.

Access: 🐾
Sat Nav: use PL13 2PX for Lansallos.
Parking: car parks at Lansallos, Lantivet Bay and Lantic Bay.

Finding out more: 01726 870146 or lansallos@nationaltrust.org.uk

Lantic Bay

near Polruan, Cornwall

🏖 ⛱ 🚻 1959

Large shingly beach on a beautiful bay, great spot for paddling and picnicking, well worth the climb back up. **Note**: sorry no toilet. Beach is down a very steep path with steps. Beware of rip tides. Nearest postcode for Sat Nav is PL23 1NP.

Finding out more: 01726 870146 or lanticbay@nationaltrust.org.uk

Lantivet Bay

between Polruan and Lansallos, Cornwall

🏖 ⛱ 🚻 🅰 1976

Great starting point for walks along this unspoilt sweep of coast, with its small rocky coves. Access to coast path. **Note**: toilets in Lantivet Bay car park (by Frogmore Farm). For Sat Nav use PL23 1NP. National Trust holiday cottages at nearby Triggabrowne Farm.

Finding out more: 01726 870146 or lantivetbay@nationaltrust.org.uk

Lawrence House

9 Castle Street, Launceston, Cornwall PL15 8BA

🏛 ♿ 1964

This Georgian town house, now a museum, hosts special exhibitions. Large display of costumes and a children's toy room. **Note**: leased to Launceston Town Council. Open weekdays 21 March to 28 October, 10:30 to 4:30 and the second Saturday of each month.

Finding out more: 01566 773277 or lawrencehouse@nationaltrust.org.uk

Levant Mine and Beam Engine

on the Tin Coast, near Pendeen, St Just, Cornwall TR19 7SX

🏠 🏛 ♨ ⚒ 1967

On the wild Cornish cliffs overlooking the Atlantic, Levant is at the heart of the Cornish Mining World Heritage Site. Uncover the story of the Tin Coast where men and boys tunnelled deep under the sea, while women and girls laboured on the surface, crushing and processing the ore. **Note**: exposed clifftop location, uneven ground.

Eating and shopping: light refreshments available, including hot and cold drinks, ice-cream and pasties. Small shop selling books, minerals, souvenirs and postcards.

Levant Mine clings dramatically to the wild cliffs of Cornwall's Tin Coast

Making the most of your day: **Indoors** Daily running of restored steam-driven beam engine. Free guided tours of mining remains. Tunnel to the man-engine shaft. Rock-breaking and mineral-washing area. **Outdoors** Waymarked walks to Geevor and Botallack. **Dogs**: welcome on leads.

Access: 🅿 🔧 🦽 ♿ 🔧 📷 ♿ ∵ ⊘ Reception 🦽 ♿ Engine house 🦽 🚻 ♿ Grounds 🦽 ➡ ♿
Parking: 328 yards.

Finding out more: 01736 786156 or levant@nationaltrust.org.uk

Levant Beam Engine		M	T	W	T	F	S	S
8 Jan–18 Mar	10:30–4	·	·	·	·	**F**	·	·
20 Mar–30 Oct	10:30–5	**M**	**T**	**W**	**T**	**F**	·	**S**
4 Nov–9 Dec	10:30–4	·	·	·	·	**F**	·	·

Engine steaming from 11.

Lizard Point

on the Lizard peninsula, near Helston, Cornwall

🏠 ♨ ⚒ 🐕 ⛵ 1935

This is mainland Britain's most southerly point, infamous as a site of shipwrecks in the past and overlooking what is still one of the busiest shipping lanes in the world. The cliffs and farmland are incredibly rich in wildlife. From the Wildlife Watchpoint (open spring to late summer) you can see seals and basking sharks, as well as the iconic Cornish choughs, which breed close by. At Bass Point, a short walk along the coast path, you'll find the tiny Lizard Wireless Station. This is dedicated to Marconi's world-changing experiments, which took place in this simple hut on the cliffs.

Eating and shopping: the highly rated Polpeor Café at Lizard Point (concession) is open all year – depending on the weather – with outside seating and great views.

Making the most of your day: take a walk along the coast path to look for marine mammals, or try one of the inland routes to search for rare plants. Polpeor Cove is good for rock-pooling. **Dogs**: welcome all around Lizard Point. Please note that in some areas livestock graze.

Access: 🅿♿🚻⛵🚶 Lizard Wireless Station ♿
Sat Nav: use TR12 7NT. **Parking**: at
Lizard Point.

Finding out more: 01326 561407 (Visitor
Services). 01326 291174 (Rangers/Wireless
Station) or lizard@nationaltrust.org.uk

Lizard Point
Telephone for opening times of the Lizard Wireless Station
at Bass Point.

Old lifeboat station at Polpeor Cove below Lizard Point

Morwenstow

near Bude, Cornwall

🏛 1956

The realm of a great Victorian character –
Parson Hawker. Hawker's Hut, driftwood-built,
is on the cliff edge near his church. **Note**: sorry
no toilets. For Sat Nav use EX23 9SR. Rectory
Tea-rooms (tenant-run) open seasonally for
cream teas and more.

Finding out more: 01208 863046 or
morwenstow@nationaltrust.org.uk

Mullion Cove

on the Lizard peninsula, near Helston, Cornwall

🏠♿🏛⛺ 1945

Originally built in the 1890s, the picturesque
harbour at Mullion Cove shelters a small fishing
fleet from powerful westerly storms.
Note: toilets are seasonal. Dogs welcome all
year. Kayaking and boat trips available.
National Trust campsite nearby at Teneriffe
Farm. For Sat Nav use TR12 7EX. Parking not
National Trust (charge including members).

Finding out more: 01326 291174 (Lizard
Rangers) or mullioncove@nationaltrust.org.uk

Northcott Mouth

near Bude, Cornwall

🏛 1981

Quiet and ruggedly beautiful, this small rocky
beach opens up to expansive sand and rock
pools as the tide drops. **Note**: sorry no toilets.
Dogs welcome everywhere, under control.
Lifeguards in high season. For Sat Nav
use EX23 9ED.

Finding out more: 01208 863046 or
northcottmouth@nationaltrust.org.uk

Penrose

near Helston, Cornwall

🏛♿🏛🐕🚂 1974

Home to Loe Pool, Cornwall's largest natural
lake, Penrose is a mix of woods, farmland,
parkland, cliffs and beaches: a great place to
explore. There are 16 miles of bridleways and
footpaths, including a trail around the pool and
many coast path links. **Note**: no watercraft on
the pool to maintain the sense of peace.

Running along one of the many paths at Penrose

Eating and shopping: Stables Café with parkland views (open daily, Easter to November, and at weekends all year). Picnics welcome in the neighbouring walled garden.

Making the most of your day: you can hire a bike at Helston, try the easy-access route from Helston to the café, or pick a downloadable trail to follow. Free Outdoors Guide and maps available. **Dogs**: welcome, please note livestock often graze in the fields.

Access: Helston Drive 🔾 ➡
Sat Nav: use TR13 0RD for Penrose Hill; TR13 0RA for Helston Drive. **Parking**: around Loe Pool (use Penrose Hill for Stables Café), and the Fairground car park (not National Trust) in Helston for Helston Drive.

Finding out more: 01326 558423 (Rangers) or penroseestate@nationaltrust.org.uk

Penrose			M	T	W	T	F	S	S
Stables Café									
25 Mar–30 Oct	10–4:30		**M**	**T**	**W**	**T**	**F**	**S**	**S**

Also open weekends and school holidays outside main season (telephone 01326 562353).

Poldhu Cove

on the Lizard peninsula, near Helston, Cornwall

🏠 🛍 🏛 ⚓ 🏕 1984

Poldhu is an unspoilt beach popular with locals and visitors. The beach, dunes and reed-beds are designated as a Site of Special Scientific Interest for their rich wildlife. South of the cove the Marconi Monument and visitor centre celebrate Poldhu's role as the site of the first transatlantic wireless signal. **Note**: car park and toilets not National Trust. Members pay for parking.

Eating and shopping: the café at Poldhu Beach is open all year (not National Trust).

Making the most of your day: popular surf school offers lessons for all the family. Want to stay in the area a bit longer? A National Trust campsite is close by at Teneriffe Farm, near Mullion. **Dogs**: council-enforced ban on beach (7 to7, Easter to 1 October). Welcome on coast path.

Access: ♿ Marconi Centre 🔾 🔾 ➡
Sat Nav: use TR12 7BU. **Parking**: on site (not National Trust).

Finding out more: 01326 291174 or poldhucove@nationaltrust.org.uk

Fun in the sand at unspoilt Poldhu Cove, near Helston

Port Quin

near Wadebridge, Cornwall

🏚️ 🛏️ 1936

Doyden Point at Port Quin, near Polzeath

Once a busy fishing port, Port Quin is now a peaceful sheltered inlet on an outstanding stretch of unspoilt coast. Nearby are the headlands of Pentire and the Rumps, with spectacular views and wild flowers; Lundy Bay at the foot of a wildlife-filled valley; and Pentireglaze Haven with great rock-pooling. **Note**: nearest toilets in Polzeath, 3 miles (not National Trust).

Eating and shopping: pubs, cafés and shops in Polzeath (not National Trust).

Making the most of your day: seals, rare bats, corn buntings and puffins to spot. Well-preserved Iron Age ramparts on the Rumps. Quirky Doyden Castle is a Trust holiday cottage. Sea kayaking and coasteering available. **Dogs**: welcome under control. Seasonal dog ban on Polzeath Beach (including Pentireglaze Haven).

Access: Coast and beach 🏃
Sat Nav: use PL29 3SU for Port Quin; PL27 6QY Pentireglaze and Pentire Farm; PL27 6QZ Lundy Bay. **Parking**: at Port Quin, Pentire Farm, Lead Mines (Pentireglaze) and Lundy Bay. Also at Polzeath (not National Trust).

Finding out more: 01208 863046 or portquin@nationaltrust.org.uk

Porth

on the Roseland peninsula, near Portscatho, Cornwall

🛶 🏚️ 🛏️ 1958

Creekside and coastal footpaths make for great walking and wildlife spotting. Towan Beach, close to Porth, is perfect for children. **Note**: for Sat Nav use TR2 5EX. Thirstea Company van (seasonal concession) serves drinks, cakes, sandwiches and ice-cream.

Finding out more: 01872 580553 or porth@nationaltrust.org.uk

Porthcurno

near Penzance, Cornwall

🍴 🏛️ 🛶 🏚️ 1994

Soft, white shell beach with popular freshwater stream, surrounded by turquoise seas. Great for watching birds, basking sharks and dolphins. **Note**: for Sat Nav use TR19 6JU. Parking and toilets not National Trust (charge including members).

Finding out more: 01736 791543 or porthcurno@nationaltrust.org.uk

St Agnes Head

near St Agnes, Cornwall

🏛️ 💺 📷 | 1967 |

A brilliant patchwork of yellow gorse and purple heather carpets this dramatic coastal landscape. Just inland is St Agnes Beacon. **Note**: nearest café and toilets at Chapel Porth. For Sat Nav use TR5 0NU.

Finding out more: 01872 552412 or stagneshead@nationaltrust.org.uk

St Anthony Head

on the Roseland peninsula, near Portscatho, Cornwall

🏛️ 💺 📷 🛏️ | 1959 |

This headland at the eastern entrance to Falmouth harbour has been strategically important for centuries. It commands magnificent views up the Fal Estuary and across Falmouth Bay towards the Lizard, and there are still plenty of historic fortifications of various eras to be explored.

Eating and shopping: many wonderful spots for picnicking. Nearby at Porth there's a seasonal Thirstea Company tea-van serving hot drinks, homemade cakes and ice-cream (concession).

Making the most of your day: many historic military remains to discover. There's a bird hide for spotting peregrine falcons and you can walk the coast path or scramble down to lovely Molunan Beach. **Dogs**: welcome.

Access: 🚾 ♿
Sat Nav: use TR2 5HA. **Parking**: on site.

Finding out more: 01872 580553 or stanthonyhead@nationaltrust.org.uk

View up the Fal Estuary from near St Anthony Head

St Michael's Mount

Marazion, Cornwall TR17 0HS

🏰 ✝ ✿ 🎐 1954

This iconic rocky island, crowned by a medieval church and castle, is home to the St Aubyn family and a 30-strong community of islanders. Visiting the Mount, you are immersed in history, islanders' tales and legends like the famous 'Jack the Giant Killer'. There's a subtropical terraced garden to explore, and spectacular views of Mount's Bay and the Lizard from the castle battlements. If the tide is high, you can take an evocative boat trip to the island harbour; at low tide you walk across the ancient cobbled causeway from Marazion on the mainland, as pilgrims have done for centuries. **Note**: steep climb to the castle over uneven, cobbled, historic pathway. St Aubyn Estates/National Trust partnership. Members have to pay for car parking and boat trips to the Mount at high tide.

Eating and shopping: Island Café for pasties, sandwiches and cream teas. Sail Loft for Newlyn fish, daily specials, cream teas, homemade breads and cakes. Both serve local ales and cider. Island Shop and Courtyard Shop sell local produce, jewellery, bags, arts and crafts.

Making the most of your day:
Indoors Children's quiz. Events, exhibitions. Find out more about the castle's history by asking our knowledgeable room guides. Sunday church services (Whitsun to September). **Outdoors** Garden trail for children. **Dogs**: assistance dogs only in castle and garden.

Access: 🅿 ♿ ♿ 🔼 🎨 🅰 Castle 🔼 Village ♿ ♿
Parking: numerous spaces in Marazion, opposite St Michael's Mount, not National Trust (charge including members).

Finding out more: 01736 710265 (information, tides and boats) or stmichaelsmount@nationaltrust.org.uk stmichaelsmount.co.uk Estate Office, King's Road, Marazion, Cornwall TR17 0EL

St Michael's Mount		M	T	W	T	F	S	S
Castle								
14 Feb–19 Feb	10:30–4	M	T	W	T	F	·	S
23 Feb–11 Mar	Tour	·	T	·	·	F	·	·
13 Mar–3 Jul	10:30–5	M	T	W	T	F	·	S
4 Jul–2 Sep	10:30–5:30	M	T	W	T	F	·	S
4 Sep–30 Oct	10:30–5	M	T	W	T	F	·	S
Garden								
11 Apr–1 Jul	10:30–5	M	T	W	T	F	·	·
7 Jul–2 Sep	10:30–5:30	·	·	·	T	F	·	·
8 Sep–30 Sep	10:30–5	·	·	·	T	F	·	·

Last admission 45 minutes before castle closes (enough time should be allowed for travel from mainland). 23 February to 11 March: tours 11:15 and 2:15. Castle winter opening: telephone for details.

Stunning cosmic display at St Michael's Mount (below), and the castle garden (opposite). Riding the waves at Sandymouth (right)

Sandymouth

near Bude, Cornwall

A popular destination, yet Sandymouth remains unspoilt and breathtakingly beautiful. You'll find an extreme difference between the beach at low tide – when it is a huge sweep of sand and rocky outcrops – and at high tide, when it shrinks back to a pebbly cove, backed by twisted cliffs. **Note**: toilets are seasonal.

Eating and shopping: Sandymouth Café (concession, open seasonally) has outdoor and indoor seating and also sells beach goods. Pubs, shops and cafés in Kilkhampton and Bude (none National Trust).

Making the most of your day: surf school. Fantastic rock-pooling and coastal walks. Look out for the waterfall and amazing geological formations backing the beach. You may also catch sight of skylarks, song thrushes and stonechats. **Dogs**: welcome everywhere, including the beach, but under close control (especially around livestock).

Access: 🅿️ 🚻 ♿ Coast and beach 🐾
Sat Nav: use EX23 9HW. **Parking**: on site.

Finding out more: 01208 863046 or sandymouth@nationaltrust.org.uk

Sandymouth
Café at Sandymouth open seasonally, telephone 01288 354286.

Tintagel Old Post Office

Fore Street, Tintagel, Cornwall PL34 0DB

🏠✖ 1903

One of the Trust's earliest acquisitions, this quaint house and garden was once in danger of being demolished. Dated *circa* 1380, it is a rare example of a medieval 'longhouse', modified over 600 years, yet retaining its charm. It has had many uses, most notably as a Victorian post office. **Note**: nearest toilet 54 yards in Trevena Square (not National Trust).

Eating and shopping: small souvenir shop in the Post Room selling stamps, crafts, gifts and books inspired by the Old Post Office's history. Picnics welcome in the cottage garden.

Making the most of your day: **Indoors** Events held over the season, including traditional craft workshops, baking demonstrations and school holiday entertainment. **Outdoors** Family trail, games and dressing-up. **Dogs**: assistance dogs only.

Access: 🚹🖐♿📷📹 Building 🔲🔳
Grounds 🔲🔳
Parking: in village car parks, not National Trust (charge including members). Nearest Trust parking at Glebe Cliff in Tintagel, ½ mile.

Tintagel Old Post Office: a rare medieval 'longhouse'

Finding out more: 01840 770024 or tintageloldpo@nationaltrust.org.uk

Tintagel Old Post Office		M	T	W	T	F	S	S
13 Feb–21 Feb	11–4	M	T	W	T	F	S	S
7 Mar–20 Mar	11–4	M	T	W	T	F	S	S
21 Mar–25 Sep	10:30–5:30	M	T	W	T	F	S	S
26 Sep–30 Oct	11–4	M	T	W	T	F	S	S

Trelissick

Feock, near Truro, Cornwall TR3 6QL

🏠🏛✖🍴🛏🍽🍷 1955

On its own peninsula, commanding magnificent views over the Fal Estuary, Trelissick (above) surely has one of the best natural settings of any estate in the country. There are 12 hectares (30 acres) of garden to explore, with twisting paths leading you through important collections of hydrangeas, rhododendrons and ginger lilies, together with woodland plants and herbaceous borders that provide year-round colour and interest. The wider countryside offers 5 miles of dog-friendly parkland, woodland and waterside walks, plus a beach for paddling and skimming stones. Trial opening of Trelissick House will continue during 2016, when the house will host occasional exhibitions.

Eating and shopping: Crofters licensed café open daily, with outdoor seating in courtyard. The Barn Restaurant open for Sunday lunch and available for function and event hire. Gift and plant shop. Second-hand bookshop. Cornish art and craft gallery. Six holiday cottages.

Making the most of your day: **Indoors** Don't miss the amazing views from Trelissick House. Christmas: house illuminated during evening openings. **Outdoors** Regular woodland activities and countryside events.
Dogs: welcome on woodland walks. Assistance dogs only in garden.

Access: ⃝⃝⃝⃝⃝⃝⃝⃝⃝⃝
Reception ⃝⃝ Stables ⃝⃝
Garden ⃝⃝⃝⃝⃝⃝
Parking: 30 yards.

Finding out more: 01872 862090 or trelissick@nationaltrust.org.uk

Commanding its own peninsula (below), Trelissick is famed for its garden, park and woodland, as well as waterside walks and a beach. The Water Tower in May (right)

Trelissick		M	T	W	T	F	S	S
Garden, café, shop, gallery and bookshop								
1 Jan–12 Feb	10:30–4:30	M	T	W	T	F	S	S
13 Feb–30 Oct	10:30–5:30	M	T	W	T	F	S	S
31 Oct–31 Dec	10:30–4:30	M	T	W	T	F	S	S
House trial opening								
1 Mar–30 Oct	10:30–5:30	·	T	W	T	F	S	S
Parkland and walks								
Open all year		M	T	W	T	F	S	S

Garden closes dusk if earlier. Closed 25 and 26 December. Some areas occasionally closed for private events.

Trengwainton Garden

Madron, near Penzance, Cornwall TR20 8RZ

[⛭] [♿] [1961]

Here in this warm and luxuriant garden, you can follow in the footsteps of the 1920s plant hunters to see plants that flowered in Britain for the first time. Award-winning magnolias and rhododendrons are still nurtured by those with a passion for plants, and subtropical species from around the world thrive in the shelter of the walled gardens, including a kitchen garden built to the dimensions of Noah's Ark. Winding wooded paths follow a half-mile incline to sea views across Mount's Bay, and the descent via the drive is bordered by a colourful stream garden and open meadows.

Vibrant colour at Trengwainton Garden, near Penzance

Eating and shopping: award-winning tea-room (not National Trust) in its own walled garden, with outdoor eating area. When it's chilly you can warm yourself by the woodburner in the shop, which sells local gifts, food and souvenirs. Large selection of Trengwainton plants for sale.

Making the most of your day: daily family trail. Events all year. You can visit the Dig for Victory plot and taste heritage apples in the newly extended orchard. Why not visit Godolphin on the same day? **Dogs**: welcome on leads.

Access: [icons] Reception [♿] Tea-room [♿] Garden [♿][▶][♿] **Parking**: 150 yards.

Finding out more: 01736 363148 or trengwainton@nationaltrust.org.uk

Trengwainton Garden		M	T	W	T	F	S	S
14 Feb–30 Oct	10:30–5	M	T	W	T	.	.	S

Open Good Friday. Tea-room opens at 10.

Trerice

Kestle Mill, near Newquay, Cornwall TR8 4PG

[🏠][⛭][♿][🔔][T] [1953]

It's easy to lose yourself in this small yet enchanting place as you soak up the tranquillity of Trerice, just a stone's throw from Newquay yet nestled in a peaceful corner of rural Cornwall. This romantic Elizabethan manor house tells a story of prosperous origins, decline, partial ruin and 20th-century restoration. Today, the peace and quiet of Trerice is occasionally pierced by shouts of excitement from the Bowling Green (surely you will want to try a game of kayling or slapcock?), bringing back some of the bustle and noise that must have typified its time as a busy manor house.

Eating and shopping: self-service restaurant offering morning coffee, locally produced lunches, cakes and desserts, as well as our famous lemon meringue pie. The shop sells a range of local products, souvenirs and plants.

Making the most of your day: Indoors Tudor-themed craft activities, costume days, introductory talks, living history and conservation events. Replica armour to try on. **Outdoors** Family activities and trails, Cornish 'kayles' and other traditional games. **Dogs**: welcome in car park only.

Access: 🅿♿♿♿♿♿♿♿ House ♿♿♿ Barn ♿♿ Garden ♿♿➡♿
Parking: 300 yards.

Finding out more: 01637 875404 or trerice@nationaltrust.org.uk

Trerice		M	T	W	T	F	S	S
House, garden, shop and tea-room								
27 Feb–30 Oct	10:30–5*	**M**	**T**	**W**	**T**	**F**	**S**	**S**
Great Hall, garden, shop and tea-room								
5 Nov–18 Dec	11–4	.	.	.	.	.	**S**	**S**

*House opens at 11 and closes at 4:30.

The east front of Trerice, near Newquay. This romantic Elizabethan manor house tells a tale of prosperity, decline and partial ruin, followed by 20th-century restoration

Wheal Coates

near St Agnes, Cornwall

🏚♿♿ 1956

Dramatic ruins on cliffs carpeted with heather and gorse, the old mine buildings of Wheal Coates are a Cornish icon. **Note**: nearest café and toilets at Chapel Porth. For Sat Nav use TR5 0NT.

Finding out more: 01872 552412 or whealcoates@nationaltrust.org.uk

Additional coastal and countryside car parks in Cornwall

Strangles Beach	EX23 0LQ	Reskajeage Downs	TR14 0JG	Predannack	TR12 7EZ
Glebe Cliff, Tintagel	PL34 0DL	Derrick Cove	TR14 0JG	Poltesco	TR12 7LR
Lundy Bay	PL27 6QZ	Fishing Cove	TR27 5EE	Nare Head	TR2 5PQ
Pentireglaze	PL27 6QY	Trencrom	TR27 6NP	Lamledra	
Park Head	PL27 7UU	Carn Galver	TR20 8YX	(Vault Beach)	PL26 6JS
Treago Mill (Polly Joke)	TR8 5QS	Cot Valley	TR19 7NS	Coombe Farm	PL23 1HW
St Agnes Beacon	TR5 0NU	Chyvarloe	TR12 7PY	Hendersick	PL13 2HZ

Devon
and Dorset

The Dart Estuary, as seen from Greenway, Devon

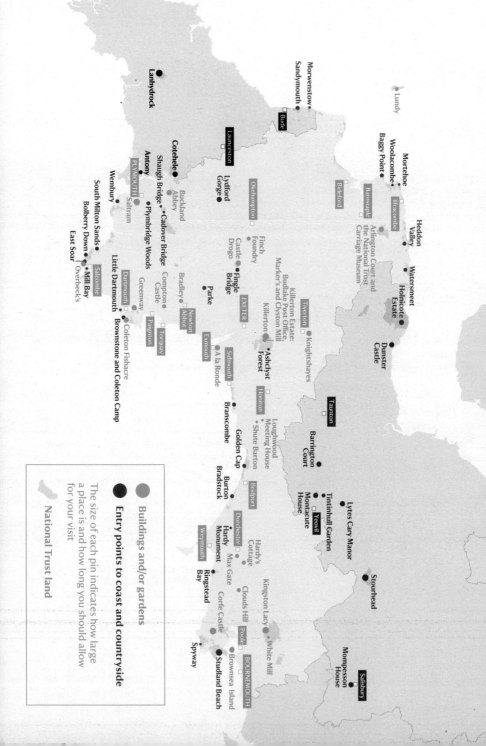

Lundy

Morwenstow
Sandymouth

Lanhydrock

Bude

Launceston

Coetehele
Antony
PLYMOUTH
Shaugh Bridge
Saltram
Wembury
South Milton Sands
Bolberry Down
East Soar
Salcombe
Mill Bay
Overbeck's

Buckland
Abbey
Cadover Bridge
Plymbridge Woods
Lydford
Gorge
Okehampton

Little Dartmouth
Dartmouth
Brownstone and Coleton Camp
Coleton Fishacre
Paignton
Torquay
Greenway
Newton
Abbot
Compton
Castle
Bradley
Parke

Mortehoe
Woolacombe
Baggy Point

Heddon
Valley
Watersmeet
Holnicote
Estate
Dunster
Castle

Ilfracombe
Arlington Court and
the National Trust
Carriage Museum
Barnstaple

Bideford

Castle
Drogo
Finch
Foundry
Fingle
Bridge
Killerton Estate:
Budlake Post Office,
Marker's and Clyston Mill
Killerton
Forest
EXETER
Ashclyst
Forest
Tiverton
Knightshayes
Taunton
Barrington
Court

Sidmouth
A la Ronde
Exmouth
Honiton
Branscombe
Golden Cap
Burton
Bradstock
Shute Barton
Loughwood
Meeting House
Bridport
Dorchester
Hardy's
Monument
Weymouth
Max Gate
Ringstead
Bay
Hardy's
Cottage
Clouds Hill
Kingston Lacy
White Mill
Corfe Castle
Poole
BOURNEMOUTH
Brownsea Island
Studland Beach
Spyway

Montacute
House
Yeovil
Tintinhull Garden
Lytes Cary Manor
Stourhead
Mompesson
House
Salisbury

A la Ronde

Summer Lane, Exmouth, Devon EX8 5BD

🏠♿ 1991

Full of creativity and treasures from around the world, this amazing 16-sided house was the work of cousins Jane and Mary Parminter in 1796. Step inside and you enter another world, one where their imaginations ran wild in design and ornamentation. They decorated walls with feathers, shells and pictures made of seaweed and sand, and every space contains mementoes from their travels. With the 360° touchscreen virtual tour, you can view the fragile shell gallery made from nearly 25,000 shells. Outside, there's a sense of harmony around the orchard, hay meadow and colourful borders, and views over the Exe Estuary. **Note**: small and delicate rooms. Photography welcome without flash.

Eating and shopping: tea-room has indoor and outdoor seating with views of the Exe Estuary. Hot and cold light lunches, homemade cakes and Devon cream teas. Picnic area in orchard. The shop features gifts, local food and keepsakes. Second-hand book sales.

A la Ronde, Devon (left and above), is full of amazing treasures from around the world

Making the most of your day: **Indoors** Self-guided tours and family trail. Gallery exhibitions. **Outdoors** Orchard, hay meadow and colourful borders. Views of Exe Estuary. Garden games and croquet. Events, including family trails and crafts. **Dogs**: dogs on leads welcome everywhere except inside house. Assistance dogs can access all areas.

Access: 🅿♿♿🅿🖼️🏠♿☕🅿
House 🏠♿🚻 Grounds 🏠➡️
Parking: on site.

Finding out more: 01395 265514 or alaronde@nationaltrust.org.uk

A la Ronde		M	T	W	T	F	S	S
30 Jan–12 Feb	Tour	M	T	W	T	F	S	S
13 Feb–21 Feb	11–5	M	T	W	T	F	S	S
22 Feb–11 Mar	Tour	M	T	W	T	F	S	S
12 Mar–30 Oct	11–5	M	T	W	T	F	S	S

Grounds, shop and tea-room open 10:30 to 5:30. Last orders in tea-room at 5. Last entry to house at 4.

Arlington Court and the National Trust Carriage Museum

Arlington, near Barnstaple, Devon EX31 4LP

🏠✝🔥❄🦽♿ 1949

Hidden in the lichen-draped landscape of North Devon, Arlington is a surprise and a delight. The house's starkly classical exterior gives no clue to what lies inside – the passions of 11 generations of the Chichester family, including shells, ships and pewter. The stable block houses a nationally important display of carriages, from grand state coaches to humble governess carts. The garden is restored to its colourful Victorian glory, and the conservatory's exotic plantings reveal the Chichesters' world travels. New 2016 exhibition: 'Happily Ever After?' explores the hidden hazards of Victorian childhood, with the supposed 'cures' sometimes worse than the illness.

Exploring the extensive estate at Arlington in Devon

Eating and shopping: seasonal produce grown in the walled garden is used in the tea-room. Reduced menu November to March. Be sure not to leave without a pot of Arlington chutney – ingredients grown on site and cooked by an award-winning producer.

Making the most of your day: **Indoors** Spy on the bats in the attic. Children's activities. **Outdoors** Bring your walking boots to explore the extensive estate, including two woodland play areas. Daily children's activities (school holidays). **Dogs**: welcome on leads in garden, Carriage Museum and wider estate.

Access: 🅿♿🦽♿♿🐕📷🎦🎨☎♿
House 🅰♿🅱 **Museum** 🅰⬆🅱 **Grounds** ➡♿🅱
Sat Nav: from South Molton, don't turn left into unmarked lane (deliveries only).
Parking: 150 yards.

Finding out more: 01271 850296 or arlingtoncourt@nationaltrust.org.uk

Arlington Court		M	T	W	T	F	S	S
13 Feb–21 Feb	11–4	M	T	W	T	F	S	S
27 Feb–6 Mar	11–4						S	S
12 Mar–30 Oct	11–5*	M	T	W	T	F	S	S
5 Nov–18 Dec	11–4						S	S

*Garden, shop and tea-room open 10:30. Grounds open dawn to dusk, all year.

Arlington's interior is full of fascinating treasures

Ashclyst Forest

near Broadclyst, Exeter, Devon

1944

One of the largest woods in East Devon, with waymarked trails for exploring. A haven for butterflies, bluebells and birds. **Note**: for Sat Nav use EX5 3DT, follow signs to Ashclyst. Part of the Killerton Estate – toilets, café and shop nearby at main Killerton car park.

Finding out more: 01392 881345 or ashclystforest@nationaltrust.org.uk

Baggy Point

near Croyde, Devon

1939

Baggy Point (above) is the impressive headland at Croyde, once owned by the Hyde family and overlooking one of the best surfing beaches in the South West. Huge coastal views, great walks and opportunities to climb, surf and coasteer make it a must-do destination for anyone visiting North Devon. **Note**: toilets (not National Trust) on main beach slipway, 500 yards from Trust car park.

Eating and shopping: Sandleigh tea-room, garden and shop (tenant-run) serving drinks and food grown in the walled garden. Open-air covered seating area overlooking garden. Tea-room is next to car park, close to beach slipway. Car park kiosk serving cold drinks and snacks.

Making the most of your day: free children's activity pack (to borrow). Walks leaflets available from car park kiosk. Arlington Court and the National Carriage Museum is nearby. **Dogs**: welcome on leads (except for seasonal ban on Croyde Beach from May to September).

Access: 🅿️ ♿ ➡
Sat Nav: use EX33 1PA. **Parking**: car park in Moor Lane, Croyde.

Finding out more: 01271 870555 or baggypoint@nationaltrust.org.uk

Baggy Point

Car park is usually staffed March to November and at busy periods, and locked at dusk.

Bolberry Down

between Salcombe and Hope Cove,
near Malborough, Devon

🏖️ ⛰️ 1938

The starting point for discovering a spectacular
stretch of coast between Salcombe and Hope
Cove, including the headlands of Bolt Head
and Bolt Tail and the sandy beach at Soar Mill
Cove. The majestic ragged cliffs have claimed
countless ships over the centuries. There's an
easy-access route over the clifftops.
Note: sorry no toilet.

Eating and shopping: refreshments and meals
available in pub and hotels in Hope Cove
(not National Trust). Walkers' Hut café
(tenant-run) at East Soar serving hot drinks
and homemade cakes.

Making the most of your day: downloadable
walks and Salcombe Estuary canoe map
guides. Canoe hire available through Singing
Paddles (not National Trust). **Dogs**: welcome
(on leads where animals grazing).

Access: 🅿️ ♿ 🚶 ➡️
Sat Nav: use TQ7 3DY. **Parking**: at Bolberry
Down and Hope Cove (not National Trust).

Finding out more: 01752 346585.
01548 561904 (Walkers' Hut) or
bolberrydown@nationaltrust.org.uk

Bradley

Totnes Road, Newton Abbot, Devon TQ12 6BN

🏛️ ✝️ ✳️ 1938

Unspoilt and fascinating medieval manor
house, still a relaxed family home, in a green
haven among riverside meadows and
woodland. Many charming original features,
such as the medieval cat hole and drip stones.
The quiet and peaceful chapel was licensed for
services in 1428. **Note**: sorry no toilet. Parking
from 10:30 on open days.

Eating and shopping: table-top shop selling
honey, souvenirs, gifts and postcards.

Making the most of your day: open-air theatre
and countryside craft events. Walks in
surrounding countryside. For a truly medieval
experience, visit nearby Compton Castle.
Dogs: welcome in meadows and woodland.
Assistance dogs only in garden and house.

Access: 🅿️ 🅿️ 🏠 🚶 👓 📷 **Building** ♿ ♿ 🚻
Grounds ♿ ♿ ➡️
Sat Nav: TQ12 1LX directs to gate lodge (follow
driveway for parking). **Parking**: in meadow
(for designated parking call 01626 354513).

Finding out more: 01803 661907 or
bradley@nationaltrust.org.uk

Bradley		M	T	W	T	F	S	S
5 Apr–29 Sep	11–5		**T**	**W**	**T**			

Branscombe

on the Jurassic Coast, near Seaton, Devon

[icons] 1965

Nestling in a valley that reaches down to the sea on East Devon's dramatic Jurassic Coast, the village of Branscombe is surrounded by picturesque countryside with miles of tranquil walking through woodland, farmland and beach. Charming thatched houses, forge and restored watermill add to the timeless magic of the place. **Note**: nearest toilets at information point, village hall and beach car park.

Eating and shopping: Old Bakery tea-room (tenant-run) serving sandwiches, homemade cakes and cream teas. Quality ironwork on sale from the Old Forge.

Making the most of your day: trail (graded as easy) winding up from the beach to the village, passing Manor Mill, Old Bakery and Old Forge. The beach is great for swimming and picnics. **Dogs**: welcome on leads in the Old Bakery garden, orchard, beach and wider countryside.

Access: [icons] Building [icons] Mill [icons] Grounds [icon]
Sat Nav: use EX12 3DB. **Parking**: next to Old Forge, limited spaces. Also village hall and beach car parks (neither National Trust).

Finding out more: 01752 346585 or branscombe@nationaltrust.org.uk

Branscombe		M	T	W	T	F	S	S
Manor Mill								
3 Apr–17 Jul	2–5							S
20 Jul–31 Aug	2–5			W				S
4 Sep–30 Oct	2–5							S
Old Forge								
Open all year	10–5*	M	T	W	T	F	S	S

*Telephone 01297 680481 to confirm forge opening times. For details of the Old Bakery tea-room opening, telephone 01297 680333.

Bradley, Devon (opposite): this unspoilt medieval manor house is still a relaxed family home

Brownsea Island (right) in Dorset, feels like another world and is perfect for a day's adventure

Brownsea Island

Poole Harbour, Poole, Dorset

[icons] 1962

The perfect day's adventure, this island wildlife sanctuary is easy to get to but feels like another world from the moment you step ashore. The island sits in the middle of Poole Harbour, with dramatic views to the Purbeck Hills. Thriving natural habitats, including woodland, heathland and a lagoon, have created havens for wildlife, such as the red squirrel and a huge variety of birds. The island is rich in history too. It is the birthplace of the Scouting and Guiding movements, and there are the remains of daffodil farming, pottery works and Maryland village to explore. **Note**: half-hourly boat service from 10 (not National Trust). Wheelchair boat service. No access to castle. Small entry fee to Dorset Wildlife Trust area (including members).

Eating and shopping: Villano Café, coffee bar and self-service drinks at the Outdoor Centre. Mobile ice-cream unit (peak periods). Engine Gift Shop selling Brownsea Island outdoors range, local produce, souvenirs and ice-cream. Scout and Guide Trading Post sells memorabilia.

Making the most of your day: family activities, tree-climbing trail, Tracker Packs and natural play area. Events. Walks and talks. Open-air theatre. Outdoor and visitor centres. Introductory walks and buggy tours for less-mobile visitors (booking advised). **Dogs**: assistance dogs only.

Access: 🚻🅿️♿🚻🐕🚗🔆📷 **Building** 🏛️
Grounds ♿🚪
Sat Nav: for Sandbanks Jetty use BH13 7QJ; for Poole Quay BH15 1HP. **Parking**: near Sandbanks and Poole Quay, not National Trust (charge including members).

Finding out more: 01202 707744 or brownseaisland@nationaltrust.org.uk

Brownsea Island		M	T	W	T	F	S	S
Hourly boat service from Poole Quay and Sandbanks*								
6 Feb–13 Mar	10–4	·	·	·	·	·	S	S
Full boat service from Poole Quay and Sandbanks								
19 Mar–30 Oct	10–5	M	T	W	T	F	S	S

Shop and Villano Café open until last boat. *Special weekend openings: boats leave every hour from Poole and Sandbanks (shop, café and visitor centre will all be open). New for winter: Poole Harbour Bird Boats from Poole Quay (booking essential).

The rugged and captivating coast at Brownstone and Coleton Camp, Devon (right)

The wildlife sanctuary of Brownsea Island, Dorset (below), sits in the middle of Poole Harbour

Brownstone and Coleton Camp

between Dart Estuary and Brixham, Devon

🏠📷♿🚶 1981

Rugged and captivating stretch of coast east of the Dart Estuary, with cliffs, beaches and traditional farmland. From Trust car parks you can easily reach the coast path for great walking and superb views. Close to Brownstone car park is one of the few remaining Second World War gun batteries. **Note**: public toilets at nearby Kingswear, or at the Trust's Coleton Fishacre (when open).

For other ways to get involved go to nationaltrust.org.uk/get-involved/volunteer

Eating and shopping: café at nearby Coleton Fishacre offering tea and homemade cakes or a hearty lunch.

Making the most of your day: spectacular views of the coast. Peregrines, seals and dolphins can be spotted from the coast path. The Froward Point area is known for its rare flora. **Dogs**: on leads near livestock and on cliff paths.

Access: ♿ 👟
Sat Nav: use TQ6 0EH for Brownstone; TQ6 0EQ Coleton Camp; TQ6 0EF Mansands and Scabbacombe. **Parking**: at Brownstone (for Froward Point and Brownstone Battery), Coleton Camp, Mansands (for Woodhuish and Mansands Beach), and Scabbacombe.

Finding out more: 01803 753010 or coletoncamp@nationaltrust.org.uk

Buckland Abbey

Yelverton, Devon PL20 6EY

🏠 ✝ ❀ ⚓ 🚻 🍴 1948

Hundreds of years ago, Cistercian monks chose this tranquil valley as the perfect spot in which to worship, farm their estate and trade. The Abbey, later converted into a house, today combines furnished rooms with museum galleries bringing to life the story of how seafaring adventurers Sir Richard Grenville and Sir Francis Drake changed the shape of Buckland Abbey and the fate of England.

Outdoors you'll find the garden, including a walled kitchen garden, Cider House garden and wild garden; the impressive medieval Great Barn; community growing areas; orchards and woodland walks with far-reaching views and late spring bluebells. **Note**: Abbey interior presented in association with Plymouth City Museum.

Eating and shopping: Ox Yard Restaurant serves freshly cooked local produce, often using ingredients grown in the kitchen garden. Picnics welcome in garden and grounds. Shop selling gifts and plants. Gallery and second-hand bookshop. Holiday cottage.

Tranquil Buckland Abbey, Devon (above and below)

Exploring the garden at Buckland Abbey, Devon

Making the most of your day: Indoors Final year of our 'Rembrandt Revealed' exhibition. **Outdoors** Higher Paddock natural play area and zip wire for younger visitors. Year-round events, estate walks and trails. **Dogs:** welcome on leads in farmland and on woodland walks. Assistance dogs only in garden.

Access: [icons]
Abbey [icons] Visitor Welcome [icons]
Grounds [icons]
Sat Nav: do not use. **Parking:** 150 yards.

Finding out more: 01822 853607 or bucklandabbey@nationaltrust.org.uk

Buckland Abbey		M	T	W	T	F	S	S
13 Feb–30 Oct	10:30–5:30*	M	T	W	T	F	S	S
5 Nov–27 Nov	11–4*						S	S
1 Dec–23 Dec	11–4*	M	T	W	T	F	S	S

*Abbey opens 30 minutes later and closes 30 minutes earlier. Last admission to Abbey one hour before closing. Estate, garden, restaurant and shop also open 2, 3 January and 27 to 31 December.

Eating and shopping: tenant-run Hive Beach Café on Chesil Bank serving local seafood.

Making the most of your day: events through the year, some especially for families. Paddling, swimming and outdoor activities. Circular and clifftop walks. Hive Beach popular for scuba diving and angling. **Dogs:** welcome. Dog-free zone on Hive Beach 1 June to 30 September.

Access: [icons]
Sat Nav: use DT6 4RF. **Parking:** on site.

Finding out more: 01297 489481 or burtonbradstock@nationaltrust.org.uk

Burton Bradstock on Dorset's Jurassic Coast

Burton Bradstock

on the Jurassic Coast, near Bridport, Dorset

[icons] 1973

One of the main gateways to Dorset's Jurassic Coast, with easy access to spectacular sandstone cliffs and miles of unspoilt beaches. Hive Beach is a hugely popular family destination, part of Chesil Bank – the largest shingle ridge in the world. Nearby, Burton Cliff glows bright gold in the sunlight.

Cadover Bridge

on Dartmoor, near Shaugh Prior, Devon

[icons] 1960

Tranquil moorland by the River Plym with pools. Starting point for walks across open moors and tors, or ancient woodland. **Note:** for Sat Nav use PL7 5EH.

Finding out more: 01752 341377 or cadoverbridge@nationaltrust.org.uk

Castle Drogo

Drewsteignton, near Exeter, Devon EX6 6PB

🏠✝❄♿☂ 1974

High above the ancient woodlands of the Teign Gorge stands Castle Drogo. Inspired by the rugged Dartmoor tors that surround it, the castle was designed and built by renowned 20th-century architect Sir Edwin Lutyens. Nothing is normal at Drogo, as the castle is currently undergoing a major conservation project to save it by making it watertight. The inside has been redisplayed by artists who have taken inspiration from the stories of Drogo, bringing to life darkened spaces and displaying the collection in creative new ways. A scaffolding viewing tower enables you to see the craftsmanship of the modern-day stonemasons. **Note**: access may be restricted or changed due to building works. Restrictions apply to viewing platform.

Eating and shopping: popular licensed café in the visitor centre, with extra outside seating, serving light meals, homemade cakes and scones. Picnics welcome in garden and grounds. Shop stocking large ranges of gifts, local beers, jams and a good-sized plant centre.

Conservation work underway at Castle Drogo, Devon (below). Walking in the Teign Gorge (above right)

Making the most of your day: Indoors Specialised guided tours, family trails and events. **Outdoors** Lutyens-designed terraced garden, games on the lawn. Walks into the Teign Gorge with views across Dartmoor and riverside paths. **Dogs**: welcome on leads in grounds and wider estate. Assistance dogs only in formal garden.

Access: 🅿♿♿♿♿♿♿♿♿♿
Building ♿♿♿ Grounds ♿♿♿➡♿
Parking: 400 yards from visitor centre.

Finding out more: 01647 433306 or castledrogo@nationaltrust.org.uk

Castle Drogo		M	T	W	T	F	S	S
Estate								
Open all year	Dawn–dusk	M	T	W	T	F	S	S
Garden, visitor centre, café and shop								
1 Jan–6 Mar	11–4	M	T	W	T	F	S	S
7 Mar–30 Oct	10–5:30	M	T	W	T	F	S	S
31 Oct–31 Dec*	11–4	M	T	W	T	F	S	S
Castle and project viewing platform								
7 Mar–30 Oct	11–5	M	T	W	T	F	S	S
5 Nov–18 Dec	Tour**	.	.	.	.	.	S	S

*Closed 24 to 26 December. **Tours 11 to 4. Viewing platform opening subject to weather conditions. During restoration project the visitor route may change.

Clouds Hill

Bovington, Dorset BH20 7NQ

🏠 1937

In this tiny woodsman's cottage you can discover the essentials and the luxuries chosen by T. E. Lawrence after he had abandoned the 'Lawrence of Arabia' persona and remodelled himself as a private in the army at Bovington Camp. The motorcycle garage has an exhibition about his life.

Eating and shopping: tea, coffee and cake available in the motorcycle garage. Shop selling gifts, books and Lawrence memorabilia.

Making the most of your day: you can visit the nearby homes of Thomas Hardy – Max Gate and Hardy's Cottage – along the very roads Lawrence himself walked. Why not follow the Lawrence Trail to Moreton church?
Dogs: welcome on leads in grounds only.

Access: 📷 Building ♿🚻 Grounds ♿
Parking: on site.

Finding out more: 01929 405616 or cloudshill@nationaltrust.org.uk

Clouds Hill		M	T	W	T	F	S	S
8 Mar–30 Oct	11–5		**T**	**W**	**T**	**F**	**S**	**S**

Open Bank Holiday Mondays. No electric light, so last admission at dusk.

Clouds Hill, Dorset: T. E. Lawrence's atmospheric retreat

Coleton Fishacre

Brownstone Road, Kingswear, Devon TQ6 0EQ

🏠❀🍴⛵🚗☕ 1982

Coleton Fishacre, Devon: 1920s Art Deco elegance

This evocative 1920s Arts and Crafts-style house, with its elegant Art Deco interiors, perfectly encapsulates the spirit of the Jazz Age. The former country home of the D'Oyly Carte family, it has a light, joyful atmosphere and inspiring views. You can glimpse life 'upstairs and downstairs' and try on 1920s clothing in the popular handling room. In the garden, paths weave through glades and past tranquil ponds and rare tender plants from New Zealand and South Africa; many exotic plants thrive beneath the tree canopy. You can also walk down to the coastal viewpoint through the valley garden.

Eating and shopping: 1920s-inspired award-winning Café Coleton serving tea and homemade cakes or a hearty lunch. Art Deco-inspired shop selling souvenir guides, china, gifts, food products, music, plants and decorative gifts.

Making the most of your day: daily guided garden walks from Easter to October, led by a member of the garden team. Events, including theatre in the garden. Family trails and new wild play area. **Dogs**: welcome on leads on designated paths (map available from reception) and outside Café Coleton.

The contents and interiors of Coleton Fishacre
(above and top) capture the spirit of the Jazz Age

Access: 🅿️ 🅳 🈂️ 🈺 🈹 🖥️ 🎵 ⠿
Building 🦽 🦽 ♿ **Grounds** 🦽 ▶️ ♿
Parking: 20 yards from reception; overflow parking 150 yards.

Finding out more: 01803 842382 or coletonfishacre@nationaltrust.org.uk

Coleton Fishacre		M	T	W	T	F	S	S
13 Feb–30 Oct	10:30–5	M	T	W	T	F	S	S
5 Nov–18 Dec	11–4	·	·	·	·	·	S	S
27 Dec–31 Dec	11–4	·	T	W	T	F	S	·

Compton Castle

Marldon, Paignton, Devon TQ3 1TA

🏰 ✝️ 🏵️ 🍽️ 🅿️ 1951

A rare survivor, this medieval fortress (below) with high curtain walls, towers and two portcullis gates, set in a landscape of rolling hills and orchards, is a bewitching mixture of romance and history. Home for nearly 600 years to the Gilbert family, including Sir Humphrey Gilbert, half-brother to Sir Walter Ralegh. **Note**: hall, sub-solar, solar, medieval kitchen, scullery, guard room and chapel open. Credit cards not accepted.

Eating and shopping: Castle Barton restaurant (not National Trust) opposite. Table-top shop selling souvenirs, gifts, souvenir guides and postcards. Picnics welcome in the orchard.

Making the most of your day: history and squirrel trails for children. 1½-mile circular footpath, accessible from opposite the castle – a great walk with wellies. Events such as Easter Egg fun. **Dogs**: welcome in the orchard. Assistance dogs only in castle and garden.

Access: 🅳 🖥️ 🎵 ⠿ **Building** 🦽 🦽 **Grounds** 🦽 🦽
Parking: on site. Hard-standing parking for campervans and overflow at Castle Barton, opposite entrance, 100 yards.

Finding out more: 01803 661906 or comptoncastle@nationaltrust.org.uk

Compton Castle		M	T	W	T	F	S	S
29 Mar–27 Oct	10:30–4:30	·	T	W	T	·	·	·
Open Bank Holiday Mondays.								

Corfe Castle

Corfe, Wareham, Dorset BH20 5EZ

[♿] [🛏] [♿] [1982]

This fairytale fortress is an iconic and evocative survivor of the English Civil War, partially demolished by the Parliamentarians in 1646. It's a favourite haunt for adults and children alike – all ages are captivated by these romantic ruins with their breathtaking views. There are 1,000 years of the castle's history as a royal palace and fortress to be discovered here. Fallen walls and secret places tell tales of treachery and treason around every corner. Corfe Castle's brooding presence is a backdrop to some of Britain's most beautiful coast and countryside. Corfe Common and Hartland Moor are close by – you can explore them by walking or cycling (top right), discovering rare wild flowers and masses of wildlife along the way. **Note**: steep, uneven slopes; steps; sudden drops throughout castle. All/parts of castle close in high winds.

Eating and shopping: 18th-century tea-room serving cream teas. Summer garden with unrivalled castle views and an open log fire in winter. Shop in village square, offering products ranging from pocket-money treats to luxury locally made gifts. Visitor centre at the car park.

Making the most of your day: our action-packed programme of fun family history events runs from April until September, with something every weekend and during school holidays. Highlights include Saxon and Viking, Civil War and medieval archery re-enactments, falconry, open-air theatre and cinema. Throughout the year, discover the castle trebuchet, our small timber-framed mason's lodge and children's quest. There's some fascinating wildlife and industrial archaeology in the area to be found by foot or bike. Landscapes range from rich chalk grassland around Corfe Castle, to the tranquil oasis of Middlebere and Hartland on the shores of Poole Harbour. Bird hides overlook the heathland and Middlebere Lake.
Dogs: welcome on short leads.

Iconic Corfe Castle, Dorset (below and right), is the backdrop to some of Britain's most beautiful countryside

East Soar

between Salcombe and Hope Cove, near Malborough, Devon

🏕️ 🏛️ 1950

This is a great starting point for exploring the isolated and rugged coast between Bolt Head and Bolt Tail. There's lots of history to discover, including the remains of Bronze Age settlements, shipwrecks and a top-secret Second World War installation. There is a waymarked one-mile route to Overbeck's, overlooking Salcombe. **Note**: sorry no toilet.

Eating and shopping: the quirky Walkers' Hut on East Soar Farm (tenant-run) serves hot drinks and homemade cakes. Nearby Overbeck's offers crab sandwiches and cream teas with sea views.

Making the most of your day: this is a good stretch of coast for wildlife-spotting – look out for cirl buntings, silver-studded blue butterflies and large flocks of swallows and house martins gathering for their autumn migration.

Access: 🚻
Sat Nav: use TQ7 3DR. **Parking**: at East Soar car park.

Finding out more: 01752 346585. 01548 561904 (Walkers' Hut) or eastsoar@nationaltrust.org.uk

Access: 🅿️🅿️♿🚻🍴🔌🎫📷📷 Grounds ♿
Sat Nav: use BH20 5EZ. **Parking**: 800 yards (uphill walk). Norden park and ride (½ mile) and West Street in village, neither National Trust (charge including members).

Finding out more: 01929 481294 (ticket office). 01929 480921 (shop). 01929 481332 (tea-room) or corfecastle@nationaltrust.org.uk

Corfe Castle		M	T	W	T	F	S	S
Castle, shop and tea-room								
1 Jan–29 Feb	10–4	M	T	W	T	F	S	S
1 Mar–31 Mar	10–5	M	T	W	T	F	S	S
1 Apr–30 Sep*	10–6	M	T	W	T	F	S	S
1 Oct–31 Oct	10–5	M	T	W	T	F	S	S
1 Nov–31 Dec	10–4	M	T	W	T	F	S	S

Tea-room closed for refurbishment 4 to 8 January. Shop closed 5 January. Castle, shop and tea-room: closed 3 March and 25 to 26 December. *Shop and tea-room close at 5:30.

Soar Mill Cove is just a short walk along the rugged coast from East Soar in Devon

Finch Foundry

Sticklepath, Okehampton, Devon EX20 2NW

⌂ ✿ ♿ 1994

The foundry was a family-run business producing a range of tools for south-west industries, including farming and mining, in the 19th century. The huge waterwheels and tilt hammer spring into action during regular demonstrations. Outside is a delightful cottage garden with Tom Pearse's summerhouse ('Widecombe Fair' fame). **Note**: narrow entrance to car park, plus height restrictions.

Eating and shopping: small tea-room serving snacks, cakes, ice-cream, tea and coffee. Small gift shop, plant sales.

Making the most of your day: **Indoors** Family activities, stories, demonstrations and tours of machinery. Live blacksmithing event on St Clement's Day (19 November). **Outdoors** Great starting point for moorland walks. **Dogs**: welcome in all areas except tea-room.

Access: 🅿♿🚻🅿🖼📷👓 Foundry ♿🏛 Grounds ♿
Parking: on site (height/width restrictions).

Finding out more: 01837 840046 or finchfoundry@nationaltrust.org.uk

Finch Foundry		M	T	W	T	F	S	S
5 Mar–30 Oct	11–5	**M**	**T**	**W**	**T**	**F**	**S**	**S**

Demonstrations of the working machinery throughout the day. Open for St Clement's Day, 19 November (patron saint of blacksmiths).

Blacksmith at work in Finch Foundry, Devon

Fingle Bridge

Teign Gorge, near Drewsteignton, Exeter, Devon

🚻 1990

This is a popular spot at the bottom of the Teign Gorge on Dartmoor, where a 17th-century bridge (above) crosses the river. There's much to explore – downstream lie 27 miles of newly reopened footpaths through Fingle Woods; upstream you can climb towards Castle Drogo on a ridge high above the river. **Note**: uneven terrain. Fingle Woods are being restored and managed in partnership with the Woodland Trust.

Eating and shopping: you're welcome to picnic in the meadow by the river. Refreshments available at the Fingle Bridge Inn (not National Trust) and at Castle Drogo café, where there is also a National Trust shop, at the top of the gorge.

Making the most of your day: abundant birdlife in Fingle Woods and the Teign Gorge, plus bats and butterflies. Iron Age hill forts, riverside walks and wonderful views. 'Wild Tribe' events in the meadow (booking essential). **Dogs**: welcome under close control.

Access: ♿🚻
Sat Nav: for Fingle Bridge car park use EX6 6PW; Castle Drogo car park EX6 6PB; Steps Bridge car park EX6 7EQ. **Parking**: Fingle Bridge (access over narrow packhorse bridge) for Fingle Woods. Additional parking Castle Drogo main car park or Steps Bridge in Teign Valley.

Finding out more: finglebridge@nationaltrust.org.uk

Golden Cap

on the Jurassic Coast, near Bridport, Dorset

⬚⬚⬚⬚ 1961

Spectacular countryside estate on the Jurassic Coast – England's only natural World Heritage Site. The great rocky shoulder of Golden Cap is the south coast's highest point, with breathtaking views in all directions. Stonebarrow Hill is a good starting point for discovering the 25 miles of footpaths around the estate.

Eating and shopping: small volunteer-run shop and information centre, with toilets and bunkhouse, in the old radar station at Stonebarrow car park, Charmouth.

Making the most of your day: play trail on Langdon Hill. Smugglers' trail on Stonebarrow Hill. Family activities and events all year. Charmouth Beach for fossils and traces of 185 million years of Earth's history. **Dogs**: welcome.

Access: ⬚
Sat Nav: for Stonebarrow use DT6 6RA; Langdon Hill DT6 6EP. **Parking**: at Stonebarrow Hill and Langdon Hill.

Finding out more: 01297 489481 or goldencap@nationaltrust.org.uk

Golden Cap

Stonebarrow shop and information centre open seasonally, Easter to October.

Breathtaking view from Golden Cap, Dorset (below), and Agatha Christie's Greenway, Devon (right)

Greenway

Greenway Road, Galmpton, near Brixham, Devon TQ5 0ES

⬚⬚⬚⬚⬚⬚ 2000

Take a glimpse into the lives of the famous and much-loved author Agatha Christie and her family. Their relaxed, atmospheric holiday home is set in the 1950s when the family would spend time here. The family were great collectors and the house is filled with archaeology, Tunbridgeware, silver, porcelain and books. There is a large and romantic woodland garden, with restored vinery and peach house, which drifts down the hillside towards the sparkling Dart Estuary and the boathouse. Please consider 'green ways' to get here: ferry (shuttle service available from quay), bus, steam train, cycling or walking.
Note: booking essential for car parking. Train halt approximately ½ mile (woodland walk or shuttle bus).

Inside Greenway, a relaxed family holiday home

Hardy Monument

Black Down, near Portesham, Dorset

🏠 ♿ 1938

Memorial to Vice-Admiral Hardy, Flag-Captain of HMS *Victory* at Trafalgar, designed to look like a spyglass. Views over the Channel. **Note**: nearest postcode for Sat Nav is DT2 9HY. Open 2 April to 30 September, Wednesday to Sunday, 11 to 4.

Finding out more: 01297 489481 or hardymonument@nationaltrust.org.uk

Eating and shopping: licensed Barn Café serving lunches, cakes and cream teas. Tack-room for takeaway options open at peak times. Agatha Christie-inspired shop selling books, Greenway merchandise, DVDs, music, local food products, gifts, plants and souvenir guides. Second-hand bookshop in café.

Making the most of your day: daily guided garden tours from March to October. New for 2016, visit the welcome and orientation space. Events, including garden workshops, open-air theatre. Family croquet, tennis, clock golf and trails. **Dogs**: welcome in garden on short leads (tethering rings available in courtyard).

Access: 🅿️ 🅿️ ♿ 🦽 🔆 🔆 🖥️ 📺 🎦 👓 🖼️
Buildings 🦽 🦽 ♿ **Garden** 🦽 ♿
Parking: spaces must be booked – same-day booking possible by telephone. No parking on Greenway Road or Galmpton.

Finding out more: 01803 842382 (Infoline and car park booking). 01803 882811 (Greenway Ferry Company). 01803 555872 (Dartmouth Steam Railway and River Boat Company) or greenway@nationaltrust.org.uk

Greenway		M	T	W	T	F	S	S
13 Feb–30 Oct	10:30–5	M	T	W	T	F	S	S
5 Nov–18 Dec	11–4						S	S
27 Dec–31 Dec	11–4		T	W	T	F	S	

Hardy's Cottage

Higher Bockhampton, near Dorchester, Dorset DT2 8QJ

🏠 ♿ 1948

The writer Thomas Hardy was born and grew up in this cottage, and wrote his early novels *Under the Greenwood Tree* and *Far from the*

Madding Crowd here. Visitors can enjoy its homely atmosphere and savour a taste of the world Hardy captured in his novels and poetry. **Note**: nearest toilet at Hardy's Birthplace Visitor Centre (near car park).

Eating and shopping: postcards, gifts and Thomas Hardy's books are sold at both Hardy's Cottage and Hardy's Birthplace Visitor Centre (near the car park). Café (not National Trust) at the visitor centre.

Making the most of your day: why not combine your visit with a trip to Max Gate, Hardy's later home in Dorchester, and Clouds Hill, the retreat of Hardy's friend T. E. Lawrence? **Dogs**: welcome on leads in garden and walks through woods only.

Access: 🅿️♿️📶📷 **Building** ♿️ **Grounds** 🏔️▶️ **Parking**: 700 yards (not National Trust). Telephone for disabled parking arrangements.

Finding out more: 01305 262366 or hardyscottage@nationaltrust.org.uk

Hardy's Cottage		M	T	W	T	F	S	S
9 Mar–30 Oct	11–5			**W**	**T**	**F**	**S**	**S**

Open Bank Holiday Mondays. Last admission 45 minutes before closing and dusk if earlier. Timed tickets may apply on certain days. Please note: Wednesdays and Sundays are busy.

Hardy's Cottage, Dorset: a taste of Thomas Hardy's world

Heddon Valley

on Exmoor, near Combe Martin, Devon

🍴🏛️📶♿️🅿️ 1963

The dramatic west Exmoor coast, favourite landscape of the Romantic poets, offers not only the beautiful Heddon Valley, but also Woody Bay and the Hangman Hills to explore. There are spectacular coastal and woodland walks, as well as a car park, shop and information centre in the Heddon Valley.

Eating and shopping: shop selling walking equipment and clothing, maps, postcards, local history books, Exmoor products, gifts and ice-cream.

Making the most of your day: all-terrain children's buggies and all-terrain mobility scooter available to borrow (call 01598 763556 to book mobility scooter). There are barbecues by the river that you're welcome to borrow. **Dogs**: welcome.

Access: 🅿️🅿️♿️📶 **Countryside** ▶️📶 **Sat Nav**: use EX31 4PY. **Parking**: opposite Trust shop.

Finding out more: 01598 763402 or heddonvalley@nationaltrust.org.uk

Heddon Valley		M	T	W	T	F	S	S
Shop								
12 Mar–30 Oct	10:30–5	**M**	**T**	**W**	**T**	**F**	**S**	**S**

Closes 4:30 in March and October.

Exploring the dramatic west Exmoor coast

Killerton

Broadclyst, Exeter, Devon EX5 3LE

[icons] 1944

Would you give away your family home for your political beliefs? Sir Richard Acland did just that with his Killerton Estate in the heart of Devon, when he gave it to the Trust in 1944. Today, you'll find a friendly Georgian house set in 2,600 hectares (6,400 acres) of working farmland, woods, parkland, cottages and orchards. There's plenty of calm space in the glorious garden, beautiful year-round with rhododendrons, magnolias, champion trees and formal lawns. You can explore winding paths, climb an extinct volcano, discover an Iron Age hill fort and take in distant views towards Dartmoor. More family home than grand mansion, the relaxed house holds the National Trust's largest fashion collection, with selected items exhibited annually.

Eating and shopping: meals served to your table in the highly rated Killerton Kitchen restaurant, or a lighter bite in the Stables Café – with dishes made using Killerton Estate produce. Picnics welcome. Plant centre, bookshop and flagship shop selling gifts and award-winning estate produce.

Making the most of your day: **Indoors** You're welcome to play the piano, read library books and sit on the chairs. Dress up in replica costumes and explore a kaleidoscope of colourful fashion in this year's exhibition: 'Fashion to dye for'. Pick up a family trail to find the hidden mice. **Outdoors** Walk, run and cycle in the parkland, woods, orchards and rolling Devon countryside. Secret garden paths to the bear's hut, ice house and chapel. There are giant redwoods, rhododendrons and far-reaching views to discover. Many events, including Easter Egg fun, cider and apple festival and Christmas at Killerton. Don't miss our seasonal family trails. **Dogs**: welcome in the parkland and estate. Assistance dogs only in garden and chapel grounds.

The glorious garden and rolling parkland at Killerton, Devon (left, above and opposite), offer space and freedom to explore and play

Killerton Estate: Budlake Post Office, Marker's and Clyston Mill

Killerton Estate, Broadclyst, Devon

🏠 ❄ 1944

Access: 🅿 🅳 🚌 🚏 🖑 🔋 🚲 🖥 📲 📷 🖼
House 🦽 🔼 🚶 **Grounds** 🦽 ➡ 🚶
Sat Nav: postcode leads to house, so follow brown signs to main car park. **Parking**: main car park 280 yards. Additional smaller car parks, including Ashclyst Forest Gate, Ellerhayes Bridge, Danes Wood.

Finding out more: 01392 881345 or killerton@nationaltrust.org.uk

Killerton		M	T	W	T	F	S	S
House and Killerton Kitchen restaurant								
13 Feb–11 Mar	11–4	M	T	W	T	F	S	S
12 Mar–30 Oct	11–5	M	T	W	T	F	S	S
19 Nov–31 Dec**	11–4	M	T	W	T	F	S	S
Chapel, garden, Stables Café, shop and plant centre								
1 Jan–12 Feb	11–4*	M	T	W	T	F	S	S
13 Feb–31 Dec**	10–5:30*	M	T	W	T	F	S	S
Park								
Open all year	8–7	M	T	W	T	F	S	S

*Open 9 on Saturday. **Special Christmas opening until 5 January 2017. Closes at 3 on 24 December, everything except park closed 25 December; house closed 26 December. Garden and park open daily until 7 or dusk if earlier.

You can get a feel for life on the wider estate by searching out Marker's, a modified medieval hall-house with unusual painted screen; the picturesque working watermill at nearby Clyston; and Budlake, a thatched cottage that once served as the village post office, with a pretty cottage garden. **Note**: nearest toilets at Broadclyst car park and Killerton visitor car park.

Eating and shopping: Clyston flour available at the mill or at the Killerton gift shop. Wide range of food and drink on offer at Killerton.

Making the most of your day: unusual and quirky things to spot, including the red telephone box and two-seater privy at Budlake. Flour ground at Clyston. Map available at Killerton. **Dogs**: on leads at Budlake and Clyston Mill. Assistance dogs only at Marker's.

Access: 🅿 🅳 🖼 Marker's 🦽 Clyston 🦽 🔼 ➡
Sat Nav: for Marker's and Clyston use EX5 3DX; for Budlake follow Killerton brown signs. **Parking**: for Marker's and Clyston use Broadclyst village car park. For Budlake use main Killerton car park.

Finding out more: 01392 881345 or killerton@nationaltrust.org.uk

Budlake, Marker's and Clyston Mill		M	T	W	T	F	S	S
26 Mar–30 Oct	1–5	M	T	W	·	·	S	S

Picturesque Budlake Post Office
on the Killerton Estate, Devon

A monument to exceptional taste, Kingston Lacy in Dorset offers treasures to enjoy both inside and out

Kingston Lacy

Wimborne Minster, Dorset BH21 4EA

🏠 🏛 ❀ 🍴 🛏 🅰 🆃 1982

Home to the Bankes family for over 300 years, Kingston Lacy is a monument to the family's exceptional taste and desire to surround themselves with beauty. After Corfe Castle fell to the Parliamentarians in the English Civil War, the family created Kingston Lacy as a beautiful Italian palace in the heart of rural Dorset. Today you can discover an internationally acclaimed art collection, including paintings by Rubens, Velázquez and Titian, exquisite carvings and lavish interiors. There's even more to explore outside, with sweeping lawns, a Japanese Garden, kitchen garden, then beyond, woodland and parkland walks – keep an eye out for the award-winning herd of Red Ruby Devon cattle – and a huge 3,500-hectare (8,500-acre) countryside estate to enjoy.

Eating and shopping: hot meals at lunchtime, light bites, cream teas and delicious cakes in the Stables Restaurant. Drinks, cakes and ice-cream available in the kitchen garden (March to October). The old kitchen shop stocks local food, plants, gifts and souvenirs. Second-hand bookshop.

Making the most of your day: **Indoors** Lavish interiors, world-class art collection, sculptures and wood carvings, winter opening for guided tours and exhibitions only. **Outdoors** See the garden change from snowdrops, spring bulbs and bluebells to summer flowers and autumn colour. You can relax in a deckchair on the lawn, explore the kitchen garden or join a garden tour. Events throughout the year, including open-air theatre, '50 things to do before you're 11¾' and Christmas lights. Across the estate there are walks and trails including a riverside walk at Eye Bridge and the Iron Age hill fort of Badbury Rings, home to 14 varieties of orchid. **Dogs**: welcome on leads in restaurant courtyard, park, woodlands and wider estate.

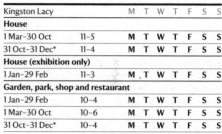

Access: ♿🚻🅿️ [icons]
Building 🏛️ Grounds [icons]

Sat Nav: unreliable, follow B3082 to main entrance. Use BH21 4EL for Eye Bridge; BH21 4EE for Pamphill Green; DT11 9JL for Badbury Rings. **Parking**: on site or at Eye Bridge, Pamphill Green and Badbury Rings, where there is a charge on point-to-point race days (including members).

Finding out more: 01202 883402 or kingstonlacy@nationaltrust.org.uk

Kingston Lacy		M	T	W	T	F	S	S
House								
1 Mar–30 Oct	11–5	M	T	W	T	F	S	S
31 Oct–31 Dec*	11–4	M	T	W	T	F	S	S
House (exhibition only)								
1 Jan–29 Feb	11–3	M	T	W	T	F	S	S
Garden, park, shop and restaurant								
1 Jan–29 Feb	10–4	M	T	W	T	F	S	S
1 Mar–30 Oct	10–6	M	T	W	T	F	S	S
31 Oct–31 Dec*	10–4	M	T	W	T	F	S	S

Last admission to house one hour before closing. Timed tickets may operate on busy days (available from visitor reception on arrival, places limited). *Closed 24 and 25 December.

Den-building at Kingston Lacy and walking on Badbury Rings (top and left); part of the internationally acclaimed art collection (below)

Knightshayes

Bolham, Tiverton, Devon EX16 7RQ

🏠 ⚿ ❀ ⛄ 🚾 ☕ 1972

One of the finest in the South West and the only existing 'garden in a wood', Knightshayes' garden is a masterpiece of architectural planting. As well as showcasing every continent's most beautiful, unusual discoveries, there are hidden glades and views across the Exe Valley. The Gothic Revival house is a rare example of the genius of William Burges, whose opulent designs are guaranteed to inspire extremes of opinion. Alongside this, the restored walled garden merges full productivity with aesthetic appeal. Practising traditional growing techniques, it's one of the best examples of a Victorian kitchen garden in the country.

Eating and shopping: Stables Café serving hot meals, made using ingredients from the kitchen garden, also soups, sandwiches, cakes and drinks. Conservatory tea-room serving snacks, cakes, ice-cream and drinks. Picnics welcome. Well-stocked shop and plant centre, with plants from the Knightshayes collection.

The garden (below and above) surrounding Knightshayes Court, Devon (top), is a model of architectural planting

Making the most of your day: **Indoors** Family home of a golfing legend. Traditional Victorian Christmas. **Outdoors** Play areas. Animal topiary. Glasshouse restoration project. Events, including outdoor music in the summer and Christmas fairs and illuminations. **Dogs**: welcome on leads in parkland and woods; in formal garden, November to February only.

Access: 🅿 ♿ 🚻 ♿ 🚹 ♿ 🔆 💻 🖼 ♿ 🅰
House 🔆 ♿ 🔆 Stables 🔆 ♿ 🔆 Gardens 🔆 ▶ 🔆
Sat Nav: do not use, follow brown signs on nearing Tiverton/Bolham. **Parking**: on site.

Finding out more: 01884 254665 or knightshayes@nationaltrust.org.uk

Knightshayes		M	T	W	T	F	S	S
House, garden, shop, plant centre and café								
1 Jan–28 Feb**	10–4*	M	T	W	T	F	S	S
29 Feb–30 Oct	10–5*	M	T	W	T	F	S	S
31 Oct–31 Dec**	10–4*	M	T	W	T	F	S	S
Parkland and woodland								
Open all year	Dawn–dusk	M	T	W	T	F	S	S

*House opens 11. **Selected rooms open in the winter. Late-night opening until 8 on 28 and 29 October and 9, 10, 11, 16, 17 and 18 December. Everything closed 24 and 25 December. Saturday 23 July: Mid-Devon Show, open as usual but expect significant delays on entry.

Little Dartmouth

near Dartmouth, Devon

🏛️🏖️🚃 1970

A gentle coastal landscape west of Dartmouth, with wonderful views, wild flowers and the ruins of a Civil War encampment. **Note**: toilets at Dartmouth Castle (not National Trust). For Sat Nav use TQ6 0JP.

Finding out more: 01752 346585 or littledartmouth@nationaltrust.org.uk

Loughwood Meeting House

Dalwood, Axminster, Devon EX13 7DU

✝️ 1969

Atmospheric 17th-century thatched Baptist meeting house dug into the hillside. **Note**: sorry no toilet. Open daily, 11 to 5. Services held twice yearly (details at Meeting House).

Finding out more: 01752 346585 or loughwood@nationaltrust.org.uk

Lundy

Bristol Channel, Devon

🏚️✝️🍽️🏛️🔥🏖️🚃🐕 1969

Undisturbed by cars, this wildlife-rich island, designated the first Marine Conservation Area, encompasses a small village with an inn, Victorian church and the 13th-century Marisco Castle. **Note**: financed, administered and maintained by the Landmark Trust. Ferry from Bideford or Ilfracombe. MS *Oldenburg* fares (including members), discounts available.

Eating and shopping: tavern serving hot and cold food and drinks. Shop selling souvenirs, Lundy stamps, snacks and ice-creams.

Making the most of your day: scuba diving, walking, letterboxing, bird and wildlife-watching. Holiday cottages (not National Trust). **Dogs**: assistance dogs only.

Access: 🚗🅿️♿ Building 🔥 Grounds ♿
Sat Nav: use EX34 9EQ for Ilfracombe; EX39 2EY for Bideford. **Parking**: at Bideford and Ilfracombe, not National Trust (charge including members).

Finding out more: 01271 863636 or lundy@nationaltrust.org.uk The Lundy Shore Office, The Quay, Bideford, Devon EX39 2LY

Lundy
MS *Oldenburg* sails from Bideford or Ilfracombe up to four times a week from the end of March until the end of October carrying both day and staying passengers. A helicopter service operates from Hartland Point from November to mid-March, Mondays and Fridays only, for staying visitors.

Wildlife-rich Lundy Island in the Bristol Channel: the first designated Marine Conservation Area

Devon and Dorset

Lydford Gorge

Lydford, near Tavistock, Devon EX20 4BH

📷 | 1947

This magical legend-rich river gorge (the deepest in the South West) offers a variety of adventurous walks. The gorge provides a truly breathtaking experience: around every corner the River Lyd plunges, tumbles, swirls and gently meanders as it travels through the steep-sided, oak-wooded valley. There are amazing features carved out by the water over thousands of years, from the 30-metre Whitelady Waterfall to the turbulent pothole called the Devil's Cauldron. Throughout the seasons there is an abundance of wildlife and plants to see, from woodland birds to wild garlic in the spring and fungi in the autumn. **Note**: rugged terrain, vertical drops.

Eating and shopping: shop selling gifts, books, local food and drink, outdoor wear. Two tea-rooms serving light lunches, soup, sandwiches, cream teas, cakes and ice-cream. Takeaway drinks and food available.

Making the most of your day: family events, wildlife-themed and bushcraft activities, children's play area, bird walk and bird hide along the old railway line. **Dogs**: welcome on leads.

Access: 🅿️ 🐕 👶 ♿ 🔄 📷 ⛺ 📷
Buildings 📷 Gorge 📷
Parking: on site.

Finding out more: 01822 820320 or lydfordgorge@nationaltrust.org.uk

Lydford Gorge		M	T	W	T	F	S	S
Gorge, shop and both tea-rooms								
5 Mar–2 Oct	10–5*	M	T	W	T	F	S	S
3 Oct–30 Oct	10–4*	M	T	W	T	F	S	S
Gorge, shop, waterfall tea-room								
5 Nov–18 Dec**	11–3:30						S	S

*Waterfall tea-room opens 11; closing dependent on weather.
**Only short walk to waterfall open: other gorge paths closed due to weather and maintenance. Short walk to waterfall also open during daylight hours in January and February.

Fun, mystery and adventure are all to be found at legend-rich Lydford Gorge in Devon (right)

Max Gate

Alington Avenue, Dorchester, Dorset DT1 2AB

🏛 ❄ 1940

Max Gate, home to Dorset's most famous author and poet, Thomas Hardy, was designed by the writer himself in 1885. This atmospheric Victorian house is where Hardy wrote some of his most famous novels, including *Tess of the d'Urbervilles* and *Jude the Obscure*, as well as most of his poetry.

The comfortable study at Max Gate

Thomas Hardy designed his home, Max Gate in Dorset

Eating and shopping: Thomas Hardy's books, souvenirs and small gifts on sale. Tea, coffee, cakes and ice-cream available.

Making the most of your day: visit nearby Hardy's Cottage, the thatched cottage in which the writer was born and grew up, and Clouds Hill, the retreat of Hardy's friend T. E. Lawrence ('Lawrence of Arabia'). **Dogs**: welcome on leads in garden only.

Access: 🖼 🔲 ⌖ Building 🔲 🔲 Garden 🔲
Sat Nav: use DT1 2AJ. **Parking**: on the roadside, 50 yards, limited (not National Trust).

Finding out more: 01305 262538 or maxgate@nationaltrust.org.uk

Max Gate			M	T	W	T	F	S	S
9 Mar–30 Oct	11–5				·	**W**	**T**	**F**	**S** **S**

Open Bank Holiday Mondays. Closes dusk if earlier.

Mill Bay

East Portlemouth, near Salcombe, Devon

🔲 🔲 1991

There are sandy beaches at Mill Bay, Sunny Cove and Seacombe Sands, with rugged walking past coastguard lookouts towards Prawle. **Note**: for Sat Nav use TQ8 8PU. Toilets and Mill Bay Beach not National Trust.

Finding out more: 01752 346585 or millbay@nationaltrust.org.uk

Mortehoe

near Ilfracombe, Devon

🔲 🔲 🔲 1909

Gateway to a wild, remote coast with a rich history of wrecking and smuggling. Amazing walking, wildlife and sunbathing seals. **Note**: use EX34 7DR for village car park and toilets, not National Trust (charge including members). Town Farmhouse (tenant-run) offers cream teas in summer.

Finding out more: 01271 870555 or mortehoe@nationaltrust.org.uk

Overbeck's

Sharpitor, Salcombe, Devon TQ8 8LW

🏠 ❋ ♨ 📐 1937

Tucked away on the cliffs above Salcombe is this hidden paradise: a subtropical garden, bursting with colour, filled with exotic and rare plants and surprises round every corner, which surrounds the seaside home of scientist and inventor Otto Overbeck. The garden's views over the Estuary and coast are truly breathtaking. Inside, among Otto's eclectic collections – glimpses of a bygone age – are his 'Rejuvenator', once believed to cure all ills, and the melodious giant music box called a polyphon (you can choose a disc to play). Generations of children return to discover Fred the friendly ghost. **Note**: entrance path and grounds are very steep in places.

Eating and shopping: licensed tea-room serving cream teas and light lunches (crab sandwiches a speciality), terrace with sea views. Shop selling unique gifts such as 'First Flight', a statuette inspired by the bronze girl in the garden, books and plants.

Making the most of your day: **Indoors** Activities, tours, trails and quizzes for children and adults. **Outdoors** Garden trails, tours. Statue garden, secret paths, woodland areas. The surrounding coast and beaches are great for exploring. **Dogs**: assistance dogs only.

Access: 🅿 💺 🔢 📶 ▢ 🎵 ◎
Building 🏛 Grounds 🔀
Sat Nav: follow brown signs through Malborough. **Parking**: small car park at top of drive and on approach lane. Additional parking at East Soar (1½ miles along coast path).

Finding out more: 01548 842893 or overbecks@nationaltrust.org.uk

Overbeck's		M	T	W	T	F	S	S
13 Feb–30 Oct	11–5	**M**	**T**	**W**	**T**	**F**	**S**	**S**
Tea-room open to 4:45.								

The exotic subtropical garden (above) at Overbeck's, Devon, surrounds the house (top) on the cliffs above Salcombe

Parke

near Bovey Tracey, Devon TQ13 9JQ

[icons] 1974

Set on the south-eastern edge of Dartmoor, this tranquil parkland (above) contains numerous delights. Riverside paths follow the course of the Bovey, as it meanders through woodlands and meadows rich in plant and wildlife. There is also a medieval weir, walled garden and historic orchard to explore.

Eating and shopping: Home Farm Café (not National Trust). Delicious, freshly cooked food from the menu board. Coffee, teas and homemade cakes.

Making the most of your day: orienteering trails to follow and geocaches to find. Events, including our apple day in October. Self-guided woodland trails leaflet available in courtyard. Productive walled garden to explore.
Dogs: welcome throughout (please put on leads where stock are grazing).

Access: [icons] Countryside [icons]
Sat Nav: use TQ13 9JQ. **Parking**: on site.

Finding out more: 01626 834748 or parke@nationaltrust.org.uk

Parke	
Open every day all year	10–5*

*Closes 4 in winter. Open Friday and Saturday evenings. Parkland, woodland and walks open dawn to dusk.

Plymbridge Woods

near Plymouth, Devon

[icons] 1968

The wooded valley of the River Plym creates a tranquil 'green bridge' from the edge of Plymouth to the heights of Dartmoor. At its lower end, Plymbridge is the starting point for footpaths that lead through the woods, alive with birdsong, and alongside the river past fascinating industrial ruins that speak of the valley's busy past. There is also the family-friendly cycle path (NCN27), which runs along an old railway line (below), and wooded mountain-bike trails along with a variety of running routes. The Upper Plym Valley climbs past rocky crags to open onto the high moors.

Eating and shopping: mobile refreshment van in Plymbridge car park (weekends). Riverside picnic spots. A short cycle ride away is Saltram, with its popular Park Café and Chapel Tea-room in the garden.

Making the most of your day: plenty of options for walkers, runners, cyclists and birdwatchers. Peregrine falcons can be watched from the viewpoint on Cann Viaduct in spring. Downloadable walking, cycling and orienteering trails available. **Dogs**: welcome under close control.

Access: [icons]
Sat Nav: use PL7 4SR for Plymbridge.
Parking: at Plymbridge.

Finding out more: 01752 341377 or plymbridgewoods@nationaltrust.org.uk

Ringstead Bay

on the Jurassic Coast, near Weymouth, Dorset

[icons] 1949

This quiet, unspoilt stretch of the Jurassic Coast in west Dorset is like the seaside of childhood memories: a perfect sweep of shingle beach with rock pools inviting you to explore, backed by farmland and cliffs covered with flowers and butterflies. The seawater is incredibly clear and safe for bathing.

Eating and shopping: picnics welcome at the Trust car park at the top of the hill, with its views of the Jurassic Coast World Heritage Site. Shop and café at the beach car park (not National Trust).

Making the most of your day: spectacular views of the bay and across to the Isle of Portland to enjoy. Why not walk out to the chalk headland of White Nothe?
Dogs: welcome everywhere, especially on the South West Coast Path.

Access: [icon]
Sat Nav: use DT2 8NQ for Southdown.
Parking: on the clifftop farmland at Southdown Farm and at beach car park (not National Trust).

Finding out more: 01297 489481 or ringsteadbay@nationaltrust.org.uk

Ringstead Bay, Dorset: a perfect sweep of shingle beach

Saltram

Plympton, Plymouth, Devon PL7 1UH

[icons] 1957

Standing high above the River Plym with magnificent views across the Estuary, Saltram's 202 hectares (500 acres) of rolling landscape parkland now provide wooded walks and open space for rest and play on Plymouth's outskirts. Saltram House was home to the Parker family from 1743 and reflects the family's increasingly prominent lifestyle during the Georgian period. Its magnificent decoration and original contents include Robert Adam's Neo-classical Saloon, original Chinese wallpapers, 18th-century Oriental, European and English ceramics and a superb country-house library. Outside, there's a tranquil garden, with 18th-century orangery and follies, to explore. After wandering along scented pathways and the magnificent lime avenue, why not treat yourself to afternoon tea in the Chapel Gallery and tea-room?

Eating and shopping: Park Café serving meals, drinks, snacks and ice-cream. The Chapel Tea-room offering light lunches and afternoon tea with waitress service. Shop selling seasonal gifts, local food, books and plants. The Chapel Gallery sells locally made arts and crafts.

Making the most of your day: **Indoors** Now open 363 days a year. Dressing-up, guided tours, baking in the kitchen, themed trails, conservation in action, 'stag bags' for children, changing exhibitions and the house dressed for Christmas. **Outdoors** Seasonal spectacles of winter snowdrops, spring daffodils, summer blooms and autumn colour in the garden. The park is ideal for anyone wanting a stroll with the dog, a run, cycle or simply to feed the ducks whatever the weather. Activities, open-air theatre, family activities, guided walks and tours throughout the year. Why not book our outdoor classroom for a Forest School session or a child's birthday? **Dogs**: very welcome in the park (identified on- and off-lead areas).

Access: P₄ D₃ 🚻 🏕 📷 ♿ ♿
House 🏠 ♿ Grounds ♿ ➡ ♿ ♿
Sat Nav: enter Merafield Road, not postcode.
Parking: 50 yards.

Finding out more: 01752 333500 or saltram@nationaltrust.org.uk

Saltram		M	T	W	T	F	S	S
House and Chapel Tea-room								
1 Jan–29 Feb*	11–3:30	M	T	W	T	F	S	S
1 Mar–31 Oct**	11–4:30	M	T	W	T	F	S	S
1 Nov–31 Dec*	11–3:30	M	T	W	T	F	S	S
Garden, Park Café and shop								
1 Jan–29 Feb	10–4	M	T	W	T	F	S	S
1 Mar–31 Oct	10–5	M	T	W	T	F	S	S
1 Nov–31 Dec	10–4	M	T	W	T	F	S	S
Park								
Open all year	Dawn–dusk	M	T	W	T	F	S	S

*Winter route in operation; house decorated over Christmas. **West Wing route only 11 to 12; whole house open from 12 (timed tickets); last admission 45 minutes before closing. Chapel Tea-room opening hours may vary depending on weather. Everything, except park, closed 25 and 26 December.

The quality of the superb library (left) at Saltram, Devon (top), reflects the importance of the family during the Georgian era. Outside is a games-friendly garden (middle) and grounds

Shaugh Bridge

on Dartmoor, near Shaugh Prior, Devon

🏛️♿👣 1960

Ancient oakwoods and mossy boulders cloak the Plym Valley; riverside walks pass the atmospheric Dewerstone Rocks and industrial ruins. **Note**: for Sat Nav use PL7 5HD. Watch out for climbers on the Dewerstone Rocks.

Finding out more: 01752 341377 or shaughbridge@nationaltrust.org.uk

Shute Barton

Shute, near Axminster, Devon EX13 7PT

🏠❄️♿ 1959

Medieval manor house, with later Tudor gatehouse and battlemented turrets – now a holiday cottage. **Note**: open weekends 21 to 22 May, 18 to 19 June, 17 to 18 September and 15 to 16 October (admission by guided tour only).

Finding out more: 01752 346585 or shute@nationaltrust.org.uk

South Milton Sands

Thurlestone, near Kingsbridge, Devon

♿🚗 1980

This popular beach – a long sweep of golden sand and rock pools – edges a sheltered bay of crystal-clear water and looks out to the iconic Thurlestone Rock offshore. The nearby wetland is home to many bird species and is an ideal place to spot rare migratory visitors.

Eating and shopping: Beachhouse café (tenant-run) serving breakfast, lunch and dinner (locally caught fish).

Seaside discovery at South Milton Sands, Devon

Making the most of your day: great for swimming and watersports (RNLI lifeguard in summer). Wetsuits, as well as windsurf and paddle boards, for hire (seasonal). The South West Coast Path offers great walks. **Dogs**: welcome on coast path and beach.

Access: 🅿️♿ Café and toilets ♿ Beach ♿
Sat Nav: use TQ7 3JY. **Parking**: behind beach.

Finding out more: 01752 346585 or southmiltonsands@nationaltrust.org.uk

South Milton Sands
Beachhouse café seasonal opening, telephone 01548 561144.

Spyway

on the Purbeck coast, Langton Matravers, near Swanage, Dorset

🏠🏛️♿♿🚗 1982

Gateway to a distinctive landscape of grassy clifftops teeming with wildlife and dramatic coast, including Dancing Ledge. Fabulous walking country. **Note**: sorry no toilet. For Sat Nav use BH19 3HG.

Finding out more: 01929 450002 or spyway@nationaltrust.org.uk

Studland Bay

Studland, near Swanage, Dorset

[icons] 1982

This glorious slice of Purbeck coastline is famed for its 4-mile stretch of golden sand, gently shelving bathing waters and views of Old Harry Rocks and the Isle of Wight. With four beaches to choose from, Studland is loved by young families and watersports fans of all ages, and it includes the most popular naturist beach in Britain. The vast swathe of heathland behind the beach is a haven for native wildlife and features all six British reptiles. Footpaths, cycle tracks and bridleways through sand dunes, woods and wild open landscape encourage you to explore. Wildlife to spot includes deer, insects and birds as well as numerous wild flowers. Studland was the inspiration for Toytown in Enid Blyton's *Noddy*. **Note**: toilets at Shell Bay, Knoll Beach and Middle Beach; also South Beach (not National Trust).

Eating and shopping: seaside café at Knoll Beach, with spectacular views of Old Harry Rocks, serves fresh, locally sourced food (inside and outside seating). Log burner in winter. Knoll Beach shop sells seaside-themed goods, including buckets and spades, swimwear and local gifts.

Studland Bay in Dorset offers inland activities (above), as well as beach fun and watersports (below)

Making the most of your day: year-round events programme, including food events, family trails and a multitude of watersports and beach sports to try – geocaching, slacklining, beach volleyball (at Shell Bay), snorkelling, swimming, diving, paddle-boarding, pedaloes, canoeing and sea kayaking, windsurfing, kite-surfing and sailing. And don't forget sandcastles and rock-pooling. You can hire bikes or go pony-trekking to explore inland. Signposted trails for walking. Look out for the Second World War remains that tell of Studland's role in the build-up to D-Day. Five bird hides overlooking Poole Harbour and

Little Sea. Discovery Centre for private hire. Coastal change interpretation hut. National Trust holiday cottages. **Dogs:** on short leads (2½ yards maximum), 1 May to 30 September. No winter restrictions.

Access: 🅿️♿🚻🏪 Grounds 🏞️♿
Sat Nav: use BH19 3AQ for Knoll Beach.
Parking: at Shell Bay (7 to 9); South Beach (9 to 11); Knoll Beach and Middle Beach (9 to 8, or dusk if earlier).

Finding out more: 01929 450500 or studlandbay@nationaltrust.org.uk

Studland Bay	M	T	W	T	F	S	S
Shop and café							
Open every day all year	9:30–5*						

*27 March to 29 October, open to 6 at weekends. Reduced hours in winter (usually 10 to 4). Shop and café closed 2 and 3 March and 25 December.

Making the most of your day: Exmoor Spotter chart for families and *Exmoor Coast of Devon* walks leaflet available. **Dogs:** allowed on leads in tea-garden.

Access: 🅿️♿ Building 🏪 Grounds 🏞️
Sat Nav: use EX35 6NT. **Parking:** pay and display (not National Trust) on Watersmeet Road; steep walk down to house. Trust car parks nearby at Combe Park and Countisbury.

Finding out more: 01598 752648 or watersmeet@nationaltrust.org.uk

Watersmeet		M	T	W	T	F	S	S
Tea-room and tea-garden								
13 Feb–21 Feb	11–3	M	T	W	T	F	S	S
12 Mar–30 Oct	10:30–5*	M	T	W	T	F	S	S

*March and October closes at 4:30. Shop opens 30 minutes after tea-room and tea-garden in main season.

Watersmeet

on Exmoor, near Lynmouth, Devon

🏠🏚️♿🏞️🛏️🍴 1955

This area, where the lush valleys of the East Lyn and Hoar Oak Water (below) tumble together, is a haven for wildlife and offers excellent walking. At the heart sits Watersmeet House, a 19th-century fishing lodge, which is now a tea-garden, shop and information point. **Note:** deep gorge, steep walk down to house.

Eating and shopping: tea-garden serving hot and cold food and drinks in a magnificent wooded setting. Shop selling Exmoor produce and gifts, walking gear and maps.

Wembury

near Wembury village, Plymouth, Devon

🏖️♿🏞️🛏️ 1939

A great beach, and more: some of the best rock pools in the country, good surfing, masses of wildlife and views of a distinctive island – the Great Mewstone. Starting point for lovely inland and coastal walks to Wembury Woods and the Yealm Estuary, as well as around Wembury Point. **Note:** toilet (not National Trust).

Eating and shopping: Old Mill Café serving coffees, homemade cakes, soups, pasties and ice-cream, as well as beach shop selling everything from spades and wetsuits to windbreaks (tenant-run). Pub in Noss Mayo (not National Trust), a walk and ferry ride away.

Making the most of your day: rock-pooling at Marine Centre, surfing, kayaking and snorkelling. **Dogs:** welcome on coast path all year, and on beach 1 October to 30 April.

Access: 🅿️♿♿ Café 🏪
Marine Centre 🏞️ Beach 🏪
Sat Nav: use PL9 0HP. **Parking:** just above beach.

Finding out more: 01752 346585.
01752 862538 (Marine Centre) or
wembury@nationaltrust.org.uk

The beach at Wembury, Devon, offers
some of the best rock pools in the country,
as well as wonderful surfing, masses of
wildlife and glorious views

Wembury

For details of the Old Mill Café seasonal opening,
telephone 01752 863280.

White Mill

Sturminster Marshall, near Wimborne Minster,
Dorset BH21 4BX

⊞ 1982

An 18th-century corn mill with original wooden
machinery, built on a Domesday Book site in a
peaceful riverside setting. **Note**: open
weekends, 19 March to 30 October, 12 to 5
(admission by guided tour, last tour 4).

Finding out more: 01258 858051 or
whitemill@nationaltrust.org.uk

Woolacombe

near Ilfracombe, Devon

🛏️🅿️ 1935

A golden beach and huge dunes, amazing
surfing, perfect coves for rock-pooling and
numerous headland walks with views of Lundy.
Note: for Sat Nav use EX34 7BG (car park).
Nearest toilets are by the beach. Neither toilets
nor car park are National Trust. Members have
to pay for parking.

Finding out more: 01271 870555 or
woolacombe@nationaltrust.org.uk

Additional coastal and countryside car parks in Devon and Dorset

Devon				
Countisbury	EX35 6NE	East Titchberry	EX39 6AU	Hembury Woods	TQ11 0HW
Combe Park	EX35 6LF	Stoke	PL8 1JG	Holne Woods	TQ13 7ST
Woody Bay	EX31 4QU	Ringmore	TQ7 4HR	Danes Wood	EX5 3LH
Trentishoe Down	EX34 0PF	Snapes Point	TQ8 8NQ	Ellerhayes	EX5 4PY
Torrs Walk,		Prawle Point	TQ7 2BX		
Ilfracombe	EX34 8BA	Scabbacombe	TQ6 0EF	**Dorset**	
Hartland:		Man Sands	TQ6 0EF	Cogden	DT6 4RJ
Brownsham	EX39 6AN	Salcombe Hill	EX10 0NY	Lambert's Castle	DT6 5QJ
Exmansworthy	EX39 6AR	Dunsland	EX22 7AA	Acton	BH19 3JN
		Steps Bridge	EX6 7EQ	Dean Hill Viewpoint	BH19 3AA

Somerset and Wiltshire

The Holnicote Estate, Somerset

Stroud
Rodborough
Woodchester Park ● Common
Minchinhampton Cirencester
Common
Newark Park ● Buscot and ● Buscot Park
Coleshill Estates
Badbury Hill

Heelis □ Swindon ● White
Horse Hill

Dyrham
Blaise Hamlet ● Park
Leigh Woods Lacock Abbey,
Clevedon Court □ Fox Talbot Museum
and Village
Tyntesfield ● BRISTOL Bath Bath ● Avebury
Bath Assembly Rooms □ Skyline
Great Chalfield Manor
Brean Down ● Prior Park ● The Courts Devizes
Cheddar Landscape Garden
Gorge Garden Westwood
King John's Manor
Hunting Lodge
Watersmeet Wells Frome Warminster
Holnicote Minehead
Estate □ Dunster Castle Stonehenge
Dunster Coleridge Landscape
Working Cottage
Watermill Bridgwater ● Glastonbury Tor
Fyne Court ● Stembridge Stourhead ● Dinton Park and
Tower Mill Philipps House
Priest's House, □ Salisbury
Muchelney ● Lytes Cary Manor Mompesson
Taunton House
Wellington Tintinhull Garden
Monument Barrington ● Yeovil
Knightshayes Court Montacute
Tiverton Treasurer's House, House
Martock
SOUTHAMPTON
Killerton Ringwood
Kingston Lacy ●

Andover

Sandh.
Memo.
Cha.

Winches
Mottisfo

Romsey

● Buildings and/or gardens

● Entry points to coast and countryside

The size of each pin indicates how large
a place is and how long you should allow
for your visit

🌿 National Trust land

Avebury

near Marlborough, Wiltshire

🏠✝🍴🏛♻♿🛏 1943

At Avebury, the world's largest prehistoric stone circle partially encompasses a pretty village. Millionaire archaeologist Alexander Keiller excavated here in the 1930s, and there is a museum bearing his name. Arranged in two parts, the Alexander Keiller Museum is divided into the Stables, displaying archaeological treasures from across the local area, and the Barn, a 17th-century threshing barn housing interactive displays and children's activities that reveal the story of this ancient landscape. Avebury forms part of the Stonehenge and Avebury World Heritage Site. Avebury Manor, on the edge of the village, was transformed in a partnership between the National Trust and the BBC, creating a hands-on experience that celebrates and reflects the lives of the people who once lived here. **Note**: English Heritage holds guardianship of Avebury Stone Circle (owned and managed by the National Trust).

Eating and shopping: Circles Café and the Manor tea-room (seasonal). Shop selling local gifts, including Avebury honey and books on the archaeology and mythology of the area.

Making the most of your day: **Indoors** Specialist talks and guided tours of the manor. Family activities in museum and events during holidays. **Outdoors** Guided tours of the stone circle all year. Talks and guided tours of the landscape. Hunt for the golden hare at Easter or for witches' cats at Hallowe'en. **Dogs**: assistance dogs only in Avebury Manor and garden and Circles Café. Elsewhere dogs on leads welcome.

The prehistoric stone circle at Avebury, Wiltshire, is the largest in the world

Access: ♿🅿🚐♿🔊🚼📷💷🚻📷 **Museum** ♿🅿 **Manor** ♿🅿🚻 **Grounds** ♿🅿▶

Sat Nav: use SN8 1RD. **Parking**: 300 yards. Please do not park on village streets.

Finding out more: 01672 539250 or avebury@nationaltrust.org.uk
National Trust Estate Office, High Street, Avebury, Wiltshire SN8 1RF

Avebury		M	T	W	T	F	S	S
Stone circle								
Open all year	Dawn–dusk	M	T	W	T	F	S	S
Manor house and garden*								
13 Feb–24 Mar	11–4	M	T	W	T	F	S	S
25 Mar–30 Oct	11–5	M	T	W	T	F	S	S
3 Nov–31 Dec	11–4**	·	·	·	T	F	S	S
Museum								
1 Jan–24 Mar	10–4	M	T	W	T	F	S	S
25 Mar–30 Oct	10–6	M	T	W	T	F	S	S
31 Oct–31 Dec	10–4**	M	T	W	T	F	S	S

Shop and café open every day. *Manor closed 20 to 22 June. Last entry one hour before closing; timed tickets during peak times. In winter, part of garden and museum may be closed, and everything closes at dusk if earlier than 4. **All except stone circle closed 24 to 26 December.

Inside the kitchen (top) at Avebury Manor (below), which offers a fascinating hands-on experience

Barrington Court

Barrington, near Ilminster, Somerset TA19 0NQ

🏠❄🦯🛏🔔🌳⛱ 1907

Colonel Lyle, whose family firm became part of Tate & Lyle, rescued the partially derelict 16th-century Court House in the 1920s, surrounding it with a productive estate. A keen collector of architectural salvage, Colonel Lyle filled the house with his collection of panelling, fireplaces and staircases. Now without furniture, the light, empty spaces provide atmospheric opportunities to explore freely. The walled White Garden, Rose and Iris Garden and Lily Garden were influenced by Gertrude Jekyll, with playing fountains, vibrant colours and intoxicating scents. The original kitchen garden supplies the restaurant and continues the Lyle family's vision of self-sufficiency. **Note**: independently run artisan workshops (opening times vary).

Eating and shopping: Strode dining and tea-rooms offering tea, homemade cakes and main meals with ingredients often grown in the kitchen garden. Children's menu available. Gift shop selling gifts, plants and award-winning cider and apple juice. Second-hand bookshop.

Barrington Court in Somerset (left and above), was rescued from dereliction in the 1920s

Making the most of your day: **Indoors** House tours and children's trail, seasonal events. Activities in artisans' workshops. **Outdoors** Trails and tours. Seasonal events, including Easter Egg hunts. Holiday cottage in Strode House. **Dogs**: assistance dogs only in formal garden.

Access: 🅿♿🚗🚻👶🖼🚪📷 Building ♿ Grounds ♿➡♿♿
Sat Nav: misdirects visitors to rear entrance – follow brown signs from Barrington village.
Parking: 200 yards.

Finding out more: 01460 241938 or barringtoncourt@nationaltrust.org.uk

Barrington Court		M	T	W	T	F	S	S
2 Jan–14 Feb	10:30–3						S	S
15 Feb–30 Oct	10:30–5	M	T	W	T	F	S	S
5 Nov–31 Dec	10:30–3						S	S

Closed 24 and 25 December.

Bath Assembly Rooms

Bennett Street, Bath, North Somerset BA1 2QH

🏠♿🍴 1931

The Assembly Rooms were at the heart of fashionable Georgian society. The Fashion Museum is on the lower ground floor. **Note**: limited access during functions. Bath Assembly Rooms is run by Bath and North East Somerset Council. Entry charge for the Fashion Museum (including members).

Finding out more: 01225 477789 or bathassemblyrooms@nationaltrust.org.uk

Bath Skyline

Bath, North Somerset

♿ 1959

One of Bath's unique features, leading to its World Heritage Site designation, is its 'green setting' – encircling meadows and wooded hillsides where you can walk and relax with grandstand views over the historic cityscape. There's a 6-mile Bath Skyline waymarked walk, plus shorter routes to follow from the city centre. **Note**: sorry no toilet or parking.

Bath Skyline, North Somerset: grandstand views

Eating and shopping: there are many great places to picnic around the Skyline. Food and snacks are available in the nearby city centre and local shops (none National Trust).

Making the most of your day: at Claverton Down – Family Discovery Trail, woodland play area (open all year), Wild Wednesdays (school holidays from 10:30). Geocaching trail. Bath Parkrun every Saturday and regular city-to-countryside guided walks.
Dogs: welcome under control (on leads in woodland play area). Cattle grazing April to November.

Access: ♿ ➡
Sat Nav: use BA2 7AD for Claverton Down; BA2 7PD for Bushey Norwood; BA2 6EP for Bathwick.
Parking: none on site, nearest city centre.

Finding out more: 01225 833977 or bathskyline@nationaltrust.org.uk

Blaise Hamlet

Henbury, Bristol BS10 7QY

🏠 1943

Delightful hamlet of nine picturesque cottages, designed by John Nash in 1809 for Blaise Estate pensioners. **Note**: access to green only; cottages not open. Sorry no toilet.

Finding out more: 01275 461900 or blaisehamlet@nationaltrust.org.uk

Brean Down

near Weston-super-Mare, North Somerset

⌂🏠♿🖼👣 1954

One of Somerset's most striking coastal landmarks: a dramatic limestone peninsula jutting out into the Bristol Channel. You can relax on the beach at the foot of the down or take a walk along this spectacular 'natural pier' (below) to the fort, which provides a unique insight into Brean's military past. **Note**: steep climbs and cliffs; please stay on main paths. Tide comes in quickly.

Eating and shopping: Cove Café – with winter woodburner or summer courtyard and picnic benches – serving cooked breakfasts, lunches or tea and cakes. Newly refurbished shop with popular ice-cream bar, buckets, spades, beach games and souvenirs.

Making the most of your day: discover the historic fort at the end of the down, and on the way you can spot birds, feral goats and flowers. Downloadable circular walk available and events all year. **Dogs**: welcome on leads.

Access: 🏢 Building 🏛
Sat Nav: use TA8 2RS. **Parking**: at Cove Café and shop.

Finding out more: 01278 751874 or breandown@nationaltrust.org.uk

Brean Down		M	T	W	T	F	S	S
Café and shop								
Open all year	10–4*	M	T	W	T	F	S	S

*Shop open 9 to 5, March to October. Car park closes at 8. Shop and café closed 25 and 26 December.

Cheddar Gorge

in the Mendips, near Wells, Somerset

♿👣 1910

At almost 400 feet deep and three miles long, Cheddar (below) is England's largest gorge. It was formed during successive Ice Ages, when glacial meltwater carved into the limestone, creating steep cliffs. The gorge is a haven for wildlife and contains many rare plants, including the Cheddar pink. **Note**: terrain is steep away from the road. Caves and car parks privately owned (charge including members).

Eating and shopping: seasonal shop and information centre providing leaflets, local information, gifts and souvenirs.

Making the most of your day: 4-mile circular gorge walk (details from shop and information centre) and Strawberry Line (NCN26) cycle route to Cheddar. **Dogs**: welcome on leads in shop and gorge.

Access: 🏛
Sat Nav: use BS27 3QE. **Parking**: car parks on both sides of gorge, not National Trust (charge including members).

Finding out more: 01934 744689 or cheddargorge@nationaltrust.org.uk

Cheddar Gorge		M	T	W	T	F	S	S
Information centre and shop								
1 Mar–31 Oct	10–5	M	T	W	T	F	S	S

Also open November and December weekends, until 18 December. Telephone to check additional opening times.

Clevedon Court, North Somerset: still a family home

Clevedon Court

Tickenham Road, Clevedon,
North Somerset BS21 6QU

🏠 ✲ 1961

Home to the lords of the manor of Clevedon for centuries, the core of the house is a remarkable survival, featuring rare domestic architecture from the medieval period. The house was bought by Abraham Elton in 1709 and it is still the much-loved family home of his descendants today. **Note**: the Elton family opens Clevedon Court for the National Trust.

Eating and shopping: kiosk serving cream teas and soft drinks.

Making the most of your day: extensive collection of Elton Ware pottery, Nailsea glass and prints of industrial archaeology. Family guide and children's quiz/trail. **Dogs**: assistance dogs only.

Access: 📶 🐕 🔊 🖥 🎧 ⠿ ⊘
Building ♿ 🏫 **Grounds** ♿
Parking: 50 yards (unsuitable for trailer or motor caravans). Alternative parking 100 yards east of entrance in cul-de-sac.

Finding out more: 01275 872257 or clevedoncourt@nationaltrust.org.uk

Clevedon Court		M	T	W	T	F	S	S
27 Mar–29 Sep	2–5	·	·	**W**	**T**	·	·	**S**

Car park opens 1:15. House entry by timed ticket, not bookable. Open Bank Holiday Mondays.

Coleridge Cottage

35 Lime Street, Nether Stowey, Bridgwater, Somerset TA5 1NQ

🏠 ✲ 1909

A visit to the award-winning former home of Samuel Taylor Coleridge offers the opportunity to immerse oneself in the sights, sounds and smells of an 18th-century cottage. Coleridge's poetry is brought to life in this simple house, the birthplace of the literary Romantic Movement, and its garden.

Eating and shopping: light refreshments in the tea-room; shop selling gifts reflecting Coleridge's life and work.

Making the most of your day: **Indoors** Regular events, special tours. Family activities and trails. Chance to get hands-on in the kitchen. **Outdoors** You can hear poetry in the garden and draw water from the well.

Access: 📷 🔊 🔊 **Building** ♿ 🏫 **Garden** ♿ ⊕
Parking: in pub or village car parks (neither National Trust).

Finding out more: 01278 732662 (Infoline). 01643 821314 or coleridgecottage@nationaltrust.org.uk

Coleridge Cottage		M	T	W	T	F	S	S
5 Mar–30 Oct	11–5	**M**	·	·	**T**	**F**	**S**	**S**
3 Dec–18 Dec	11–3	·	·	·	·	·	**S**	**S**

Step back in time at Coleridge Cottage in Somerset

The Courts Garden in Wiltshire is a hidden gem, consisting of garden rooms in different styles

The Courts Garden

Holt, near Bradford on Avon,
Wiltshire BA14 6RR

🔲 1943

This curious English country garden is a hidden gem. Garden rooms of different styles, shaped by the vision of past owners and gardeners, reveal themselves at every turn. You'll find herbaceous borders, quirky topiary, a peaceful water garden, arboretum, kitchen garden, naturally planted spring bulbs and a redesigned sunken garden.

Eating and shopping: seasonal produce grown in the kitchen garden for sale, as well as a small selection of gifts and guidebooks. Sales from the second-hand bookshop support conservation work. Rose Garden tea-room serving lunch and afternoon tea. Picnics welcome in the arboretum.

Making the most of your day: discover garden history and seasonal highlights in the Orchard Room. Trails and a hidden wildlife garden for young explorers. Keen gardeners can pick up tips from the friendly team. **Dogs**: assistance dogs only.

Access: 🔲🔲🔲🔲🔲🔲 Garden 🔲🔲🔲🔲
Parking: 80 yards in village hall car park (not National Trust). Follow signs for overflow parking. Please avoid parking on village streets.

Finding out more: 01225 782875 or courtsgarden@nationaltrust.org.uk

The Courts Garden		M	T	W	T	F	S	S
Garden and tea-room								
6 Feb–28 Feb	11–5:30						S	S
29 Feb–30 Oct*	11–5:30	M	T		T	F	S	S

*Special evening openings of the garden on Thursdays in June: 5:30 to 9 (tea-room not open). Garden closes at dusk in winter if earlier. Garden access out of season by appointment only. Tea-room last orders 4:45.

Dinton Park and Philipps House

Dinton, Salisbury, Wiltshire SP3 5HH

🔲🔲🔲 1943

Neo-Grecian house in a tranquil park, designed by Jeffry Wyatville for William Wyndham in 1820. **Note**: the house will be closed in 2016. The park is open daily all year. Sorry no toilet.

Finding out more: 01672 538014 or sw.customerenquiries@nationaltrust.org.uk

Dunster Castle

Dunster, near Minehead, Somerset TA24 6SL

🏰❄♿🔔⛔☂ 1976

Dramatically sited on top of a wooded hill, a
castle has existed here since at least Norman
times. Its impressive medieval gatehouse and
ruined tower are a reminder of its turbulent
history. The castle that you see today, owned
by the Luttrell family for over 600 years,
became an elegant country home during the
19th century. The terraced garden displays
varieties of Mediterranean and subtropical
plants, while the tranquil riverside wooded
garden below, with its natural play area, leads
to the historic working watermill. There are
panoramic views over the Bristol Channel
and surrounding countryside from the
castle and grounds.

Eating and shopping: 17th-century stables
shop selling local and regional gifts and
guidebooks. Light refreshments available at the
Camellia House. Riverside tea-room and shop
selling stoneground flour at Dunster Working
Watermill. Places to eat and drink in Dunster
village (not National Trust).

The dramatic location and exterior of Dunster Castle, Somerset (below), is matched by its elegant interior (above and right)

Making the most of your day: **Indoors**
Interactive exhibitions and 'Chapters' bring stories to life. Tours of kitchens and behind the scenes. Explore the vaulted Victorian reservoir beneath the Keep Garden. **Outdoors** Events, including open-air theatre and re-enactments. **Dogs**: welcome in parkland and garden on short leads.

Access: [icons]
Castle [icons] Stables [icons] Grounds [icons]
Parking: 300 yards (enter from A39).

Finding out more: 01643 823004 (Infoline). 01643 821314 or dunstercastle@nationaltrust.org.uk

Dunster Castle		M	T	W	T	F	S	S
Castle								
5 Mar–30 Oct	11–5*	M	T	W	T	F	S	S
4 Dec–18 Dec	11–3	.	.	.	.	.	S	S
Garden, park and shop								
1 Feb–4 Mar	11–4	M	T	W	T	F	S	S
5 Mar–30 Oct	10–5	M	T	W	T	F	S	S
31 Oct–31 Dec	11–4	M	T	W	T	F	S	S

*Last entry to castle 45 minutes before closing. 'Dunster by Candlelight': castle open 4 to 9, Friday 2 and Saturday 3 December. Shop also open 1 January and then weekends only in January; closed 25 and 26 December.

Dunster Working Watermill

Mill Lane, Dunster, near Minehead, Somerset TA24 6SW

[icon] 1976

Close to Dunster Castle on the peaceful River Avill is this fully operating 18th-century watermill, built on the site of a mill mentioned in the Domesday Survey of 1086. With the recent installation of a new second waterwheel, this is now a very rare surviving example of a double-overshot mill. **Note**: admission to watermill inclusive with a Dunster Castle garden ticket.

Eating and shopping: the mill produces stoneground wholemeal flour from organic wheat, and the milling team packs porridge oats, jumbo oats and their own muesli mix – all for sale in the shop. The riverside tea-room and garden serves light lunches and afternoon teas.

Making the most of your day: milling often takes place on the first Wednesday of every month from April until September. A one-mile circular walk suitable for families takes in the mill and Dunster Castle. **Dogs**: welcome in the Watermill tea-room garden.

Access: [icon] Building [icons]
Parking: at Dunster Castle car park, 800 yards (enter from A39).

Finding out more: 01643 821759 (mill). 01643 821314 (Dunster Castle) or dunstercastle@nationaltrust.org.uk

Dunster Working Watermill		M	T	W	T	F	S	S
5 Mar–30 Oct	10–5*	M	T	W	T	F	S	S

*Tea-room opens 10:30. 'Dunster by Candlelight': mill and tea-room open 4 to 9, 2 and 3 December.

The 18th-century Dunster Working Watermill, Somerset, is fully operational and now has a new second waterwheel

Fyne Court

near Bridgwater, Somerset

🏠 ❄ ♿ 👤 1967

A hidden Somerset gem in the Quantock Hills. While the house (the former home of amateur scientist Andrew Crosse) no longer stands, the site, within woods and meadows, is simply beautiful. A great place for gentle walks, splashing in streams, building dens and discovering ruins. Information room in courtyard.

Eating and shopping: Courtyard tea-room serving light lunches, cream teas and cakes.

Making the most of your day: events, including open-air theatre, Wild Wednesdays for families in school holidays and free Thursday tours of the grounds in the summer. Three walking trails and a children's play trail. **Dogs**: welcome on leads.

Access: 🅿 ♿ 🅿 Grounds 🅿 ➡
Sat Nav: use TA5 2EQ. **Parking**: on site.

Fyne Court, Somerset: hidden in the Quantock Hills

Finding out more: 01643 862452 or fynecourt@nationaltrust.org.uk

Fyne Court		M	T	W	T	F	S	S
Estate								
Open all year		M	T	W	T	F	S	S
Tea-room								
5 Mar–30 Oct	10:30–4*	M	T	W	T	F	S	S

*Extended opening hours in the school holidays. Opening times vary according to weather conditions.

Glastonbury Tor

near Glastonbury, Somerset

✝ ♿ 1933

Iconic tor, topped by a 15th-century tower offering spectacular views of the Somerset Levels, Dorset and Wiltshire. **Note**: sorry no toilet. For Sat Nav use BA6 8YA for nearest car park, not National Trust (charge including members).

Finding out more: 01278 751874 or glastonburytor@nationaltrust.org.uk

Great Chalfield Manor and Garden

near Melksham, Wiltshire SN12 8NH

🏠 ✝ ❄ ♿ 1943

A monkey, soldiers and griffins adorn the rooftops of this moated medieval manor, looking over the terraces of the romantic garden with topiary houses, rose garden and spring-fed fish-pond. All is lovingly looked after by the Floyd family. The manor recently featured in the BBC drama *Wolf Hall*.
Note: home to the donor family tenants, who manage it for the National Trust. Members attending annual plant fair before normal opening times pay for admission.

Eating and shopping: guidebooks, postcards and plants for sale. You can help yourself to tea and coffee in the Motor House for a small donation.

Places may occasionally close for events or bad weather

Making the most of your day: visits to the house are by guided tour (limited). The garden and parish church can be enjoyed at any time. Maps for cross-country walk to The Courts Garden are available. **Dogs**: assistance dogs only.

Access: ⃞ ⃞ ⃞ ⃞ ⃞ ⃞ ⃞
Manor ⃞ ⃞ **Garden** ⃞ ⃞
Parking: 100 yards, on grass verge outside manor gates.

Finding out more: 01225 782239 or greatchalfieldmanor@nationaltrust.org.uk

Great Chalfield		M	T	W	T	F	S	S
Manor								
27 Mar–30 Oct	Tour*	·	T	W	T	·	·	S
Garden								
27 Mar–30 Oct	2–5	·	·	·	·	·	·	S
29 Mar–27 Oct	11–5	·	T	W	T	·	·	·

*Manor admission by 45-minute guided tour only (places limited, not bookable). Tuesday, Wednesday and Thursday at 11, 12, 2, 3 and 4; Sunday at 2, 3 and 4. Group visits welcome Friday and Saturday (not Bank Holidays) by written arrangement with donor family tenant, Mrs Robert Floyd (charge including members).

Great Chalfield Manor and Garden, Wiltshire: this moated medieval manor looks out on a romantic garden, complete with topiary and rose garden

Heelis

Kemble Drive, Swindon, Wiltshire SN2 2NA

⃞ 2005

The Trust's award-winning central office is a remarkable example of an innovative and sustainable building. **Note**: admission to offices by booked guided tour only. Telephone for café and shop opening arrangements.

Finding out more: 01793 817575 or heelis@nationaltrust.org.uk

Holnicote Estate

on Exmoor, near Minehead, Somerset

✝ 🏛 ♨ 🏞 🐾 🚶 1944

Set within Exmoor National Park, Holnicote was part of the Acland bequest, together with Killerton – one of the largest estates ever given to the National Trust. There are 20 square miles of spectacular landscape to explore, with five pretty villages and vast tracts of moorland, including Dunkery Beacon, Somerset's highest point. Ancient Horner Wood has many species of bat, fungi and lichen. With more than 150 miles of paths, including the South West Coast Path, this is a fantastic area for walking, horse-riding, cycling and orienteering. Wildlife highlights include red deer, Exmoor ponies and the heath fritillary butterfly. **Note**: toilets at Bossington and Horner car parks; also at Selworthy (not National Trust).

Eating and shopping: Periwinkle tea-room on Selworthy Green serves light lunches or cream teas. Shop selling gifts and information on exploring the estate. Barbecues welcome in picnic field at Bossington car park.

Making the most of your day: Selworthy and Webber's Post orienteering trails. Downloadable walks or walk packs available from shop. **Dogs**: welcome on leads.

Holnicote Estate, Somerset (above and below), is set within Exmoor National Park

Access: 🎧 Grounds 🚶 ♿
Sat Nav: use TA24 8TP for Selworthy; TA24 8HY for Horner Wood; TA24 8TB for Webber's Post (follow signs to Webber's Post); TA24 8HF for Bossington. **Parking**: at Selworthy, Horner, Webber's Post, Bossington, Allerford, Dunkery and North Hill.

Finding out more: 01643 862452 or holnicote@nationaltrust.org.uk

Holnicote Estate		M	T	W	T	F	S	S
Tea-room								
5 Mar–24 Jul	10:30–5			T	W	T	F	S	S
25 Jul–4 Sep	10:30–5	M	T	W	T	F	S	S
6 Sep–30 Oct	10:30–5			T	W	T	F	S	S

Open Bank Holiday Mondays. Hours vary according to weather. Estate office open Monday to Friday, 9 to 5.

King John's Hunting Lodge

The Square, Axbridge, Somerset BS26 2AP

🏠 1968

This early Tudor timber-framed wool merchant's house (*circa* 1500) provides a fascinating insight into local history. **Note**: run as a local history museum by Axbridge and District Museum Trust. Open daily 1 April to 31 October, 1 to 4.

Finding out more: 01934 732012 or kingjohns@nationaltrust.org.uk

Lacock Abbey, Fox Talbot Museum and Village

Lacock, near Chippenham, Wiltshire SN15 2LG

🏛️ ✝️ 🍽️ ❄️ ♿ 📷 1944

You can see why Ela of Salisbury chose this spot for her abbey in 1232: nestled alongside the River Avon in a rolling Wiltshire landscape, Lacock invites you to stay. The Abbey bears testament to a legacy of almost 800 years of past owners with sophisticated taste, who sensitively turned it from a nunnery into a quirky family home, furnished with well-loved mementoes and furniture. Seasonal colour can be discovered in the wooded grounds, botanic garden, greenhouse and orchard. The museum celebrates William Henry Fox Talbot, who created the first photographic negative and established this as a birthplace of photography. Lacock has a homely feel, and the village, with its timber-framed cottages, is to this day a bustling community.

Note: during winter please check the opening times for the first-floor furnished Abbey rooms.

Eating and shopping: lots of places to eat and drink in Lacock village, including The Stables tea-room with changing seasonal menu. Two National Trust shops and a variety of other retail options make Lacock a great place for shopping.

Making the most of your day: **Indoors** The Abbey offers two distinct experiences: peaceful ground-floor monastic cloisters and first-floor furnished rooms. The museum provides an insight into the history of photography which appeals to all ages and includes changing exhibitions. The birthplace of photography story is also brought to life through exciting displays in the Abbey and museum. **Outdoors** The level grounds are great for picnics and walks. For families there are outdoor play features and changing trails. Special events cater for all interests and ages. Lacock is also a famous filming location and its appearances include *Harry Potter*, *Wolf Hall* and *Pride and Prejudice*. **Dogs**: on short leads welcome in Abbey grounds from 1 November to 31 March.

Lacock Abbey in Wiltshire: once a nunnery, the house bears testament to almost 800 years of sophisticated owners

Access: ⓟ♿🚲♿♿🅿️🔢⬚📷·•🅰️
Abbey 🦽🔼 Museum 🔼🔃♿
Grounds 🔼🦽➡️♿♿

Sat Nav: may direct down closed road. Set to Hither Way, Lacock, for car park. **Parking**: 220 yards. No visitor parking on village streets.

Finding out more: 01249 730459 or lacockabbey@nationaltrust.org.uk

Lacock Abbey		M	T	W	T	F	S	S
Abbey cloisters and grounds, museum, tea-room and shop*								
2 Jan–12 Feb	11–4	M	T	W	T	F	S	S
13 Feb–30 Oct	10:30–5:30	M	T	W	T	F	S	S
31 Oct–31 Dec**	11–4	M	T	W	T	F	S	S
Abbey rooms (first floor)								
2 Jan–7 Feb†	11:30–3:30	·	·	·	·	·	S	S
13 Feb–30 Oct	11–5	M	T	W	T	F	S	S
5 Nov–27 Nov†	11:30–3:30	·	·	·	·	·	S	S
1 Dec–31 Dec†	11:30–3:30	·	·	·	T	F	S	S

Last admission to Abbey rooms 45 minutes before closing. *Shop and tea-room open 10 in main season, in winter tea-room opens 10:30 and cloisters and grounds may close at dusk. **All closed 25 and 26 December (except tea-room, open 26 December) †Great Hall only; closed 25 and 26 December. Village businesses open and close at various times.

Leigh Woods

Bristol

🏛️📷♿👶 1909

The cloisters at Lacock Abbey, Wiltshire (left). Tranquil Leigh Woods (above), overlooking Bristol

A tranquil wilderness on Bristol's doorstep, with woodland, wildlife, prehistoric fort and wonderful views of the Avon Gorge and suspension bridge. Excellent network of paths, including a 1¾-mile easy-access trail, links to the National Cycle Network and popular 'Yer Tiz' off-road cycle trail. Unique whitebeam trees grow in these woods. **Note**: sorry no toilet.

Eating and shopping: picnics welcome.

Making the most of your day: natural play area. Permanent orienteering course (map available from office). Iron Age hill fort, called Stokeleigh Camp, with great views. Listen for the calls of ravens and peregrine falcons overhead. **Dogs**: welcome (but be aware of cattle).

Access: 🦽
Sat Nav: use BS8 3QB for Leigh Woods car park. **Parking**: limited, on site (not National Trust).

Finding out more: 0117 973 1645 or leighwoods@nationaltrust.org.uk

The entrance to medieval Lytes Cary Manor in Somerset

Access: [icons]
Building [icons] Grounds [icons]
Parking: 40 yards.

Finding out more: 01458 224471 or
lytescarymanor@nationaltrust.org.uk

Lytes Cary Manor		M	T	W	T	F	S	S
House								
5 Mar–30 Oct	11–4:30	M	T	W	T	F	S	S
Garden, tea-room and shop								
5 Mar–30 Oct	10:30–5	M	T	W	T	F	S	S
Estate walks								
Open all year	Dawn–dusk	M	T	W	T	F	S	S

Limited access to garden on frosty and wet days.
Tea-room open to 4:45.

Inside the Great Hall at Lytes Cary Manor

Lytes Cary Manor

near Somerton, Somerset TA11 7HU

[icons] 1949

This intimate medieval manor house, with its
beautiful Arts and Crafts-inspired garden, was
originally the family home of the Elizabethan
herbalist Henry Lyte. After years of neglect
Lytes Cary was lovingly restored in the 20th
century by Sir Walter Jenner and is arranged as
it was in his time. A stroll around the garden
rooms, divided by high yew hedges, reveals
collections of topiary (including the 12
Apostles), sensuous herbaceous borders and
manicured lawns. A visit to this harmonious
manor is wonderfully relaxing and uplifting.

Eating and shopping: small tea-room
offering light refreshments. Picnic tables in
the courtyard. Shop selling gifts, garden
accessories and plants. Second-hand
books available.

Making the most of your day: tranquil walks
on the wider estate and children's outdoor
natural play area. Allotments are bursting with
creative and colourful designs. West wing is
available as a holiday rental. **Dogs**: welcome on
leads on estate walks only.

Mompesson House

The Close, Salisbury, Wiltshire SP1 2EL

🏠❄️🍽️ 1952

Access: 🔲📷🔜🎦🔲📶📟🔳
Building 🔲🔲 Grounds 🔲🔲
Parking: 260 yards in city centre, not National Trust (charge including members).

Finding out more: 01722 420980 (Infoline). 01722 335659 or mompessonhouse@nationaltrust.org.uk

Mompesson House		M	T	W	T	F	S	S
12 Mar–27 Jul	11–5	M	T	W	.	.	S	S
28 Jul–7 Sep	11–5	M	T	W	T	F	S	S
10 Sep–30 Oct	11–5	M	T	W	.	.	S	S
26 Nov–18 Dec*	11–3:30	.	.	.	.	.	S	S

*'The Christmas House' – downstairs rooms open and decorated. Open Good Friday.

When walking into the celebrated Cathedral Close in Salisbury, visitors step back into a past world, and on entering Mompesson House (above), featured in the film *Sense and Sensibility*, the feeling of leaving the modern world behind deepens. The tranquil atmosphere is enhanced by the magnificent plasterwork, fine period furniture and graceful oak staircase, which are the main features of this perfectly proportioned Queen Anne house. The Turnbull collection of 18th-century drinking glasses is of national importance. The delightful walled garden has a pergola and traditional herbaceous borders. The new exhibition features work by renowned artist and printmaker Rena Gardiner (1929–99).

Eating and shopping: tea-room serving locally baked scones and cakes, light lunches and teas. National Trust shop only 60 yards away. Turnbull Glass Collection catalogue for sale.

Making the most of your day: regular croquet sessions on the lawn and occasional live music, including Northumbrian Pipers.
Dogs: assistance dogs only.

Montacute House

Montacute, Somerset TA15 6XP

🏠❄️🍽️🛏️ 1931

Built in golden Ham stone, Montacute House commands a central position in the picturesque village sharing its name. A beacon of Elizabethan pomp and style, it contains oak-panelled rooms, tapestries, samplers and Britain's longest remaining Long Gallery, hosting potraits from the National Portrait Gallery. The surrounding clipped lawns, wobbly hedges, hidden paths and parkland all entice exploration. Edward Phelips – a wealthy, ambitious lawyer and MP – built this grand mansion to advertise his lofty positon and success. Now, over 400 years later, he may well have enjoyed the fact that it featured as Henry VIII's Greenwich Palace in BBC2's *Wolf Hall*.

Eating and shopping: café serving a variety of homemade seasonal lunches and tempting cakes to be enjoyed inside or out. Gift shop and plant sales. Monthly farmers' markets all year, 10 to 2.

Montacute House, Somerset: this beacon of Elizabethan pomp and style is surrounded by an enticing garden, with clipped lawns, wobbly hedges and hidden paths

Making the most of your day: **Indoors** National Portrait Gallery exhibition 'After Holbein'. **Outdoors** Regular 'Elizabethan Welcome' outdoor tours and seasonal events. Family trails and swings. Tintinhull Garden and Barrington Court nearby. **Dogs**: welcome in garden on short leads (on gravel paths only).

Access: 🅿️♿🏠🔈🎬📷 ▪️🔊 Building ♿🏠♿
Grounds ♿➡️♿
Parking: on site.

Finding out more: 01935 823289 or montacute@nationaltrust.org.uk

Montacute House		M	T	W	T	F	S	S
House								
2 Jan–28 Feb*	12–3	·	·	·	·	·	S	S
5 Mar–30 Oct	11–4:30	M	T	W	T	F	S	S
5 Nov–31 Dec*	12–3	·	·	·	·	·	S	S
Garden, parkland, café and shop								
1 Jan–4 Mar	11–4	·	·	W	T	F	S	S
5 Mar–30 Oct	10–5	M	T	W	T	F	S	S
2 Nov–31 Dec	11–4	·	·	W	T	F	S	S

*Some rooms may not be open. Everything closed 24 and 25 December.

Priest's House, Muchelney

Muchelney, Langport, Somerset TA10 0DQ

🏠 1911

Medieval hall-house, built in 1308. **Note**: private home. Sorry no toilet. Open Sunday and Monday, 13 March to 25 September, 2 to 5 (admission by guided tour only).

Finding out more: 01458 253771 or priestshouse@nationaltrust.org.uk

Prior Park Landscape Garden

Ralph Allen Drive, Bath, Somerset BA2 5AH

🧩 1993

Perched on a hillside overlooking Bath, this elevated spot was chosen by Ralph Allen to show off his estate to the city. The magical landscape garden he created captures a moment in time: 1764, the year of Allen's death. There is a lot to discover, from winding paths leading to hidden retreats, to views over Bath. There are seasonal family trails and a natural play area, and you can even walk over the Palladian Bridge, one of only four in the world. A tea-garden provides a picturesque refreshment stop at the bottom of the garden by the lakes. **Note**: house not accessible. Steep slopes, steps and uneven paths.

Eating and shopping: Tea Shed by the lakes serving light snacks, cakes and refreshments (please note outdoor seating only, in tea-garden). Small shop next to visitor reception selling outdoor-related products and pocket-money gifts.

Making the most of your day: events and activities all year. Free guided tours and seasonal trails. Natural play area and swing. The Bath Skyline 6-mile circular walk is just minutes from the garden. **Dogs**: welcome on short leads.

Access: ♿ 🅿 📷 📖 ♿ 🔊 ⊙ Grounds ♿ 🔊
Parking: for disabled visitors only. Car parks in city centre, 1 mile (steep, uphill walk). Frequent bus services from bus station, Abbey and Manvers Street (by bus station).

Finding out more: 01225 833977 or priorpark@nationaltrust.org.uk

Prior Park Landscape Garden		M	T	W	T	F	S	S
2 Jan–31 Jan	10–4	·	·	·	·	·	S	S
1 Feb–30 Oct	10–5:30	M	T	W	T	F	S	S
5 Nov–31 Dec	10–4	·	·	·	·	·	S	S

Last admission one hour before closing. Closes dusk if earlier than 5:30. Tea Shed opening times vary.

Prior Park Landscape Garden, Somerset, sits on a steep hillside overlooking Bath. Its Palladian Bridge (opposite), is one of only four in the world

Stembridge Tower Mill

High Ham, Somerset TA10 9DJ

🏚 1969

Built in 1822, this is the last remaining thatched windmill in England – the only survivor of five in the area. **Note**: please respect the tenants' privacy in adjoining cottage. Sorry no toilet, limited parking, assistance dogs only. Mill interior open first and third Sunday of the month, March to September, 1 to 4.

Finding out more: 01935 823289 or stembridgemill@nationaltrust.org.uk

Stonehenge Landscape

near Amesbury, Wiltshire

🏛 🖼 1927

You can wander freely through thousands of acres of downland within the Stonehenge and Avebury World Heritage Site (below). The landscape around the famous stones is studded with ancient monuments, such as the Avenue and Cursus, and abounds with wildlife. The shuttle from the visitor centre also stops at Fargo woodland. **Note**: English Heritage manages stone circle, visitor centre/car park. Bookings via english-heritage.org.uk. Trust members enter free (excluding International National Trust or affiliate membership organisation members). Pay and display car park free to members (booking essential).

Eating and shopping: café and shop at visitor centre (not National Trust).

Making the most of your day: guided walks and family activities throughout the year. **Dogs**: welcome on leads and under close control. Assistance dogs only at stone circle.

Access: 🅿 🏛 ♿
Sat Nav: use SP3 4DX. **Parking**: at visitor centre (English Heritage), free to Trust members displaying Trust sticker. Booking essential to guarantee space. Limited parking at Woodhenge.

Finding out more: 0870 333 1181 (English Heritage). 01980 664780 (National Trust) or stonehenge@nationaltrust.org.uk

Stourhead

near Mere, Wiltshire BA12 6QF

🏠➕🍴🏛♻♿🛂▲🔔🍽 1946

'A living work of art' is how Stourhead was described when it first opened over 250 years ago. The world-famous landscape garden surrounds a glistening lake. There are towering trees, exotic rhododendrons, classical temples and a magical grotto to explore. Stourhead House was one of the first in the country to showcase Palladian architecture. With a unique Regency library, Chippendale furniture and inspirational paintings, this was a grand family home, shaped by generations of the Hoare family. Outside, views stretch across the Wiltshire countryside, and the lawns are perfect for picnics. Great for walking and wildlife spotting, with 1,072 hectares (2,650 acres) of chalk downs, ancient woods, Iron Age hill forts and farmland to explore.

Stourhead, Wiltshire: the garden (above) is a 'living work of art', while the grand house (below) is a Palladian showcase

Eating and shopping: large shop with local food, crafts, gifts and enticing garden and plant selection. Award-winning restaurant. 18th-century Spread Eagle Inn. Ice-cream parlour serving takeaway snacks and refreshments, Red Lion country pub, farm shop and art gallery (not National Trust). Picnics welcome.

Making the most of your day: Indoors The house is a great place to start your 'Harry's Story' journey. You can find out about the tragedies and joys of family life for Henry, Alda and their son Harry, the last owners of Stourhead. Alda wrote her letters in the Gothic Cottage, and you can share your memories there today. **Outdoors** The landscape garden changes in harmony with the seasons. From spring blooms and fresh greens of summer, to spectacular autumn colours and exposed winter views. There's lots to see in the productive walled garden. 'Harry's Story' trail reveals his family's garden paradise. **Dogs**: in garden on leads after 4 (March to October) and 3 (November), all day (December to February).

Tintinhull Garden

Farm Street, Tintinhull, Yeovil,
Somerset BA22 8PZ

[icons] 1953

The vision of Phyllis Reiss, amateur gardener, lives on in this small yet perfectly formed garden (below). You can stroll among clipped lawns, glinting pools and welcome shaded areas that punctuate 'living rooms' of colour and scent. It's just the place to sit, relax and get away from it all.

Eating and shopping: quaint tea-room serving cakes and cream teas. Small shop and plant sales.

Making the most of your day: village history exhibition (Tintinhull Archaeological Society). Why not combine with a visit to Montacute House or Lytes Cary Manor? Manor house available as holiday let. **Dogs**: welcome in courtyard only (reception has details of local walks).

Access: [icons]
Building [icons] Gardens [icons]
Parking: 150 yards.

Finding out more: 01935 823289 or tintinhull@nationaltrust.org.uk

Tintinhull Garden		M	T	W	T	F	S	S
19 Mar–29 May	11–5	·	·	W	T	F	S	S
31 May–31 Jul	11–5	·	T	W	T	F	S	S
3 Aug–30 Oct	11–5	·	·	W	T	F	S	S

Open Bank Holiday Mondays.

Access: [icons]
House [icons] Landscape Garden [icons]
Parking: 400 yards. King Alfred's Tower, 100 yards.

Finding out more: 01747 841152 or stourhead@nationaltrust.org.uk

Stourhead		M	T	W	T	F	S	S
Garden, shop and restaurant								
1 Jan–31 Mar	9–5*	M	T	W	T	F	S	S
1 Apr–31 Oct	9–6*	M	T	W	T	F	S	S
1 Nov–31 Dec	9–5*	M	T	W	T	F	S	S
House								
27 Feb–23 Oct	11–4:30	M	T	W	T	F	S	S
24 Oct–13 Nov	11–3:30	M	T	W	T	F	S	S
26 Nov–21 Dec**	11–3:30	M	T	W	T	F	S	S
Entrance Hall								
9 Jan–7 Feb	11–3	·	·	·	·	·	S	S
13 Feb–21 Feb	11–3	M	T	W	T	F	S	S
Behind Closed Doors Tours								
11 Jan–12 Feb	Vary	M	T	W	T	F	·	·
King Alfred's Tower								
5 Mar–30 Oct	12–4	·	·	·	·	·	S	S

*Shop opens at 10. **'The Christmas House': selected rooms open and decorated. Everything closed 25 December. King Alfred's Tower also open Bank Holidays.

Treasurer's House, Martock

Martock, Somerset TA12 6JL

🏠 1971

Completed in 1293, this medieval house includes a Great Hall, 15th-century kitchen and an unusual wall-painting. **Note**: private home. Sorry no toilets or parking. Open 13 March to 25 September, Monday, Tuesday and Sunday, 2 to 5.

Finding out more: 01935 825015 or treasurersmartock@nationaltrust.org.uk

Tyntesfield

Wraxall, Bristol, North Somerset BS48 1NX

🏠✝🖼🛏🚻☕ 2002

At its heart Tyntesfield is a Victorian country house and estate, which serves as a backdrop to the remarkable story of four generations of the Gibbs family. Their tale charts the accumulation of wealth from the guano trade, transformation of a Georgian house to a Victorian Gothic masterpiece and the collection of over 50,000 objects. Their achievements are celebrated through ornate Gothic carvings, flower-filled terraces and an expansive estate amid the Somerset countryside. With each visit you'll experience a new side of Tyntesfield, as we close one door and open another. In 2016 we continue 'Changing times – Antony Gibbs at Tyntesfield': an exploration into the life of the second generation of the family who called this special place 'home'. **Note**: house tickets sell out very quickly during holiday periods. Booking via website advised.

Eating and shopping: Home Farm visitor centre offers year-round homemade dishes using estate-grown ingredients. Shop with plant sales, second-hand bookshop and small play area. For light bites while exploring, try the Pavilion Café.

Four generations of the Gibbs family lived at Tyntesfield, North Somerset (above and opposite)

Making the most of your day: **Indoors** The house is open every day (except 25 December). From March to October you can explore the treasures of Victorian owner Antony Gibbs. Guided tours take you behind the scenes (check times on arrival). Step back in time with 'A very Victorian Christmas at Tyntesfield', featuring fabulous Victorian festive fun. **Outdoors** Free garden and greenhouse tours all year (check times on arrival). For young explorers we have three play areas, including a woodland adventure and sculpture trail. Packed activities programme, including open-air theatre, food and craft markets (first Sunday of each month, April to November) and living history. **Dogs**: welcome on two signposted woodland walks all year; in formal garden (November to February).

Access: 🅿♿🚻🦽🔄📷🚶👓🅿
House 🦽🏠🔢🚹♿ Grounds 🦽🏠🔄♿
Parking: 550 yards.

Finding out more: 0344 800 4966 (Infoline). 01275 461900 or tyntesfield@nationaltrust.org.uk

Tyntesfield		M	T	W	T	F	S	S
1 Jan–28 Feb	10–5*	M	T	W	T	F	S	S
29 Feb–30 Oct	10–6*	M	T	W	T	F	S	S
31 Oct–31 Dec	10–5*	M	T	W	T	F	S	S

Last entry to house one hour before closing. Timed tickets to house (limited numbers): booking via Tyntesfield website advised. Everything closed on 25 December. 24 and 31 December house closes at 2; garden, estate, restaurant and shop at 3. *House open 11 to 3, 1 January to 28 February and 31 October to 31 December and 11 to 5, 29 February to 30 October. Shop and restaurant close 30 minutes before estate.

Wellington Monument

near Wellington, Somerset

[icon] 1934

A striking memorial to the Duke of Wellington, in an informal rural setting on the edge of the Blackdown Hills. **Note**: for Sat Nav use TA21 9PB. Sorry no toilet.

Finding out more: 01643 862452 or wellingtonmonument@nationaltrust.org.uk

Westwood Manor

Westwood, near Bradford on Avon, Wiltshire BA15 2AF

[icons] 1960

Are you seeing double? Take a look at the topiary sculpture alongside this small Jacobean manor house, and see what you think.

Inside the house, virtually untouched since 1650, there is decorative plasterwork, fine period furniture and tapestries. Particular highlights are two rare keyboard instruments: a spinet and a virginal. **Note**: Westwood Manor is a family home, administered by the tenants. Sorry no toilet.

Eating and shopping: guidebook telling the fascinating history of Westwood, postcards and CD of Elizabethan music recorded on the virginal and spinet for sale.

Making the most of your day: children's quizzes (house suitable for over fives). Perfect for a short visit (one to two hours), so why not explore other Trust places nearby?

Access: [icons] Manor [icons] Garden [icon]
Parking: 90 yards.

Finding out more: 01225 863374 or westwoodmanor@nationaltrust.org.uk

Westwood Manor	M	T	W	T	F	S	S
27 Mar–28 Sep	2–5		**T**	**W**			**S**

Groups (eight people plus): please contact the tenant to arrange a private tour outside normal opening hours.

A rare 16th-century virginal at Westwood Manor, Wiltshire

Additional coastal and countryside car parks in Somerset and Wiltshire

Somerset		King's Wood,		Wiltshire	
Sand Point	BS22 9UD	Mendip Hills	BS25 1DH	Whitesheet Hill	BA12 6RP
Staple Plain,		Ivy Thorn,		Win Green Hill	SP5 5AW
Quantock Hills	TA4 4DQ	Polden Hills	BA16 0TZ	Overton Hill	SN8 1QG
Holford	TA5 1SE	Walton Hill,		Pepperbox Hill	SP5 3QL
Quarts Moor	EX15 3UZ	Polden Hills	BA16 9RD	Cley Hill	BA12 7QU

Places may occasionally close for events or bad weather

The Cotswolds, Buckinghamshire and Oxfordshire

Newark Park,
Gloucestershire

Coughton Court

Warwick

NORTHAMPTON

Charlecote Park

Canons Ashby

Greyfriars' House and Garden

WORCESTER

Upton House and Gardens

Bedford

Croome

Evesham

Banbury

Milton Keynes

Hidcote

Stowe

Snowshill Manor and Garden

Chastleton House

Buckingham

Buckingham

Chantry Chapel

Buckingham

Ashleworth Tithe Barn

Chipping Norton

Claydon

Ascott

Dunstable Downs and the Whipsnade Estate

Cheltenham

Stow-on-the-Wold

Crickley Hill

Waddesdon Manor

King's Head

Pitstone Windmill

Westbury Court Garden

Gloucester

Chedworth Roman Villa

Boarstall Duck Decoy

Boarstall Tower

Ashridge Estate

Haresfield Beacon

Stroud

Lodge Park and Sherborne Estate

Long Crendon Courthouse

Aylesbury

Coombe Hill

Rodborough Common

Cirencester

Hartwell House Hotel, Restaurant and Spa

Woodchester Park

Minchinhampton Common

Buscot Park

OXFORD

Newark Park

Buscot and Coleshill Estates

Buscot Old Parsonage

West Wycombe Park, Village and Hill

Hughenden

Great Coxwell Barn

High Wycombe

Badbury Hill

Priory Cottages

Nuffield Place

Cliveden

Dorneywood Garden

Swindon

White Horse Hill

Dyrham Park

Leigh Woods

BRISTOL

Ashdown House

Greys Court

Maidenhead and Cookham Commons

Basildon Park

Windsor

Tyntesfield

Bath

Bath Skyline

Lacock Abbey, Fox Talbot Museum and Village

READING

Avebury

Runnymede

Prior Park Landscape Garden

Great Chalfield Manor

Devizes

Sandham Memorial Chapel

Westwood Manor

The Courts Garden

The Vyne

● **Buildings and/or gardens**

● **Entry points to coast and countryside**

The size of each pin indicates how large a place is and how long you should allow for your visit

🟫 **National Trust land**

Majestic tree-lined avenue at Ascott, Buckinghamshire

Ascott

Wing, near Leighton Buzzard,
Buckinghamshire LU7 0PR

🏠 ❀ 1949

This half-timbered Jacobean farmhouse, transformed by the de Rothschilds towards the end of the 19th century, houses an exceptional collection of paintings, fine furniture and superb oriental porcelain. The extensive gardens are an attractive mix of formal and natural, with specimen trees, shrubs and beautiful herbaceous borders.

Eating and shopping: tea-room with indoor and outdoor seating serving light refreshments. When available, plants and produce from the garden are for sale.

Making the most of your day: free information leaflet with map available at the kiosk showing key points of interest and unusual garden features. **Dogs**: assistance dogs only.

Access: 🅿️ 🚐 ♿ 🏛 🔟 ♿
Building 🔟 ♿ ♿ Grounds ♿ ♿ ♿
Parking: 220 yards.

Finding out more: 01296 688242 or
ascott@nationaltrust.org.uk

Ascott		M	T	W	T	F	S	S
22 Mar–1 May	2–6			T	W	T	F	S	S
3 May–30 Jun	2–6			T	W	T			
1 Jul–11 Sep	2–6			T	W	T	F	S	S

Open Good Friday and Bank Holiday Mondays. Gardens open in aid of National Gardens Scheme 2 May and 29 August (£5 for garden entry, including members).

Ashleworth Tithe Barn

Ashleworth, Gloucestershire GL19 4JA

🏠 1956

Barn, with immense stone-tiled roof, picturesquely situated close to the River Severn. **Note**: sorry no toilet.

Finding out more: 01452 814213 or
ashleworth@nationaltrust.org.uk

Badbury Hill

Coleshill, near Swindon, Oxfordshire

🚶 2011

An Iron Age hill fort giving stunning views over the Upper Thames Valley. Varied circular walks and footpaths through the woodland to explore. New cycle trails opening this year.

Access: 🚶 ♿
Sat Nav: use SN7 7NJ. **Parking**: at countryside car park.

Finding out more: 01793 762209 or
badburyhill@nationaltrust.org.uk

Sunrise at Badbury Hill, Oxfordshire

Boarstall Duck Decoy

Boarstall, near Bicester,
Buckinghamshire HP18 9UX

[icons] 1980

One of the very few remaining decoys in the country, providing fascinating insights into a rare aspect of rural life. **Note**: open Monday, Wednesday, Saturday and Sunday, 5 March to 6 November, 11 to 5 (also open Good Friday, 11 to 5).

Finding out more: 01280 817156 or boarstalldecoy@nationaltrust.org.uk

Boarstall Tower

Boarstall, near Bicester,
Buckinghamshire HP18 9UX

[icons] 1943

Charming 14th-century moated gatehouse set in beautiful gardens, retaining original fortified appearance. Grade I listed. **Note**: access to upper levels is via a spiral staircase. Open Wednesdays, 9 March to 28 September, 2 to 5 (also Saturdays and Mondays of Bank Holiday weekends, 11 to 5).

Finding out more: 01280 817156 or boarstalltower@nationaltrust.org.uk

Buckingham Chantry Chapel

Market Hill, Buckingham,
Buckinghamshire MK18 1JX

[icons] 1912

Atmospheric 15th-century chapel, restored by Sir Gilbert Scott in 1875. Today it is a thriving coffee shop and second-hand bookshop.

Note: open Tuesday, Friday and Saturday, 1 January to 16 December (volunteer-run, so please telephone before visiting).

Finding out more: 01280 817156 or buckinghamchantry@nationaltrust.org.uk

The Buscot and Coleshill Estates

Coleshill, near Swindon

[icons] 1956

These countryside estates on the western border of Oxfordshire include the attractive, unspoilt villages of Buscot and Coleshill, each with a thriving tea-room. There are circular walks of differing lengths and a series of footpaths criss-crossing the estates, with breathtaking countryside and wildlife at Buscot Lock and Badbury Hill. **Note**: toilets in Coleshill Estate office yard and next to village shop and tea-room in Buscot.

Exploring at The Buscot and Coleshill Estates

Eating and shopping: Buscot tea-room offering lunches and afternoon tea. Locally sourced produce served at Coleshill shop and tea-room and The Radnor Arms (award-winning ales and microbrewery).

Making the most of your day: guided walks throughout the year, including tours of the Second World War bunker. **Dogs**: on leads only.

Access: [icon]
Sat Nav: use SN6 7PT. **Parking**: at Buscot village and by Coleshill Estate office.

Finding out more: 01793 762209 or buscotandcoleshill@nationaltrust.org.uk

The Buscot and Coleshill Estates
Coleshill Watermill open second Sunday of the month: April to October, 2 to 5.

Buscot Park, Oxfordshire: the elegant Peto Water Garden

Buscot Old Parsonage

Buscot, Faringdon, Oxfordshire SN7 8DQ

[icons] 1949

Beautiful early 18th-century house with small walled garden, on the banks of the Thames. **Note**: sorry no toilets. Open Wednesdays, 6 April to 26 October, 2 to 6, by written appointment with tenant (please mark envelope National Trust booking).

Finding out more: 01793 762209 or buscot@nationaltrust.org.uk

Buscot Park

Faringdon, Oxfordshire SN7 8BU

[icons] 1949

Lord Faringdon's family live in the house, maintain its interior, curate its contents on behalf of the Trustees of The Faringdon Collection and manage and develop the grounds and gardens. This unusual arrangement for a National Trust property gives it an idiosyncratic air and a different take on taste and presentation. As a result the whole entity becomes more fluid and more surprising. New works of art mingle with the old within the house, and new alleys and vistas stride out within the grounds. Paintings, statuary and objects by contemporary artists reinvigorate the whole – refreshing the spirit. **Note**: access to house may be limited due to major conservation work on the roof.

Eating and shopping: tea-room (not National Trust), serving cream teas, cakes, ice-cream and a selection of hot and cold drinks. Local honey and cider, peppermints, plants and kitchen garden produce (when available). Ice-cream also available in ticket office. Picnic area.

Making the most of your day: occasional events in grounds and theatre (available for hire). **Dogs**: in Paddock (overflow car park) only.

Access: ⓟⓓⓔ♿ⓐⓙ⊡ **House** ♿Ⓧ
Grounds ♿ⓐ♿➡❤♿
Parking: on site.

Finding out more: 01367 240932 (Infoline).
01367 240786 or
buscotpark@nationaltrust.org.uk
buscotpark.com

Buscot Park		M	T	W	T	F	S	S
House, grounds and tea-room								
25 Mar–30 Sep	2–6	·	·	**W**	**T**	**F**	·	·
Grounds only								
29 Mar–27 Sep	2–6	**M**	**T**	·	·	·	·	·

Weekend opening: 26, 27 March, 9, 10, 23, 24, 30 April,
1, 14, 15, 28, 29 May, 11, 12, 25, 26 June, 9, 10, 23, 24 July,
13, 14, 27, 28 August, 10, 11, 24, 25 September, 2 to 6
(tea-room 2 to 5:30). Last admission to house one hour
before closing. Open Bank Holiday Mondays.

Chastleton House

Chastleton, near Moreton-in-Marsh,
Oxfordshire GL56 0SU

🏠❄ 1991

Jacobean country house and garden built in
the early 17th century by Walter Jones as an
impressive statement of wealth and power. The
house remained essentially unchanged for 400
years, as the family who owned the house until
1991 struggled financially, leaving a unique and
fascinating time capsule. **Note**: last entry one
hour before closing (timed tickets on arrival).

Eating and shopping: plants and home-grown
seasonal garden produce for sale. Honey from
our hives and local ice-cream. Stables
second-hand books. Light refreshments
available in the local church (not National
Trust), Wednesday to Saturday. Sunday tea
and cake from Chastleton Brewhouse.

Making the most of your day: **Indoors**
Conservation in action and Family Explorer
packs. **Outdoors** Introductory video, croquet
on the lawn, garden tours and Garden Explorer
packs. **Dogs**: on leads in car park and Dovecote
Field. Assistance dogs only in garden.

Chastleton House in Oxfordshire (above),
inside and out, remained virtually unchanged
for 400 years, so is a fascinating time capsule

Access: ⓟⓓⓔⓐⓥⓙ⊡
Building ♿ **Garden** ♿
Sat Nav: misleading, follow brown signs.
Parking: 270 yards (steep path to house).

Finding out more: 01494 755560 (Infoline).
01608 674981 or
chastleton@nationaltrust.org.uk

Chastleton House		M	T	W	T	F	S	S
2 Mar–31 Mar	1–4	·	·	**W**	**T**	**F**	**S**	**S**
1 Apr–30 Oct	1–5	·	·	**W**	**T**	**F**	**S**	**S**
3 Dec–18 Dec	11–3	·	·	·	·	·	**S**	**S**

Timed-ticket system on arrival during peak times.
Last entry one hour before closing.

Chedworth Roman Villa

Yanworth, near Cheltenham,
Gloucestershire GL54 3LJ

🏛 1924

At the head of a secluded Cotswold valley are the remains of one of the largest Roman villas in Britain, rediscovered by Victorians over 150 years ago. Leading the way in archaeology and conservation, Chedworth is midway through an exciting five-year summer excavations programme. A modern conservation building gives you exceptional access to the extensive mosaic floors, hypocaust systems and bathhouse rooms, while the refurbished museum houses a range of finds and artefacts from the villa. As well as all of this, the tranquil setting, idyllic views and rich wildlife haven provide plenty of opportunities for walks or simply relaxation.

The extensive mosaics (left) and remains (above) at Chedworth Roman Villa, Gloucestershire, are exceptional

Eating and shopping: café serving sandwiches, cakes, snacks, hot and cold drinks and ice-cream. Shop offering Roman-themed souvenirs, books and games, as well as seasonal plants and gifts.

Making the most of your day: **Indoors** Updated guidebook and audio guides. Activities, including Roman dressing-up for children. Costumed interpreters and living history events. **Outdoors** Family activities and trails (weekends and school holidays). **Dogs**: assistance dogs only.

Access: 🅿 🐕 🖾 🖾 🖾 🎥 🖾 🎵 Reception 🖾 ♿
West Range 🖾 ⬆ ♿ Grounds 🖾 🖾 ➡ ♿
Parking: on lane at entrance, plus woodland overflow (March to October).

Finding out more: 01242 890256 or chedworth@nationaltrust.org.uk

Chedworth Roman Villa		M	T	W	T	F	S	S
13 Feb–24 Mar	10–4	M	T	W	T	F	S	S
25 Mar–29 Oct	10–5	M	T	W	T	F	S	S
30 Oct–27 Nov	10–4	M	T	W	T	F	S	S

Claydon

Middle Claydon, near Buckingham,
Buckinghamshire MK18 2EY

🏠✝🌸♨🔔⊤ 1956

Nestled in peaceful parkland, this Georgian
exterior hides a lavish interior that left the
18th-century Verney family facing financial
ruin. Rococo carvings frame portraits of
interesting characters, from Civil War heroes to
buccaneers. A truly inspirational place, where
Florence Nightingale, sister of Lady Verney,
spent her summers. **Note**: garden entry
charges apply (including members).

Eating and shopping: second-hand bookshop,
courtyard shops, seasonal kitchen garden
produce and tea-room (not National Trust).
Picnics welcome.

Making the most of your day: **Indoors** Talking
pictures and costume exhibition. Children's
activities, trails and dressing-up. **Outdoors** The
classic English garden opened by the Verney
family. **Dogs**: welcome on leads in the park.

Access: 🅿️🅱️♿♿🐕🔦📷📹♿
House 🦽♿🅱️ Grounds 🦽♿➡️
Parking: on site.

Finding out more: 01296 730349 or
claydon@nationaltrust.org.uk

Claydon		M	T	W	T	F	S	S
5 Mar–6 Nov	11–5	M	T	W			S	S

Garden and tea-room open as house (telephone 01296
730252 for details). Whole property open Good Friday.

Classically Georgian Claydon in Buckinghamshire

Cliveden

Cliveden Road, Taplow, Maidenhead,
Buckinghamshire SL1 8NS

🏠🌸♨🏞️ 1942

Nestled high above the River Thames with
panoramic views over the Berkshire
countryside, these gardens capture the
grandeur of a bygone age. Over the course of
300 years, each family that fell in love with this
place added their own extravagant touch,
creating a series of distinct gardens. From
carpets of spring bulbs and vibrant floral
displays on the elaborate Parterre, to the
intimate Rose Garden and rich autumn colour
in the oriental Water Garden, each area is
designed purely for pleasure. Miles of walks
meander through majestic beech woodlands
and along riverbank paths, while a giant
yew-tree maze, storybook-themed play area
and acres of space to run around in, help make
this a great place to play. **Note**: mooring
charge on Cliveden Reach, £9 per 24 hours
(including members), does not include entry.

Eating and shopping: Dovecote Coffee Shop serving morning coffee and afternoon tea. Lunch (12 to 2:30) and snacks available at the Orangery Café. Doll's House Café beside play area designed especially with families in mind. Shop, including plant sales. Picnic areas.

Making the most of your day: Indoors Short guided tour of part of the house (now a hotel) on certain days. Introductory film. Greys Court and Hughenden nearby. **Outdoors** More than 30,000 plants create striking displays on the Parterre in spring and summer, with thousands more flowers filling the Long Garden each season. The Rose Garden blooms from late June. Walking and fitness trails. Highlights for families include a play area, maze, free seasonal trails, woodland play trail and den-building area. Events include open-air theatre, family fun days, guided garden walks and workshops. Boat trips on the Thames, April to October (additional charge including members). **Dogs**: welcome under close control in woodlands only.

Access: [access icons]
House (hotel) [icons] Garden [icons]
Sat Nav: for gardens use Cliveden Road and SL1 8NS. For woodlands use SL6 0HJ.
Parking: on site.

Finding out more: 01628 605069 or cliveden@nationaltrust.org.uk

Cliveden		M	T	W	T	F	S	S
Garden, shop, café and woodland*								
13 Feb–31 Dec	10–5:30**	M	T	W	T	F	S	S
Woodland only								
1 Jan–12 Feb	10–4	M	T	W	T	F	S	S
House (part), chapel								
3 Apr–28 Aug	3–5				T			S

*Café last orders 30 minutes before closing. **Closes dusk if earlier. Property closed 24 and 25 December. Admission to house by timed ticket only from Information Centre.

Set high above the Thames with far-reaching views, miles of walks and several distinctly different gardens, Cliveden, Buckinghamshire (left, above and below) offers fun for all

Coombe Hill

Butler's Cross, near Wendover, Buckinghamshire

🏛️🅿️🚻🐕 1918

Nationally important chalk grassland site and the highest viewpoint in the Chilterns. Stunning views over the Aylesbury Vale. **Note**: sorry no toilet. For Sat Nav use HP17 0UR.

Finding out more: 01494 755573 (Hughenden Estate Office) or coombehill@nationaltrust.org.uk

Crickley Hill

Birdlip, Gloucestershire

🐕 1935

Sitting high on the Cotswold escarpment with views towards the Welsh hills, Crickley Hill overlooks Gloucester and Cheltenham. **Note**: visitor centre and car park (charge including members) not National Trust. For Sat Nav use GL4 8JY.

Finding out more: 01452 814213 or crickleyhill@nationaltrust.org.uk

Dorneywood Garden

near Burnham, Buckinghamshire SL1 8PY

🌸 1942

Ministerial residence with country garden. Afternoon teas. Open selected afternoons (dates may change at short notice). **Note**: no photography. Visitor details recorded for security reasons. Open daily 9 to 20 July, 2 to 4:30 (booking essential). Garden also open most Wednesdays and Thursdays in April, May, June, August and September, 2 to 4.

Finding out more: dorneywood@nationaltrust.org.uk

Dyrham Park

Dyrham, near Bath,
South Gloucestershire SN14 8ER

🏛️✝️🌸🐕 1961

Join us as we rediscover Dyrham after the roofing project and celebrate the year of the garden. From May the scaffolding will be removed and we'll be spending the season unpacking the collection. The sensory journey through 'Mr Blathwayt's apartment' allows you to step back in time and find out more about the intriguing William Blathwayt. Outside we'll be working to re-create some aspects of his 17th-century garden, and you can find out more about the story behind this spectacular landscape in a new exhibition in the house. The newly opened 'lost terraces' are perfect for a stroll. Beyond the garden, the 110-hectare (270-acre) park provides plenty of space for exploration, as well as far-reaching views towards the Welsh hills. **Note**: re-roofing project may cause disruption.

Eating and shopping: tea-room serving lunch, cakes and refreshments. Courtyard and garden kiosks (with outdoor seating) offering drinks, ice-cream and snacks on summer and busy days. Shop selling plants, books, local products and crafts. Indoor and outdoor picnic tables in the Old Lodge.

Making the most of your day: Indoors Events and activities all year, including behind-the-scenes tours. **Outdoors** Guided tours of the park and garden. New family trail through the park, with natural play zones and fun things to find along the way. Children can play at Old Lodge or borrow a Tracker Pack to help explore nature. The Cotswold Way passes Dyrham, for walking further afield. Nearby Prior Park Landscape Garden offers great views and access to the Bath Skyline, where you can enjoy a six-mile circular walk encompassing beautiful woodlands, meadows and historic features. **Dogs**: welcome in car park only (exercise area at far end).

Access: ⬛♿⬛⬛⬛⬛⬛⬛
House ⬛⬛⬛ **Grounds** ⬛➡
Sat Nav: use SN14 8HY and enter via A46.
Parking: 20 yards from visitor centre.

Finding out more: 0117 937 2501 or dyrhampark@nationaltrust.org.uk

Dyrham Park		M	T	W	T	F	S	S
House								
5 Mar–30 Oct	10–5	M	T	W	T	F	S	S
Garden, basement, shop and tea-room								
2 Jan–7 Feb	10–4	·	·	·	·	·	S	S
13 Feb–31 Dec**	10–5	M	T	W	T	F	S	S
Park								
Open all year**	10–5	M	T	W	T	F	S	S

Last admission one hour before closing. Closes at dusk if earlier than 5. Whole place closed until 1 on 7 and 21 September, 2, 9, 16, 23 and 30 November, 7 December. **Except 25 December.

Dyrham Park, South Gloucestershire: meeting the park residents (below), the garden (left) and a pair of precious Delftware pyramid tulip vases (opposite)

Great Coxwell Barn

Great Coxwell, Faringdon, Oxfordshire SN7 7LZ

🏠 1956

Former 13th-century monastic barn, a favourite of William Morris, who would regularly bring his guests to wonder at its structure.
Note: sorry no toilet; narrow access lanes leading to property. Open daily, dawn to dusk.

Finding out more: 01793 762209 or greatcoxwellbarn@nationaltrust.org.uk

Greys Court

Rotherfield Greys, Henley-on-Thames, Oxfordshire RG9 4PG

🏠✺🍴 1969

Set in the rolling hills of the Chilterns, Greys Court is a picturesque Tudor manor house surrounded by layers of history, intimate walled gardens and glorious wooded parkland. The house is warm and welcoming, unfurling the memories of the Brunner family through the rooms of their comfortable home. Across the perfect lawn, a medieval tower and patchwork of mellow brick buildings conceals an English country garden. Through an ancient arch, seasonal blooms are revealed, from bright bulbs through clematis and wisteria to glorious peonies and roses in the summer. Winter walks in the woodland are a must.

Eating and shopping: tea-room serving morning coffee, afternoon tea, lunches and snacks. Shop selling books, gifts, souvenirs and plants. Seasonal organic produce and plants from the gardens (when available).

Making the most of your day: you could savour the delights of Greys Court in the morning, refreshing yourself with a delicious lunch in the tea-room, then visit nearby Nuffield Place in the afternoon. **Dogs**: welcome on leads (excluding the walled gardens and children's play area).

Greys Court, Oxfordshire: this picturesque Tudor manor house is warm and welcoming both inside (above) and out (top)

Access: 🅿♿♿🚽♿📷💺📷
House ♿ Tea-room ♿ Grounds ♿♿
Parking: 220 yards.

Finding out more: 01491 628529 or greyscourt@nationaltrust.org.uk

Greys Court		M	T	W	T	F	S	S
Garden, tea-room and shop								
Open all year	10–5*	M	T	W	T	F	S	S
House guided tours**								
1 Jan–29 Feb	11–3†	M	T	W	T	F	S	S
1 Mar–31 Oct	11–12	M	T	W	T	F	S	S
1 Nov–30 Nov	11–3†	M	T	W	T	F	S	S
House								
1 Mar–31 Oct	1–5	M	T	W	T	F	S	S
1 Dec–31 Dec	1–5	M	T	W	T	F	S	S

*Closes dusk if earlier. Closed 24 and 25 December.
**House tickets available from visitor reception (places limited). †Weekend tours in January, February and November at 11 and 12; free-flow from 1.

Haresfield Beacon

near Stroud, Gloucestershire

🏛️♿ 1931

Prominently positioned on three spurs of the
Cotswold escarpment. Views across the Severn
Estuary towards the Forest of Dean and Brecon
Beacons. The wildlife is some of the best in
the Cotswolds and there's a wealth of
archaeological features, including long and
round barrows, a hill fort and cross dyke.
Note: Cotswold Way National Trail runs
through estate.

Eating and shopping: pubs in Randwick and
Haresfield (not National Trust). Ice-cream
vendor (not Trust) in Shortwood car park on
sunny days. Picnics welcome.

Making the most of your day: wildlife to spot,
from bluebells to butterflies, as well as superb
veteran beech trees on the slopes of
Shortwood. Great place to fly a kite and watch
buzzards and kestrels. **Dogs**: welcome on
lead near livestock. Dog bins available in
Shortwood car park.

Access: 👣
Sat Nav: use GL6 6PP for Shortwood car park.
Parking: at Shortwood.

Finding out more: 01452 814213 or
haresfieldbeacon@nationaltrust.org.uk

Golden autumn day at Haresfield Beacon, Gloucestershire

Elegant Hartwell House Hotel in Buckinghamshire

Hartwell House Hotel, Restaurant and Spa

Oxford Road, near Aylesbury,
Buckinghamshire HP17 8NR

🏛️❄️♿🛏️🔔🍽️ 2008

Elegant Grade I listed stately home, having
both Jacobean and Georgian façades, contains
magnificent main hall with rococo ceiling and
elegant drawing-rooms serving morning coffee
or afternoon tea. Set in beautifully landscaped
grounds, including ruined Gothic church, lake,
bridge and 36 hectares (90 acres) of parkland.
Only one hour from central London.
Note: access is for paying guests of the
hotel, including for luncheon, afternoon tea
and dinner. Children over the age of six
welcome. Held on a long lease from the
Ernest Cook Trust.

Finding out more: 01296 747444.
01296 747450 (fax) or
info@hartwell-house.com hartwell-house.com

Hidcote

Hidcote Bartrim, near Chipping Campden, Gloucestershire GL55 6LR

[✤][♠][T] 1948

This world-famous Arts and Crafts garden nestles in a north Cotswolds hamlet. Created by the talented and wealthy American horticulturist Major Lawrence Johnston, Hidcote's colourful and intricately designed outdoor 'rooms' are full of surprises, which change in harmony with the seasons. Many of the unusual plants found growing in the garden were collected from Johnston's plant-hunting trips to faraway places. Wandering through the maze of narrow paved pathways you come across secret gardens, unexpected views and plants that burst with colour. The Wilderness with its secluded stretch of tall trees is just right for a picnic.

Eating and shopping: Barn Café, plus Winthrop's Café and conservatory. Largest Trust plant centre. Shop selling exclusive Hidcote souvenirs.

Making the most of your day: daily introductory talks. Exclusive evening Head Gardener tours and open-air theatre events. Themed family activities and workshops. **Dogs**: assistance dogs only.

Access: [icons]
Visitor reception [icons] Grounds [icons]
Parking: 100 yards.

Finding out more: 01386 438333 or hidcote@nationaltrust.org.uk

Hidcote		M	T	W	T	F	S	S
13 Feb–28 Feb	11–4	.	.	.	.	.	S	S
29 Feb–27 Mar	10–5	M	T	W	T	F	S	S
28 Mar–2 Oct	10–6	M	T	W	T	F	S	S
3 Oct–30 Oct	10–5	M	T	W	T	F	S	S
5 Nov–18 Dec	11–4	.	.	.	.	.	S	S

Last admission to garden one hour before closing. Barn Café closed during November and December.

Sunshine and flowers at Hidcote, Gloucestershire (above and below): an Arts and Crafts gardening 'tour de force' which is famous throughout the world

Hughenden

High Wycombe, Buckinghamshire HP14 4LA

🏠➕🔊♿🍴 1947

It's hardly surprising that the unconventional Victorian Prime Minister Benjamin Disraeli so loved Hughenden. His handsome home, set in an unspoiled Chiltern valley with its views of ancient woods and rolling hills, is full of the fascinating personal memorabilia of this charismatic and colourful statesman. Disraeli's hillside retreat later became the headquarters for a top-secret, Second World War operation that put Hughenden high on Hitler's target list. The basement exhibition, 1940s living room and ice-house bunker bring wartime Britain to life. The estate also offers a variety of walks, rewarding visitors with perfect views of the Chiltern Hills.

Eating and shopping: Stableyard café serving hot meals, sandwiches, cakes and drinks. Dizzy's tea-room serving sandwiches, cakes and drinks, weekends only. Shop stocks local produce, ales and honey, as well as Disraeli and 'Hillside' memorabilia. Second-hand bookshop, plants and estate produce also available.

Making the most of your day: **Indoors** Morning guided tour, followed by historical introductory talks throughout the day. **Outdoors** Woodland walks, children's trails in Walled Garden and woodland play at the top of the picnic orchard. **Dogs**: welcome in orchard, park and woodland. Assistance dogs only in formal and walled gardens.

Handsome Hughenden, Buckinghamshire (above and top)

Access: 🅿️🔊🔊♿🔊🔊🔊📷🔊 ⊡
Manor 🔊🔊🔊 Grounds 🔊🔊➡🔊
Parking: on site.

Finding out more: 01494 755565 (Infoline). 01494 755573 or hughenden@nationaltrust.org.uk

Hughenden	
Open every day all year	10–5*

*Closes dusk if earlier. Shop and manor open at 11. 4 January to 12 February, weekday manor visits by guided tour only, 12 to 4. Closed 24 and 25 December.

King's Head

King's Head Passage, Market Square, Aylesbury, Buckinghamshire HP20 2RW

🏠🍴 1925

Historic public house dating back to 1455, with a pleasant family atmosphere. This is one of England's best-preserved coaching inns. **Note**: Farmers' Bar leased by Chiltern Brewery. Open Monday to Saturday, 11 to 11, and Sundays, 12 to 10:30. Closed 25 December.

Finding out more: 01296 718812 (Farmers' Bar). 01280 817156 (National Trust) or kingshead@nationaltrust.org.uk

Lodge Park and Sherborne Estate

Aldsworth, near Cheltenham,
Gloucestershire GL54 3PP

🏠🧺🛏️🔔🍽️ 1983

Within the tranquil Sherborne Park Estate sits England's only surviving 17th-century deer-coursing grandstand (above). Lodge Park was built in 1634 to satisfy John 'Crump' Dutton's love of gambling and entertaining. Now an enchanting place to explore, discover, picnic and play. Don't miss the dramatic views from the roof. **Note**: toilets at Lodge Park only.

Eating and shopping: tea and cake and plants for sale at Lodge Park on open days. Tea-room in Sherborne village (not National Trust).

Making the most of your day: living history, family events, children's quizzes, lawn games, historic shepherd's hut, woodland play trail and beautiful walks in Bridgeman landscape at Lodge Park. Country walks across the wider estate. **Dogs**: on leads in Lodge Park grounds and near livestock. Under control at all times.

Access: 🅿️ 🚗 📶 🎧 🏠 **Building** ♿🔼
Sat Nav: for Lodge Park use GL54 3PP; for Sherborne Estate use GL54 3DT (Ewe Pen Barn) or GL54 3DL (Water Meadows). **Parking**: on site for Lodge Park. For Sherborne Estate use either Ewe Pen Barn or Water Meadows car parks.

Finding out more: 01451 844130 or lodgepark@nationaltrust.org.uk

Lodge Park and Sherborne Estate		M	T	W	T	F	S	S
Lodge Park								
4 Mar–29 May	11–4					**F**	**S**	**S**
3 Jun–26 Sep*	11–4	**M**				**F**		**S**
30 Sep–30 Oct	11–4					**F**	**S**	**S**
Sherborne Estate								
Open all year	Dawn–dusk	**M**	**T**	**W**		**T**	**F**	**S**	**S**

Open Bank Holiday Mondays. *June to September, Monday entry may be by tour (bookable). Lodge Park occasionally closes for private functions (telephone to confirm openings).

Long Crendon Courthouse

Long Crendon, Aylesbury,
Buckinghamshire HP18 9AN

🏠 1900

Superb example of a 14th-century courthouse with a wealth of local history – the second building acquired by the National Trust. **Note**: extremely steep stairs. Sorry no toilet. Parking limited. Open Wednesday, Saturday and Sunday, 5 March to 6 November, 11 to 5 (volunteer-run, so opening subject to availability).

Finding out more: 01280 817156 or longcrendon@nationaltrust.org.uk

Minchinhampton and Rodborough Commons

near Stroud, Gloucestershire

🏛️🧺 1913

These historic Cotswold commons, traditionally grazed, are famed for rare flowers and butterflies, prehistoric remains and far-reaching views. Minchinhampton Common contains a nationally important complex of Neolithic and Bronze Age burial mounds, while Rodborough Common's limestone grasslands have abundant wild flowers, including rare pasqueflowers and many varieties of orchid.

Eating and shopping: many great picnic spots (no picnic tables). The historic Winstones ice-cream factory is on Rodborough Common and ice-cream vans are usually found in the Reservoir car park in summer. Several pubs around the edge of both commons (none National Trust).

Making the most of your day: the commons are great places to walk, picnic, spot butterflies or fly a kite, and there are events throughout the year. Downloadable Rodborough Common butterfly walk available. **Dogs**: welcome everywhere (under close control near livestock). Dog bins in car parks.

Access: 🔾
Sat Nav: use GL5 5BJ for Minchinhampton; GL5 5BP Rodborough. **Parking**: at Reservoir car park on Minchinhampton Common; Rodborough Fort car park on Rodborough Common.

Finding out more: 01452 814213 or minchinhampton@nationaltrust.org.uk

Newark Park

Ozleworth, Wotton-under-Edge, Gloucestershire GL12 7PZ

🏠 ❄ 🛏 🚌 1949

With splendid views from the Cotswold escarpment, Newark Park is a secluded estate with a country home at its heart. From Tudor beginnings to dramatic rescue by a 20th-century Texan, the house has many stories to tell and the informal garden and estate provide space to play, explore and contemplate. **Note**: toilets in car park (accessible toilet in house).

Eating and shopping: shop in visitor reception selling a range of souvenirs, gifts and plants. Pavilion café in garden serving light lunches, cakes, drinks and ice-cream. There is outdoor seating, and some indoor seating available in Newark House.

Making the most of your day: waymarked walks and geocaching on the estate. Open-air theatre events and croquet on the lawn, with peacocks for company. Seasonal garden specials include snowdrops and wild garlic. **Dogs**: welcome on leads in the garden and estate (please mind grazing livestock).

Access: 🅿🔾🔾🔾🔾🔾🔾🔾🔾
Building 🔾🔾 Grounds 🔾
Sat Nav: only works from north, follow brown signs from Wotton-under-Edge and A46 from south. **Parking**: 100 yards.

Finding out more: 01453 842644 or newarkpark@nationaltrust.org.uk

Newark Park		M	T	W	T	F	S	S
13 Feb–29 Feb	11–4	**M**	·	**W**	**T**	**F**	**S**	**S**
2 Mar–31 Oct	11–5	**M**	·	**W**	**T**	**F**	**S**	**S**
3 Dec–11 Dec	11–4	·	·	·	·	·	**S**	**S**

Estate walks open daily dawn to dusk (weather permitting).

Rescued from decline, the house at secluded Newark Park, Gloucestershire, has many stories to tell

Nuffield Place

Huntercombe, near Henley-on-Thames, Oxfordshire RG9 5RY

🏠 ✿ 2011

Though he left school at 15, William Morris went on to become an international figure and one of the richest men in the world. As founder of Morris Motors he changed not only the industrial, but social landscape with his philanthropic benefactions. Despite his great wealth, Morris, later Lord Nuffield, lived in a pleasant but unostentatious home in the Oxfordshire countryside. Perched on the Ridgeway, this house and garden typify early 20th-century taste and thrift, and reveal the home life of a couple who with a fortune behind them, still enjoyed the simpler things in life.

Eating and shopping: tea-room serving light lunches and afternoon tea. Shop selling unique Nuffield Place mementoes, gifts, books and postcards. Seasonal produce and plants grown in the garden (when available).

Making the most of your day: Indoors Immerse yourself in the wonderful storytelling of our passionate volunteers. **Outdoors** Charming Arts and Crafts-style gardens with

interesting details that are being beautifully restored. Greys Court nearby. **Dogs**: welcome on leads in the gardens and woodlands.

Access: 🅿️ House 🔽 Shop 🔽 Grounds 🔽
Parking: on site.

Finding out more: 01491 641224 or nuffieldplace@nationaltrust.org.uk

Nuffield Place		M	T	W	T	F	S	S
29 Feb–30 Oct	11–5	**M**	**T**	**W**	**T**	**F**	**S**	**S**

Closed 8 May, 26 June and 12 July. On busy days timed tickets in operation (limited, first-come, first-served).

Pitstone Windmill

Ivinghoe, Buckinghamshire LU7 9EJ

🌾 ⚒ 1937

Believed to be the oldest postmill in England. Stunning views of the Chilterns. **Note**: access to windmill 262 yards via a grassy field track. Sorry no facilities. Limited parking.
Open Sundays, 15 May to 28 August, 2 to 5 (also 16 May and 29 August).

Finding out more: 01442 851227 or pitstonemill@nationaltrust.org.uk

Priory Cottages

1 Mill Street, Steventon, Abingdon, Oxfordshire OX13 6SP

🏠 1939

Now converted into two houses, these former monastic buildings were gifted to the National Trust by the famous Ferguson's Gang.
Note: Priory Cottage South only open. Administered by a tenant. Sorry no toilet. Great Hall open Tuesdays, 5 April to 27 September, 2 to 6 (by written appointment with tenant).

Finding out more: 01793 762209 or priorycottages@nationaltrust.org.uk

Secret built-in workshop at Nuffield Place, Oxfordshire

Snowshill Manor and Garden

Snowshill, near Broadway,
Gloucestershire WR12 7JU

🏠 ✣ 🛏 1951

Charles Wade had a passion. From the age of seven, he collected and restored beautiful and interesting objects, living his whole life according to his motto 'Let nothing perish'. Seeing the true value of craftsmanship, colour and design, he housed his curious and unlikely finds in the Manor, and laid them out pictorially 'to inspire a thousand fancies'. Next to the manor house is the Priest's House, Charles Wade's humble home, set in a beautiful terraced garden with lovely views of the Cotswolds. Snowshill Manor and Garden is a quirky place, a world away from ordinary. **Note**: entry by timed ticket (including members), places limited.

Eating and shopping: tea-room serving cream teas, homemade cakes and lunches using home-grown produce where possible. Shop selling gifts, plants and local produce. Second-hand bookshop. Picnic tables.

The garden and many collections at Snowshill Manor and Garden, Gloucestershire (below and right), will delight all

Making the most of your day: **Indoors** Special tours and family trails. Handling collection. **Outdoors** Free children's trails and model village. Introductory and garden talks. Special events, including Apple Festival. Downloadable circular walk. **Dogs**: assistance dogs only.

Access: 🅿️♿🚻🚼🍴🏠📷♿
Manor 🦽 Garden 🦽♿
Sat Nav: follow signs from centre of village.
Parking: 500 yards.

Finding out more: 01386 852410 or snowshillmanor@nationaltrust.org.uk

Snowshill Manor and Garden		M	T	W	T	F	S	S
Manor and Priest's House								
14 Mar–30 Oct	11–5:30	M	T	W	T	F	S	S
5 Nov–27 Nov	Tour*	·	·	·	·	·	S	S
Garden, shop and tea-room								
14 Mar–30 Oct	11–5:30	M	T	W	T	F	S	S
5 Nov–27 Nov	10:30–3:30	·	·	·	·	·	S	S

Manor admission by non-bookable timed tickets (may run out on busy days). Last admission one hour before closing. *Winter weekend tours at 11:15, 12:15, 1:15, 2:15. Priest's House opens at 11.

Places may occasionally close for events or bad weather

Visitors find perfect spots to relax and enjoy the picture-perfect views at Stowe, Buckinghamshire (above and opposite)

Stowe

Buckingham, Buckinghamshire MK18 5EQ

🎭 ❄ ♨ 🔔 ⊥ 1990

The beauty of Stowe has attracted visitors since 1717. Picture-perfect views, lakeside walks and temples create a monumental landscape that changes with the seasons. Full of hidden meaning and classical references, the garden remains an earthly paradise. You can follow in the footsteps of 18th-century tourists and begin your visit at the New Inn (now a visitor centre), from where it is a short walk or buggy-ride to the garden, where another world awaits. Join us to celebrate 'Capability' Brown's 300th anniversary, as we continue to restore areas of the garden back to their former glory. The sheer size and scale is perfect for either a steady stroll or vigorous ramble, and will leave you overwhelmed by its awe-inspiring splendour.

Eating and shopping: café inside New Inn, serving fresh homemade food – light lunches, cakes, soups and scones. Shop selling local products inspired by Stowe, as well as gifts, plants, and Restoration Ale. New second-hand bookshop. Picnics welcome.

Making the most of your day: Indoors 18th-century tavern rooms in the New Inn. Stowe House (not National Trust) – New Inn visitor centre provides details about visiting Stowe House State Rooms. New visitor centre open, includes exhibition and family friendly activities. St Mary's church open for visits.
Outdoors Crisp winter walks, blooming spring displays, lazy summer days and vivid autumn colour – Stowe is forever changing. Fun family activities and outdoors event programme. We are restoring paths, statues and opening new garden areas all year, so there will be more to explore on every new visit. **Dogs**: welcome on leads (downloadable dog trail available). Tie-up points and water provided.

Access: 🅿️ ♿ 🚻 🔼 📷 📹 Visitor centre ♿ 🛗 👶
Grounds ♿ ➡ 🦽
Parking: 545 yards.

Finding out more: 01280 817156 or stowe@nationaltrust.org.uk

Stowe		M	T	W	T	F	S	S
Gardens, shop, café and parlour rooms								
Open all year*	10–6**	M	T	W	T	F	S	S
Parkland								
Open all year	Dawn–dusk	M	T	W	T	F	S	S

*Gardens closed 28 May but visitor centre, parkland, café and shop open. **Closes dusk if earlier. Recommended last entry to the gardens 90 minutes before closing. Closed 24 and 25 December.

Waddesdon Manor

Waddesdon, near Aylesbury,
Buckinghamshire HP18 0JH

🏛️ 🍴 ❄️ ♿ 🔺 🍷 1957

Baron Ferdinand de Rothschild started building Waddesdon Manor in 1874 to display his outstanding collection of art treasures and entertain fashionable society. His choice of French-château style, typical of the Loire Valley, surprises many visitors. The highest quality 18th-century French decorative arts are displayed alongside magnificent English portraits and Dutch Old Master paintings in more than 40 elegant interiors. Outside is one of the finest Victorian gardens in Britain, famous for its parterre and ornate working aviary, and enhanced with classical and contemporary sculpture. Today, the Manor continues its tradition of entertainment and hospitality with events celebrating food and wine. Visitors can explore Waddesdon's history, collections and gardens through changing exhibitions, talks and tours. **Note**: advance booking for house tickets essential for weekends and holidays for all visitors, including members.

Eating and shopping: two licensed restaurants for lunches and afternoon teas. Snacks and drinks at the Summer House or Coffee Bar. Gift shop, wine shop and old-fashioned sweet shop with fudge made in our kitchens at the Stables (managed by the Rothschild Foundation).

Finding out more: 01296 653226 or
waddesdonmanor@nationaltrust.org.uk

Waddesdon Manor		M	T	W	T	F	S	S
Gardens, aviary, playground, wine cellars, shops, restaurant								
9 Jan–20 Mar	10-5						S	S
13 Feb–21 Feb	10-5	M	T	W	T	F	S	S
23 Mar–3 Apr	10-5	M	T	W	T	F	S	S
6 Apr–27 May	10-5	·	·	W	T	F	S	S
28 May–5 Jun	10-5	M	T	W	T	F	S	S
8 Jun–21 Oct	10-5	·	·	W	T	F	S	S
22 Oct–30 Oct	10-5	M	T	W	T	F	S	S
2 Nov–23 Dec	10-5	·	·	W	T	F	S	S
27 Dec–31 Dec	10-5	M	T	W	T	F	S	S
House*								
23 Mar–3 Apr	12-4	M	T	W	T	F	S	S
6 Apr–27 May	12-4	·	·	W	T	F	S	S
28 May–5 Jun	12-4	M	T	W	T	F	S	S
8 Jun–23 Oct	12-4	·	·	W	T	F	S	S
Christmas House (partial opening)*								
9 Nov–23 Dec	12-4	·	·	W	T	F	S	S
27 Dec–31 Dec	12-4	M	T	W	T	F	S	S

Open Bank Holiday Mondays. *House admission by timed
ticket (advance booking at busy times recommended),
available at waddesdon.org.uk or by calling 01296 653226
(£3 telephone booking fee). House: open 11 to 4 at weekends
and Bank Holiday Mondays. Recommended last entry 2:30;
last tickets available 3:10. Christmas later opening in the
garden to 7, Friday to Sunday, 18 November to 1 January.
Closed 24, 25 and 26 December.

From the opulent splendour of its façade (above), to its
fine Victorian gardens (right top), Waddesdon Manor,
Buckinghamshire, is a wonder. Viewed from the
air (bottom right) its sheer scale becomes apparent

Making the most of your day: **Indoors** Wide
range of free activities on aspects of the house,
collection and special exhibitions with experts.
Rolling presentation on the Rothschilds and
Waddesdon. Wine cellar tours and tastings.
Outdoors Guided walks in the gardens and
tours of the aviary. Woodland playground and
Miss Alice's Drive nature trail, ideal for children.
Family events, open-air film and theatre. Food
festivals and fairs. **Dogs**: assistance dogs only.

Access: 🅿️🚻♿🔥🔊👁️🗺️📷🎧🔆
Building ♿⬆️🔽 **Grounds** ♿➡️🔽
Parking: ¾ mile (free shuttle).

West Wycombe Park, Village and Hill

West Wycombe, Buckinghamshire

🏠✝🍴🎣 1943

Alongside this historic village lies an exquisite Palladian mansion. This lavish home and serene landscape garden reflect the wealth and personality of its creator, the infamous Sir Francis Dashwood, founder of the Hellfire Club. Still home to the Dashwood family and their fine collection, it remains a busy, private estate. **Note**: opened in partnership with the Dashwood family. The Hellfire Caves and café are privately owned and National Trust members receive a discount on the admission charge.

Eating and shopping: refreshments available at the Hellfire Caves and café (not National Trust), where members receive a discount. Variety of shops and pubs in the National Trust village, offering refreshments and local produce (none National Trust).

Making the most of your day: Indoors Mansion guided tours, Monday to Thursday (free-flow access Sundays). **Outdoors** Centuries-old village with historic cottages and coaching inns. West Wycombe Hill, iconic Dashwood mausoleum and church with golden ball. **Dogs**: welcome on West Wycombe Hill. Assistance dogs only in park.

Access: 🅿🅿♿🚾📷🎫📍 Building 🔦🔦♿
Sat Nav: use HP14 3AJ. **Parking**: 250 yards.

Finding out more: 01494 755571 (Infoline). 01494 513569 or westwycombe@nationaltrust.org.uk

West Wycombe		M	T	W	T	F	S	S
House and grounds								
1 Jun–31 Aug	2–6*	M	T	W	T	·	·	S
Grounds only								
3 Apr–31 May	2–6	M	T	W	T	·	·	S

*House entry Monday to Thursday by guided tour (timed tickets). Free-flow on Sundays and Bank Holidays. Last admission 45 minutes before closing.

Westbury Court Garden

Westbury-on-Severn, Gloucestershire GL14 1PD

🌳 1967

Originally laid out between 1696 and 1705, this is the only restored Dutch water garden in the country. There are canals, clipped hedges, working 17th-century vegetable plots and many old varieties of fruit trees.

Making the most of your day: evening garden tours, Easter Egg fun, Apple Day. **Dogs**: welcome on short leads at all times.

White Horse Hill

Uffington, Oxfordshire

🏛️ ⬆️ ♿ 1979

The White Horse at Uffington is part of an ancient landscape, steeped in history and mythology. It's the oldest chalk figure in the country, dated to the late Bronze Age about 3,000 years ago. Its linear form dominates the landscape, yet no one knows how it was made. The walls of an Iron Age hill fort are visible on the hilltop, the highest point in Oxfordshire. You can also look down on a valley known as The Manger and a natural outcrop known as Dragon Hill, where St George was said to have fought and slain the dragon. **Note**: archaeological monuments under English Heritage guardianship. Sorry no toilet.

Making the most of your day: guided walks and events to re-chalk the White Horse. Stunning views can be enjoyed from the top of the hill. **Dogs**: under close control at all times (stock grazing).

Access: 🅿️ ♿
Sat Nav: use SN7 7QJ. **Parking**: on site.

Finding out more: 01793 762209 or whitehorsehill@nationaltrust.org.uk

Westbury Court Garden, Gloucestershire (above), and White Horse Hill, Oxfordshire (below)

Access: 🅿️ 🅻 🖥️ 👓 Grounds ♿ ♿ ♿
Parking: 300 yards.

Finding out more: 01452 760461 or westburycourt@nationaltrust.org.uk

Westbury Court Garden		M	T	W	T	F	S	S
9 Mar–30 Jun	10–5	·	·	W	T	F	S	S
1 Jul–30 Sep	10–5	M	T	W	T	F	S	S
1 Oct–23 Oct	10–5	·	·	W	T	F	S	S

Open Bank Holiday Mondays. Open other times by appointment.

Woodchester Park

Nympsfield, near Stroud, Gloucestershire

🖼 1994

This tranquil wooded valley contains a 'lost landscape': remains of an 18th- and 19th-century landscape park with a chain of five lakes. The restoration of this landscape is an ongoing project. Waymarked trails (steep in places) lead through picturesque scenery, passing an unfinished Victorian mansion. **Note**: mansion managed by Woodchester Mansion Trust. Toilet not always available. Mansion not National Trust, admission charges apply (including members).

Eating and shopping: seasonal café, shop and toilet facilities available at Woodchester Mansion (not National Trust).

Numerous waymarked trails run through the picturesque scenery at Woodchester Park, Gloucestershire

Making the most of your day: waymarked trails through valley and popular woodland play trail for children built along shortest route, which includes rope swings, see-saw, balance beams and zip wire. Events throughout the year. **Dogs**: under close control, on leads where requested.

Access: Grounds 🔖
Sat Nav: nearest GL10 3TS, then follow signs.
Parking: accessible from Nympsfield road, 300 yards from junction with B4066.

Finding out more: 01452 814213 or woodchesterpark@nationaltrust.org.uk

Additional countryside car parks in Gloucestershire and Buckinghamshire

Gloucestershire

Mayhill	GL18 1JS
Dover's Hill	GL55 6PN

Buckinghamshire

Ivinghoe Beacon	HP4 1NF
Pulpit Wood	
Whiteleaf Fields	HP27 0NB

Berkshire, Hampshire and the Isle of Wight

Mottisfont, Hampshire

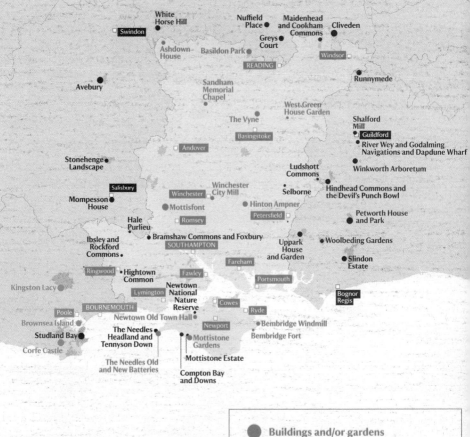

White Horse Hill

Nuffield Place

Maidenhead and Cookham Commons

Cliveden

Swindon

Greys Court

Ashdown House

Basildon Park

Windsor

READING

Avebury

Runnymede

Sandham Memorial Chapel

West Green House Garden

Shalford Mill

Guildford

River Wey and Godalming Navigations and Dapdune Wharf

The Vyne

Basingstoke

Andover

Ludshott Commons

Winkworth Arboretum

Stonehenge Landscape

Salisbury

Winchester City Mill

Selborne

Hindhead Commons and the Devil's Punch Bowl

Mompesson House

Winchester

Mottisfont

Hinton Ampner

Petworth House and Park

Hale Purlieu

Romsey

Petersfield

Ibsley and Rockford Commons

Bramshaw Commons and Foxbury

SOUTHAMPTON

Uppark House and Garden

Woolbeding Gardens

Slindon Estate

Ringwood

Hightown Common

Fawley

Fareham

Kingston Lacy

Lymington

Newtown National Nature Reserve

Portsmouth

Bognor Regis

BOURNEMOUTH

Cowes

Ryde

Poole

Newtown Old Town Hall

Newport

Bembridge Windmill

Brownsea Island

The Needles Headland and Tennyson Down

Mottistone Gardens

Bembridge Fort

Studland Bay

Mottistone Estate

Corfe Castle

The Needles Old and New Batteries

Compton Bay and Downs

● Buildings and/or gardens

● Entry points to coast and countryside

The size of each pin indicates how large a place is and how long you should allow for your visit

National Trust land

Ashdown House

Lambourn, Newbury, Berkshire RG17 8RE

🏛️🏚️❄️♿ 1956

Unique 17th-century chalk-block hunting lodge, with doll's-house appearance, built for the Queen of Bohemia by the Earl of Craven. The guided tour, which reveals an intriguing family history, leads up the staircase hung with fine 17th-century paintings. Outstanding rooftop views across three counties.
Note: access to roof via 100-step staircase.

Making the most of your day: guided tour.
Dogs: on leads in woodland only.

Access: 🅿️📷🔲 Building ♿ Grounds 🏢
Sat Nav: follow local brown signs from B4000.
Parking: in main estate car park, 437 yards.

Finding out more: 01494 755569 (Infoline). 01793 762209 or ashdownhouse@nationaltrust.org.uk

Ashdown House		M	T	W	T	F	S	S
House								
2 Apr–29 Oct	Tour*	·	·	**W**	·	·	**S**	·
Woodland								
2 Jan–31 Dec		**M**	**T**	**W**	**T**	·	**S**	**S**

*House admission by guided tour only, 2:15, 3:15 and 4:15 (advance booking not necessary).

Basildon Park

Lower Basildon, Reading, Berkshire RG8 9NR

🏛️❄️♿🍽️ 1978

Lovingly restored and on a grand scale; Lord and Lady Iliffe made it their life's work to bring this fine Georgian mansion back to its full glory, dressing it with carefully chosen antique fine furnishings and important Old Master paintings. By contrast, 'below stairs' the 1950s kitchen and laundry are utterly of their period, and the everyday homeware and equipment provide nostalgic hands-on fun for visitors of all ages. Outside, the informal gardens and extensive parkland, inspired by 'Capability' Brown, offer family activities and seasonal trails that everyone will enjoy. Recently featured in *Downton Abbey*. **Note**: entrance to main show rooms of mansion on first floor – 21 steps from ground level.

Eating and shopping: mansion tea-room serves hot lunches between 12 and 2:30, with homemade cakes and cream teas available all day. The Parlour in the stableyard offers tasty treats and drinks. The shop sells books, plants, local food, ice-cream and much more.

Making the most of your day: **Indoors** New exhibition, 'At Home with Art, Treasures of the Ford Collection'. Guided house tours. **Outdoors** Woodland and parkland walks. Wild Play and family activities. **Dogs**: welcome on leads in grounds. Assistance dogs only in house.

Access: 🅿️♿🅿️🚹♿📷🔲📺♫👓 Mansion ♿ Grounds ➡️
Sat Nav: not reliable, please follow brown tourist signs. **Parking**: 400 yards.

Finding out more: 01491 672382 or basildonpark@nationaltrust.org.uk

Basildon Park	
Open every day all year	10–5*

*House open 11 to 5 (tours only from 11 to 12). Between November and March access to house may be by guided tours only (telephone for details). Closes dusk if earlier. Closed 24 and 25 December.

Basildon Park, Berkshire: restoration on a grand scale

Bembridge Fort

Bembridge Down, near Bembridge,
Isle of Wight PO36 8QY

🏰 ♿ 🎫 1967

In a commanding position on top of Bembridge Down, this unrestored Victorian fort is open for volunteer-run guided tours. **Note**: sorry no toilets. Not suitable for children under ten. Open Tuesdays, 5 April to 25 October, 2 to 3:30 (access by guided tour only, booking essential).

Finding out more: 01983 741020 or bembridgefort@nationaltrust.org.uk c/o Longstone Farmhouse, Strawberry Lane, Mottistone, Isle of Wight PO30 4EA

Iconic Bembridge Windmill on the Isle of Wight

Bembridge Windmill

High Street, Bembridge,
Isle of Wight PO35 5SQ

✕ ♿ 1961

This little gem, the only surviving windmill on the Isle of Wight, is one of the island's most iconic images. Built *circa* 1700 and last operated in 1913, it still has most of its original machinery intact. Climb to the top and follow the milling process down its four floors.

Eating and shopping: reception kiosk with hot and cold drinks, including tea, hot chocolate and various coffees. Ice-creams, postcards, sweets, gifts and souvenirs. Picnic tables in grounds.

Making the most of your day: walks, including the start of Culver Trail. Nature trails (school holidays). Bembridge Fort (booking essential) nearby. **Dogs**: welcome in grounds on leads. Assistance dogs only in windmill.

Access: ♿🅿️🎦📷🚜👓 Building 🔦👨‍👩‍👧♿
Sat Nav: do not use, look for brown signs.
Parking: free (not National Trust), 100 yards in lay-by.

Finding out more: 01983 873945 or bembridgemill@nationaltrust.org.uk

Bembridge Windmill		M	T	W	T	F	S	S
12 Mar–30 Oct	10:30–5	**M**	**T**	**W**	**T**	**F**	**S**	**S**

Closes dusk if earlier. Conducted school groups and special visits March to end October (telephone or email to book).

Bramshaw Commons and Foxbury

near East Wellow, Hampshire

♿ 1928

Wide open spaces, gentle hillsides and hidden ponds can be discovered while exploring these recovering landscapes and their wildlife. This is a fragile conservation site for wildlife and we only allow access for special seasonal events.

Access: 🐾
Sat Nav: use SO51 6AQ and look out for the Omega signs. **Parking**: on Blackhill Road.

Finding out more: 01425 650035 or bramshaw@nationaltrust.org.uk

There's plenty of space to splash and play on the sandy beach of Compton Bay, Isle of Wight

Compton Bay and Downs

Compton, Isle of Wight

1961

Compton Bay offers a great day out, there's plenty of space on the sandy beach, and it's a prime site for fossil-hunting. The multi-coloured cliffs provide a wonderful backdrop, with fine views. A self-guided trail runs along part of this ridge, which is rich in wild flowers and butterflies.

Eating and shopping: licensed van selling hot and cold snacks, drinks and ice-cream.

Making the most of your day: one of the best spots on the Isle of Wight for swimming and surfing, or just taking time out. Why not search for dinosaur foot casts in the rocks? **Dogs**: welcome on beach between Hanover Point and Brook Chine all year.

Access: Compton Bay
Sat Nav: use PO30 4HB. **Parking**: on site.

Finding out more: 01983 741020 or comptonbay@nationaltrust.org.uk

Hale Purlieu

Hale, near Fordingbridge, Hampshire

1947

This wild heathland is especially atmospheric on a misty morning, when the glorious bird song will send your spirits soaring. **Note**: please stick to well-worn tracks, as some areas can be very boggy. For Sat Nav use SP6 2QZ. Look out for our Omega signs.

Finding out more: 01425 650035 or halepurlieu@nationaltrust.org.uk

Hightown Common

Ringwood, Hampshire

1929

Small but perfectly formed, this is the New Forest in miniature – a great place to explore with four-legged friends. **Note**: for Sat Nav use BH24 3HH.

Finding out more: 01425 650035 or hightowncommon@nationaltrust.org.uk

Hinton Ampner

Hinton Ampner, near Alresford,
Hampshire SO24 0LA

🏠✚⚙️🎫☕ 1986

Hinton Ampner is the fulfilment of one man's vision. After a catastrophic fire in 1960, Ralph Dutton rebuilt his home in the light and airy Georgian style he loved. A passionate collector, he filled the sunny rooms with ceramics and art. Outside, Dutton designed a series of tranquil garden rooms, each with their own distinctive planting still apparent today. Geometric topiary, exotic-coloured dahlias and borders of repeat-flowering roses lead onto terraces with panoramic views across the South Downs. Extensive lawns, a park with ancient oaks and beech woodland provide plenty of space to stroll, play, relax and picnic.

Eating and shopping: Stables tea-room serving seasonal dishes, homemade cakes and cream teas, made using produce grown in our walled garden. Shop selling many locally sourced products, including estate-grown plants. Second-hand bookshop. Picnics welcome.

Making the most of your day: **Indoors** Conservation demonstrations throughout the year. **Outdoors** Estate walking trails and free seasonal garden walks. Children's trails and events. Uppark House and Garden and Winchester City Mill nearby. **Dogs**: welcome on leads in parkland, estate walks and tea-room courtyard (no access to formal gardens).

Access: 🅿️♿🚶♿🐕📷📱♿📱
Building ♿🅱️ **Grounds** ♿➡️🅱️
Sat Nav: use SO24 0NH – takes you to Hinton Arms pub, 21 yards west of main entrance.
Parking: on site.

Finding out more: 01962 771305 or hintonampner@nationaltrust.org.uk

Hinton Ampner		M	T	W	T	F	S	S
Estate, garden, shop and tea-room*								
Open all year	10–5**	M	T	W	T	F	S	S
House								
13 Feb–19 Dec†	11–4:30††	M	T	W	T	F	S	S
Exhibition in main hall								
1 Jan–7 Feb	11–4:30††	M	T	W	T	F	S	S
27 Dec–31 Dec	11–4:30††		T	W	T	F	S	

Closed 24 and 25 December. *Tea-room: last service 4:30.
**Closes dusk if earlier. †House: closed 28 November to 2 December. ††House: last entry 45 minutes before closing.

From its elegant exterior (below) to its light and airy Georgian interior (above), Hinton Ampner, Hampshire, is a delight

Places may occasionally close for events or bad weather

Ibsley and Rockford Commons

near Ringwood, Hampshire

🦅 1999

Wild expanses of purple heather and scented yellow gorse, littered with rambling paths in a centuries-old landscape shaped by man. **Note**: steep hills and hidden tracks. Park at Moyles Court car park. For Sat Nav use BH24 3NF. Look out for our Omega signs.

Finding out more: 01425 650035 or ibsleyandrockford@nationaltrust.org.uk

Ludshott Commons

near Headley Down, Hampshire

🦅👟 1908

One of the largest remaining heaths in Hampshire, dotted with footpaths through ancient heathland, wood-pasture and wetlands brimming with wildlife. **Note**: for Sat Nav GU26 6JE.

Finding out more: 01428 751338 or ludshott@nationaltrust.org.uk

Maidenhead and Cookham Commons

near Maidenhead, Berkshire

🏛🦅 1934

Dotted around Maidenhead and Cookham, these attractive areas of common land are popular spots for walking, horse-riding and picnicking.

Eating and shopping: numerous shops, restaurants, pubs and cafés in nearby Cookham, Cookham Dean, Golden Ball, Pinkneys Green and Maidenhead (none National Trust).

Making the most of your day: butterfly trail around Maidenhead Thicket. **Dogs**: welcome (please be mindful of ground-nesting birds and cattle grazing).

Access: 🔗
Sat Nav: use SL6 6QD for Pinkneys Green.
Parking: numerous on site.

Finding out more: 01628 605069 or maidenheadandcookham@nationaltrust.org.uk

Maidenhead and Cookham Commons, Berkshire, are perfect for so many leisure activities

Mottisfont

near Romsey, Hampshire SO51 0LP

🏯 ❊ ⚲ 1957

Visitors enjoying Mottisfont, Hampshire (this page), and scented blooms (opposite)

Once across the crystal-clear river, visitors enter a garden paradise. Ancient trees, babbling brooks and rolling lawns frame this lovely old house. An 18th-century home with a medieval priory at its heart, Mottisfont inspired a 1930s dream of creativity. Artists came here to relax and create works, some of which are still visible in our historic rooms. We continue those artistic traditions today, with major exhibitions in our top-floor gallery. Outside, carpets of spring bulbs, a walled rose garden, rich autumn leaves and a colourful winter garden create a feast for the senses all year round. New for 2016 – Beatrix Potter exhibition in summer, and house open during the winter. **Note**: National Collection of Old-fashioned Roses (usually flowering June).

Eating and shopping: new visitor welcome facilities, including spacious shop and plant sales. Kitchen Café serving hot meals, and new Coach House Café opening in early 2016, serving light refreshments. Ice-cream parlour and second-hand bookshop.

Making the most of your day: open-air theatre and events throughout the year. Free daily guided walks and talks. Family fun activities, including building dens, make-and-take days and a new wild play trail. Five major exhibitions in the art gallery every year, including a summer family show with a creative challenge quest trail. Seasonal variety in the Winter Garden, with spring bulbs and late summer borders. Wider estate to explore on foot or by bike. **Dogs**: welcome on short leads at all times in most of grounds and garden.

Access: 🅿♿🚼🚻♿🚼🎨🖼🚻⛽♿
House and gallery 🚶♿♿ Grounds ♿➡♿
Sat Nav: use SO51 0LN. **Parking**: on site.

Finding out more: 01794 340757 or mottisfont@nationaltrust.org.uk

Mottisfont		M	T	W	T	F	S	S
Garden, shop, café and art gallery*								
Open all year	10–5**	M	T	W	T	F	S	S
House								
1 Mar–31 Dec	11–5†	M	T	W	T	F	S	S

*Gallery opens 11 and closes for short periods to change exhibitions. **Closes dusk if earlier. Closed 24 and 25 December. Late opening during rose season (except house and café), telephone for details. †Timed tickets may apply at certain times. House and gallery close at 4 from 1 November.

Why not share your pictures with us? #nationaltrust

Mottistone Estate

Mottistone, near Brighstone,
Isle of Wight PO30 4ED

[icons] 1965

A farmed landscape rich in wildlife, with
well-marked paths and coastal views from the
Long Stone. **Note**: toilets available within
Mottistone Gardens.

Finding out more: 01983 741020 or
mottistoneestate@nationaltrust.org.uk

Mottistone Gardens

Mottistone, near Brighstone,
Isle of Wight PO30 4ED

[icons] 1965

Set in a sheltered south-facing valley, these
gardens are full of surprises, with shrub-filled
banks, hidden pathways and colourful
herbaceous borders. Surrounding an attractive
manor house (tenanted, not open), these
20th-century gardens have a Mediterranean-
style planting scheme to take advantage of its
southerly location, including drought-tolerant
plants from subtropical regions. Other
surprises include a monocot border, a small
organic kitchen garden and a traditional
tea-garden alongside The Shack, a unique cabin
retreat designed as their summer drawing
office by architects John Seely (2nd Lord
Mottistone) and Paul Paget. There are also
delightful walks across the adjoining
Mottistone Estate. **Note**: manor house open
two days a year.

Eating and shopping: shop selling gifts, books,
cards, postcards and ice-cream. Plant stall.
Second-hand books. Tea-garden serving hot
and cold drinks, soup, sandwiches, cake, cream
teas and light refreshments.

Mottistone Gardens on the Isle of Wight:
full of surprises, these gardens benefit from their
position in a sheltered, south-facing valley

Making the most of your day: family events
and garden tours. Flowerpot trail and estate
walks. Newtown Old Town Hall and The
Needles Old Battery and New Battery nearby.
Dogs: welcome on leads.

Access: [icons]
The Shack [icons] Garden [icons]
Parking: 50 yards.

Finding out more: 01983 741302 or
mottistonegardens@nationaltrust.org.uk

Mottistone Gardens		M	T	W	T	F	S	S
Gardens and shop								
13 Mar–27 Oct	10:30–5	M	T	W	T	.	.	S
Shop								
3 Nov–10 Dec	11–3	.	.	.	T	F	S	.
11 Dec	11–3	.	.	.	.	.	.	S

Closes dusk if earlier. Manor house open two days only:
29 May by guided tour 9:30 to 12 (timed ticket, available on
day); free-flow 1 to 5, and 30 May, 10:30 to 5 by free-flow
(additional charges apply).

The Needles Old Battery and New Battery

West High Down, Alum Bay,
Isle of Wight PO39 0JH

🏛️♿🎦🏠 1975

Perched high above The Needles, amid acres of unspoilt countryside, is The Needles Old Battery, a Victorian fort built in 1862 and used throughout both World Wars. The Parade Ground has two original guns, and the fort's fascinating military history is brought to life with displays and models, plus a series of vivid cartoons by acclaimed comic book artist Geoff Campion. An underground tunnel leads to a searchlight emplacement with dramatic views over The Needles rocks. The New Battery, further up the headland, has an exhibition on the secret British rocket tests carried out there during the Cold War. **Note**: steep paths and uneven surfaces. Spiral staircase to tunnel. Toilet at Old Battery only.

Unbeatable views from The Needles Old Battery, Isle of Wight

The Needles Headland and Tennyson Down

West High Down, Alum Bay,
Isle of Wight PO39 0JH

🏛️♿🎦🏠 1975

Tennyson Down (above) is probably one of the most popular places to walk on the island. You can enjoy it just for the great leg-stretch from Freshwater Bay to the Needles Headland, and drink in the salt-laden air that so inspired Tennyson. **Note**: toilets at the Needles Old Battery (seasonal). Bus from Alum Bay car park to Batteries, not National Trust (discount for members).

Eating and shopping: when you've reached the Needles Headland, satisfy your hunger and thirst at the Needles New Battery (open March to October, 11 to 4).

Making the most of your day: the best view of the Needles is from our viewpoint just down from the Needles New Battery. The clifftop walks and coastal views are the best on the island. **Dogs**: welcome under close control as the downs are grazed by sheep and cattle.

Access: 🅿
Sat Nav: use PO39 0JH. **Parking**: at High Down car park and Alum Bay. Also at Freshwater Bay (not National Trust).

Finding out more: 01983 754772 or needlesheadland@nationaltrust.org.uk

The Needles Headland, Isle of Wight

Newtown National Nature Reserve

Town Lane, Newtown, Isle of Wight PO30 4PA

[icons] 1963

Wander past flower-filled hay meadows and through ancient woodlands with rare butterflies and red squirrels down to the picturesque harbour. **Note**: parking at Visitor Point opposite Newtown Old Town Hall.

Eating and shopping: clifftop 1940s-style tea-room serving soup, jacket potatoes, sandwiches, cakes, cream teas and light refreshments. Picnic tables. Gift shop selling confectionery, gifts and souvenirs. Drinks, snacks and ice-cream available at New Battery kiosk.

Making the most of your day: Indoors Family activity packs. Inspector and soldier trails. **Outdoors** Clifftop walks to Tennyson Monument and beyond. **Dogs**: welcome on leads, although assistance dogs only in tea-room.

Access: [icons]
Old Battery [icons] New Battery [icons]
Parking: no parking on site (limited disabled parking by arrangement). Nearest at Alum Bay, ¾ mile, not National Trust (minimum charge £4, including members). Freshwater Bay, 3½ miles (not National Trust), or Highdown (196:SZ325856) 2 miles.

Finding out more: 01983 754772 or needlesoldbattery@nationaltrust.org.uk

Finding out more: 01983 741020 or newtownnaturereserve@nationaltrust.org.uk

Newtown Old Town Hall

Newtown, near Shalfleet, Isle of Wight PO30 4PA

[icons] 1933

Tucked away in a tiny hamlet adjoining the National Nature Reserve, this small and quirky 17th-century building (below) is the only remaining evidence of Newtown's former importance. It's hard to believe that this tranquil corner of the island once held what were often turbulent elections before sending two Members to Parliament. **Note**: nearest toilet in car park.

The Needles Batteries		M	T	W	T	F	S	S
Old Battery and tea-room*								
12 Mar–30 Oct	10:30–5	M	T	W	T	F	S	S
New Battery								
12 Mar–30 Oct	11–4	M	T	W	T	F	S	S
Tea-room								
2 Jan–28 Feb	11–3						S	S
13 Feb–21 Feb	11–3	M	T	W	T	F	S	S
5 Nov–11 Dec	11–3						S	S

*Closes dusk if earlier. Property closes in high winds. 15 May: no disabled vehicular access due to Walk the Wight. 2 July: Old Battery early opening for Round the Island Yacht Race.

Eating and shopping: postcards and souvenirs available.

Making the most of your day: **Indoors** Children's quiz sheet. Exhibitions by local artists. **Outdoors** National Nature Reserve walks. Bird hide (April to September). Family activities run by Newtown Ranger from nearby Visitor Point.

Access: 🅿🗎🗒📖🖼🔊📷 **Building** ♿
Parking: 15 yards.

Finding out more: 01983 531785.
01983 531622 (Visitor Point) or
oldtownhall@nationaltrust.org.uk

Newtown Old Town Hall		M	T	W	T	F	S	S
13 Mar–20 Oct	2–5	·	T	W	T	·	·	S

Last admission 15 minutes before closing. Closes dusk if earlier.

Sandham Memorial Chapel, Hampshire:
a tranquil yet powerful place

Sandham Memorial Chapel

Harts Lane, Burghclere, near Newbury,
Hampshire RG20 9JT

✚ ❋ 1947

This tranquil yet powerful place contains an outstanding series of paintings by artist Stanley Spencer, inspired by his experiences as a First World War medical orderly and soldier. An exhibition tells the story of Sandham, while outside the garden provides space to reflect and picnic.

Eating and shopping: small shop selling books, postcards, plants and local products. Picnics welcome.

Making the most of your day: new exhibition contextualising the paintings. **Dogs**: in grounds on leads only.

Access: 🅿🗎🖥🔊🖼🚻📷 **Chapel** ♿
Visitor reception/exhibition ♿ **Grounds** ♿♿➡
Parking: opposite entrance to chapel.

Finding out more: 01635 278394 or
sandham@nationaltrust.org.uk

Sandham Memorial Chapel		M	T	W	T	F	S	S
2 Mar–3 Apr	11–4	·	·	W	T	F	S	S
6 Apr–30 Sep	11–4	·	·	W	T	F	·	·
9 Apr–2 Oct	11–5	·	·	·	·	·	S	S
5 Oct–30 Oct	11–4	·	·	W	T	F	S	S

Open Bank Holiday Mondays, 11 to 4.

Selborne

near Alton, Hampshire

🏞🚶 1933

These beechwood hangers and flower-filled meadows inspired the pioneering naturalist Gilbert White, and are havens for wildlife and walkers alike. **Note**: traditional management with grazing animals in operation.
For Sat Nav use GU34 3JR.

Finding out more: 01428 751338 or
selborne@nationaltrust.org.uk

The Vyne

Vyne Road, Sherborne St John, Basingstoke, Hampshire RG24 9HL

🏠✝❄🐾🐕♿☂ 1956

Once an important Tudor palace, this atmospheric mansion has some illustrious connections, from Henry VIII to Jane Austen and J. R. R. Tolkien. Rare 16th-century interiors mix with elaborate 18th-century architecture, and there are rooms filled with treasures, including an ancient cursed ring and jewel-encrusted casket. Outside, acres of wildlife-rich gardens, meadows and woods create a wonderful space for relaxation and exploration, and a unique 'Hidden Realm' play space gives children freedom to let their imaginations take them on fantasy adventures. Sweeping lawns offer lakeside picnicking, and a short stroll reveals a cosy bird hide overlooking the water meadows. **Note**: major repair works starting this year, visitor route may change. Whole house will be scaffolded.

Eating and shopping: tea-room serving light lunches, soup, sandwiches, cakes and scones. Gift shop. Second-hand bookshop in house, plant sales. Picnics welcome.

Making the most of your day: **Indoors** Events and activities all year. Free guided tours, exhibitions and themed days. **Outdoors** Open-air theatre. Seasonal garden tours, trails and woodland walks. Geocaching, orienteering and inspirational 'Hidden Realm' playground.

Dogs: welcome on short leads in woodlands and most of gardens.

Access: 🅿♿♿♿♿♿♿📷🖥♿👓🔦
Building ♿🅱 **Grounds** ♿🅱
Sat Nav: not reliable, follow brown tourist signs. **Parking**: on site.

Finding out more: 01256 883858 or thevyne@nationaltrust.org.uk

The Vyne	
Open every day all year	10–5*

*Closes dusk if earlier. House opens 11 for visit by tour or timed ticket (telephone for details). Shop opens 11. Last entry one hour before closing. Closed 24 and 25 December.

The Vyne, Hampshire: interior splendour (above), and so much space to explore outside (below)

West Green House Garden

West Green, Hartley Wintney,
Hampshire RG27 8JB

❖ 1957

Four seasons of beauty, contrast and
inspiration. Created by acclaimed garden
designer and writer Marylyn Abbott.
Note: maintained on behalf of the National
Trust by Marylyn Abbott. Facilities not National
Trust. Open Wednesday to Sunday, 2 March to
30 October, 11 to 4:30 and daily 16 November
to 18 December, 11 to 4.

Finding out more: 01252 844611 or
westgreenhouse@nationaltrust.org.uk

Winchester City Mill

Bridge Street, Winchester,
Hampshire SO23 9BH

🏠❖☂ 1929

This fully restored working watermill has stood
at the heart of the city of Winchester for a
millennium and is probably the oldest working
watermill in the UK. As the official Gateway to
the South Downs National Park, City Mill
provides information for visitors wishing
to explore local walks and attractions.
Note: nearest toilet 220 yards
(not National Trust).

Eating and shopping: shop selling local
produce, gifts and books, as well as our freshly
milled wholemeal flour.

Making the most of your day: tours,
workshops and exhibitions. School holiday
quizzes and trails and seasonal events for the
whole family, including Easter Egg hunts.
Flour-milling demonstrations every weekend
and regular baking demonstrations.
Dogs: assistance dogs only.

Access: 🅿🖼📷📱♿☂⋮📷 **Building** ♿
Sat Nav: do not use. **Parking**: at Chesil car
park or park and ride, neither National Trust
(charge including members).

Finding out more: 01962 870057 or
winchestercitymill@nationaltrust.org.uk

Winchester City Mill		M	T	W	T	F	S	S
1 Jan–24 Dec	10–4	**M**	**T**	**W**	**T**	**F**	**S**	**S**

15 February to 30 October, open to 5.

**Winchester City Mill, Hampshire: the
watermill (top) and internal machinery**

Kent, Surrey
and Sussex

Box Hill, Surrey

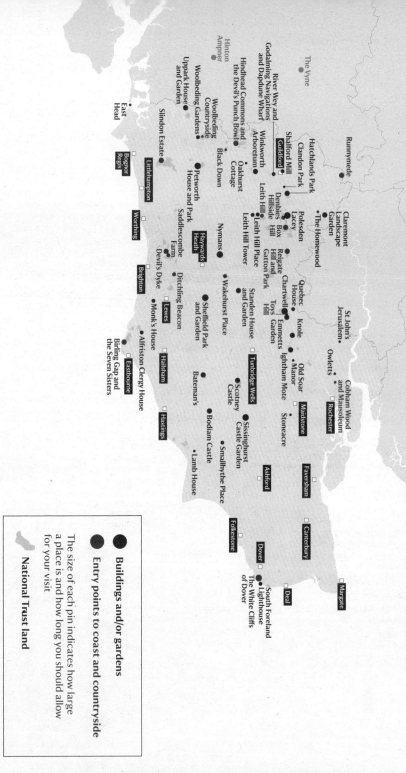

Hinton
Ampner

The Vyne

East
Head

River Wey and
Godalming Navigations
and Dapdune Wharf

Hindhead Commons and
the Devil's Punch Bowl

Uppark House
and Garden

Woolbeding
Countryside

Woolbeding Gardens

Black Down

Slindon Estate

Bognor
Regis

Littlehampton

Worthing

Clandon Park

Shalford Mill

Guildford

Hatchlands Park

Winkworth
Arboretum

Oakhurst
Cottage

Leith Hill

Polesden
Lacey

Denbies
Hillside

Box
Hill

Petworth
House and Park

Saddlescombe
Farm

Devil's Dyke

Brighton

Runnymede

Claremont
Landscape
Garden

The Homewood

Quebec
House

Reigate
Hill and
Gatton Park

Chartwell

Emmetts
Garden

Leith Hill Place

Leith Hill Tower

Nymans

Hayward's
Heath

Monk's House

Lewes

Ditchling Beacon

Wakehurst Place

Sheffield Park
and Garden

Standen House
and Garden

Toys
Garden

Knole

Old Soar
Manor

Ightham Mote

St John's
Jerusalem

Owlets

Cobham Wood
and Mausoleum

Tunbridge Wells

Scotney
Castle

Sissinghurst
Castle Garden

Stoneacre

Maidstone

Rochester

Halsham

Eastbourne

Alfriston Clergy House

Birling Gap and
the Seven Sisters

Bateman's

Bodiam Castle

Lamb House

Smallhythe
Place

Hastings

Ashford

Faversham

Folkestone

Canterbury

Dover

South Foreland
Lighthouse

The White Cliffs
of Dover

Deal

Margate

The size of each pin indicates how large
a place is and how long you should allow
for your visit

● ● Buildings and/or gardens

● ● Entry points to coast and countryside

National Trust land

Alfriston Clergy House

The Tye, Alfriston, Polegate,
East Sussex BN26 5TL

🏠 ❄ 1896

The pretty garden at Alfriston Clergy House, East Sussex

This rare 14th-century Wealden 'hall-house' was the first building to be acquired by the National Trust, in 1896. The thatched, timber-framed house is in an idyllic setting, with views across the River Cuckmere, and is surrounded by a tranquil cottage garden full of wildlife. **Note**: nearest toilet in village car park.

Eating and shopping: shop selling souvenirs.

Making the most of your day: **Indoors** Children's quizzes and trails. Varied events all year. **Outdoors** Short circular walks and longer hikes over the South Downs.

Access: 🅿️🗺️🖥️👓🅿️
Building 🦽🚶 **Grounds** 🦽🚶
Parking: 500 yards in village car parks (not National Trust).

Finding out more: 01323 871961 or alfriston@nationaltrust.org.uk

Alfriston Clergy House		M	T	W	T	F	S	S
27 Feb–13 Mar	10:30–5	·	·	·	·	·	S	S
14 Mar–30 Oct	10:30–5	M	T	W	·	·	S	S
31 Oct–18 Dec	11–4	M	T	W	·	·	S	S
Open Good Friday.								

Bateman's

Bateman's Lane, Burwash,
East Sussex TN19 7DS

🏠🖼️❄🍴🛍️ 1940

Rudyard Kipling loved this place; it was his personal paradise, and somewhere he could enjoy family life. Surrounded by the wooded landscape of the Sussex Weald, this 17th-century house, with mullion windows, pretty secluded garden and acres of countryside, provided a tranquil sanctuary. The atmospheric oak-beamed rooms remain much as he left them. Outside, winding paths take in manicured lawns, a wildflower meadow and Kipling's 1928 Rolls-Royce Phantom 1, while beside the river sits a 17th-century watermill.

Eating and shopping: shop selling Kipling souvenirs, specialist second-hand Kipling books and plants from the garden. Tea-room offering seasonal lunches (made using fresh produce from the kitchen garden), homemade cakes and light bites.

Garden giants at Bateman's in East Sussex

Set in the Sussex Weald, Bateman's was Rudyard Kipling's personal paradise

Making the most of your day: **Indoors** Children's house guide. **Outdoors** Re-enactment weekends, garden and countryside walks. Family fun days. Children's Tracker Packs, quizzes, trails and storytelling. Scotney Castle and Bodiam Castle nearby. **Dogs**: welcome in the gardens on a short lead.

Access: 🅿️♿🐕🚾👶📷📺♿🚻♿
Building ♿♿♿ Grounds ♿▶️♿
Parking: 30 yards.

Finding out more: 01435 882302 or batemans@nationaltrust.org.uk

Bateman's		M	T	W	T	F	S	S
House								
1 Jan–26 Feb	11:30–3:30	M	T	W	T	F	S	S
27 Feb–30 Oct	11–5*	M	T	W	T	F	S	S
31 Oct–31 Dec	11:30–3:30*	M	T	W	T	F	S	S
Garden, shop and tea-room								
Open all year	10–5*	M	T	W	T	F	S	S

*Closes at dusk if earlier. Closed 24 and 25 December.

Birling Gap and the Seven Sisters

near Eastbourne, East Sussex

🚻🛏️♿🍷 1931

For drama, nothing beats the point where the sheer chalk cliffs of the South Downs meet the sea. One of the south coast's longest undeveloped stretches, the Seven Sisters are truly iconic. If you venture down the steps onto the beach, you can discover fascinating rock pools and the intricate wave-cut platform. Our visitor centre, with its café and shop, is a delightful place to start or end your peaceful downland walk. Before you explore the rare chalk heath and grassland, why not pick up a Tracker Pack or get some friendly advice from a volunteer in the visitor centre?

Eating and shopping: clifftop café serving coffee, tea, fish and chips, cream teas, cakes and soup. Seaside shop selling local and seasonal items. Picnic area outside shop.

Making the most of your day: events and activities for all ages. Chyngton Farm, Frog Firle Farm, Alfriston Clergy House and Monk's House nearby. **Dogs**: welcome, on leads in café, shop and visitor centre or near livestock.

Birling Gap and the Seven Sisters in East Sussex (above and opposite): these astonishing sheer chalk cliffs are truly iconic

Access: [P] [icons] Café [icon] Shop [icon]
Sat Nav: use BN20 0AB. **Parking**: at Birling Gap.

Finding out more: 01323 423197 or
birlinggap@nationaltrust.org.uk

Birling Gap and the Seven Sisters	M	T	W	T	F	S	S
Café and shop							
Open all year*	10–4:30**	M	T	W	T	F	S	S

*Closed 24 and 25 December. Extended hours in summer.
**Closes dusk if earlier.

Black Down

Haslemere, Surrey

[icon] 1944

Highest point on the South Downs with breathtaking views. The heathland and woodland offer a true sense of the wild.
Note: sorry no toilet. For Sat Nav use GU27 3AF.

Finding out more: 01428 652359 or
blackdown@nationaltrust.org.uk

Bodiam Castle

Bodiam, near Robertsbridge,
East Sussex TN32 5UA

🏰 🏛 ⚓ 🍽 1926

A brooding symbol of power for over 700 years, the strong stone walls of Bodiam Castle rise up proudly from the peaceful river-valley setting. A wide moat encircles the seemingly untouched medieval exterior. Once inside, spiral stairways, tower rooms and battlements with dizzying viewpoints are ripe for exploration. The ruins of the inner rooms are brought to life through stories told by a range of medieval characters and audio adventure – 'A Knight's Peril'. **Note**: popular with schools. Toilets in car park only.

Eating and shopping: shop selling gifts, castle-themed products and local produce. Tea-room serving homemade lunches, teas, snacks and ice-cream. Seasonal coffee shop overlooking the castle.

Making the most of your day: medieval character talks, trails and activities. Choose your own interactive adventure, 'A Knight's Peril'. Events, including Building Bodiam, Easter trail and family activities throughout the year. **Dogs**: welcome on leads in grounds only.

Access: 🅿️ 🚻 🚼 ♿ ⬆️ 🛗 🔄 💻 🎧 👓 🖼
Castle 🚶 🏛 ⬆️ ♿ **Grounds** ➡️ ♿
Parking: 400 yards.

Finding out more: 01580 830196 or bodiamcastle@nationaltrust.org.uk

Bodiam Castle	
Open every day all year	10–5*

*Closes dusk if earlier. Castle opens 10:30. Closed 24 and 25 December.

Moated and castellated Bodiam Castle, East Sussex, has been a brooding symbol of power for more than 700 years

Box Hill

Tadworth, Surrey

 1914

A great place for family adventures: exploring the woods, braving the natural play trail, finding the tower or paddling in the River Mole at the stepping stones. On a clear day you can see for miles from the top of Box Hill, so if you're hiking up, the view is well worth it. You can pick up free walks guides from the shepherd's hut and café or find your own way along our many footpaths. Borrow a kite or a children's Tracker Pack to explore the wild and make the most of the weather.

Eating and shopping: the Box Hill café, with its pretty crockery, has indoor and outdoor seating and serves light lunches, snacks and afternoon teas. Servery offers takeaway hot drinks, cakes, sandwiches and the famous 'revival' flapjack!

Making the most of your day: school holiday activities and walks guides available; you are welcome to borrow a kite or Tracker Pack from the shepherd's hut. **Dogs**: under close control where livestock is grazing.

Enjoying the sunset at Box Hill, Surrey (above). Children have fun paddling and exploring the fresh springtime woodland (right)

Access: ⭤⭤⭤⭤⭤
Café and Discovery Zone ⭤ Grounds ⭤
Sat Nav: use KT20 7LB. **Parking**: off the Box Hill Zig Zag road (short walk to café and viewpoint).

Finding out more: 01306 888793.
01306 878554 (learning and events) or boxhill@nationaltrust.org.uk

Box Hill		M	T	W	T	F	S	S
Countryside								
Open all year		M	T	W	T	F	S	S
Shop, café, Discovery Zone and servery								
1 Jan–24 Mar	10–4	M	T	W	T	F	S	S
25 Mar–30 Oct	9–5	M	T	W	T	F	S	S
31 Oct–31 Dec	10–4	M	T	W	T	F	S	S

Servery, shop, café and Discovery Zone may close early in bad weather. Closed 25 December.

Chartwell

Mapleton Road, Westerham, Kent TN16 1PS

🏠♿️♨️🔔⚓️🍽️ 1946

Chartwell was a home and a place that truly inspired Sir Winston Churchill. The house is still much as it was when the family lived here, with pictures, books and personal mementoes. The studio is home to the largest collection of Churchill's paintings. The garden reflects Churchill's love of the landscape and nature including the lakes he created, the kitchen garden and the Marycot, a playhouse designed for his youngest daughter Mary. Make the most of our six swings leading to the woodland estate, which offers family walks, trails, den-building, a Canadian camp and opportunities to stretch your legs. You may come across our resident cat, Jock, making his daily inspection of the grounds. **Note**: house entrance by timed ticket only, available on the day from the visitor welcome centre.

Chartwell, Kent: the Churchill family (opposite), and the house, outside and in (above and below)

Eating and shopping: Landemare Café serving seasonal dishes, hot food, salads, light bites, cream teas and delicious cakes. Shop stocking Churchill memorabilia, books, garden ornaments, plants and local produce. Plus a special range of Jock the cat items. Picnics welcome.

Making the most of your day: **Indoors** Daily talks in the studio about Sir Winston's paintings. New temporary exhibitions in the winter months – January and February 'Into the Trenches', then in November and December 'Child of the Commons'. **Outdoors** Family adventure trails around the garden and estate throughout the season. Tours of Churchill's family garden on selected days. The woodland trail offers great views of the house and connects with the hilly five-mile circular Weardale Walk to Emmetts Garden. Why not pick up some takeaway food from the Landemare Café and enjoy a picnic on the lower lawns by the lakes? **Dogs**: welcome on short leads in the gardens and estate.

Access: 🅿️🅳🔥🏛️🔔🔟🖼️🎥🎬🔄📷
Building 🔥🏛️🔟 Grounds 🔥🏛️🔟
Parking: on site.

Finding out more: 01732 868381 or chartwell@nationaltrust.org.uk

Chartwell		M	T	W	T	F	S	S
House								
27 Feb–30 Oct	11–5*	·	·	·	·	·	S	S
29 Feb–28 Oct	11:30–5*	M	T	W	T	F	·	·
3 Dec–18 Dec	11–3*	·	·	·	·	·	S	S
Garden, exhibition, studio, shop and café								
Open all year	10–5**	M	T	W	T	F	S	S

*Entry to house by timed ticket (places limited) available from the visitor centre. Last entry 45 minutes before closing.
**Studio opens daily, times vary, closed in January, tours only in February. Exhibition closes for short periods to change display. Closes dusk if earlier. Whole site closed 24 and 25 December.

Clandon Park

West Clandon, Guildford, Surrey GU4 7RQ

Until a major fire in April 2015, Clandon Park was one of the country's most complete Palladian mansions. Although the fire has devastated Clandon, we are hopeful that we can rebuild in some shape or form. For up-to-date information, including future opening arrangements, please contact the property.

Finding out more: 01483 222482 or clandonpark@nationaltrust.org.uk

Claremont Landscape Garden

Portsmouth Road, Esher, Surrey KT10 9JG

❀ 1949

Hidden in the heart of Surrey, this green oasis (below) has always been a place to escape everyday life and enjoy simple pleasures with family and friends. For centuries the garden was a sanctuary for some of the wealthiest, most influential people in the country, but today everyone can enjoy it. The impressive turf amphitheatre offers wonderful views over the lake. Walks take in interesting features like the grotto and camellia terrace. As a child Queen Victoria loved relaxing here and the tradition of play continues today, with nine-pin bowling, two play areas and a cottage full of toys and games. **Note**: limited parking during busy times. Please park considerately to maximise spaces available.

A gentle stroll at Claremont Landscape Garden, Surrey

Eating and shopping: café (licensed) serving lunches and freshly baked homemade cakes, biscuits and scones. Outside terraced seating area overlooking lake. Café is outside the pay barrier and close to the car park at the main entrance. Shop area within café. Free wi-fi.

Making the most of your day: events throughout the year, including children's trails, crafts and activities during school holidays. Guided walks. Belvedere Tower open on selected dates (April to October).
Dogs: welcome on short leads between 1 October and 31 March only.

Access: ⓟ♿♿♿♿♿♿ Grounds ♿➡♿
Sat Nav: unreliable, instead follow brown signs from Cobham and Esher. **Parking**: main car park at entrance. Space limited at busy times – use car park in West End Lane opposite.

Finding out more: 01372 467806 or claremont@nationaltrust.org.uk

Claremont Landscape Garden		M	T	W	T	F	S	S
1 Jan–31 Jan	10–5*	M	T	W	T	F	S	S
1 Feb–31 Mar	10–5	M	T	W	T	F	S	S
1 Apr–31 Oct	10–6	M	T	W	T	F	S	S
1 Nov–31 Dec	10–5*	M	T	W	T	F	S	S

Café and shop close 30 minutes earlier than garden.
*Closes at dusk if earlier, local closing times posted at the property. Closed 24 and 25 December.

Cobham Wood and Mausoleum

near Cobham, Kent

🏠♿ 2014

Sitting proud in historic woodland pasture, the 18th-century Darnley Mausoleum commands stunning views across the North Kent Downs. **Note**: for Sat Nav use DA12 3BS. Woodland open every day all year, dawn to dusk. Mausoleum open first Sunday of the month, April to September, 12:30 to 4:30 (normally also open one weekday). South Lodge Barn first Sunday of the month, April to September, 12 to 5.

Finding out more: 01732 810378 or cobham@nationaltrust.org.uk

Denbies Hillside

near Dorking, Surrey

♿ 1963

Denbies Hillside is a dramatic chalk escarpment with panoramic views of the Surrey countryside. It's a great place for walking, picnics and wildlife-watching – you may even spot chalk downland species such as the Adonis blue and chalkhill blue butterflies.

Eating and shopping: picnic area with benches in Steers Field.

Far-reaching view from Denbies Hillside in Surrey

Why not share your pictures with us? #nationaltrust

Making the most of your day: self-guided trail, spectacular views and several Second World War pillboxes to discover. Why not visit nearby Hackhurst Downs? **Dogs**: welcome, on leads when livestock are grazing.

Access: 🅿️ ♿
Sat Nav: use RH5 6SR. **Parking**: at Ranmore West car park and Denbies Hillside.

Finding out more: 01306 887485 or denbieshillside@nationaltrust.org.uk

Devil's Dyke

near Brighton, West Sussex

🎫 🏛️ ♿ 1995

At nearly a mile long, the Dyke Valley (above) is the longest, deepest and widest 'dry valley' in the UK. Legend has it that the Devil dug this chasm to drown the parishioners of the Weald. On the other hand, scientists believe it was formed naturally just over 10,000 years ago in the last ice age. The walls of the Iron Age hill fort can be seen when you walk around the hill, and there is a carpet of flowers and a myriad of colourful insects to discover in the valley.

Eating and shopping: Devil's Dyke pub (not National Trust) beside car park.

Making the most of your day: self-guided walks leaflet, orienteering course map and family Discovery Packs available from information trailer (open April to September, weekends and some weekdays). Numerous bridleways offer great cycling.

Access: 🅿️ 🅳 ♿ 🦮 🚶 ♿ ➡️
Sat Nav: use BN1 8YJ. **Parking**: on site.

Finding out more: 01273 857712 or devilsdyke@nationaltrust.org.uk

Ditchling Beacon

near Ditchling, Westmeston, East Sussex

🏛️ ♿ 1953

Just 7 miles north of Brighton, at 248 metres above sea level, Ditchling Beacon is the highest point in East Sussex and offers panoramic views (below) all around the summit. To the south visitors can see the sea, while to the north you look across the Weald or east-west across the Downs. The site also has the remains of an Iron Age hill fort. Situated on the South Downs Way, it makes an excellent place to start a walk heading west towards Devil's Dyke or east towards Black Cap and Lewes.

Eating and shopping: refreshments available from ice-cream van. Picnics welcome.

Making the most of your day: great for bracing walks with amazing views on the South Downs. Traces of the rampart and ditch of the hill fort to discover. Why not visit nearby Ditchling Down? **Dogs**: welcome but must be kept on leads at all times.

Access: 🅿️ ♿
Sat Nav: use BN6 8XG. **Parking**: off Ditchling Road.

Finding out more: 01323 423197 or ditchlingbeacon@nationaltrust.org.uk

East Head

near Chichester, West Sussex

[icons] 1966

One of the last surviving areas of natural coastline in West Sussex, with unspoilt sand dunes and fabulous views. **Note**: for Sat Nav use PO20 8AJ.

Finding out more: 01243 814730 or easthead@nationaltrust.org.uk

Emmetts Garden

Ide Hill, Sevenoaks, Kent TN14 6BA

[icons] 1965

Every season brings its own delights at colourful Emmetts Garden in Kent (above and below)

Emmetts is a garden to enjoy with friends and family. If you delve a little deeper, there are exotic plants collected from around the world and a host of stories to be discovered. Emmetts is known for its beautiful bluebells and amazing spring colour, summer brings the romantic rose garden, followed by vibrant autumn foliage – there is something to see all year round. It is a place where you can let off steam, play games, picnic in our meadow or simply sit back and relax. Far-reaching views across the Weald of Kent can be enjoyed from our countryside walks.

Eating and shopping: the Old Stables serving cakes, bakes and light refreshments. Shop selling a variety of gifts, including children's toys, sweets, jams and souvenirs. Venture outside to the plant area for an array of garden gifts.

Making the most of your day: children's trails during the school holidays and December. Children's activities can be found in the Discovery Cabin. Garden tours (selected days). Walk guides available for the surrounding countryside. **Dogs**: welcome on short leads in gardens and in the wider countryside.

Access: [icons] Grounds [icons]
Parking: 100 yards.

Finding out more: 01732 751507 or emmetts@nationaltrust.org.uk

Emmetts Garden			M	T	W	T	F	S	S
27 Feb–31 Dec	10–5*		**M**	**T**	**W**	**T**	**F**	**S**	**S**

*Last entry 45 minutes before closing. Closes dusk if earlier. All winter opening weather permitting. Closed 24 and 25 December.

Hatchlands Park

East Clandon, Guildford, Surrey GU4 7RT

🏠 ✥ ♨ 1945

With open fields, ancient woodland and wildflower meadows, the parkland is perfect for relaxation and exploration. Our natural adventure area is a great place for families and, new for this year, both young and old can climb to our tree house and get even closer to nature. Nestled in the parkland is a Georgian country house, home to Alec Cobbe and his superb collection of paintings and the Cobbe Collection, Europe's largest array of keyboard instruments – including some which inspired such world-famous composers as J. C. Bach, Elgar and Chopin. **Note**: only six ground-floor rooms are open to the public.

Eating and shopping: café in the original kitchen. Gift shop. Picnic areas.

Bluebells light up the woods at Hatchlands Park, Surrey

Making the most of your day: **Indoors** Guided mansion tours most Thursdays. Cellar tours (selected days). Cobbe Collection concerts. **Outdoors** Children's adventure area, Sylvanian Families trail, open-air theatre. NGS Quiet Garden. **Dogs**: welcome under close control in designated parkland areas.

Access: 🅿️ 🏛 🚻 ♿ 🔄 📷 ♿ ∴ 🏞
Building 🏛 🏛 ♿ **Grounds** 🏞 ➡ ♿
Sat Nav: misleading, instead follow brown signs to main entrance on A246 (grid reference TQ06349 51580). **Parking**: 300 yards.

Finding out more: 01483 222482 or hatchlands@nationaltrust.org.uk

Hatchlands Park		M	T	W	T	F	S	S
House and garden†								
27 Mar–30 Oct*	2–5:30	·	T	W	T	·	·	S
Shop, café, park walks and NGS Quiet Garden								
1 Jan–26 Mar††	10:30–4	M	T	W	T	F	S	S
27 Mar–30 Oct**	10:30–5:30	M	T	W	T	F	S	S
31 Oct–31 Dec††	10:30–4	M	T	W	T	F	S	S

*Also open Fridays in August.†Garden open 10:30 to 6 on house open days. Open Bank Holiday Mondays. ††Closes dusk if earlier. Closed 24 and 25 December. **Park walks and NGS Quiet Garden open to 6.

Hindhead Commons and the Devil's Punch Bowl

near Hindhead, Surrey

1906

Spectacular views from Hindhead Commons and uninterrupted walks to the Devil's Punch Bowl make this an unforgettable place to relax and take in some of the best countryside in the South East. Since the opening of the A3 tunnel, paths, cycle routes and bridleways have been reconnected and natural contours restored. Peace and calm now reign and the glorious landscape, with its carpets of purple heather in the summer and grazing Highland cattle, is there to enjoy. Borrow a children's Tracker Pack to explore the wild and make the most of your visit.

Two very different views of Hindhead Commons and the Devil's Punch Bowl in Surrey

Eating and shopping: café with indoor and outdoor seating, serving hot food, sandwiches and cakes.

Making the most of your day: walks leaflets available from the café and shepherd's hut. Children's Tracker Packs available to hire from the shepherd's hut at weekends. **Dogs**: under very close control during bird-nesting season (March to October).

Access:
Café and shop Grounds
Sat Nav: use GU26 6AB. **Parking**: off the London Road.

Finding out more: 01428 681050 (Rangers). 01428 608771 (café) or hindhead@nationaltrust.org.uk

Hindhead Commons		M	T	W	T	F	S	S
Café								
Open all year	9–4	**M**	**T**	**W**	**T**	**F**	**S**	**S**

Extended café opening during fine weather and school holidays. Closed 25 December.

The Homewood

Portsmouth Road, Esher, Surrey KT10 9JL

🏠 ⊞ 1999

Patrick Gwynne's extraordinary early
20th-century family home is a masterpiece of
Modernist design in the midst of a picturesque
garden. **Note**: administered on behalf of the
National Trust by a tenant. **Access is via
minibus from Claremont Landscape Garden
only**. Sorry no toilet. Additional charge for
minibus and guided tour (including members).
Open first and third Friday and the second and
fourth Saturday of every month, 1 April to
29 October. 45-minute guided tours at 10:30,
11:30, 12:30, 2 and 3 (entry by booked tours
only). Garden open day: 19 October.

Finding out more: 01372 476424 or
thehomewood@nationaltrust.org.uk
c/o Claremont Landscape Garden,
Portsmouth Road, Esher, Surrey KT10 9JG

Ightham Mote

Mote Road, Ivy Hatch, Sevenoaks,
Kent TN15 0NT

🏠 ⊞ 🛏 🚻 T 1985

Ightham Mote (above and below): this perfectly preserved
medieval manor house sits in a secluded Kent valley

Hidden away in a secluded Kent valley is this
perfectly preserved medieval moated manor
house. Emerging from the natural landscape
almost 700 years ago, Ightham Mote is built
from Kentish ragstone and great Wealden oaks.
While its architecture and decoration trace the
development of the English country house, its
owners provide the stories of a once-cherished
family home, evoking a deep sense of history. In
the tranquil gardens there are streams and lakes
fed by natural springs, an orchard, flower borders
and a cutting garden. The wider estate offers
walks with secret glades and countryside views.
Note: very steep slope from visitor reception –
passenger buggy or lower drop-off available.

Eating and shopping: Mote café serving hot
lunches, sandwiches, cream teas, cakes and
hot, cold, alcoholic and non-alcoholic
beverages. Picnic facilities available. Shop
selling gifts, local produce and plants.

Making the most of your day: **Indoors**
Year-round events, including theatre
productions, themed dining evenings,
behind-the-scenes events, arts and crafts
courses. **Outdoors** Countryside walks,
activities and family fun days. Children's
natural play area and discovery den.
Dogs: welcome on café patio and unticketed
areas; assistance dogs only in ticketed areas.

Access: ⬚⬚⬚⬚⬚⬚⬚⬚⬚⬚⬚
Building ⬚⬚⬚⬚⬚ Grounds ⬚⬚
Parking: 200 yards.

Finding out more: 01732 810378 or
ighthammote@nationaltrust.org.uk

Ightham Mote		M	T	W	T	F	S	S
House								
29 Feb–30 Oct	11–5	M	T	W	T	F	S	S
5 Nov–20 Nov	11–3	·	·	·	·	·	S	S
26 Nov–31 Dec	11–3	M	T	W	T	F	S	S
Garden, café, exhibition and shop								
Open all year**	10–5	M	T	W	T	F	S	S

Closed 24 and 25 December. **Closes dusk if earlier. Partial
access to house and grounds in winter months.

Knole

Sevenoaks, Kent TN15 0RP

⬚ ⬚ ⬚ 1946

Knole is a house full of hidden treasures. Built as
an archbishop's palace and nestled in a medieval
deer-park, the house passed through royal hands
and into those of the Sackville family, who still
live here 400 years on. A major conservation
project is taking place at Knole, with the support
of the Heritage Lottery Fund. This exciting
project brings changes to the visitor experience
and facilities throughout the year. In 2016 new
spaces will be opening, including a conservation
studio, new café, learning centre and the
gatehouse tower. **Note**: visitor routes will be
altered during the conservation project,
please check before visiting.

Eating and shopping: temporary outdoor café
serving refreshments in the park until the new
café opens later in year. The bookshop also
offers coffee and cake (limited seating available).

Making the most of your day: **Indoors**
Year-round events revealing project work and
Knole's stories. Children's trails and drop-in
activities.**Outdoors** Ancient parkland to
explore. Special entry to the private garden
(Tuesdays, 5 April to 27 September).
Dogs: welcome in parkland and courtyards
on leads.

Access: ⬚⬚⬚⬚⬚⬚⬚⬚ State Rooms ⬚
Orangery ⬚⬚⬚ Park/garden ⬚⬚⬚
Sat Nav: use TN13 1HU and follow brown signs.
Parking: 60 yards. Additional parking in
town centre.

Finding out more: 01732 462100 or
knole@nationaltrust.org.uk

Knole		M	T	W	T	F	S	S
State Rooms								
5 Mar–30 Oct*	11–4	·	T	W	T	F	S	S
Green Court: visitor centre, bookshop, orangery, old estate								
Open all year**	10–5	M	T	W	T	F	S	S
Parkland								
Open all year		M	T	W	T	F	S	S

*Guided tours only 11 to 12; free-flow from 12. State Rooms
open Bank Holiday Mondays, except 26 December.
**Closes dusk if earlier. Closed 24 and 25 December.
Private gardens open Tuesdays only, 5 April until
27 September, 11 to 4.

**Exciting things are happening at Knole, Kent.
Built as an archbishop's palace before passing
through royal hands to the Sackville family, this
enormous house contains many hidden treasures.
This year new areas will be opening to
make visiting even more enjoyable**

Lamb House

West Street, Rye, East Sussex TN31 7ES

🏠 ❀ 1950

Georgian home of writers Henry James and E. F. Benson, who depicted the property in the *Mapp and Lucia* stories. **Note**: maintained on the National Trust's behalf by a tenant. Sorry no toilet. Open Tuesday, Friday and Saturday, 19 March to 29 October, 11 to 5.

Finding out more: 01580 762334 or lambhouse@nationaltrust.org.uk

Eating and shopping: hot and cold food and drinks available at Leith Hill Tower (not National Trust), or at Leith Hill Place when open. Picnics welcome, but no barbecues please.

Making the most of your day: walks leaflets available on site to help you explore the estate. Don't miss a visit to Leith Hill Tower, the bird hide at the Rhododendron Wood or Leith Hill Place. **Dogs**: on leads on heathland (April to July).

Access: 🔬
Sat Nav: for Rhododendron Wood and Starveall Corner use RH5 6LU; for Windy Gap RH5 6LX; for Landslip RH5 6HG. **Parking**: on site.

Finding out more: 01306 712711 or leithhill@nationaltrust.org.uk

Leith Hill

near Coldharbour village, Dorking, Surrey

🏠 ⚓ 1923

Glorious walking country featuring iconic views of heathland, pine woodland and farmland landscapes. Every season is a riot of colour – don't miss spring bluebells at Frank's Wood, early summer colour at the Rhododendron Wood or stunning displays of autumn golds and reds.

Leith Hill Place

Leith Hill Lane, near Coldharbour, Dorking, Surrey RH5 6LY

🏠 ⚓ 1945

Childhood home of English composer Ralph Vaughan Williams, once owned by the Wedgwood family and regularly visited by Charles Darwin. Opened to the public in 2013 for the first time in 40 years, it is a work in progress with an unusually informal atmosphere. Glorious views over the South Downs. **Note**: parking access across sloping field (often muddy). Cash or cheques only – no credit-card facilities.

Eating and shopping: no café, but volunteer bakers provide freshly made cakes and cream teas by donation. Original AGA in use and visitors can sit in the stone-flagged dining-room or outside on the terrace or the courtyard garden.

Making the most of your day: free soundscape audio tour (timed tickets). Everyone is welcome to play the piano, listen to music (often live), explore the cellar graffiti and children's trails. Summer concerts. **Dogs**: welcome on leads in grounds and house, except kitchen and soundscape.

The view from Leith Hill in Surrey

Leith Hill Place, Surrey: illustrious owners and visitors

Access: [icons] House [icon]
Courtyard garden/south terrace [icons]
Sat Nav: use RH5 6LU.
Parking: Rhododendron Wood car park, 437 yards, in Tanhurst Lane.

Finding out more: 01306 711685 or leithhillplace@nationaltrust.org.uk

Leith Hill Place		M	T	W	T	F	S	S
4 Mar–30 Oct*	11–5	M	·	·	·	F	S	S
3 Dec–4 Dec**	11–3:30	·	·	·	·	·	S	S

*Closed 31 July for Ride London cycle race. Closes at 4 on 30 October. **Christmas concerts must be booked.

Leith Hill Tower

near Coldharbour village, Dorking, Surrey RH5 6LU

[icons] 1923

Built in 1765 by Richard Hull of Leith Hill Place, the tower is the highest point in south-east England. From the top there are unbeatable views north to the high-rise buildings of London and to the south it's possible to see the sea sparkling through Shoreham Gap.
Note: steep spiral stairs to the top of tower; no toilet and no parking at tower.

Eating and shopping: hot drinks and snacks available from the servery (not National Trust). Picnics welcome but no barbecues please.

Making the most of your day: Indoors Small exhibition room outlining the history of the tower. **Outdoors** Two free telescopes at top of the tower and walks leaflets covering the Leith Hill estate. **Dogs:** on leads on heathland (April to July).

Access: Tower [icons]
Sat Nav: for Rhododendron Wood and Starveall Corner use RH5 6LU; for Windy Gap RH5 6LX; for Landslip RH5 6HG.
Parking: on site.

Finding out more: 01306 712711 or leithhilltower@nationaltrust.org.uk

Leith Hill Tower	
Open every day all year	10–3*

*Open weekends and Bank Holidays (daylight permitting), 9 to 5. Closed 25 December.

Leith Hill Tower, Surrey: highest point in the South East

Monk's House

Rodmell, Lewes, East Sussex BN7 3HF

🏠 ❄️ 🦽 1980

The sitting-room at Monk's House in East Sussex

This small 17th-century weatherboarded cottage in the village of Rodmell was the country retreat of novelist Virginia Woolf and her husband Leonard and a meeting place for the Bloomsbury Group. The garden features the room where she created her best-known works and includes cottage garden borders, orchard, allotments and ponds. **Note**: no access to Rodmell from A26.

Eating and shopping: gift shop offering Woolf and Bloomsbury-related products.

Making the most of your day: why not try your hand at a game of bowls? One of the favoured pastimes of the Woolfs.
Dogs: allowed in garden on leads.

Access: 🏠 Building 🦽 🏛️ Grounds 🦽
Sat Nav: do not use. **Parking**: 100 yards (height restriction barrier).

Finding out more: 01273 474760 or monkshouse@nationaltrust.org.uk

Monk's House		M	T	W	T	F	S	S
23 Mar–30 Oct*	1–5**		·	**W**	**T**	**F**	**S**	**S**

Last admission to house 15 minutes before closing.
*Open Bank Holiday Mondays. **Admission to garden 12:30 to 5:30.

Nymans

Handcross, near Haywards Heath, West Sussex RH17 6EB

🏠 ❄️ 🦽 🛏️ 🔔 🍴 1954

One of the National Trust's premier gardens, Nymans (below) was a country retreat for the creative Messel family, and has views stretching out across the Sussex Weald. Today you can recharge your batteries here, while you explore this beautiful place, discovering hidden corners through stone archways, walking along tree-lined avenues while surrounded by lush green countryside. From vibrantly colourful summer borders, to the tranquillity of ancient woodland, Nymans is a place of experimentation with constantly evolving planting designs and a rare and unusual plant collection. The comfortable yet elegant house, a partial ruin, reflects the personalities and stories of the talented Messel family, from the Countess of Rosse to Oliver Messel and photographer Lord Snowdon.

Eating and shopping: large shop, plant and garden centre selling a collection of plants grown at Nymans. Café serving a choice of seasonal food. Grab & Go kiosk open during busy periods. Woodland craft sales. Second-hand bookshop.

Making the most of your day: **Indoors** Small gallery in the house with changing exhibitions for every season. **Outdoors** Free, daily guided walks. Contemporary art installations during January and February. Mobility buggy tours of the garden and woods. Daily family programme includes '50 things' activities, seasonal trails, natural play and geocaching. Seasonal programming includes gardening and creative workshops. Walks and talks in the woodland and garden. Summer open-air theatre and jazz. Woodland trails. **Dogs**: in woodland only, on leads during bird-nesting season (1 March to 31 July).

Access: ⓟ🅳🦽♿🚻🅹📷🖼🎵
House 🦽♿🍴♿ Gallery 🦽 Garden 🦽♿♿♿
Parking: on site.

Nymans, West Sussex, in spring: a family enjoys the blossom and gentle sunshine (above), while glorious wisteria brightens a stone wall (right)

Petworth House and Park, West Sussex (opposite)

Finding out more: 01444 405250 or nymans@nationaltrust.org.uk

Nymans	
Open every day all year	10–5*

Gallery closed for short periods to change exhibitions.
*Closes dusk if earlier. 1 November to 29 February, house closed for winter conservation. Closed 24 and 25 December.

Oakhurst Cottage

Hambledon, near Godalming, Surrey GU8 4HF

🏠 ✳️ 1952

Timber-framed home offering a rare insight into domestic life in the mid-19th century, with a traditional cottage garden to explore.
Note: sorry no toilet. Access by booked guided tour only (maximum six visitors). Open Wednesday, Thursday, Saturday and Sunday, 2 April to 29 September, 2 to 5, and 1 to 30 October, 2 to 4.

Finding out more: 01483 208936 or oakhurstcottage@nationaltrust.org.uk

Old Soar Manor

Plaxtol, Borough Green, Kent TN15 0QX

🏠 1947

Dating from 1290, the remaining rooms of this knight's house offer a glimpse back to the time of Edward I. **Note**: sorry no toilet or tea-room. Narrow lanes, limited off-road parking. Open Monday to Thursday and weekends, 2 April to 29 September, 10 to 6.

Finding out more: 01732 810378 or oldsoarmanor@nationaltrust.org.uk

Owletts

The Street, Cobham, Gravesend, Kent DA12 3AP

🏠 ✳️ 1938

An architect's 17th-century family home with a varied history and architectural features, set within a relaxing, traditional garden. **Note**: open Sundays, 3 April to 25 September, 11 to 5.

Finding out more: 01732 810378 or owletts@nationaltrust.org.uk

Petworth House and Park

Petworth, West Sussex GU28 0AE

🏠 ♿ 🍴 1947

Shaped by a family of collectors over the past 800 years, this 17th-century 'house of art' inspired countless artists, including England's greatest landscape painter J. M. W. Turner. The finest collection of art and sculpture in the National Trust, including world-famous paintings by Van Dyck, Reynolds, Blake and Turner, is displayed in the opulent state rooms and North Gallery. In contrast the atmospheric servants' quarters evoke the hustle and bustle of 'below stairs' life. Outdoors is a woodland Pleasure Ground and acres of 'Capability' Brown landscaped deer-park with glorious views of the South Downs National Park.
Note: additional charge may apply for some events, including Winter Art Exhibition.

Eating and shopping: Servants' Hall coffee shop serving barista-style coffee and tempting treats. Audit Room serving light lunches, afternoon teas and homemade cakes. Gift shop, second-hand bookshop and plant sales.

Making the most of your day: **Indoors** Free daily introductory talks, specialist talks, costumed interpretation (monthly) and snapshot tours (Thursday and Friday). Trilingual multimedia guide (English, French and German) at small additional charge. Children's activities. **Outdoors** 283 hectares (700 acres) of deer-park in which to relax and let off steam. Downloadable walks. Events throughout the seasons. **Dogs**: under close control in Petworth Park. Assistance dogs only in Pleasure Grounds.

Access: ⯗⯗⯗⯗⯗⯗⯗⯗⯗⯗⯗⯗
Building ⯗⯗⯗
Sat Nav: use GU28 9LR. **Parking**: on A283, 700 yards. Separate car park for Petworth Park.

Finding out more: 01798 342207 or petworth@nationaltrust.org.uk

Petworth House and Park		M	T	W	T	F	S	S
House*								
19 Mar–6 Nov	11–5	**M**	**T**	**W**	**T**	**F**	**S**	**S**
Pleasure Ground, shop and café								
Open all year	10–5**	**M**	**T**	**W**	**T**	**F**	**S**	**S**

*Thursdays and Fridays partially open (specialist tours available). **Closes dusk if earlier. Closed 24 and 25 December.

The grounds at Petworth House and Park, West Sussex (above and below)

An opulent interior (above) and rolling parkland (below) at Polesden Lacey, Surrey

Polesden Lacey

Great Bookham, near Dorking, Surrey RH5 6BD

⌂ ✿ ♿ ⊟ ⊺ 1942

'This is a delicious house…' remarked Queen Elizabeth, the Queen Mother, on her honeymoon at Polesden Lacey. Mrs Greville's Edwardian party house, set in an Area of Outstanding Natural Beauty, boasts captivating views across the rolling Surrey Hills. Visitors can enjoy the changing seasons with a waymarked walk across Ranmore Common, part of the 566-hectare (1,400-acre) estate. The glittering gold room, designed to impress kings and maharajas, and the extensive collection of fine and decorative arts, ranging from world-famous Dutch Old Masters to sparkling Fabergé, are breathtaking. Outside, the gardens offer something for every season, including an idyllic rose garden, one of the longest double herbaceous borders in the country, and a winter garden bursting with yellow aconites. **Note**: a weekday visit will avoid the crowds. An additional charge (including members) apply to certain events and our holiday trails.

Eating and shopping: Granary Café and Cowshed Coffee Shop offering home cooking, drinks and snacks. Home and giftware, souvenirs and plants available to buy, all located outside the pay perimeter. Second-hand bookshop in the grounds.

Making the most of your day: **Indoors** House tours explore fascinating pieces in the collection, such as the Greville tiara, stories about Edwardian society and conservation work. Pianists play in the gold room on weekends and throughout the summer, and the halls are decked in glorious festive style for our annual Christmas event. **Outdoors** Set in an Area of Outstanding Natural Beauty, the estate offers some of the most idyllic picnic spots in Surrey. Explore Ranmore Common, a Site of Special Scientific Interest, on waymarked walks across our huge estate. Free garden tours from March until November. **Dogs**: on short leads in designated areas, under control on landscape walks, estate and farmland.

Access: 🅿️♿🏠🪑👓🔔👜📷🏛️🎧
House 🦽♿♿ **Grounds** ♿➡️🐕♿
Parking: 200 yards.

Finding out more: 01372 452048 or polesdenlacey@nationaltrust.org.uk

Polesden Lacey		M	T	W	T	F	S	S
House[1]								
9 Jan–20 Mar	Tour[2]	·	·	·	·	·	S	S
25 Mar–30 Oct	11–5*	M	T	W	T	F	S	S
31 Oct–31 Dec**	11–4*	M	T	W	T	F	S	S
Gardens, Granary Café, shop and coffee shop								
Open all year	10–5**	M	T	W	T	F	S	S

[1]Admission by timed tickets at certain times; last entry one hour before closing. [2]Winter tours 11 to 3. *Weekday access by guided tour, 11 to 12:30, then free-flow. **Closes dusk if earlier. Whole property closed 24 and 25 December.

A family enjoys Polesden Lacey's garden

Quebec House

Quebec Square, Westerham, Kent TN16 1TD

🏠♿ 1918

Simple and charming Quebec House, Kent

The childhood home of General James Wolfe, this 18th-century house retains much of its original charm and family feel, with a replica bed and examples of traditional pastimes the Wolfes would have enjoyed. An exhibition tells of the dramatic battle for North America, which tragically ended in General Wolfe's death. **Note**: Coach House closed 9 May to 2 August for essential building work.

Eating and shopping: second-hand books. Souvenirs and guidebooks for sale in the Coach House, as well as hot and cold drinks and a selection of cakes.

Making the most of your day: house guided tours at 12 and 12:30 (book on arrival). Every Sunday we re-create Mrs Wolfe's recipes in the Georgian kitchen. Exhibition on the North American campaign. **Dogs**: welcome on short leads in the gardens.

Access: ♿🔔👜🏛️🎧📷🐕
Building ♿♿ **Grounds** ♿♿
Parking: 80 yards in main town car park on A25 (not National Trust).

Finding out more: 01732 868381 or
quebechouse@nationaltrust.org.uk

Quebec House	M	T	W	T	F	S	S
House, garden and exhibition							
27 Feb–8 May	11–5*	·	·	**W**	**T**	**F**	**S**	**S**
3 Aug–30 Oct	11–5*	·	·	**W**	**T**	**F**	**S**	**S**
5 Nov–18 Dec	1–4	·	·	·	·	·	**S**	**S**
House							
14 May–31 Jul	12–5*	·	·	·	·	·	**S**	**S**

*House opens at 12 (access by tour only, 12 to 1).
Open Bank Holiday Mondays. Closes dusk if earlier.

Reigate Hill and Gatton Park

near Reigate, Surrey

🏞 1912

Reigate Hill commands sweeping views across the Weald to the South Downs. It's a great spot for walking, family picnics and wildlife-watching. A short walk away is the 19th-century Reigate Fort. The complex is open every day and the fort buildings open for special events. To the east of Reigate Hill is Gatton Park, designed by Lancelot 'Capability' Brown. 2016 marks the 300th anniversary of the birth of 'Capability' Brown. **Note**: areas of Gatton Park open once a month by the Gatton Trust.

Eating and shopping: picnics welcome. Tea kiosk (not National Trust).

Making the most of your day: free walks leaflets available from the noticeboards. Chalk downland species, such as the Adonis blue butterfly, to spot, as well as mysterious military structures on Reigate Hill. **Dogs**: welcome, on leads when livestock grazing.

Access: 🚻 ♿
Sat Nav: use RH2 OHX. **Parking**: at Wray Lane car park.

Finding out more: 01342 843036 or reigate@nationaltrust.org.uk

Reigate Hill and Gatton Park, Surrey: standing stone circle (top), and sweeping views (right)

River Wey and Godalming Navigations and Dapdune Wharf

Navigations Office and Dapdune Wharf, Wharf Road, Guildford, Surrey GU1 4RR

🏠🍴🍸 1964

A hidden haven where you can take a boat trip, explore a restored barge, or enjoy scenic walks. Dapdune Wharf in Guildford brings to life stories of this historic waterway (below), along 20 miles of waterside towpath. A great place for children to have fun – and raid our dressing-up box. **Note**: boat trip charges, mooring and fishing fees apply to members.

Eating and shopping: small tea-room serving sandwiches, cakes, ice-cream and drinks. Shop with plant sales. Picnic areas at Dapdune Wharf.

Making the most of your day: **Indoors** Dressing-up clothes for children. **Outdoors** Year-round events, including activities for children at Dapdune and guided walks along towpath and beyond. River Festival in September. Overnight moorings available. **Dogs**: on leads at Dapdune Wharf and lock areas; elsewhere under control.

Access: 🅿️♿♿♿:♿🔄 Grounds 🚶
Parking: at Dapdune Wharf.

Finding out more: 01483 561389 or riverwey@nationaltrust.org.uk

River Wey and Dapdune Wharf		M	T	W	T	F	S	S
Dapdune Wharf								
12 Mar–6 Nov	11–5*	M			T	F	S	S

Open daily during local school half-term and summer holidays. *24 October to 6 November: closes one hour earlier. River trips from Dapdune Wharf 11 to 4 (conditions permitting). Access to towpath during daylight hours all year.

Runnymede

Egham, near Old Windsor, Surrey

🏠🚲♿🚻🍸 1931

Seen by many as the birthplace of modern democracy, this picturesque open landscape beside the Thames was witness to King John's historic sealing of the Magna Carta more than 800 years ago. Today Runnymede offers the ideal space to enjoy ancient woodlands, countryside walks or picnics by the river, all within easy reach of the M25. Along with Lutyens' impressive Fairhaven Lodges, the peaceful landscape is also home to memorials for the Magna Carta, John F. Kennedy and Commonwealth Air Forces, making it the perfect place to remember and reflect upon important moments in world history. **Note**: toilets available only when tea-room open. Mooring and fishing (during fishing season) available for additional fee (including members).

Eating and shopping: tea-room and shop serving freshly baked homemade produce, morning coffee, light lunches and afternoon teas.

Making the most of your day: events throughout the year. River boat trips available with French Brothers Boat Hire (01784 439626). **Dogs**: welcome on leads near livestock.

Access: [P] [⛲] [♿] Tea-room [♿] Grounds [♿] [♿]
Sat Nav: use TW20 0AE. **Parking**: either side of A308. Seasonal opening, check website for closing times.

Finding out more: 01784 432891 or runnymede@nationaltrust.org.uk

Runnymede		M	T	W	T	F	S	S
Tea-room								
Open all year	10–5:30*	M	T	W	T	F	S	S

*Closes dusk if earlier. Car parks: locked at 7, April to October; at dusk in winter. Closed 24 and 25 December.

Saddlescombe Farm

near Brighton, West Sussex

[🏛] [📷] [⛱] [⛺] [1995]

Saddlescombe Farm is a gem on the South Downs Way 5 miles from Brighton, a unique downland farm showing a changing way of life throughout the centuries. Newtimber Hill offers the finest chalk grassland with many varieties of downland flowers and wildlife, ancient lime trees and 19th-century graffitied beech trees.
Note: Saddlescombe is a working farm and is fully open only on special open days.

Eating and shopping: Hiker's Rest café (not National Trust) serving teas, cakes and light lunches (open Wednesday to Sunday. Closed January to mid-March).

Making the most of your day: circular route to Devil's Dyke and walks up Newtimber Hill through ancient woodland. Cycling along the South Downs Way. Open days and events throughout the year. **Dogs**: welcome, on leads where livestock grazing.

Access: [♿] [♿] Buildings [♿] [♿] [♿]
Sat Nav: use BN45 7DE. **Parking**: at Devil's Dyke. Very limited parking in lay-by opposite farm entrance (no parking in farm).

Finding out more: 01273 857712 or saddlescombe@nationaltrust.org.uk

Historic Runnymede, Surrey (left and top), and Saddlescombe Farm on the South Downs, West Sussex (above)

St John's Jerusalem

Sutton-at-Hone, Dartford, Kent DA4 9HQ

✚ ✿ 1943

Set within a secluded moated garden is this rare example of a 13th-century chapel built by the Knights Hospitaller. **Note**: private residence, maintained and managed by a tenant on behalf of the National Trust. Sorry no toilet or tea-room. Open Wednesdays, 6 April to 28 September, 2 to 6, and 5 to 26 October, 2 to 4.

Finding out more: 01732 810378 or stjohnsjerusalem@nationaltrust.org.uk

Scotney Castle

Lamberhurst, Tunbridge Wells, Kent TN3 8JN

🏛 🏠 ☕ ✿ ♿ 1970

The medieval moated Old Scotney Castle lies in a peaceful wooded valley. In the 19th century its owner Edward Hussey III set about building a new house, partially demolishing the Old Castle to create a romantic folly, the centrepiece of his picturesque landscape. From the terraces of the new house, sweeps of rhododendrons and azaleas cascade down the slope in summer, followed by highlights of autumn leaf colour, mirrored in the moat. In the house three generations have made their mark, adding possessions and character to the homely Victorian mansion which enjoys far-reaching views out across the estate.

Eating and shopping: the coach house tea-room offers a selection of hot meals and sandwiches, as well as homemade cakes and scones. Take home your own part of Scotney with local honey, Scotney Ale and plant sales available in the shop.

Comfortable Scotney Castle, Kent (above and left): a place where medieval and Victorian meet

Shalford Mill

Shalford, near Guildford, Surrey GU4 8BS

🏛 1932

You can sense the evocative stories of the past in the very structure of the mill, although the machinery no longer works. The wonderful story of the Ferguson's Gang is waiting for you – eccentric young women from the 1930s, determined to save the fabric of England for the future. **Note**: sorry no toilet.

Making the most of your day: **Indoors** Regular guided tours, evening talks and children's events. **Outdoors** Geocaching kits available on Sundays. **Dogs**: assistance dogs only.

Access: 🖵 :• **Building** 🏨
Parking: none on site, off-street parking available near church.

Finding out more: 01483 561389 or shalfordmill@nationaltrust.org.uk

Shalford Mill		M	T	W	T	F	S	S
23 Mar–30 Oct	11–5	·	·	**W**	·	·	·	**S**

Open Bank Holiday Mondays and Saturdays on Bank Holiday weekends.

Making the most of your day: **Indoors** Children's guided trails around house. **Outdoors** Garden tree trails in spring and autumn. Natural play. Estate trails. **Dogs**: welcome on leads in the garden and on the estate.

Access: 🅿♿🍼👶🚼📷🖵📖
House 🏨♿♿ **Grounds** 🏨▶♿
Parking: 130 yards (limited), overflow parking 440 yards.

Finding out more: 01892 893820 (Infoline). 01892 893868 or scotneycastle@nationaltrust.org.uk

Scotney Castle	
Open every day all year	10–5*

*Closes dusk if earlier. House opens at 11. All visitors require timed ticket to visit house (places limited, early sell-outs possible). Estate walks available every day. Property may close during adverse weather. Closed 24 and 25 December.

Shalford Mill, Surrey: you can discover the story of the Ferguson's Gang at this picturesque building

Sheffield Park and Garden, East Sussex: vibrant colours, scents and gentle natural sounds provide a sensory feast

Sheffield Park and Garden

Sheffield Park, Uckfield, East Sussex TN22 3QX

🏵️🐾🍸 1954

Colour, perfume and sound excite your senses as you enjoy winding paths, majestic trees, ponds and dappled glades. Falls, cascades and bridges are integral to the garden design. Planting is reflected in ponds so clear that the eye is tricked into thinking up is down. Bold and grand planting has a sculptural form in winter. Spring and summer bring vibrant blooms, fragrant arbours and splashes of colour. Autumn is a blazing kaleidoscope of greens, flame-reds, burnt oranges and bright yellows, planted for their combined display. The encircling park and woodland provide opportunities for further adventure. Dragonflies skit across the meadows, buzzards circle in the sky, kingfishers flash across the ponds and eels pass from river to lake.

Eating and shopping: tea-room serving homemade cakes, sandwiches, hot lunches and cream teas. Catering buggy in garden, weather permitting. Shops in reception building and Coach House selling gifts, local products, gardening items, outdoor accessories and plants. Second-hand bookshop in Coach House.

Exploring Sheffield Park and Garden

Making the most of your day: '50 things' self-led activities for families all year, with extra events and trails in the school holidays. Natural playtrail in Ringwood Toll – try tree-climbing, den-building, balance beams and much more. Over 121 hectares (300 acres) of parkland, with circular walks, River Ouse and lock remains, flood meadow and wildlife haven. Cricket matches most summer weekends. Carpets of bluebells in spring and outstanding autumn colour display. Guided garden tours on Tuesdays and Thursdays. Pulham Falls waterfall (12 to 1, Tuesdays and Fridays). Bluebell Railway nearby with Sheffield Park station just a short walk across the parkland (weekend bus link operates spring/summer). **Dogs**: on short leads in parkland and after 2:30 in garden. Off-lead in East Park.

Access: 🅿️♿🚻🚹🚼🎦📷♿👶📱📷
Reception ♿♿ **Tea-room** ♿♿
Garden ♿♿➡️♿♿
Parking: on site (overflow car park 600 yards).

Finding out more: 01825 790231 or sheffieldpark@nationaltrust.org.uk

Sheffield Park and Garden	M	T	W	T	F	S	S
Garden, shop and tea-room							
Open all year 10–5*	M	T	W	T	F	S	S
Parkland							
Open all year	M	T	W	T	F	S	S

Last admission to garden one hour before closing.
*Closes dusk if earlier. Garden, shop and tea-room closed 24 and 25 December.

Sissinghurst Castle Garden

Biddenden Road, near Cranbrook,
Kent TN17 2AB

🏠🔊♿🚼🛏️🔔🍴 1967

Sissinghurst Castle Garden sits within the ruin of a great Elizabethan house – all surrounded by the rich Kentish landscape of woods, streams and farmland. The famous garden, with its fairytale tower, is the result of the creative tension between the formal design of Harold Nicolson and the lavish planting of Vita Sackville-West. The colour schemes, intimacy of the different garden 'rooms' and rich herbaceous borders are the epitome of an English garden. The wider estate, which includes a vegetable garden, lakes and rich variety of wildlife, is waiting to be explored, while our year-round exhibitions tell Sissinghurst's stories and show how history and landscape have combined to shape this special place. **Note**: limited access for buggies and wheelchairs.

Sissinghurst Castle Garden in Kent

Eating and shopping: restaurant serving lunch and afternoon tea made with produce from our vegetable garden and farm. The Old Dairy, offering sandwiches, cakes and drinks. Second-hand bookshop and plant shop selling produce grown in the Sissinghurst nursery.

Making the most of your day: **Indoors** Exhibitions and daily talks. The Library contains the National Trust's most significant collection of 20th-century literature, and visitors can learn how we conserve it. **Outdoors** Talks and activities, including dawn chorus, gardener and bluebell walks and '50 things' activities. Packs available from visitor reception to help you explore. Acres of ancient woodland and lakes. Panoramic views across the Wealden countryside. Open-air theatre and farmers' markets in the summer. Smallhythe Place, Lamb House and Stoneacre nearby. **Dogs**: welcome on leads on estate. Assistance dogs only in garden and vegetable garden.

Access: ![icons]
Building ![icons] Grounds ![icons] ➡
Parking: 315 yards.

Finding out more: 01580 710700 or sissinghurst@nationaltrust.org.uk

Sissinghurst Castle Garden		M	T	W	T	F	S	S
Garden								
12 Mar–31 Oct	11–5:30*	M	T	W	T	F	S	S
Shop and restaurant								
Open all year	10–5:30*	M	T	W	T	F	S	S
Estate								
Open all year	Dawn–dusk	M	T	W	T	F	S	S
Exhibition**								
16 Jan–28 Feb	11–4	M	T	W	T	F	S	S
1 Nov–31 Dec	11–4	M	T	W	T	F	S	S

4 to 15 January and 29 February to 11 March: estate, shop and restaurant only open. Closed 24 and 25 December. *Closes dusk if earlier. Last entry 45 minutes before closing. Due to its fragile nature we are unable to allow food, drink or buggies in the garden (carriers provided). **Please check website for details.

Slindon Estate

near Arundel, West Sussex

🏠🏛🎥♿🛏🚻⛺ 1950

The ancient Slindon Estate is an expansive patchwork of woodland, downland, farmland and parkland, with an unspoilt Sussex village at its centre. Countless historic features cover the landscape, such as Stane Street, the Roman road from Chichester to London soldiers once marched along. Slindon has a rich and wonderfully varied wildlife, and its sun-dappled woods are filled with wild flowers, with badgers and bats hunting there at dusk. The meadows are great places to spot butterflies and downland flowers, while expansive views take in the Weald and South Downs, continuing across the coastal plain to the sea.

Eating and shopping: The Forge in Slindon village (tenant-run) stocks everything from locally baked bread, deli items, fruit and vegetables, to sandwiches, biscuits and cakes. Fresh coffee and tea, beer, light breakfasts, lunches and afternoon tea are also available.

Making the most of your day: there are more than 25 miles of rights of way to explore on the estate, as well as the village to discover. **Dogs**: welcome under close control.

Access: ♿➡
Sat Nav: use BN18 0QY for Park Lane; BN18 0SP Duke's Road; BN18 1PH Bignor Hill. **Parking**: at Park Lane, Duke's Road and Bignor Hill.

Sissinghurst Castle Garden (opposite and above). Slindon Estate, West Sussex (below)

Finding out more: 01243 814730 or slindonestate@nationaltrust.org.uk

Smallhythe Place

Smallhythe, Tenterden, Kent TN30 7NG

🏠 ❖ 🔔 ⊤ 1939

Nestled in the beautiful Weald of Kent, this early 16th-century cottage is full of the vibrant spirit of the adored Victorian actress Ellen Terry, and contains her fascinating theatrical collection. Voices of famous names who have graced the stage echo through our thatched Barn Theatre in the garden.

Two Kent gems: Smallhythe Place (below), and South Foreland Lighthouse (right)

Eating and shopping: vintage-style tea-room (licensed) attached to Barn Theatre selling soup, sandwiches, cakes and drinks.

Making the most of your day: **Indoors** Wide range of plays and music in the Barn Theatre. **Outdoors** Open-air theatre in the garden. Sissinghurst Castle, Lamb House and Stoneacre nearby. **Dogs**: allowed on leads in grounds.

Access: 🅿🖥♿🚻🅰 **Building** 🔸🔸
Grounds 🔸➡
Parking: 50 yards (not National Trust).

Finding out more: 01580 762334 or smallhytheplace@nationaltrust.org.uk

Smallhythe Place		M	T	W	T	F	S	S
2 Mar–30 Oct	11–5*		·	**W**	**T**	**F**	**S**	**S**

*Tea-room opens 30 minutes later and closes 30 minutes earlier. Open Bank Holiday Mondays 11 to 5. Closes dusk if earlier.

South Foreland Lighthouse

The Front, St Margaret's Bay, Dover, Kent CT15 6HP

🏠 ⚓ 🚂 🛏 ⊤ 1989

This historic landmark, dramatically situated on the White Cliffs, guided ships past the infamous Goodwin Sands and has a fascinating tale to tell. It was the first lighthouse powered by electricity and the site of the first international radio transmission. **Note**: no access for cars.

Eating and shopping: loose-leaf tea and homemade cakes served in Mrs Knott's tea-room. Shop selling ice-cream, cold drinks and gifts.

Making the most of your day: **Indoors** Tours run by knowledgeable guides. Interactive and hands-on displays. **Outdoors** Family fun with kite-flying and games. **Dogs**: in grounds only.

Access: [icons] Lighthouse [icons]
Tea-room [icons] Grounds [icons]
Parking: none on site. Nearest at White Cliffs, 2 miles, or St Margaret's, 1 mile.

Finding out more: 01304 853281 or southforeland@nationaltrust.org.uk

South Foreland Lighthouse		M	T	W	T	F	S	S
Lighthouse								
1 Jan	11–3	.	.	.	.	F	.	.
21 Mar–30 Oct	11–5:30*	M	.	.	.	F	S	S
Tea-room								
1 Jan	11–3	.	.	.	.	F	.	.
6 Feb–20 Mar	11–3	.	.	.	.	.	S	S
21 Mar–4 Sep	11–5	M	T	W	T	F	S	S
5 Sep–30 Oct	11–5*	M	.	.	.	F	S	S

*Open daily during local school holidays. 30 October: closes 3.

South Foreland Lighthouse: shiny brass machinery

Standen House and Garden, West Sussex: idyllic setting

Standen House and Garden

West Hoathly Road, East Grinstead, West Sussex RH19 4NE

[icons] 1973

Nestled in the Sussex countryside with views across the High Weald, James and Margaret Beale chose an idyllic location to build their rural retreat. Designed by Philip Webb, Standen is one of the most complete examples of Arts and Crafts workmanship, with Morris & Co. interiors and a story of family life in 1925. Mrs Beale's passion for gardening inspires a major restoration of her 5-hectare (12-acre) hillside garden. Each garden room has a distinct character and offers something for every season, from spring bulbs to autumn colour. The wider estate offers footpaths leading into woodlands and perfect for exploring. **Note**: seasonal tours to top of water tower, £2 (suggested donation).

Eating and shopping: shop selling William Morris-inspired gifts and cards. Plant centre selling the Standen Collection. Barn Café serving seasonal menus with free wi-fi. Takeaway drinks and snacks in garden. Second-hand bookshop, woodland produce and kitchen garden barrow sales. Picnics welcome.

Corner of a bedroom at Standen House and Garden

Making the most of your day: **Indoors** Family Christmas. Changing exhibitions. **Outdoors** New for 2016: Rosery Garden and winter walk. Event highlights – 8,000 spring tulips. Play area and school holiday trails. Seasonal tours and talks.
Dogs: welcome on short leads in formal garden and wider estate (seasonal cattle grazing).

Access: ⬚⬚⬚⬚⬚⬚⬚⬚⬚⬚
House ⬚⬚⬚ Gardens ⬚⬚⬚
Parking: 200 yards (steep hill).

Finding out more: 01342 323029 or
standen@nationaltrust.org.uk

Standen House and Garden		M	T	W	T	F	S	S
House, garden, café and shop*								
Open all year[1]	10–5**	M	T	W	T	F	S	S
House tours								
4 Jan–29 Jan	11–2:30	M	T	W	T	F	·	·
31 Oct–25 Nov	11–3	M	T	W	T	F	·	·

*House: opens 11, last entry one hour before closing.
[1]Monday to Friday, house admission by guided tour at certain times. **Closes dusk if earlier. Closed 24 and 25 December.

Stoneacre

Otham, Maidstone, Kent ME15 8RS

⬚⬚ 1928

Medieval farmhouse surrounded by garden, orchard, rolling meadows and woodland. Home to famous designer and critic Aymer Vallance. **Note**: no parking on site. Open by tenants on behalf of the National Trust, Saturdays, 19 March to 24 September, 11 to 5:30 (and Bank Holiday Mondays).

Finding out more: 01622 863247 or stoneacre@nationaltrust.org.uk

Toys Hill

near Brasted Chart, Kent

⬚ 1898

Acres of mixed ancient woodland overlooking the Weald of Kent, with abundant wildlife and idyllic for peaceful walks. **Note**: for Sat Nav use TN16 1QG.

Finding out more: 01732 868381 (Chartwell) or toyshill@nationaltrust.org.uk

Uppark House and Garden

South Harting, Petersfield,
West Sussex GU31 5QR

🏠 ✿ ♿ 1954

Perched on its vantage point high on the South Downs ridge, Uppark commands views as far south as the English Channel. Outside, the intimate gardens are being gradually restored to their original 18th-century design, with plenty of space in the adjacent meadow to play and relax with a picnic. The nearby woodland is great for exploring and den-building. Uppark's Georgian interiors illustrate the comfort of life 'upstairs', in contrast to the 'downstairs' world of its servants. Highlights include one of the best examples of an 18th-century doll's-house in the country.

Eating and shopping: shop selling local products and peat-free plants. Café (licensed) serving light lunches and cakes.

Making the most of your day: free garden tour every Thursday. Quiz trails for families and outdoor toy chest on South Meadow. Harting Down (countryside), Hinton Ampner and Petworth House nearby. **Dogs**: on leads on woodland walk only. Please note: no shaded parking.

Uppark's interiors illustrate the comfort of life 'upstairs'

Access: 🅿 🅳 🚾 🏸 🔊 🎥 🎨 📷 🧑
House 🦽 ⬆ 🧑 ♿ **Gardens** 🌿 🦽 ➡ ♿
Parking: 300 yards.

Finding out more: 01730 825857 or uppark@nationaltrust.org.uk

Uppark House and Garden	
Open every day all year	10–5*

*House open at 11 and closes at 4. Ground floor: 5 March to 31 October open 12:30 to 4; Print Room: March to October open first Wednesday of month. Café: last service 30 minutes before closing. Closes dusk if earlier. Garden tours every Thursday, March to October. Closed 24 and 25 December.

Uppark House and Garden, West Sussex: the north entrance

Wakehurst Place

Ardingly, Haywards Heath,
West Sussex RH17 6TN

🏠 ✿ ♿ 🌳 🏛 🍵 1964

Wakehurst, the country estate of the Royal Botanic Gardens, Kew, is internationally significant for collections, scientific research and plant conservation. The gardens, wetland and woodland are delightful, and there is also a nature reserve. You can also visit Kew's unique Millennium Seed Bank to see science and horticulture working side-by-side.
Note: funded and managed by the Royal Botanic Gardens, Kew. International National Trust membership cards not accepted.
Parking charges apply (including members).

Eating and shopping: Seed Café serving tea, coffee, cakes, bacon sandwiches, teacakes and soup. Stables Restaurant offering hot and cold food, plus homemade cakes served all day with fresh bread from the Wakehurst Bakery. Gift shop. Plant centre (not National Trust).

Making the most of your day: free daily guided tours. Seasonal festival programme. Courses. Events all year. Willow sculpture trail. Adventurous Journeys and natural play areas for families. Seasonal soup and stroll. Kingfisher/badger/bat-watching (charges apply). **Dogs**: assistance dogs only.

Access: 🅿️♿🦽🔲👁🖐
Buildings 🏛♿🍴♿ **Grounds** 🏔➡🚗♿
Parking: 50 yards.

Finding out more: 01444 894066 or wakehurst@kew.org. kew.org

Wakehurst Place		M	T	W	T	F	S	S
Garden								
1 Jan–29 Feb	10–4:30	M	T	W	T	F	S	S
1 Mar–31 Oct	10–6	M	T	W	T	F	S	S
1 Nov–23 Dec	10–4:30	M	T	W	T	F	S	S
26 Dec–31 Dec	10–4:30	M	T	W	T	F	S	.

Mansion and Millennium Seed Bank close one hour earlier. Shop closes 4:30 from 2 January to February, 5:30 March to October, 5 from November to 1 January 2017. Catering facilities available until 4 from 2 January to February, 5:30 March to October, 4:15 November to 1 January 2017. Property closed 24 and 25 December. Shop closed Easter Sunday. UK National Trust members free (reciprocal agreements made between the Trust and other parties do not apply).

The labyrinth at Wakehurst Place, West Sussex (below), and The White Cliffs of Dover, Kent (opposite)

The White Cliffs of Dover

Langdon Cliffs, Dover, Kent

🏠♿🚗🍴 1968

There can be no doubt that The White Cliffs of Dover are one of this country's most spectacular natural features. They are an official icon of Britain and have been a symbol of hope for generations. You can appreciate their beauty and enjoy their special appeal through the seasons by taking one of the country's most dramatic clifftop walks, which offer unrivalled views of the busy English Channel and the French coast while savouring the rare flora and fauna found only on this chalk grassland. You can also learn more about the fascinating military history of The White Cliffs by taking a torch-lit tour of Fan Bay Deep Shelter, a labyrinth of forgotten Second World War tunnels. **Note**: toilets available until 7.

Eating and shopping: shop selling gifts and outdoor goods. Coffee shop serving lunches, homemade cakes and afternoon teas.

Making the most of your day: waymarked trail to South Foreland Lighthouse, just 2 miles away, with lighthouse guided tours and homemade cakes and loose-leaf tea available in Mrs Knotts tea-room. Why not pick up a timed ticket for a torch-lit tour of Fan Bay Deep Shelter and the newly uncovered sound mirrors? Spectacular viewpoints and photo opportunities. Events, talks and guided walks held throughout the year. **Dogs**: under close control at all times (stock grazing).

Access: 🅿️♿🦽🔲🚻👁🖐📷 Visitor centre 🏔♿
Fan Bay Deep Shelter 🏔 **Countryside** 🏔➡♿
Sat Nav: use CT15 5NA. **Parking**: on site.

Finding out more: 01304 202756 or whitecliffs@nationaltrust.org.uk

The White Cliffs of Dover		M	T	W	T	F	S	S
Visitor centre								
1 Jan–28 Feb	11–4	M	T	W	T	F	S	S
29 Feb–30 Oct	10–5*	M	T	W	T	F	S	S
31 Oct–31 Dec	11–4**	M	T	W	T	F	S	S

*4 July to 4 September, open to 5:30. **Closed 24 and 25 December.

Kent, Surrey and Sussex

Winkworth Arboretum

Hascombe Road, Godalming, Surrey GU8 4AD

❀ ♨ 1952

The National Trust's only arboretum is the result of one man's vision and passion. Dr Wilfrid Fox used the wooded valley and its lakes as a canvas to experiment with planting trees to 'paint a picture'. The fruits of his labour are now an award-winning collection of over 1,000 different plants, which offer stunning combinations of colour with every changing season. Famous for vibrant autumnal foliage and endless carpets of bluebells in spring; the azaleas, magnolias, witch hazel and snowdrops mean Winkworth is worth visiting all year for beautiful scenery, a picnic or the fun family events. **Note**: steep slopes; banks of lake and wetlands only partially fenced.

Eating and shopping: small tea-room offering freshly baked scones, cakes and light lunches.

Making the most of your day: events and guided walks throughout the year.
Dogs: welcome on leads.

Access: ♿ ♿ ♿ ♿ Grounds ♿ ➡
Parking: 100 yards.

Finding out more: 01483 208477 or winkwortharboretum@nationaltrust.org.uk

Winkworth Arboretum		M	T	W	T	F	S	S
1 Jan–31 Jan	10–5*	M	T	W	T	F	S	S
1 Feb–31 Mar	10–5	M	T	W	T	F	S	S
1 Apr–31 Oct	10–6	M	T	W	T	F	S	S
1 Nov–31 Dec	10–5*	M	T	W	T	F	S	S

Tea-room closes 30 minutes earlier than arboretum.
*Closes at dusk if earlier; local closing times posted at the property. Car-park gates locked at closing time.
Closed 24 and 25 December.

Glorious Winkworth Arboretum, Surrey, is the result of one man's vision and desire to plant trees to 'paint a picture'

Places may occasionally close for events or bad weather

Woolbeding Countryside

Harting Down, near Midhurst, West Sussex

🚻♿👓🐕🏠 1958

Wide horizons and secluded places, you can wander and lose yourself among this rich blend of habitats and landscape views. **Note**: sorry no toilet. For Woolbeding Parkland use GU29 9RR.

Finding out more: 01730 816638 or woolbedingcountryside@nationaltrust.org.uk

Woolbeding Gardens

Midhurst, West Sussex GU29 9RR

❀ 1956

Woolbeding Gardens, West Sussex (above and top)

Woolbeding delights at every turn, with distinctive garden rooms set against manicured hedges and thoughtfully composed colour-themed borders. Formal lawns melt into the rural landscape, and beyond the meadow you will find a waterfall, Gothic summerhouse and enchanting landscape garden. **Note**: access by park-and-ride minibus from Midhurst only (booking essential).

Eating and shopping: Orchard Café serving barista-style coffee, speciality teas, and a selection of tempting treats. Shop selling gardening books, gifts and plants.

Making the most of your day: introductory talks and croquet lawn. Nearby properties include Petworth House and Park, Uppark House and Garden, and Hinton Ampner. **Dogs**: assistance dogs only.

Access: 🅿️♿📶 Reception ♿♿ Garden ♿➡️♿
Parking: none available. Access by complimentary park-and-ride minibus from Midhurst only.

Finding out more: 0844 249 1895 or woolbedinggardens@nationaltrust.org.uk

Woolbeding Gardens		M	T	W	T	F	S	S
7 Apr–30 Sep	10:30–4:30	·	·	·	**T**	**F**	·	·

Advance booking essential. Access by park and ride only from Midhurst.

London

Rainham Hall, Rainham

● **Buildings and/or gardens**

● **Entry points to coast and countryside**

The size of each pin indicates how large
a place is and how long you should allow
for your visit

LP London Partners, see pages 192 to 195

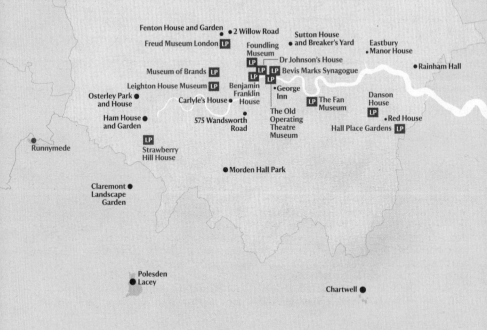

Fenton House and Garden
● 2 Willow Road
Sutton House
● and Breaker's Yard
Eastbury
Manor House
Freud Museum London **LP**
Foundling
Museum
LP
Dr Johnson's House
Museum of Brands **LP**
LP **LP** Bevis Marks Synagogue
LP
● Rainham Hall
Leighton House Museum **LP**
Benjamin
Franklin
House
Osterley Park ●
and House
Carlyle's House ●
● George
Inn
Danson
House
LP The Fan
Museum
LP
Ham House ●
and Garden
575 Wandsworth
Road
The Old
Operating
Theatre
Museum
● Red House
Hall Place Gardens **LP**
● Runnymede
LP
Strawberry
Hill House
● Morden Hall Park
Claremont ●
Landscape
Garden
Polesden
● Lacey
Chartwell ●

Carlyle's House

24 Cheyne Row, Chelsea, London SW3 5HL

🏠✿ 1936

'Let no woman who values peace of soul ever dream of marrying an author!' wrote Jane Carlyle in 1837. Her amusing letters about her husband, the sage of Chelsea, their friends (including Charles Dickens), impossible servants, noisy neighbours, builders, burglars and bedbugs bring this Victorian home to hilarious life.

Access: 📷📖 Building 🔍🕴 Grounds 🔍
Parking: limited on street (metered).

Finding out more: 020 7352 7087 or carlyleshouse@nationaltrust.org.uk

Carlyle's House		M	T	W	T	F	S	S
9 Mar–30 Oct	11–4:30	·	·	**W**	**T**	**F**	**S**	**S**

Open Bank Holiday Mondays.

Carlyle's House in Chelsea as it appeared in 1859

Eastbury Manor House

Eastbury Square, Barking IG11 9SN

🏠✿🔔🍷 1918

Elizabethan gentry house *circa* 1573. Little-altered, featuring 17th-century wall-paintings and garden with bee-boles. Tours, re-enactments, family days and crafts. **Note**: managed by London Borough of Barking and Dagenham. Some rooms are occasionally closed for private functions. Independent tea-room and shop selling Tudor pottery and books. Special events and activities are charged at an additional cost. Open Sundays, 27 March to 11 December, 12 to 5, and Thursday and Friday, 31 March to 16 December, 10 to 4.

Finding out more: 020 8227 2942 or eastburymanor@nationaltrust.org.uk

Fenton House and Garden

Hampstead Grove, Hampstead, London NW3 6SP

🏠✿🍷 1952

This 1686 town house, overlooking London from the top of Hampstead's Holly Hill, is filled with world-class collections of ceramics, paintings, textiles, musical instruments and furniture. The ever-changing horticultural gem that is our garden, includes an orchard, kitchen garden, rose garden, formal terraces and lawns, and never fails to delight.

Eating and shopping: small shop area selling local and National Trust items, garden plants and produce.

Fenton House and Garden, Hampstead: delightful formality

Making the most of your day: collections talks, music and garden events, including annual Apple Weekend. Joint tickets with 2 Willow Road available. Why not combine your visit with one of our London Partner attractions? **Dogs**: assistance dogs only.

Access: 🗝 🏠 ⛅ 🎧 **Building** 🦽 🪜 🚶 **Grounds** 🦽
Parking: none on site.

Finding out more: 020 7435 3471 or fentonhouse@nationaltrust.org.uk

Fenton House and Garden	M	T	W	T	F	S	S
2 Mar–30 Oct	11–5		·	**W**	**T**	**F**	**S**	**S**

Open Bank Holiday Mondays, Good Friday and selected dates in December for Christmas.

George Inn

The George Inn Yard, 77 Borough High Street, Southwark, London SE1 1NH

🏠 🍷 1937

This public house, dating from the 17th century, is London's last remaining galleried inn. **Note**: leased to a private company. No table bookings (telephone for details). Open daily (apart from 25 and 26 December), 11 to 11.

Finding out more: 020 7407 2056 or georgeinn@nationaltrust.org.uk

Ham House and Garden

Ham Street, Ham, Richmond TW10 7RS

🏛 ❀ 🔔 🍽 1948

On the banks of the River Thames, Ham is one of London's secret treasure houses. With a substantial collection of 17th-century paintings, furniture and textiles, Ham reveals what life looked like during the reigns of Charles I and II. You can learn how later generations protected their heritage by caring for their ancestors' treasured heirlooms. Outside, there are statues, parterres and avenues to be explored in the formal Cherry Garden, refuge to be sought in the Wilderness and seasonal produce in the Kitchen Garden. **Note**: to protect our fragile textiles, some rooms have low light levels.

Eating and shopping: the café serves lunches, teas and delicious cakes with produce harvested from the Kitchen Garden. Picnics are welcome and some tables are provided. The gift shop sells gifts for all occasions and plants, some grown on site.

Making the most of your day: **Indoors** Behind-the-Scenes house tours on set days. Art activities during school holidays and weekends. Christmas ghost tours and visit Father Christmas. **Outdoors** Garden history tours, trails for children. **Dogs**: assistance dogs only.

Access: [icons] House [icons] [icons] Café [icons] Grounds [icons]
Sat Nav: takes you to stables on Ham Street nearby. **Parking**: 380 yards (not National Trust) and on street.

Finding out more: 020 8940 1950 or hamhouse@nationaltrust.org.uk

Ham House and Garden		M	T	W	T	F	S	S
House								
1 Jan–4 Mar	12–4*	M	T	W	T	F	S	S
5 Mar–9 Oct	12–4	M	T	W	T	F	S	S
10 Oct–31 Dec	12–4*	M	T	W	T	F	S	S
Garden, café and shop								
Open all year	10–5**	M	T	W	T	F	S	S

*Selected rooms open, by guided tour at certain times.
**Closes dusk if earlier. Closed 24 and 25 December.

Fun in the Cherry Garden (below) and treasures in the Green Closet (left) at Ham House and Garden, Richmond

Morden Hall Park

Morden Hall Road, Morden, London SM4 5JD

[icons] 1942

Hoping for a catch at Morden Hall Park, South London

Hidden behind Grade II listed walls lies an Arcadian country estate, now surrounded by London but saved by a far-sighted philanthropist. The River Wandle meanders serenely throughout this former deer-park and its many habitats, creating a haven for an abundance of wildlife. Peace and tranquillity is never far away and, for the more active, adventure and fun is just around each corner; tree-climbing, paddling, family activities and a natural play area allow the whole family an opportunity to play. With the National Trust's first garden centre now open there really is something for everyone. **Note**: parking for visitors to Morden Hall Park only (including members). Admission charges do apply to some events including for members.

Eating and shopping: our exciting new garden centre is now open – pick up a beautiful gift or start your gardening journey with some exquisite plants and shrubs. Potting Shed café serving delicious hot lunches, teas and cake and our Stables coffee shop.

Wintry grace at peaceful Morden Hall Park

Osterley Park and House

Jersey Road, Isleworth, London TW7 4RB

🏠 ❖ ♣ 🔔 ▲ 🍽 1949

A suburban palace caught between town and country, Osterley Park and House is one of the last surviving country estates in London. Only a short distance from the big city, you can explore the 18th-century house designed by architect Robert Adam and fashioned for show and entertaining. Elegant pleasure gardens and hundreds of acres of parkland are perfect for a spot of table tennis or whiling away a peaceful afternoon. With our park, gardens and café now open all year you can snooze in deckchairs on the Temple Lawn in summer and enjoy brisk walks in the vibrant Winter Garden.

Eating and shopping: Stables Café, serving light meals and homemade cakes with indoor and outdoor seating. Gift shop, second-hand bookshop and plant sales in the Stables courtyard. Free wi-fi. Picnics welcome in the park and gardens.

Making the most of your day: events throughout the year, including annual country show, open-air cinema and theatre. Natural play area and regular park tours focusing on the historic and natural significance of the park. **Dogs**: welcome on leads around buildings and mown grass, including rose garden. Within sight elsewhere.

Access: 🅿️ 🅿️ ♿ 🔄 📷 🚻 ⬆️ 🖥 ♨ ⬇️ ◑
Snuff Mill 🔄 ♿ 🍴 ♿ Visitor centre, café and garden centre ♿ ♿ Parkland ♿ ♿ ➡ ♿
Sat Nav: use SM4 5JD and follow signs to Morden Hall Park Garden Centre.
Parking: 25 yards, next to garden centre.

Finding out more: 020 8545 6850 or mordenhallpark@nationaltrust.org.uk

Morden Hall Park	Open every day all year

Potting Shed café open 9 to 6. Garden centre open Monday to Saturday, 9 to 6, and Sunday 10 to 4. Rose garden and stable yard open 8 to 6. 1 November to 1 March: Potting Shed café and garden centre close at 5 and rose garden and stable yard close at 4. Closed 24 and 25 December.

Osterley Park and House, Isleworth: suburban palace

Sweet scents in the garden at Osterley Park and House

Making the most of your day: **Indoors** Year-round events and family activities, including free daily talks. **Outdoors** Adventure play trail and rope swings in the garden. **Dogs**: welcome in parkland areas, with designated on and off-lead areas.

Access: [icons] House [icons] Garden [icons]
Sat Nav: enter Jersey Road and TW7 4RD.
Parking: 400 yards.

Finding out more: 020 8232 5050 or osterley@nationaltrust.org.uk

Osterley Park and House		M	T	W	T	F	S	S
House and shop								
27 Feb–30 Oct	11–5*	M	T	W	T	F	S	S
3 Dec–18 Dec	11–4*	·	·	·	·	·	S	S
Garden and café								
Open all year	10–5†	M	T	W	T	F	S	S

*House: last entry one hour before closing. †Closes dusk if earlier. Closed 25 and 26 December.

Rainham Hall

The Broadway, Rainham, London RM13 9YN

[icons] 1949

A charming early 18th-century house, Rainham Hall has been home to a rich array of individuals over its history. One by one, we will be bringing their stories to life, starting with Captain John Harle (1688–1742), the merchant who built the Hall.

Eating and shopping: the Stables Café serves seasonally inspired light lunches, home-baked cakes, barista coffee, teas and soft drinks. Gifts, guidebooks and postcards available.

Making the most of your day: **Indoors** Regular events, including talks, family activities and Christmas festivities. **Outdoors** Nearly 1.5 hectares (3 acres) of urban green space and wide open skies. **Dogs**: assistance dogs only.

Access: [icons] House [icons]
Café [icons] Garden [icons]
Parking: 300 yards, not National Trust.

Finding out more: 01708 525579 or rainhamhall@nationaltrust.org.uk

Rainham Hall		M	T	W	T	F	S	S
Stables Café and garden								
2 Jan–31 Dec	10–5*	M	T	W	T	F	S	S
House								
17 Feb–30 Oct	10–5	·	·	W	T	F	S	S
4 Nov–18 Dec	10–5	·	·	·	·	F	S	S

*Gardens close dusk if earlier. Café and garden closed 25 and 26 December. Dates and times subject to change (**telephone before visiting**).

Visitors at Rainham Hall, Rainham

Red House, Bexleyheath: a William Morris gem

Red House

Red House Lane, Bexleyheath DA6 8JF

🏠 ❀ 2003

The only house commissioned, created and lived in by William Morris, founder of the Arts and Crafts Movement, Red House is a building of extraordinary architectural and social significance. An ongoing conservation project is gradually revealing Red House's secrets, including original Pre-Raphaelite wall-paintings and Morris's first decorative schemes.

Eating and shopping: William Morris shop housed in our Grade I listed Coach House. Café in original kitchen serving light lunches and a selection of cakes. Picnics welcome in the orchard.

Making the most of your day: **Indoors** Exhibition of Philip Webb's personal effects. Wombat trails in school holidays. Guided tours. Carols at Christmas. **Outdoors** Events, including summer arts and crafts fair and autumn Apple Day. **Dogs**: assistance dogs only.

Access: 🅿️🚻♿🎫📷🚶 Building 🏛
Grounds 🦽➡️
Sat Nav: use DA6 8HL – Danson Park car park.
Parking: at Danson Park, just over ½ mile.
Charge at weekends and Bank Holidays (including members).

Finding out more: 020 8304 9878 or redhouse@nationaltrust.org.uk

Red House		M	T	W	T	F	S	S
2 Mar–30 Oct	11–5			**W**	**T**	**F**	**S**	**S**
4 Nov–18 Dec	11–4					**F**	**S**	**S**

Admission by guided tour only at 11, 11:30, 12, 12:30 and 1 (booking essential); free-flow 1:30 to 5. Last admission 45 minutes before closing. Tea-room: last serving 4:30 (4 in winter). Open Bank Holiday Mondays.

Sutton House and Breaker's Yard

2 and 4 Homerton High Street, Hackney, London E9 6JQ

🏠 ▲ 🍴 1938

A Tudor courtier's mansion full of twists, turns and surprises in the heart of Hackney. With linenfold oak-panelled chambers, a great hall, cellars, Georgian, Victorian and Squatter rooms, all arranged around a tranquil courtyard and tea-room. Our new garden celebrates the site's industrial past as a car breaker's yard.

Eating and shopping: afternoon tea and cake are served on vintage crockery in the Georgian-styled tea-room – overlooked by prints of Hogarth's *A Harlot's Progress* – or in the courtyard, second-hand bookshop or among upcycled vehicles of the Breaker's Yard garden.

Making the most of your day: **Indoors** Panels open to show hidden features, such as 500 years of graffiti. Toy treasure chests playfully reveal secret, adventurous and refined stories.

Tudor Sutton House and Breaker's Yard in Hackney

Outdoors Breaker's Yard playground. Christmas events. **Dogs**: assistance dogs only.

Access: ♿🚼🔆🅿️🖼️💻🚻📷 Building ♿🔆🔆♿
Parking: none on site. Limited nearby, not National Trust (charge including members).

Finding out more: 020 8986 2264 or suttonhouse@nationaltrust.org.uk

Sutton House		M	T	W	T	F	S	S
3 Feb–18 Dec*	12–5	·	·	**W**	**T**	**F**	**S**	**S**

*Open daily in August. Open Bank Holiday Mondays and Good Friday. Property regularly used by local community groups – rooms always open as advertised, but call if you would like to visit during a quiet time. Occasional 'Museum Lates' opening.

575 Wandsworth Road

575 Wandsworth Road, Lambeth, London SW8 3JD

🏠 2010

Khadambi Asalache (1935–2006) turned this modest Grade II listed Georgian terraced house into a work of art. Featuring hand-carved fretwork throughout, the house and collections continue to inspire all who visit. **Note**: sorry no toilets or café. Access by booked guided tour only.

Delicate fretwork at 575 Wandsworth Road, Lambeth

Access: House ♿🚻
Parking: none on site.

Finding out more: 0844 249 1895 (bookings). 020 7720 9459 (enquiries) or 575wandsworthroad@nationaltrust.org.uk

575 Wandsworth Road		M	T	W	T	F	S	S
2 Mar–2 Nov	Tour	·	·	**W**	·	**F**	**S**	**S**

*House closed last Sunday of every month. Admission by booked guided tour only, booking essential (places limited). Tours on Wednesdays at 6:30, Fridays at 1:30 and 3:30, and Saturdays and Sundays at 11, 1:30 and 3:30.

2 Willow Road

Hampstead, London NW3 1TH

🏠⊤ 1994

This late 1930s house, an architect's vision of the future, paints a vivid picture of the creative and social circles in which Ernö and Ursula Goldfinger moved. Today you can explore the intimate and evocative interiors, innovative designs, intriguing personal possessions and impressive 20th-century art collection. **Note**: nearest toilet at local pub.

Eating and shopping: a small table in the entrance hall has property-related items available for sale.

Making the most of your day: events, including late openings and tours. Fenton House nearby (joint tickets available). Why not combine your visit with one of our London Partner attractions? **Dogs**: assistance dogs only.

Access: 🅿️🔆🖼️💻🚻📷 Building ♿🚻
Parking: very limited on-street parking nearby, not National Trust (charge including members).

Finding out more: 020 7435 6166 or 2willowroad@nationaltrust.org.uk

2 Willow Road		M	T	W	T	F	S	S
2 Mar–30 Oct	11–5*	·	·	**W**	**T**	**F**	**S**	**S**

*Entry by one-hour guided tour only, 11, 12, 1 and 2 (places limited, tickets available on day at door only). Wednesday to Friday, tours at 11 occasionally booked by groups. 3 to 5, self-guided viewing (timed entry when busy). Open Bank Holiday Mondays and Good Friday.

National Trust
Partner

London partners

'National Trust Partner' is an exciting venture between the National Trust and a selection of small, independent heritage attractions and museums within London. The Partnership aims to bring enhanced benefits to National Trust members living in London or for those visiting the capital for a day out, helping to provide increased opportunities to explore our rich and diverse heritage.

Entry charges: 50 per cent discount for members on presentation of a valid membership card. For full visiting information (and access), please see individual National Trust Partner websites.

Benjamin Franklin House

The world's only remaining home of Benjamin Franklin, featuring a unique 'Historical Experience'.

Underground: Charing Cross or Embankment.
Train: Charing Cross.

Finding out more: 020 7925 1405 or benjaminfranklinhouse.org

Bevis Marks Synagogue

Dated 1701, Britain's oldest surviving synagogue contains Cromwellian and Queen Anne furniture.

Underground: Liverpool Street or Aldgate.
Train: Liverpool Street.

Finding out more: 020 7626 1274 or bevismarks.org.uk

Danson House

Beautiful Georgian villa with sumptuous interiors, built for pleasure and entertaining.

Train: Bexleyheath.

Finding out more: 020 8303 7777 or bexley.gov.uk

The Fan Museum

Unique collection of more than 4,000 fans, housed in elegant Georgian buildings.

Train: Cutty Sark (DLR) or Greenwich.

Finding out more: 020 8305 1441 or thefanmuseum.org.uk

Dr Johnson's House

Late 17th-century townhouse, once home to lexicographer and wit Samuel Johnson.

Underground: Chancery Lane or Blackfriars. **Train**: Blackfriars.

Finding out more: 020 7353 3745 or drjohnsonshouse.org

Foundling Museum

Nationally important collection of 18th-century art, interiors, social history and music.

Underground: Russell Square, King's Cross St Pancras or Euston. **Train**: King's Cross, St Pancras or Euston.

Finding out more: 020 7841 3600 or foundlingmuseum.org.uk

Freud Museum London

The final home of pioneering psychoanalysts Sigmund Freud and his daughter Anna.

Underground: Finchley Road.
Train: Finchley Road & Frognal.

Finding out more: 020 7435 2002 or freud.org.uk

Leighton House Museum

Restored home of Victorian painter Lord Leighton, with priceless Islamic tile collection.

Underground: High Street Kensington or Holland Park.

Finding out more: 020 7602 3316 or leightonhouse.co.uk

Hall Place and Gardens

Stunning Tudor house with magnificent gardens.

Train: Bexley.

Finding out more: 01322 526574 or hallplace.org.uk

Museum of Brands

Intense experience of consumer culture: journey from Victorian times to your childhood.

Underground: Ladbroke Grove.

Finding out more: 020 7908 0880 or museumofbrands.com

The Old Operating Theatre Museum

Unique, atmospheric museum, hidden in the timbered Herb Garret of St Thomas's church.

Underground: London Bridge.
Train: London Bridge.

Finding out more: 020 7188 2679 or thegarret.org.uk

Strawberry Hill House

Horace Walpole's beautifully restored Gothic-revival castle by the Thames in Twickenham.

Train: Strawberry Hill.

Finding out more: 020 8744 1241 or strawberryhillhouse.org.uk

National Trust *Partner*

London partners

Entry charges: 50 per cent discount for members on presentation of a valid membership card. For full visiting information (and access), please see individual National Trust Partner websites.

Blickling Estate, Norfolk

Buildings and/or gardens

Entry points to coast and countryside

The size of each pin indicates how large
a place is and how long you should allow
for your visit

National Trust land

Brancaster
Estate

Brancaster
Activity
Centre

Blakeney
National
Nature
Reserve

West Runton
and Beeston
Regis Heath

Sheringham
Park

Cromer

Felbrigg Hall,
Gardens and Estate

Horsey
Windpump

Blickling Estate

King's Lynn

St George's Guildhall

Heigham Holmes

Peckover
House and
Garden

Swaffham

NORWICH

Great Yarmouth

Elizabethan
House
Museum

Peterborough

Oxburgh
Hall

Lyveden

Darrow
Wood

Ramsey Abbey
Gatehouse

Wicken
Fen National
Nature Reserve

Dunwich Heath
and Beach

Houghton Mill and
Waterclose Meadows

Newmarket

Bury St Edmunds

Theatre Royal
Bury St Edmunds

Ickworth

Orford Ness
National
Nature
Reserve

Anglesey Abbey,
Gardens and
Lode Mill

CAMBRIDGE

Lavenham
Guildhall

Bedford

Wimpole
Estate

Kyson Hill

Sutton
Hoo

Willington
Dovecote
and Stables

Melford Hall

IPSWICH

Pin Mill

Flatford

Sundon Hills
Country Park

Sharpenhoe
Moleskin and Markham Hills

Totternhoe
Knolls

Luton

Hatfield
Forest

Grange
Barn

Colchester

Bourne Mill

Dunstable Downs and the Whipsnade Estate

Paycocke's
House and
Garden

Copt Hall Marshes

Whipsnade
Tree
Cathedral

Shaw's
Corner

Hertford

Ashridge
Estate

Chelmsford

Northey Island

Morven Park

Danbury Commons
and Blakes Wood

Rayleigh Mount

Osterley Park
and House

Anglesey Abbey, Gardens and Lode Mill

Quy Road, Lode, Cambridge,
Cambridgeshire CB25 9EJ

🏠 🖼 ❄ 1966

When you step into this elegant home, you journey back to a golden age of country-house living. The Domestic Wing (below) shows how the staff serving the meticulous Lord Fairhaven ran his household like clockwork. The celebrated garden, with its sweeping avenues, classical statuary and flower borders, offers captivating views, vibrant colours and delicious scents whatever the season. Children can play, explore and discover nature in the Wildlife Discovery Area. A visit to the historic working watermill and famous Winter Garden will complete your day.

Eating and shopping: Redwoods restaurant serving seasonal, local menu. Light refreshments and snacks in gardens during peak times. Shop selling local products and gifts. Freshly milled wholemeal flour available from the historic watermill. Plant centre selling plants and garden furniture. Second-hand bookshop.

Anglesey Abbey, Gardens and Lode Mill, Cambridgeshire

Making the most of your day: **Indoors** Guided tours. Hands-on activities and demonstrations in Domestic Wing (Thursday and Friday). **Outdoors** Family activities. Weekday garden tours. Winter Lights: special event lighting the gardens at night (December weekends). **Dogs**: assistance dogs only.

Access: 🅿🚐♿🔊📷🖊🚲🖼
Abbey and mill 🔦🖼 Grounds 🖼➡🔎♿
Parking: 50 yards.

Finding out more: 01223 810080 or angleseyabbey@nationaltrust.org.uk

Anglesey Abbey		M	T	W	T	F	S	S
Garden, restaurant, shop and plant centre								
1 Jan–27 Mar	10–4:30	M	T	W	T	F	S	S
28 Mar–30 Oct	10–5:30	M	T	W	T	F	S	S
31 Oct–31 Dec	10–4:30	M	T	W	T	F	S	S
House								
9 Mar–27 Mar	11–3	·	·	W	T	F	S	S
30 Mar–30 Oct	11–4	·	·	W	T	F	S	S
House (guided tours)								
8 Mar–25 Oct	11–3:30	·	T	·	·	·	·	·
Lode Mill								
1 Jan–27 Mar	10:30–3:30	·	·	W	T	F	S	S
30 Mar–30 Oct	10:30–4	·	·	W	T	F	S	S
2 Nov–31 Dec	10:30–3:30	·	·	W	T	F	S	S

Mill and house: open Bank Holiday Mondays and daily during school holidays; house children's tours and domestic wing open Mondays and Tuesdays from Easter (Tuesday house tours every 30 minutes). Timed tickets to house on busy days. Last house entry one hour before closing. Closed 24 to 26 December. Snowdrop season: 25 January to 28 February.

Ashridge Estate

near Berkhamsted, Hertfordshire

⚔ 🏛 👜 1926

This special place has been enjoyed for centuries by everyone from pilgrims to picnickers. With its rich wildlife, diverse habitats and varied history, there is plenty to uncover at Ashridge. From the scent of the bluebells in spring, glorious birdsong and spectacular views from the chalk downland of the Pitstone Hills in summer, the rutting fallow deer in autumn and crisp walks on swathes of open common in winter, Ashridge has a landscape for every season. Waymarked trails and walks leaflets from the visitor centre. Wildwood Den natural play area for children. Climb the Bridgewater Monument for fantastic views. **Note**: toilets available only when café open.

Eating and shopping: our shop offers an ever-changing array of local and seasonal gifts, maps and books. The Brownlow Café (concession) serves homemade meals and snacks to eat in our outdoor courtyard.

Autumn at the Ashridge Estate, Hertfordshire

The Bridgewater Monument on the Ashridge Estate

Making the most of your day: events and children's activities throughout the year. Special exhibition and trail around 'Capability' Brown's Golden Valley, a jewel at the heart of Ashridge Park, from March to October.
Dogs: under close control at all times for the safety of wildlife and visitors.

Access: 🅿️♿ 🐕 🚾 📷 ♫
Visitor centre ♿ Grounds ♿ ➡️ ♿
Sat Nav: use HP4 1LT for the visitor centre and Bridgewater Monument (points to the end of the drive). **Parking**: at the visitor centre, Ivinghoe Beacon and many other parts of the estate.

Finding out more: 01442 851227 or ashridge@nationaltrust.org.uk

Ashridge Estate		M	T	W	T	F	S	S
Estate								
Open all year	Dawn–dusk	M	T	W	T	F	S	S
Visitor centre, Brownlow Café and shop*								
1 Mar–31 Oct	10–5	M	T	W	T	F	S	S
1 Nov–31 Dec	10–4	M	T	W	T	F	S	S
Bridgewater Monument (weather dependent)								
25 Mar–31 Oct	12–4:30	M	T	W	T	F	S	S

*Visitor centre and shop closed 24 and 25 December. Café opens at 8 and closes at 5 during March to October and 4 during November to December, closed 25 December. Estate may close in very high winds.

Blakeney National Nature Reserve

near Morston, Norfolk

🏠 🏛 ⚓ 🚶 ♿ 1912

Blakeney National Nature Reserve boasts wide open spaces and uninterrupted views of the beautiful Norfolk coastline. Internationally important, summer displays of terns and winter breeding grey seals (below) ensure delight for visitors all year round. Great for walkers, sightseers and wildlife enthusiasts alike; guaranteeing a memorable visit no matter the season. **Note**: nearest toilet at Morston Quay and Blakeney Quay (not National Trust).

Eating and shopping: new Grab & Go catering offer at Morston Quay. Nearby pubs and hotels (not National Trust) offering locally themed menus.

Making the most of your day: visitor centres at Morston Quay and Lifeboat House on Blakeney Point. Extensive coastal walks on the Norfolk Coast Path. Guided walks available. Ferry trips (not National Trust) to Blakeney Point. **Dogs**: some restrictions (particularly Blakeney Point), 1 April to mid-August.

Access: 🅿 🆅 Information centre ♿ 🅿
Lifeboat House ♿ 🅿
Sat Nav: use NR25 7BH for Morston Quay.
Parking: at Green Way Stiffkey Saltmarshes, Morston Quay and Blakeney Quay (not National Trust).

Finding out more: 01263 740241 or blakeneypoint@nationaltrust.org.uk

Blakeney		M	T	W	T	F	S	S
Nature Reserve								
Open all year		M	T	W	T	F	S	S
Morston Quay Information Centre and refreshments								
1 Mar–31 Oct	11–3	M	T	W	T	F	S	S
Lifeboat House (Blakeney Point)								
1 Mar–31 Oct	Dawn–dusk	M	T	W	T	F	S	S

Blickling Estate

Blickling, Aylsham, Norfolk NR11 6NF

🏛 🍴 ❄ ⚓ 🛏 🔔 1940

You'll never forget your first sight of Blickling. Sitting in a magnificent garden within a park is a breathtaking mansion, flanked by ancient yew hedges. Past owners have used the estate as a refuge while performing on the world's political stage. Philip Kerr, the last private owner, helped shape the National Trust's history, using his influence to find a way of saving great country houses for future generations to enjoy. Until his death in 1940 he used the house for entertaining his prominent guests; and photographs, sounds and objects help to tell his story. Outside, the formal garden is the result of three centuries of inspired planting, and the gently undulating historic parkland is great for exploring.

Eating and shopping: three cafés and a pub (not National Trust). Large second-hand bookshop, stamp shop, gift shop, plant and garden centre and exhibition gallery.

Blickling Estate, Norfolk: perfect for cycling

Making the most of your day: **Indoors**
Nationally important book collection in the Long Gallery. Changing local art, craft and photography exhibitions. Year-round activities for all ages, including family quizzes, games and trails. Living history performances. A variety of house and garden tours. RAF museum. **Outdoors** Cycling and walking along waymarked parkland routes (guides available from visitor reception). Permit fishing June to March. Events such as open-air cinema and summer music concerts. Pyramid mausoleum. Eight holiday cottages on the estate. Felbrigg Hall and Sheringham Park nearby.
Dogs: welcome on leads in park and courtyard café. Assistance dogs only elsewhere.

Access: [icons]
House [icons] Gardens [icons]
Parking: 400 yards.

Finding out more: 01263 738030 or blickling@nationaltrust.org.uk

Blickling Estate: the magnificent mansion

Blickling Estate		M	T	W	T	F	S	S
House*								
5 Mar–30 Oct**	12–5	M		W	T	F	S	S
5 Nov–20 Nov	12–4						S	S
25 Nov–4 Dec	2–8					F	S	S
Garden, shops and cafés								
1 Jan–4 Jan	11–3	M				F		
6 Jan–28 Feb†	11–4			W	T	F	S	S
29 Feb–30 Oct	10–5	M	T	W	T	F	S	S
2 Nov–18 Dec	11–4			W	T	F	S	S
19 Dec–23 Dec	11–4	M	T	W	T	F		
27 Dec–31 Dec	11–3		T	W	T	F	S	
Garden shop								
5 Mar–30 Oct	10–5	M	T	W	T	F	S	S

*Last entry one hour before closing. **Also open 29 March, 5 April, 31 May, 26 July, 2, 9, 16, 23, 30 August and 25 October (timed tickets on busy days). †Garden, shop and cafés also open 15 and 16 February. Muddy Boots café open 26 December. Park and woodland: open dawn to dusk. Fishing: 1 January to 14 March and 16 June to 31 December, 7 to 6 (or dusk if earlier).

Bourne Mill

Bourne Road, Colchester, Essex CO2 8RT

🏚 1936

Picturesque watermill (below) with working waterwheel in tranquil grounds. A delightful piece of late Elizabethan playfulness, used at different times for banqueting, milling flour and 'fulling' wool cloth. Large millpond, Tudor Physic Garden, wildlife area with ponds and babbling stream. Pond-dipping and garden games. Special events and family activities.

Eating and shopping: light refreshments available. Pond-side seating area. Shop selling locally designed/produced goods. Art exhibitions. Plant sales.

Making the most of your day: you can view the mill's workings, then explore the wildlife area and see how many '50 things' activities you can tick off. **Dogs**: welcome on leads.

Access: 🐕⬛⬛⬛⬛⬛⬛⬛
Building 🔲🔲 **Grounds** 🔲🔲
Parking: on site (limited), or on street.

Finding out more: 01206 549799 or bournemill@nationaltrust.org.uk

Bourne Mill		M	T	W	T	F	S	S
16 Mar–30 Oct	11–5				**W**	**T**	**F**	**S**	**S**

Whole property, including café, also open Bank Holiday Mondays, March to October. Closes 4 from 28 September.

Brancaster Activity Centre

Dial House, Harbour Way, Brancaster Staithe, Norfolk PE31 8BW

🏚⬛⬛⬛⬛⬛ 1984

Our newly refurbished outdoor learning centre offers residential experiences for schoolchildren, who can enjoy coastal-themed activities (below). Located in Brancaster Staithe Harbour, we're an ideal base for exploring the Norfolk coast and countryside. Outside the school term, special interest groups and families can enjoy a comfortable stay with us.

Eating and shopping: meals for school groups prepared freshly on site, using locally sourced produce whenever possible. Take-away drinks and light snacks available weekends and holidays.

Making the most of your day: range of coastal discovery activities and adventurous pursuits. **Dogs**: please contact the centre.

Access: ⬛ **Activity Centre** 🔲
Parking: limited within Harbour Way, Brancaster Staithe (not National Trust).

Finding out more: 01485 210719 (general enquiries/school bookings). 0344 335 1296 (group bookings) or brancaster@nationaltrust.org.uk

Brancaster
Please contact the centre for more information on residential group bookings.

---

nationaltrust.org.uk

Brancaster Estate

near Brancaster, Norfolk

🏠♿🚲🐕🚻 1923

Brancaster Estate boasts wide expanses of golden sands, wildlife-rich salt-marshes and the site of a historic Roman fort. **Note**: for beach car park (not National Trust) use Sat Nav PE31 8AX. Nearest toilet Brancaster Beach. Natural England manages Scolt Head Island National Nature Reserve.

Finding out more: 01263 740241 or brancaster@nationaltrust.org.uk

Copt Hall Marshes

near Little Wigborough, Essex

✝♿♿🚲🐕 1989

Working farm on the remote and beautiful Blackwater Estuary – a fantastic birdwatching spot, important for overwintering species. **Note**: for Sat Nav use CO5 7RD.

Finding out more: 01376 565450 or copthall@nationaltrust.org.uk

Danbury Commons and Blakes Wood

near Danbury, Essex

🏠♿🐕 1953

Varied countryside, ranging from the lowland heath of Danbury Common to ancient woodland with stunning spring flowers at Blakes Wood. **Note**: sorry no toilets. Sat Nav: for Danbury Commons use CM3 4JH and for Blakes Wood use CM3 4AU. Danbury Commons main car park closes dusk.

Finding out more: 01245 227662 or danbury@nationaltrust.org.uk

Darrow Wood

Darrow Green Road, Alburgh, Norfolk

🎖🏠♿ 1990

Darrow Wood is a small, hedge-enclosed, lightly wooded pasture field containing earthworks including a compact motte and bailey castle. **Note**: very limited off-road parking. Sorry no toilet. Do not use Sat Nav, no postcode available.

Finding out more: darrowwood@nationaltrust.org.uk

Why not share your pictures with us? #nationaltrust

Dunstable Downs and the Whipsnade Estate

near Dunstable, Bedfordshire

🏛 ♿ 👤 ⊤ 1928

'The Downs' have so much to offer all year round. The best kite-flying and picnicking site for miles around. A haven for wildlife; home to orchids, butterflies, birds and much more. Enjoy the ever-changing view from the Chilterns Gateway Centre with a refreshing drink or delicious meal. **Note**: Chilterns Gateway Centre is owned by Central Bedfordshire Council and managed by the National Trust.

Dunstable Downs and the Whipsnade Estate, Bedfordshire (above). The Chilterns Gateway Centre (left)

Eating and shopping: shop selling a wide range of kites, homemade fudge and Dunstable Downs branded products. The view café serves light lunches, snacks, hot and cold drinks with the option to eat in or take away.

Making the most of your day: events, including the annual Kite Festival in July. Nature trail and playscape in Chute Wood. Waymarked routes. History to discover and wildlife to spot. **Dogs**: under close control, on leads in car parks, near livestock and ground-nesting birds.

Access: 🅿 ♿ 🚻 ♿ ♿
Chilterns Gateway Centre 🅰 ♿ **Dunstable Downs** ➡
Sat Nav: use LU6 2GY (or LU6 2TA for older equipment). **Parking**: at Dunstable Downs, off B4541, and Bison Hill off the B4540.

Finding out more: 01582 500920 or dunstabledowns@nationaltrust.org.uk

Dunstable Downs		
Chilterns Gateway Centre: open 9:30 to 5 until November. November to February closes at 4. Closed 24 and 25 December. Please contact the centre for extended opening times in July and August.		

Dunwich Heath and Beach

Dunwich, Saxmundham, Suffolk

[icons] 1968

A precious landscape on the Suffolk coast, Dunwich Heath offers a true sense of being at one with nature. Set in the very middle of an Area of Outstanding Natural Beauty, there is an abundance of wildlife to discover, including such rare birds as the Dartford warbler and nightjar. There are many opportunities throughout the year to deepen your understanding of this special place, from guided walks to one of the many '50 things' activities, such as bug-hunting and pond-dipping. Our free app will help you make the most of your visit – search 'Dunwich Heath'.

Eating and shopping: clifftop tea-room serving breakfast, lunch, cream teas, homemade cakes (gluten-free available) and ice-cream. Gift shop selling local products, National Trust bestsellers, coastal-themed gifts and Dunwich branded items.

Three views of Dunwich Heath and Beach in Suffolk

Making the most of your day: self-guided and guided walks. Family activities, including pond-dipping, bug-hunting and nature trails. Heath Barn discovery area and family beach. Quarterly Sconeathon (there are dozens of flavours to try). **Dogs**: welcome, including in the tea-room (*Woof* guide available).

Access: [icons] Grounds [icons]
Sat Nav: use IP17 3DJ. **Parking**: on site.

Finding out more: 01728 648501 or dunwichheath@nationaltrust.org.uk

Dunwich Heath and Beach		M	T	W	T	F	S	S
Tea-room and shop								
1 Jan–3 Jan	10:30–3					F	S	S
9 Jan–7 Feb	10:30–3						S	S
13 Feb–21 Feb	10:30–4	M	T	W	T	F	S	S
27 Feb–27 Mar	10:30–4			W	T	F	S	S
28 Mar–30 Sep	10–5	M	T	W	T	F	S	S
1 Oct–23 Oct	10:30–4			W	T	F	S	S
24 Oct–30 Oct	10:30–4	M	T	W	T	F	S	S
5 Nov–18 Dec	10:30–3						S	S
26 Dec–31 Dec	10:30–3	M	T	W	T	F	S	

Visitor facility openings dependent on weather conditions.

Elizabethan House Museum

4 South Quay, Great Yarmouth,
Norfolk NR30 2QH

🏠⬆️☂️ 1943

A 16th-century quayside home, set out to
reflect day-to-day domestic life from Tudor to
Victorian times. **Note**: managed by Norfolk
Museums Service. Open Monday to Friday and
Sundays, 27 March to 30 October, 10 to 4.

Finding out more: 01493 855746 or
elizabethanhouse@nationaltrust.org.uk

Felbrigg Hall, Gardens and Estate

Felbrigg, Norwich, Norfolk NR11 8PR

🏠➕❄️♿️🚐 1969

Felbrigg Hall is a surprising mixture of opulence
and homeliness, where the stories of its owners
unfold through the completeness of its original
contents (right). Why not pick up some
inspiration from the Walled Garden? Once it
provided fruit and vegetables for the kitchens,
now it provides flowers for the Hall and is a
tranquil place to escape and relax. The rolling
landscape park, with a lake, ancient woodland
and miles of waymarked trails, is a great place
to explore nature, spot wildlife, or just to get
away from it all.

Eating and shopping: you can relax indoors
and out at the Squire's Pantry tea-room
(licensed), with a wide choice of hot and cold
drinks, sandwiches, soup and cakes. The gift
shop and second-hand bookshop offer a wide
range of goods, plants and books.

Making the most of your day: **Indoors**
Occasional attics and cellars tours. Children's
trails. Hall at Christmas event. **Outdoors**
Natural play area in Walled Garden. Events,
including Chilli Fiesta and Honey Fair. **Dogs**: on
leads in parkland when stock grazing, under
close control in woodland.

Access: 🅿️♿️♿️♿️♿️🚻♿️👶🐕
Hall ♿️♿️ Gardens ♿️♿️➡️♿️♿️
Sat Nav: use NR11 8PP. **Parking**: 100 yards.

Finding out more: 01263 837444 or
felbrigg@nationaltrust.org.uk

Felbrigg Hall		M	T	W	T	F	S	S
House and bookshop								
27 Feb–22 Oct	11–5	M	T	W	·	·	S	S
18 Jul–2 Sep*	11–5	M	T	W	T	F	S	S
23 Oct–30 Oct	11–4	M	T	W	·	·	S	S
Gardens								
27 Feb–22 Oct	11–5:30	M	T	W	T	F	S	S
23 Oct–30 Oct	11–4	M	T	W	T	F	S	S
3 Nov–18 Dec	11–3	·	·	·	T	F	S	S
Refreshments and shop								
2 Jan–21 Feb	11–3	·	·	·	·	·	S	S
27 Feb–22 Oct	10:30–5	M	T	W	T	F	S	S
23 Oct–30 Oct	10:30–4	M	T	W	T	F	S	S
3 Nov–18 Dec	11–3	·	·	·	T	F	S	S
27 Dec–31 Dec	11–3	·	T	W	T	F	S	·

House and bookshop open Good Friday. *18 July to
2 September: access to some areas of house may be limited
on Thursdays and Fridays. House open daily in local school
holidays (March to October). Parkland: open every day all
year, dawn to dusk.

Flatford

Flatford, East Bergholt, Suffolk CO7 6UL

🏠 ♿ 🚻 1943

Flatford sits beside the River Stour (below and right) in the heart of the countryside of Dedham Vale Area of Outstanding Natural Beauty. The locations which inspired many of Constable's iconic paintings surround Flatford, so that you can stand in the very same places as John Constable and enjoy views that he painted 200 years ago. Our small exhibition will give you an insight into Constable's paintings. While you are here, you could explore the countryside on foot following a circular path or hire a boat and row along the river to immerse yourself in the history and beauty of Flatford. **Note**: no public access inside Flatford Mill, Valley Farm and Willy Lott's House.

Eating and shopping: riverside tea-room serving homemade cakes and light lunches. Shop selling plants, gifts and souvenirs.

Making the most of your day: volunteer guides offer tours sharing their passion for Constable and show some of the locations he used. Waymarked circular walks and family trails around Flatford. **Dogs**: welcome, but please be aware of livestock in fields.

Access: 🅿 🅿 🚶 🐕 📷 🚻 ♿ ♿ 🚻 ⓐ
Bridge Cottage 🚻 ♿ **Grounds** 🚻 ♿ ♿
Parking: 100 yards.

Finding out more: 01206 298260 or flatford@nationaltrust.org.uk

Flatford		M	T	W	T	F	S	S
2 Jan–28 Feb	10:30–3:30						S	S
2 Mar–27 Mar	10:30–5			W	T	F	S	S
28 Mar–24 Apr	10:30–5	M	T	W	T	F	S	S
25 Apr–2 Oct	10:30–5:30	M	T	W	T	F	S	S
3 Oct–30 Oct	10:30–5	M	T	W	T	F	S	S
2 Nov–23 Dec	10:30–3:30			W	T	F	S	S

For other ways to get involved go to nationaltrust.org.uk/get-involved/volunteer

Grange Barn

Grange Hill, Coggeshall, Colchester,
Essex CO6 1RE

🏠 🔔 🍷 1989

One of Europe's oldest timber-framed
buildings, Grange Barn (below) stands as a
lasting reminder of the once powerful
Coggeshall Abbey. With oak pillars soaring up
to a cathedral-like roof, bearing the weight of
centuries, this 13th-century building has truly
stood the test of time.

Eating and shopping: takeaway refreshments,
ice-cream, limited range of souvenirs and
second-hand books available. Coffee shop
at nearby Paycocke's House and Garden.
Picnics welcome.

Making the most of your day: exhibition on
the life and work of local woodcarver Bryan
Saunders. Paycocke's House and Garden
nearby. **Dogs**: welcome on leads in grounds.

Access: 🅿️🚶 💺 Building 🔼 Grounds 🔼
Parking: on site.

Finding out more: 01376 562226 or
grangebarncoggeshall@nationaltrust.org.uk

Grange Barn		M	T	W	T	F	S	S
16 Mar–25 Sep	11–4		·	W	T	F	S	S
28 Sep–30 Oct	11–3		·	W	T	F	S	S

Open Bank Holiday Mondays.

Hatfield Forest

near Bishop's Stortford, Essex

🏠 🏚 🐕 💪 👣 ⚋ 1924

When Henry I established a Royal Hunting Forest here in 1100, he could little have guessed that almost a millennium later it would be the best survivor of its kind in the world. The ancient trees are managed using traditional techniques and the forest is home to more than 3,500 species of wildlife, including fallow deer descended from the original herd. You can walk across wide open plains, grazed by Red Poll cows, or enjoy family days out. With over 405 hectares (1,000 acres), there are many places for imaginative play or a spot of quiet relaxation.

Eating and shopping: café, with outdoor dining area, serving hot and cold refreshments, ice-creams and drinks. Shop selling local gifts, guidebook and maps, plus Hatfield Forest venison and Red Poll beef (when in season).

Making the most of your day: events, including open-air theatre. Rowing boat hire available in the summer. Download our free mobile app with interactive map (iTunes/android) before you visit, or borrow a pre-loaded tablet.
Dogs: welcome under close control. On leads in lake area and near livestock.

Hatfield Forest, Essex, was once a royal hunting forest

Access: 🅿️ 🚻 🛗 📷 ♿ 📷
Shell House 🛗 🍴 **Forest** ➡️ 🚲 ♿
Sat Nav: use CM22 6NE. **Parking**: on site (limited in winter).

Finding out more: 01279 874040 (Infoline). 01279 870678 or hatfieldforest@nationaltrust.org.uk

Hatfield Forest		M	T	W	T	F	S	S
Café								
1 Jan–20 Mar	10–3:30	·	·	W	T	F	S	S
21 Mar–30 Oct	9–5	M	T	W	T	F	S	S
2 Nov–31 Dec	10–3:30	·	·	W	T	F	S	S

Shell House and Elgin's car park open 21 March to 30 October, 10 to 4:30, Monday to Friday, and 9 to 4:30, Saturday and Sunday (conditions permitting). Café closed 25 December. Shop closed 25 and 26 December.

Heigham Holmes

near Martham, Norfolk

💪 👣 1987

Remote island nature reserve, with grazing marshes and ditches, supporting the wildlife of this internationally important and vast broadland landscape. **Note**: admission by guided visits only (booking essential), due to restricted access via floating river crossing. Charge (including members).

Finding out more: 01263 740241 or heighamholmes@nationaltrust.org.uk

Horsey Windpump

Horsey, Great Yarmouth, Norfolk NR29 4EF

⊠ 🛉 🏛 🛉 ⟊ 1948

Finding out more: 01493 393904 or horseywindpump@nationaltrust.org.uk Norfolk Coast Office, Friary Farm, Cley Road, Blakeney, Norfolk NR25 7NW

Horsey Windpump		M	T	W	T	F	S	S
Windpump Restoration Project								
29 Feb–31 Jul	10–4:30	M	T	W	T	F	S	S
Windpump								
1 Aug–31 Oct	10–4:30	M	T	W	T	F	S	S
Horsey Staithe Stores								
29 Feb–31 Oct	10–4:30	M	T	W	T	F	S	S

Car park open all year, dawn to dusk.

Currently undergoing an exciting restoration project, Horsey Windpump (above) is an iconic building with a fascinating past and the perfect gateway to experience the connection between man and nature. Standing sentinel over the surrounding Broadland landscape, a climb to the top is rewarded with beautiful panoramic views of Horsey Mere. **Note**: surrounded by Horsey Estate – managed by Buxton family. Windpump closed for restoration to end July. Horsey Gap car park, not National Trust (charge including members).

Eating and shopping: Horsey Staithe Stores (next to Horsey Windpump) serving light refreshments and selling local gifts, souvenirs and books.

Making the most of your day: see the windpump restoration in progress. Walking routes to Horsey Mere and the beach. Boat trips (not National Trust) across Horsey Mere (May to September). **Dogs**: welcome (on leads near wildlife and livestock).

Access: 🅿️ 👟 👥 👟 🏞 🖨 🖨 🖊
Windpump 🔥 🔥 🔥 Grounds 🔥 ➡️
Parking: on site. Alternatively, at Horsey Gap car park, 1 mile, not National Trust (charge including members).

Houghton Mill and Waterclose Meadows

Houghton, near Huntingdon, Cambridgeshire PE28 2AZ

🏛 🛉 🅰 🛎 1939

In a stunning riverside setting, surrounded by meadow walks, Houghton Mill is the oldest working watermill on the Great Ouse. There are hands-on activities for all the family, as well as milling demonstrations, and you can buy our flour, ground in the traditional way by our French burr millstones.

Eating and shopping: riverside tea-room serving snacks, cakes and scones made with our traditional stoneground flour. Houghton wholemeal flour and gifts for sale in our new shop.

Making the most of your day: **Indoors** Milling demonstrations (Sundays) and baking days. Family events. **Outdoors** Open-air theatre. Children's trails, activities and summer holiday events. Access to surrounding meadows via public footpaths. National Trust riverside campsite. **Dogs**: Assistance dogs only please in mill but all dogs welcome in grounds on leads.

Access: 🅿️ 👟 👟 👟 🖨 🖨 🖊 ∷
Building 🔥 🔥 🔥 Grounds ➡️
Parking: 20 yards.

Finding out more: 01480 301494 or houghtonmill@nationaltrust.org.uk

basement, 1930s domestic service is portrayed through memories of former staff. The Italianate garden mirrors the house architecture, with clipped hedges and Mediterranean planting, while an extensive Victorian stumpery, planted with shade-loving ferns, creates an air of mystery. Parkland walking and cycling routes have pastoral views with ancient oaks. **Note**: accommodation and dining – Ickworth Hotel (part of the Luxury Family Hotel Group), 01284 735350.

Eating and shopping: West Wing Café, Court Bar and Orangery serving seasonal lunches, afternoon tea and snacks. Porter's Lodge outdoor café serving light snacks and refreshments. Roving catering buggy. Gift shop. Second-hand bookshop. Plant centre in main car park.

Houghton Mill		M	T	W	T	F	S	S
Mill								
19 Mar–30 Oct	11–5	.	.	.	.	.	S	S
21 Mar–20 Jul	1–5	M	T	W	.	.	.	.
25 Jul–9 Sep	1–5	M	T	W	T	F	.	.
12 Sep–26 Oct	1–5	M	T	W	.	.	.	.
Tea-room								
2 Jan–13 Mar	10:30–4	.	.	.	.	.	S	S
19 Mar–27 Apr	10:30–5	M	T	W	.	.	S	S
30 Apr–31 Oct	10:30–5	M	T	W	T	F	S	S
5 Nov–18 Dec	10:30–4	.	.	.	.	.	S	S

Open Bank Holiday Mondays and Good Friday, 11 to 5.
Caravan and campsite: now National Trust, open 18 March to 31 October (01480 466716). Car park: closes 8 or dusk if earlier.

Ickworth

The Rotunda, Horringer, Bury St Edmunds, Suffolk IP29 5QE

🏠 ✝ 🐾 ❀ 🏕 🛏 🔔 ▼ 1956

Classical Italy brought to Suffolk. Close to Bury St Edmunds, this estate reflects the Hervey family's passion for everything Italian, influenced by their European grand tours. The Rotunda is a Neo-classical showcase, intended by the 4th Earl of Bristol to house treasures; indeed an extensive collection of silver contains the finest examples by Huguenot silversmiths. Family history is documented in portraits by artists such as Gainsborough and Reynolds, while in the

Making the most of your day: Indoors
'Ickworth Lives' experience and 1930s Living History days. Cooking workshops. Paintings by Titian, Velázquez, Reynolds, Kaufmann, Vigée Le Brun and Gainsborough, as well as an extensive Georgian silver collection, Regency furniture, historic books and Italian porcelain.
Outdoors Events and activities all year, including snowdrops, heritage daffodils, lambing and Easter Egg fun. Open-air theatre, archery and wildlife days. Summer Wool Fair, Wood and Country Craft Fair and family Christmas weekends. Historic Walled Kitchen Garden and seasonal flower meadow to explore. Guided and waymarked walks through extensive parkland. Cycle routes, geocache sites and trim trail. Children's play area.
Dogs: welcome on leads at all times. Assistance dogs only in the Italianate gardens.

Access: 🅿️ 🔠 ♿ 🚻 🅿️ 🔊 📷 House ♿ ⬆️ 🚶
West Wing ♿ ⬆️ 🍴 ♿ Grounds ♿ ♿ 🚲 ♿
Parking: on site.

Finding out more: 01284 735270 or ickworth@nationaltrust.org.uk

Ickworth		M	T	W	T	F	S	S
House								
5 Mar–30 Oct*	11–5	M	T	·	T	F	S	S
28 Mar–10 Apr*	11–5	M	T	W	T	F	S	S
30 May–5 Jun*	11–5	M	T	W	T	F	S	S
25 Jul–31 Aug*	11–5	M	T	W	T	F	S	S
24 Oct–30 Oct*	11–5	M	T	W	T	F	S	S
5 Nov–18 Dec**	11–4	·	·	·	·	·	S	S
Shop and café								
1 Jan–4 Mar	10:30–4	M	T	W	T	F	S	S
5 Mar–30 Oct	10:30–5	M	T	W	T	F	S	S
31 Oct–31 Dec	10:30–4	M	T	W	T	F	S	S
Plant and garden shop								
5 Mar–30 Oct	11–5	M	T	W	T	F	S	S
5 Nov–18 Dec	12–3	·	·	·	·	·	S	S
Porter's Lodge outdoor café								
2 Jan–18 Dec	10–4	·	·	·	·	·	S	S
5 Mar–30 Oct	10–5	M	T	W	T	F	S	S

Italianate gardens, parkland, woods and children's playground: open daily, 9 to 5:30 (dusk if earlier). *Access by tour only, 11 to 12 and 4 to 5 (except Bank Holidays). **Entrance hall and basement only open weekends in December. Last house entry 45 minutes before closing. Closed 25 December. Plant and garden shop may close earlier in winter. Porter's Lodge outdoor café may close in adverse weather.

Hands-on fun at Houghton Mill (opposite). The Rotunda at Ickworth, Suffolk (left), and visitors warm up with hot drinks (below)

Kyson Hill

Broomheath, Woodbridge, Suffolk

🏃 🏛 1934

Diminutive Kyson Hill, with its grassy slopes, specimen trees and estuarine views, is a favourite destination for walking or relaxation. **Note**: sorry no toilet. No postcode available for Sat Nav. Car park 546 yards (not National Trust).

Finding out more: 01394 389700 (Sutton Hoo) or kysonhill@nationaltrust.org.uk

Lavenham Guildhall

Market Place, Lavenham, Sudbury, Suffolk CO10 9QZ

🏠 ✤ 1951

Lavenham Guildhall in Suffolk (left and above)

Set in the lovely village of Lavenham, the Guildhall of Corpus Christi tells the story of one of the best-preserved and wealthiest towns in Tudor England. When you step inside this fine timber-framed building, you'll feel the centuries melt away. You can discover the stories of the people who have used the Guildhall through almost 500 years at the heart of its community, and learn about the men and women who have shaped the fortunes of this unique village. Then you can explore the picturesque streets of Lavenham, lined with shops, galleries and more than 320 buildings of historic interest.

Eating and shopping: tea-room serving light lunches, cream teas and hot and cold drinks. Shop selling local gifts, souvenirs, books and plants.

Making the most of your day: Indoors Children's trails and dressing-up costumes. Changing exhibitions. **Outdoors** Guided walks and talks in summer.

Access: 🐕♿🔊💬📖♿⚪🅰
Guildhall ♿♿ Garden ♿♿
Parking: in village.

Finding out more: 01787 247646 or lavenhamguildhall@nationaltrust.org.uk

Lavenham Guildhall		M	T	W	T	F	S	S
9 Jan–6 Mar	11–4	·	·	·	·	·	S	S
7 Mar–30 Oct	11–5	M	T	W	T	F	S	S
3 Nov–23 Dec	11–4	·	·	·	T	F	S	S

Parts of the property close occasionally for community use.
2 to 4 December: Lavenham Christmas Fair (free).

Melford Hall

Long Melford, Sudbury, Suffolk CO10 9AA

🏛♿♿ 1960

There are many stories to discover in this eclectic family home. Melford Hall has had its fair share of trials and tribulations, from being ransacked during the Civil War to being devastated by fire in 1942. It is thanks to the many generations who have left their mark that it continues to survive. It remains the Hyde Parker's much-loved family home and it is their stories of family life, from naval exploits to visits from their cousin Beatrix Potter, which makes this house more than mere bricks and mortar.

Melford Hall, Suffolk: garden (below), and interior (right)

Eating and shopping: small tea-room or Park Room serving sandwiches and cream teas. Gatehouse shop selling souvenirs, gifts, books, souvenir story books and plants.

Making the most of your day: **Indoors** Talks. Spot-it quiz for children under eight and Spy Catcher trail for older children (up to 13). **Outdoors** Garden games. Walks, talks and family events. **Dogs**: welcome on leads in car park and park walk only.

Access: 🅿🐕♿🔊🔊📖♿🅰
Building ♿♿🚻🚼♿ Grounds ♿♿
Parking: on site.

Finding out more: 01787 376395 (Infoline). 01787 379228 or melford@nationaltrust.org.uk

Melford Hall		M	T	W	T	F	S	S
23 Mar–30 Oct	12–5	·	·	W	T	F	S	S

Open Bank Holiday Mondays. House: 12 to 1, entry by short taster tour, then free-flow. Gardens, tea-room and shop: fully open from 12.

Moleskin and Markham Hills

near Streatley, Bedfordshire

♿♿ 2001

Wildlife-rich chalk grassland, beech woodland and meadows managed as a nature reserve. **Note**: parking in the Sharpehoe car park. For Sat Nav use LU3 3PR for car park.

Finding out more: 01582 873663 or moleskinmarkhamhills@nationaltrust.org.uk

Morven Park

Great North Road, near Potters Bar,
Hertfordshire

🖼 1928

On the site of the original Potters Bar, these
eight hectares (20 acres) of parkland are
over 150 years old. **Note**: sorry no toilet.
For Sat Nav use EN6 1HS.

Finding out more: 01582 873663 or
morvenpark@nationaltrust.org.uk

Northey Island

near Maldon, Essex

🖼🖼🖼🖼 1978

A peaceful retreat in the Blackwater Estuary,
important for overwintering birds, Northey is
also the oldest recorded battlefield in Britain.
Note: access by causeway, so restricted by
tides. Telephone in advance to arrange your
visit. For Sat Nav use CM9 6PP (CM9 5JQ
for parking).

Finding out more: 01621 853142 or
northeyisland@nationaltrust.org.uk

Orford Ness National Nature Reserve

Orford Quay, Orford, Woodbridge,
Suffolk IP12 2NU

🖼🖼🖼🖼 1993

This is Suffolk's secret coast, only reached by
National Trust ferry. Wild, remote and exposed,
the 'Island' contains the ruined remnants of a
disturbing past. Ranked among the most
important shingle features in the world, rare
and fragile wildlife thrives where weapons,
including atomic bombs, were once tested and
perfected. **Note**: limited tickets. Steep, slippery
steps, long distances. Hazardous debris.
Limited access: 'pagodas' only on tours. Charge
for ferry crossing (including members).

Eating and shopping: shops, cafés and pubs in
village (none National Trust). Fresh fish
available at quay. Local smokehouses.

Making the most of your day: guided tours on
wildlife and history, and photography tours
give access to Atomic Weapons Research
Establishment site (booking essential for all
tours). Bird-ringing and moth mornings. Meet
our sheep. **Dogs**: assistance dogs only.

Access: 🖼🖼🖼 Buildings 🖼🖼 Trails 🖼🖼
Parking: at Riverside Car Park, Quay Street,
not National Trust (charge including members),
150 yards to Trust Orford Quay office to buy
ferry ticket.

Finding out more: 01728 648024 (Infoline).
01394 450900 (tour bookings) or
orfordness@nationaltrust.org.uk

Orford Ness		M	T	W	T	F	S	S
26 Mar–25 Jun	10–2	·	·	·	·	·	S	·
28 Jun–1 Oct	10–2	·	·	T	W	T	F	S
8 Oct–29 Oct	10–2	·	·	·	·	·	S	·

Only access is by National Trust ferry from Orford Quay –
boats cross regularly between 10 and 2 only; last ferry leaves
the Ness at 5. Main visitor trail (Red Route) always available,
other routes open seasonally.

**Orford Ness National Nature Reserve on Suffolk's wild and
remote secret coast. Oxburgh Hall, Norfolk (opposite)**

Oxburgh Hall

Oxborough, near Swaffham, Norfolk PE33 9PS

🏠✝♿♨🛏🍴 1952

No one forgets their first sight of Oxburgh. Built in 1482 by the Catholic Bedingfeld family, it is the enduring legacy of their survival through turbulent times. There are 500 years of history to explore and hidden doors, rooftop views and a secret priest's hole to discover. Victorian Gothic interiors reflect a romantic view of Oxburgh's medieval past. The collections include embroideries worked by Mary, Queen of Scots, and colourful wallpapers from the mid-19th century. The moated Hall is surrounded by nearly 28 hectares (70 acres), containing gardens with seasonal interest, streams and woodland walks.

Eating and shopping: tea-room in old Kitchen and Servants' Hall. The Pantry is a seasonal kiosk serving light refreshments. Picnic in the grounds or the area by the car park. Gift shop selling gifts, games and local products. Plant sales. Second-hand bookshop.

Making the most of your day: Indoors Introductory talks most days, March to October. Family trails. **Outdoors** Daily guided garden tours, March to October. Winter weekend snowdrop walks. Children's activities, including woodland den-building area. Year-round events. **Dogs**: assistance dogs only.

Access: 🅿♿🚐🛗🔊🎨📷📺♿
Hall 🔊♿🚻♿ Chapel ♿ Garden ♿➡♿
Parking: on site.

Finding out more: 01366 328258 or oxburghhall@nationaltrust.org.uk

Oxburgh Hall		M	T	W	T	F	S	S
Garden, shop and tea-room								
2 Jan–7 Feb	11–4						S	S
13 Feb–21 Feb	11–4	M	T	W	T	F	S	S
22 Feb–4 Mar	11–4	M	T	W		F	S	S
House								
13 Feb–21 Feb	12–3	M	T	W	T	F	S	S
22 Feb–4 Mar	12–3	M	T	W		F	S	S
House, garden, shop and tea-room								
5 Mar–25 Mar*	11–5	M	T	W		F	S	S
26 Mar–10 Apr*	11–5	M	T	W	T	F	S	S
11 Apr–29 May*	11–5	M	T	W		F	S	S
30 May–5 Jun*	11–5	M	T	W	T	F	S	S
6 Jun–17 Jul*	11–5	M	T	W		F	S	S
18 Jul–4 Sep*	11–5	M	T	W	T	F	S	S
5 Sep–2 Oct*	11–5	M	T	W		F	S	S
3 Oct–23 Oct*	11–4	M	T	W		F	S	S
24 Oct–30 Oct*	11–4	M	T	W	T	F	S	S
Garden, shop and tea-room								
5 Nov–18 Dec	11–4						S	S

*Admission to garden, shop and tea-room from 10:30.

Paycocke's House and Garden

25 West Street, Coggeshall, Colchester, Essex CO6 1NS

🏠❀ 1924

Exquisitely carved half-timbered Tudor cloth merchant's house, with a beautiful and tranquil cottage garden. Visitors can follow the house's changing fortune, see how it was saved from demolition and restored to its former glory. You can admire carved timbers, architectural features and discover details about Coggeshall White cloth. **Note**: toilet on first floor.

Eating and shopping: coffee shop serving cream teas, coffee, cakes and soft drinks (courtyard and garden). Picnics welcome. Ice-cream available. Shop selling gifts, local and gardening products. Plants for sale at our garden stall. Second-hand bookshop.

Making the most of your day: **Indoors** Events all year, including changing annual exhibition. Children's activities and costumes. **Outdoors** Relax or play garden games. Why not combine with a visit to nearby Coggeshall Grange Barn? **Dogs**: welcome in garden only.

Access: 🅿️♿🏠🖼️ Building 🔼 Grounds 🔼♿
Parking: at Coggeshall Grange Barn, ½ mile, or at Stoneham Street car park, ¼ mile (not National Trust). Limited roadside parking.

Finding out more: 01376 561305 or paycockes@nationaltrust.org.uk

Paycocke's		M	T	W	T	F	S	S
16 Mar–30 Oct	11–5*		·	·	**W**	**T**	**F**	**S**	**S**

*Garden open 10:30 to 5; coffee shop open 11 to 4:30.
Open Bank Holiday Mondays.

Peckover House and Garden

North Brink, Wisbech, Cambridgeshire PE13 1JR

🏠❀🛏️🔔☕☂️ 1943

While its riverside setting at Wisbech was popular among merchants, imposing Peckover House stood apart as an oasis of calm, reflecting the Quaker way of life. As you wander through the intimate rooms, you can imagine the family reading in the Library and talking with friends in the Drawing Room. The Peckovers were bankers and added a specially designed wing to the house; an exhibition tells its story. They also loved their garden, and you can discover its delights as you explore the unexpected 0.8 hectare (two acres), discovering borders, summerhouses, an orangery and 60 varieties of rose. **Note**: Octavia Hill's Birthplace House open opposite (not National Trust).

Eating and shopping: set in the corner of the garden, the Reed Barn is the ideal place for light lunch or afternoon tea. You can browse through the second-hand bookshop, take home a special plant from the garden and enjoy our gift shop.

Making the most of your day: **Indoors** Grand piano to play. Behind-the-scenes tours. Handling collection and children's trails. Georgian Wisbech exhibition. Octavia Hill's Birthplace House opposite. **Outdoors** Free garden tours. Croquet and lawn games (summer). **Dogs**: assistance dogs only.

Access: 🅿️🥾♿️🖼️🏠📺🎵
House 🅰️♿️ Garden ♿️➡️🚻
Sat Nav: use PE13 1RG or PE13 2RA for nearest car parks. **Parking**: nearest is Chapel Road or Somers Road, 500 yards (not National Trust).

Finding out more: 01945 583463 or peckover@nationaltrust.org.uk

Peckover House and Garden		M	T	W	T	F	S	S
Garden, shop and tea-room*								
16 Jan–21 Feb	12–4	·	·	·	·	·	S	S
House, garden, shop and tea-room								
27 Feb–20 Mar	11–5**	M	T	W	·	·	S	S
21 Mar–10 Apr	11–5**	M	T	W	T	F	S	S
11 Apr–26 Jun	11–5**	M	T	W	·	·	S	S
27 Jun–3 Jul	11–5**	M	T	W	T	F	S	S
4 Jul–23 Oct	11–5**	M	T	W	·	·	S	S
24 Oct–30 Oct	11–5**	M	T	W	T	F	S	S
10 Dec–18 Dec	11–5	M	T	W	T	F	S	S

*16 January to 21 February: admission to house at 2 by timed conservation talk only. **House open 12 to 4.

Peckover House and Garden, Cambridgeshire (below and right): heaven for rose lovers

Pin Mill

near Chelmondiston, Suffolk

🏞️ 1978

A woodland and heathland restoration site. A number of footpaths from the village with panoramic views over the River Orwell. **Note**: for Sat Nav use IP9 1JW. Parking in Pin Mill village, not National Trust (charge including members), or Chelmondiston.

Finding out more: 01206 298260 or pinmill@nationaltrust.org.uk

Ramsey Abbey Gatehouse

Abbey School, Ramsey, Huntingdon, Cambridgeshire PE26 1DH

🏛️ 1952

This fascinating medieval gatehouse, along with the Lady Chapel, are all that remain of the great Benedictine Abbey at Ramsey. **Note**: sorry no toilet. Gatehouse and Lady Chapel in Abbey open first Sunday of the month, April to September, 1 to 5.

Finding out more: 01284 747500 or ramseyabbey@nationaltrust.org.uk

Rayleigh Mount

Rayleigh, Essex

🏰 1923

Medieval motte-and-bailey castle site, with adjacent windmill housing historical exhibition. **Note**: exhibition in windmill operated by Rochford District Council. For Sat Nav use SS6 7ED. Parking at Bellingham Road – adjacent to main entrance (not National Trust).

Finding out more: 01284 747500 or rayleighmount@nationaltrust.org.uk

St George's Guildhall

29 King Street, King's Lynn, Norfolk PE30 1HA

🏠 1951

The largest surviving medieval guildhall in England, with many original features – now a theatre. **Note**: managed by King's Lynn and West Norfolk Borough Council and King's Lynn Arts Centre Trust. Parking at Tuesday Market Place (not National Trust). Access by appointment during normal working hours.

Finding out more: 01553 779095. 01553 764864 (box office) or stgeorgesguildhall@nationaltrust.org.uk

Sharpenhoe

Sharpenhoe Road, Streatley, Bedfordshire

🏰👪🐾 1939

Dominating the landscape, this steep chalk escarpment is crowned with beech woodland and traces of an Iron Age hill fort. **Note**: sorry no toilets. For Sat Nav use LU3 3PR.

Finding out more: 01582 873663 or sharpenhoe@nationaltrust.org.uk

Shaw's Corner

Ayot St Lawrence, near Welwyn, Hertfordshire AL6 9BX

🏠✳ 1944

You can follow in the footsteps of one of the world's greatest playwrights, George Bernard Shaw, as you explore his fascinating home and enjoy the beauty and tranquillity of his inspiring garden. **Note**: access roads very narrow.

Eating and shopping: souvenir and gift shop. Second-hand bookshop. Ice-cream and soft drinks available in garden. Pre-1950s varieties of plants for sale.

Making the most of your day: events, including open-air performances of George Bernard Shaw's plays (summer). **Dogs**: assistance dogs only.

Access: 🅿♿📷🚗📱🚻
House 🔦🔥🚹♿ Grounds 🔦🔥♿
Sat Nav: use AL6 9BX (some routes might take you through a ford and a route not signposted to Shaw's Corner). **Parking**: very limited (not suitable for large vehicles).

Finding out more: 01438 829221 (Infoline). 01438 820307 or shawscorner@nationaltrust.org.uk

Shaw's Corner		M	T	W	T	F	S	S
25 Mar–30 Oct	12–5			**W**	**T**	**F**	**S**	**S**
Open Bank Holiday Mondays.								

Sheringham Park

Upper Sheringham, Norfolk NR26 8TL

🝖 ❖ ♨ ♒ ⛵ 1987

Using the undulating landscape laid down by glaciers 430,000 years ago, Humphry Repton created views of the North Norfolk coast that can still be enjoyed today. His 1812 design stated 'Sheringham Park had more natural beauty and advantages than any place he had ever seen'. The Upcher family added an extensive rhododendron collection to Repton's design, bringing an array of colour to the wild garden in the spring. A walk may be interrupted by the drumming of a woodpecker, the song of skylarks as they spiral above you, or the sound of a steam train travelling through the park. **Note**: Sheringham Hall is privately occupied. April to September: limited access by written appointment with leaseholder.

Eating and shopping: gift shop selling guidebooks, local gifts and souvenirs. Plant sales, including rhododendrons. Courtyard Café serving sandwiches, cake and ice-cream. A range of gluten-free food is also available. Picnics welcome.

Making the most of your day: self-guided trails and guided walks (suggested routes downloadable from website). Climb to top of Gazebo tower to see coastal views enjoyed

Glorious Sheringham Park, Norfolk (above and below)

since Napoleonic times. Free use of children's Tracker Packs. **Dogs**: welcome under control. On leads near livestock and visitor facilities.

Access: 🅿 ♿ 🚻 📖 👜 ♨ ☕ 🗺
Building 🅰 🅱 Grounds 🅰 ➡ 🚶 🅱
Parking: 60 yards.

Finding out more: 01263 820550 or sheringhampark@nationaltrust.org.uk

Sheringham Park		M	T	W	T	F	S	S
Park								
Open all year	Dawn–dusk	M	T	W	T	F	S	S
Visitor centre and Courtyard Café								
2 Jan–6 Mar	11–4	·	·	·	·	·	S	S
12 Mar–30 Oct	10–5	M	T	W	T	F	S	S
5 Nov–31 Dec	11–4	·	·	·	·	·	S	S

Courtyard Café open from 8:45 and visitor centre from 9:30 every Saturday. Visitor centre and Courtyard Café open daily 13 to 21 February and 28 to 31 December, 11 to 4. Closed 24 and 25 December.

Sundon Hills Country Park

Harlington Road, Upper Sundon, Bedfordshire

⚹🏃 2000

Wildlife-rich chalk grassland, beech woodland, open meadows and a picnic site with views north towards the Greensand Ridge. **Note**: sorry no toilets. For Sat Nav use LU3 3PE.

Finding out more: 01582 873663 or sundonhills@nationaltrust.org.uk

Sutton Hoo

Tranmer House, Sutton Hoo, Woodbridge, Suffolk IP12 3DJ

🏠🏛⚹🕊️🥄 1998

Shortly before the outbreak of the Second World War, the ship burial of an Anglo-Saxon king and his extraordinary treasures were unearthed by archaeologist Basil Brown. These ancient graves kept their secrets for 1,300 years, but what was found here changed our perceptions of the past for ever. The atmospheric burial mounds, breathtaking replica treasures, original finds and reconstruction of the king's burial chamber bring this fascinating story to life. Edith Pretty's country house takes you back to that remarkable discovery, while relaxing in true 1930s style. Walks across this Anglo-Saxon landscape offer stunning views over the River Deben.

Sutton Hoo, Suffolk: ancient graves (left and opposite), and a striking Anglo Saxon mask sculpture (above)

Eating and shopping: café serving hot meals, snacks, children's menu and cream teas (outdoor seating and views to the River Deben). You'll be inspired by the range of gifts in our shop, including exclusive locally made pottery. Second-hand bookshop in stables.

Making the most of your day: **Indoors** Exhibition – introductory video, information panels, audio recordings, dressing-up, replica treasures, burial reconstruction. House – 1930s decoration, gramophone, children's quiz, Basil's workshop. **Outdoors** Burial mound tours, circular walks. Children's play area. **Dogs**: welcome on leads in reception, shop, café terrace and countryside only.

Access: 🅿️👿🚻♿🔔🎧🦽👀
Buildings ♿🦽 Grounds ♿➡️👀🦽
Parking: on site.

Finding out more: 01394 389700 or suttonhoo@nationaltrust.org.uk

Sutton Hoo		M	T	W	T	F	S	S
1 Jan–3 Jan	10:30–4	·	·	·	·	**F**	**S**	**S**
9 Jan–7 Feb	10:30–4	·	·	·	·	·	**S**	**S**
13 Feb–30 Oct	10:30–5	**M**	**T**	**W**	**T**	**F**	**S**	**S**
5 Nov–18 Dec	10:30–4	·	·	·	·	·	**S**	**S**
27 Dec–31 Dec	10:30–4	·	**T**	**W**	**T**	**F**	**S**	·

Estate walks open daily, 9 to 6 (except for some Thursdays, November to end January).

East of England

Theatre Royal Bury St Edmunds

Westgate Street, Bury St Edmunds, Suffolk IP33 1QR

🏠🔔🍴 1974

Grade I listed theatre, one of the country's most significant theatre buildings and the only surviving Regency playhouse in Britain. **Note**: managed by Bury St Edmunds Theatre Management Ltd. Admission charges apply to live shows and selected guided tours (including members). Please call before visiting, as opening times may vary due to performances.

Finding out more: 01284 769505 or theatreroyal@nationaltrust.org.uk

Totternhoe Knolls

Castle Hill Road, Totternhoe, Bedfordshire

🏛🏞🐾 2000

The dramatic earthworks of a Norman castle rise from important chalk grassland habitat, sitting high above the surrounding landscape. **Note**: sorry no toilets. For Sat Nav use LU6 1RG.

Finding out more: 01582 873663 or totternhoeknolls@nationaltrust.org.uk

West Runton and Beeston Regis Heath

near West Runton, Norfolk

🏛🏞 1925

A lovely place to walk among heath and woods, with fine views of the North Norfolk coast. **Note**: sorry no toilets. For Sat Nav use NR27 9ND.

Finding out more: 01263 820550 or westrunton@nationaltrust.org.uk

Whipsnade Tree Cathedral

Whipsnade, Dunstable, Bedfordshire

🏞 1960

Peaceful place with trees planted in shape of medieval cathedral. Created after the First World War to commemorate fallen comrades. **Note**: administered by Trustees of Whipsnade Tree Cathedral. Dogs under close control. Car park open 9 to 4 (winter); 9 to 7 (summer). For Sat Nav use LU6 2LQ. Donations welcome.

Finding out more: 01582 872406 or whipsnadetc@nationaltrust.org.uk

Wicken Fen, Cambridgeshire (above and opposite)

Wicken Fen National Nature Reserve

Lode Lane, Wicken, Ely, Cambridgeshire

❌ ♿ 👤 1899

With vast skies above flowering meadows, sedge and reedbeds, Wicken Fen is a window onto a lost fenland landscape. A wealth of wildlife is at home in this important wetland, including rarities such as hen harriers and bitterns, numerous dragonflies, moths and wildfowl. The landscape feels wild, though people have managed it for years, as revealed by the fenman's yard, windpump and cottage. The Wicken Fen Vision, an ambitious landscape-scale conservation project, is opening up new areas for wildlife and for you to explore. Grazing herds of Highland cattle and Konik ponies help create a diverse range of new habitats. **Note**: some paths may be subject to seasonal closure.

Eating and shopping: shop in the visitor centre selling wildlife and outdoor books, as well as local food and crafts. Café serving homemade soup, light lunches and afternoon teas. Picnics welcome.

Making the most of your day: all-weather boardwalk and longer paths allow exploration of the heart of the Fen by foot. Seasonal boat trips offer an alternative view. Cycle the Lodes Way across the wider reserve. **Dogs**: welcome on leads on reserve and in visitor centre.

Access: 🅿 🅳 ♿ 🚻 🏷 📷 📶 🖼
Building ♿ 🅶 Grounds ♿ 🅶
Sat Nav: use CB7 5XP. **Parking**: 120 yards.

Finding out more: 01353 720274 or wickenfen@nationaltrust.org.uk

Wicken Fen		M	T	W	T	F	S	S
Reserve, visitor centre and shop								
Open all year	10–5	M	T	W	T	F	S	S
Café								
1 Jan–14 Feb	10–4:30	·	·	W	T	F	S	S
15 Feb–30 Oct	10–5	M	T	W	T	F	S	S
2 Nov–31 Dec	10–4:30	·	·	W	T	F	S	S

Closed 25 December. Café open 26, 27 December. Access to reserve dawn to dusk. Visitor centre closes dusk in winter.

Willington Dovecote and Stables

Willington, Church End, near Bedford, Bedfordshire MK44 3PX

✠ ♿ 1914

A hidden gem in a tranquil setting; were these magnificent Tudor stone buildings built for Henry VIII's 1541 visit? **Note**: admission by appointment with the volunteer team, contact Mrs J. Endersby, 21 Chapel Lane, Willington MK44 3QG (01234 838278). Exterior open daily. Open last Sunday of the month, April to September, 1 to 5.

Finding out more: 01480 301494 or willingtondovecote@nationaltrust.org.uk

Wimpole Estate

Arrington, Royston, Cambridgeshire SG8 0BW

🏛️✝️🏛️🔊✳️🦋🔔📶 1976

It will take at least a day to discover Wimpole's acres of parkland, miles of walks, Walled Kitchen Garden and Home Farm. There is also the Hall to explore, where intimate rooms contrast with beautiful Georgian interiors. With its various owners driven by passions and purposeful agendas, Wimpole is both a place to escape to and a place to get involved. We continue the 3rd Earl of Hardwicke's passion for trail-blazing food production and design, celebrating the estate's past magnificence and echoing Elsie Bambridge's 20th-century revival. As owners changed, a roll-call of ingenious architects, artists and landscape designers cultivated magnificence. Wimpole is an 'all-year-round' place to visit, reflecting the changing seasons, with something to captivate and inspire all visitors.

Eating and shopping: Old Rectory Restaurant, Farm Café and Stables Café, using produce from the Walled Garden and Home Farm. Large shop with local food, gifts, crafts, homeware, gardenware, plants and books. Wimpole rare-breed meat, flour and eggs. Second-hand bookshop, toy shop.

Making the most of your day: **Indoors** Explore the Hall at your own pace on a one-way route. Bookable basement tours. Top Hat and Mob Cap trail for families. **Outdoors** Seasonal spectaculars, including daffodils, spring blossom, summer parterre, herbaceous borders and autumn trees. Free guided walks in the parkland and geocaching. Contemporary art installation. Daily farm activities: grooming the donkey, meeting the Shire horse, rabbits, feeding the pigs and milking the cow. Lambing time. Celebrating 'Capability' Brown's 300th birthday. Open-air theatre, literary festival, '50 things to do before you're 11¾', craft fair and Christmas events. Sporting activities, including running and walking groups, cycle and running trails.
Dogs: welcome on leads in park.

Access: [access icons] Hall [icons]
Farm [icons] Gardens [icons]
Sat Nav: entrance via A603, not A1198.
Parking: 275 yards.

Finding out more: 01223 206000 or
wimpole@nationaltrust.org.uk

Wimpole Estate		M	T	W	T	F	S	S
Garden, Old Rectory Restaurant and stable block								
1 Jan–12 Feb	11–4	M	T	W	T	F	S	S
13 Feb–30 Oct	10–5	M	T	W	T	F	S	S
31 Oct–31 Dec	11–4	M	T	W	T	F	S	S
Home Farm and Farm Café								
2 Jan–7 Feb	11–4	·	·	·	·	·	S	S
13 Feb–30 Oct	10:30–5	M	T	W	T	F	S	S
5 Nov–31 Dec	11–4	·	·	·	·	·	S	S
Hall								
13 Feb–30 Oct	11–5	M	T	W	T	·	S	S
Hall (guided basement tour)								
5 Nov–27 Nov	11–3	·	·	·	·	·	S	S

Park: open every day all year dawn to dusk. Hall: also open
Fridays in the school holidays. Home Farm: open 1 to
4 January and 27 to 31 December, daily, 11 to 4. Estate: closed
25 and 26 December, except park and stable block (servery
and gift shops) open 26 December, 11 to 4. Bookshop as shop,
but closed Monday mornings. Car park: open 7:30 to 6:30.

Wimpole Estate, Cambridgeshire: there is so much to see and do, that a day is barely enough

East Midlands

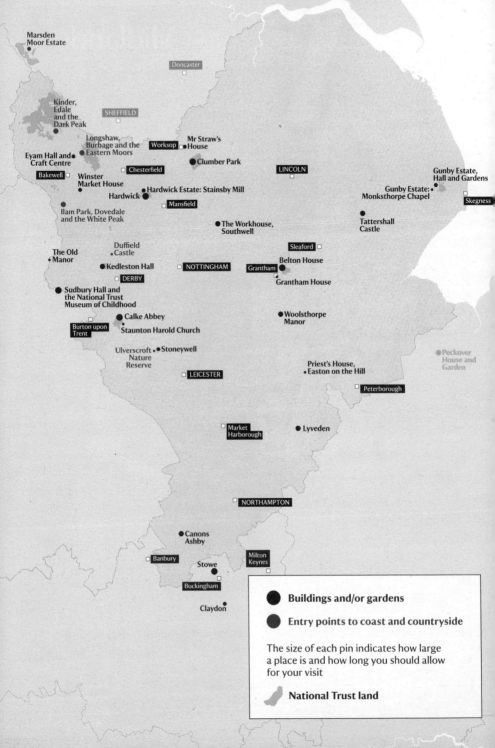

KINGSTON UPON HULL ⬜ ●Maister House

Marsden
Moor Estate

Doncaster ⬜

Kinder,
Edale
and the
Dark Peak ●

SHEFFIELD ⬜

Longshaw,
Burbage and the
Eastern Moors ● | Worksop ⬜ ●Mr Straw's
House

Eyam Hall and
Craft Centre ●

Bakewell ⬜ | Chesterfield ⬜ | ●Clumber Park

LINCOLN ⬜

Winter
Market House

Hardwick Estate: Stainsby Mill

Gunby Estate,
Hall and Gardens ●

Hardwick ● | Mansfield ⬜

Gunby Estate:
Monksthorpe Chapel ●

Skegness ⬜

Ilam Park, Dovedale
and the White Peak ● | ●The Workhouse,
Southwell

Tattershall
Castle ●

The Old
●Manor | Duffield
Castle ● | Sleaford ⬜

Belton House ●

Kedleston Hall ● | NOTTINGHAM ⬜ | Grantham ⬜ ●

DERBY ⬜ | Grantham House

Sudbury Hall and
the National Trust
Museum of Childhood ●

Calke Abbey ● | ●Woolsthorpe
Manor

Burton upon
Trent ⬜

Staunton Harold Church

Ulverscroft ●Stoneywell
Nature
Reserve | Peckover
House and
Garden ●

LEICESTER ⬜ | Priest's House,
●Easton on the Hill

Peterborough ⬜

Market
Harborough ⬜ | ●Lyveden

NORTHAMPTON ⬜

●Canons
Ashby

Banbury ⬜ | Milton
Keynes ⬜

Stowe ●

Buckingham ⬜

Claydon ●

Surrounded by elegant gardens and an ancient deer-park, Belton House, Lincolnshire, contains many fine collections

Belton House

Grantham, Lincolnshire NG32 2LS

🏛 ✝ ♣ ♨ 🔔 🍸 1984

Belton is often cited as being the perfect example of an English country-house estate. The 17th-century Carolean mansion features fine collections of silver and porcelain, an extensive library and is surrounded by elegant formal gardens and an ancient deer-park. In 2016, Belton explores the role played by Peregrine Cust, the 6th Baron, in the royal abdication of 1936. 'Perry' was close friend and Lord in Waiting to King Edward VIII and stood by his side in the crisis that rocked the nation. Uncover the story of Belton during this time of political upheaval with events and exhibitions throughout the year. Revamped in 2015, the outdoor adventure playground is a must for families looking for a fun day out. **Note**: all visitors (including members) need to obtain an admission sticker from visitor reception on arrival.

Eating and shopping: Stables Restaurant serving hot meals (between 12 and 2), including Belton's award-winning venison (in season). Snacks and light meals served in Ride Play Café. Two shops selling gifts, plants and local produce. Extensive second-hand bookshop.

Making the most of your day: **Indoors** You can enjoy the mansion at your own pace with no set visitor route and discover more about Belton with themed interpretation and guided tours. Why not pick up a timed ticket to hear about life 'below stairs' for Belton's servants? Indoor adventure play café open every day and Discovery Centre for family activities on weekends and school holidays. **Outdoors** Downloadable walks and family trails. Open-air cinema, theatre evenings and markets. Lincolnshire's largest outdoor adventure playground. Seasonal colour in the gardens throughout the year. Easter, Hallowe'en and Christmas activities. Woolsthorpe Manor, home of Sir Isaac Newton, is nearby.
Dogs: welcome on leads in parkland and stableyard. Assistance dogs only in gardens and playground.

Access: 🅿 ♿ 🏛 🚻 ⓘ 🍴 🎥 🛗 🐕 ⓓ
House 🏛♿🅖 Grounds 🏛➡♿🅖
Sat Nav: use NG32 2LW. **Parking**: on site.

Finding out more: 01476 566116 or belton@nationaltrust.org.uk

Belton House		M	T	W	T	F	S	S
House								
12 Mar–30 Oct	12:30–5			W	T	F	S	S
Shops, restaurant, Ride Play Café, adventure playground								
1 Jan–28 Feb	9:30–4	M	T	W	T	F	S	S
29 Feb–30 Oct	9:30–5:30	M	T	W	T	F	S	S
31 Oct–31 Dec	9:30–4	M	T	W	T	F	S	S

House: open Bank Holiday Mondays (March to October); no set visitor route. Specialist tours most days and timed tickets for 'below stairs' tours daily from the Marble Hall. Park and garden: open as shops and restaurant. Bellmount Woods: open daily, access from separate car park. Bellmount Tower and Boathouse open occasionally. House closes in poor light. Closed 25 December.

With extensive grounds, family trails and an adventure playground, Belton House (above and below) is perfect for families

Entry is still possible at most places up to 30 minutes before closing

Calke Abbey, Derbyshire: a place of curious contrasts

Calke Abbey

Ticknall, Derby, Derbyshire DE73 7LE

🏛 ✝ 🔊 ❄ ♿ 🐕 ⛺ 🍽 1985

Calke Abbey tells the story of the dramatic decline of the Harpur-Crewe's grand country estate. The house and stables have been preserved as we found them. Grand rooms are crammed full of collections, from art to natural history, which contrast with abandoned rooms and objects no longer used. The overgrown stable courtyards, with their peeling paintwork, are great for exploring. Throughout the year the gardens yield flowers and produce, while faded garden buildings such as the Orangery hint at former fortunes. The Pleasure Grounds provide some great spots for a stroll and picnics. For the adventurous, the historic and fragile habitats of Calke Park and its National Nature Reserve await discovery, together with the limeyards, wetlands, ancient trees and ponds. **Note**: everyone requires admission tickets for house and garden, including members. House admission by timed ticket.

Eating and shopping: restaurant serving meals including estate-reared meat. Café open every weekend and at peak times. Coffee van and barbecue at peak times. Large gift shop selling seasonal gifts, plants and local food.

Making the most of your day: **Indoors** Family activities in Squirt's Stable at weekends and during school holidays from February to October. Children's activity sheets for the house. **Outdoors** Events all year, whatever the weather, including guided park and garden walks. Children's play areas. Park play map available from the ticket office. Tramway cycling and walking circuit suitable for all the family. We also offer Tracker Packs and discovery trails. **Dogs**: welcome on leads in parkland and stableyards; assistance dogs only the house and gardens.

Access: 🅿️� ♿ 🚻 ⬆️ 🔆 📷 🏛️ 🎦 🎵 👓
House 🔆♿♿ Stables ♿♿ Grounds 🔆♿➡️
Sat Nav: use DE73 7JF. **Parking**: on site.

Finding out more: 01332 863822 or calkeabbey@nationaltrust.org.uk

Calke Abbey's collections (below) never fail to enthral, while outside (above), there is plenty of space to let off steam

Calke Abbey		M	T	W	T	F	S	S
Calke Park National Nature Reserve††								
Open all year	7:30–7:30	M	T	W	T	F	S	S
House*								
20 Feb–30 Oct	11–5	M	T	W	T	F	S	S
Garden and stables								
13 Feb–30 Oct	10–5	M	T	W	T	F	S	S
Restaurant and shop[1]								
Open all year	10–5	M	T	W	T	F	S	S

††Closes dusk if earlier; closed 25 December. *House: ground floor taster visit between 11 and 12:30; house opens fully 12:30 (admission by timed ticket). [1]Stables, restaurant and shop: close at 4 in January, February, November and December. Whole property closed 25 December.

Places may occasionally close for events or bad weather

Canons Ashby

near Daventry, Northamptonshire NN11 3SD

🏠✝🏛❋⚡ 1981

Tranquil Elizabethan manor house set in beautiful 18th-century gardens. Built by the Drydens using the remains of a medieval priory, the house and gardens have survived largely unaltered since 1710 and are presented as they were during the time of Sir Henry Dryden, a Victorian antiquary, passionate about the past. The warm and welcoming house features grand rooms, stunning tapestries and Jacobean plasterwork, contrasting with the domestic detail of the servants' quarters. Strolling through the historic parkland, you will glimpse early medieval landscapes, while a wander through the priory church reveals the story of the canons of Canons Ashby. **Note**: admission by timed tickets on busy days.

Tranquil Canons Ashby, Northamptonshire (above and left), was built on the remains of a medieval priory

Eating and shopping: Stables tea-room and pretty tea-gardens with daily home baking and light meals. Coach House shop selling home and garden gifts and seasonal home-grown plants. Well-stocked second-hand bookshop (donations welcome).

Making the most of your day: Indoors Events all year, including costumed weekends. **Outdoors** Live music in the gardens and priory. Guided walks. Family fun activities on Mothering Sunday, Easter, Hallowe'en, Christmas and school holidays. **Dogs**: welcome on leads in car park, paddock, tea-garden and parkland only.

Access: 🅿♿♿♿♿♿♿ VT ♿♿
Building 🏠👪 Church 🏠 Grounds 🏠♿
Parking: 218 yards.

Finding out more: 01327 861900 or canonsashby@nationaltrust.org.uk

Canons Ashby		M	T	W	T	F	S	S
Tea-room, gardens, shop, church and parkland*								
13 Feb–4 Mar	10:30–3:30	M	T	W	T	F	S	S
5 Mar–31 Oct	10:30–5	M	T	W	T	F	S	S
1 Nov–18 Dec	10:30–3:30	M	T	W	T	F	S	S
27 Dec–31 Dec	10:30–3:30	·	T	W	T	F	S	·
House*								
13 Feb–4 Mar	11–3	M	T	W	·	F	S	S
5 Mar–31 Oct†	1–5†	M	T	W	·	F	S	S
5 Nov–4 Dec	11–3	·	·	·	·	·	S	S
10 Dec–18 Dec	11–3	M	T	W	T	F	S	S

House: closed Thursdays, except 15 December. †House taster tours: 11 to 1 (30 minutes, showing three rooms), tickets on arrival. *Some garden areas and house rooms may be closed during winter months for conservation needs. Tea-room, shop, gardens, church, parkland open 1 January 2017.

Clumber Park

Worksop, Nottinghamshire S80 3BE

✚ ✱ ♨ ▲ ⊤ 1946

Carved out of the ancient forest of Sherwood, the Dukes of Newcastle created a space of playfulness and pleasure on a grand scale. Clumber Park is true to its spirit as a place of recreation; there are 20 miles of cycle routes and 1,537 hectares (3,800 acres) of parkland, woodland and heathland to explore – havens for wildlife. The beauty of the Gothic Revival chapel, with its original stained-glass windows, reveal a rich historic past. The Pleasure Grounds frame the magnificent lake, making a perfect place to stroll or picnic. The Walled Kitchen Garden, with its National Collection of Rhubarb, provides a variety of fruit and vegetables to the café and colourful herbaceous borders during the summer.

Eating and shopping: café serving hot meals, snacks, cream teas and a children's menu. Garden Tea House. Barbecue at peak times. Large gift shop and plant sales. Second-hand bookshop; cycle hire, servicing and sales. Picnics welcome and designated barbecue site.

Three views of Clumber Park, Nottinghamshire: playfulness and pleasure on a grand scale

Making the most of your day: Indoors Year-round activities for all ages and interests, including workshops, art, history and wildlife exhibitions at the Discovery Centre, chapel, glasshouse and Museum of Gardening Tools, Burrow play area for under threes and Willow Tree Farm. **Outdoors** Seasonal highlights include spring bluebells, rhododendrons and apple blossom, late-summer-flowering heathers and autumn tree colour. The Discovery Centre and Walled Kitchen Garden are great places to explore the '50 things' activities. There are downloadable walks, woodland play areas, cycle hire, a programme of outdoor events and a campsite.
Dogs: welcome, some restrictions apply. Covered refreshment area for dog walkers. Downloadable *Woof* guide.

Access: ⓟ 🖼 🚽 🔂 ⚗ 🎵
Buildings 🏛 ♿ Grounds 🏛 ➡ ♿ ♿
Parking: 250 yards.

Finding out more: 01909 544917 or clumberpark@nationaltrust.org.uk

Clumber Park		M	T	W	T	F	S	S
Visitor facilities*								
1 Jan–26 Mar	10–4	M	T	W	T	F	S	S
27 Mar–29 Oct	10–5	M	T	W	T	F	S	S
30 Oct–31 Dec	10–4	M	T	W	T	F	S	S
Walled Kitchen Garden								
2 Jan–7 Feb	11–3						S	S
13 Feb–26 Mar	11–3	M	T	W	T	F	S	S
27 Mar–29 Oct	10–5	M	T	W	T	F	S	S
30 Oct–6 Nov	10–4	M	T	W	T	F	S	S
12 Nov–18 Dec	11–3						S	S

*Visitor facilities close at 6 on Saturday and Sunday. Visitor facilities include café, shop, plant sales, cycle hire, chapel, Discovery Centre and woodland play park. Open daily except 25 December. Café: open daily at 9. Tea House open Saturday and Sunday, 11 to 4, and daily in school summer holidays, 10 to 4.

Duffield Castle

Duffield, Derbyshire

🏰 🏛 1899

One of England's largest 13th-century castles – today you can see its foundations, imagine the stories and savour the views. **Note**: sorry no toilets. Steep steps. For Sat Nav use DE56 4DW.

Finding out more: 01332 842191 or duffieldcastle@nationaltrust.org.uk

Eyam Hall and Craft Centre

Main Street, Eyam, Derbyshire S32 5QW

🏛 ❄ ♿ 2013

Eyam Hall is an unspoilt example of a gritstone Jacobean manor house, set within a walled garden. Completed in 1672, it was home to the Wright family for 11 generations. Explore the legendary plague history of the village and the surrounding Peak District countryside.

Eating and shopping: gift and craft shops. Buttery café (not National Trust) serving lunch and refreshments.

Making the most of your day: **Indoors** Seasonal events and themed workshops. **Outdoors** 'Thought walks', exploring some of the village stories and plague history, and guided walks. Hardwick Hall nearby. **Dogs**: welcome on 'thought walks'. Assistance dogs only in house and walled gardens.

Access: 📶 🅿 ♿ 🚹 📷 🎦 🚻 Building ♿ ♿ 🚶 ♿ **Parking**: 43 yards.

Finding out more: 01433 639565 or eyam@nationaltrust.org.uk

Arches garlanded with fragrant roses at Eyam Hall and Craft Centre, Derbyshire (above)

Eyam Hall and Craft Centre		M	T	W	T	F	S	S
Craft Centre								
Open all year*	10:30–4:30	·	T	W	T	F	S	S
Hall and garden								
13 Feb–30 Oct*	10:30–4:30	·	·	W	T	F	S	S
26 Nov–23 Dec**	10:30–3:30	·	·	W	T	F	S	S

Independent craft shops and café opening hours may vary from National Trust. *Open Bank Holidays, April to August. **Reduced number of rooms available to view in December.

Grantham House

Castlegate, Grantham, Lincolnshire NG31 6SS

🏛 ❄ 1944

Handsome town house, one of the oldest buildings in Grantham, with riverside walled garden. **Note**: leased by the National Trust and the lessee is responsible for arrangements and facilities. Open by appointment only, Wednesdays and Thursdays, April to October, 2 to 5 (appointments not required in June).

Finding out more: 01476 564705 or granthamhouse@nationaltrust.org.uk

Gunby Estate, Hall and Gardens

Gunby, Spilsby, Lincolnshire PE23 5SS

🏠✚🏛️❖🐾🖼️🔔 1944

The Massingberd family home from 1700 until 1967, Gunby Hall still feels cherished and lived-in. Exploring three floors, you can easily imagine you'll bump into one of the family at any moment. Enjoy garden colour whatever the season: abundant spring flowers, summer roses, autumn borders and plentiful fruit and vegetables.

Eating and shopping: courtyard tea-room offering cakes, sweet treats, savoury snacks, hot and cold drinks. Well-stocked second-hand bookshop in the basement. Seasonal plants and produce for sale when available.

Gunby Estate, Hall and Gardens, Lincolnshire

Making the most of your day: events throughout year, from open-air theatre to Regency re-enactments and apple days. Public footpaths run across the wider historic park and estate: ask for directions and maps in the tea-room. **Dogs**: welcome on leads in the gardens, courtyard tea-room terrace and grounds.

Access: 🅿♿ Building ♿🏛️ Grounds ♿🐕
Sat Nav: may misdirect – entrance is off roundabout (not beyond or before).
Parking: on site.

Finding out more: 01754 890102 or gunbyhall@nationaltrust.org.uk

Gunby Estate		M	T	W	T	F	S	S
House*								
26 Mar–30 Oct	11–5	M	T	W	·	·	S	S
26 Nov–11 Dec	11–3	·	·	·	·	·	S	S
Gardens and tea-room**								
24 Mar–30 Oct	11–5	M	T	W	T	F	S	S
26 Nov–11 Dec	11–3	·	·	·	·	·	S	S
Parkland and car park								
Open all year	11–5	M	T	W	T	F	S	S

*House: last admission one hour before closing.
On busy days admission to the house may be by timed ticket.
**Tea-room: last service 4:30. May close dusk or earlier.

Gunby Hall Estate: Monksthorpe Chapel

Monksthorpe, near Spilsby, Lincolnshire PE23 5PP

✚ 2000

Monksthorpe Chapel, dated 1701, was made to look like a barn to avoid detection and features a rare open-air baptistry. **Note**: chapel open daily, 24 March to 30 October, 11 to 4 (access by key, obtained from Gunby Hall tea-room, £20 refundable deposit required). Grounds open daily, 11 to 5.

Finding out more: 01754 890102 or monksthorpe@nationaltrust.org.uk

Hardwick

Doe Lea, Chesterfield, Derbyshire S44 5QJ

🏠❄️🎿🐾🔔🍽 1959

The Hardwick Estate is made up of stunning houses and beautiful landscapes that have been created by a cast of thousands. It was the formidable Bess of Hardwick who first built Hardwick Hall in the late 16th century, and in the centuries since then, gardeners, builders, decorators, embroiderers and craftsmen of all kinds have contributed and made Hardwick their creation. This year we take a closer look at the life of Duchess Evelyn, the 'last lady of Hardwick'. Her newly restored bedroom completes the family rooms on the middle floor. You can discover more about the life of a duchess, her pioneering conservation work and the dramatic changes she made to the east view landscape. **Note**: Old Hall owned by the National Trust and administered by English Heritage (01246 850431).

Eating and shopping: Great Barn Restaurant serving hot meals, seasonal specials and homemade cakes. Stables shop selling gifts, souvenirs and local produce. Outdoors shop and plant sales (many propagated in the nursery at Hardwick). Picnic areas in the stableyard and parkland.

Making the most of your day: Indoors
Seasonal events, including Easter and
Christmas. **Outdoors** Open-air films during the
summer and themed tours and talks. You can
see the garden highlights including the new
stumpery and spring bulbs. There are also
walking trails around the estate and
surrounding countryside. Family woodland trail
and Tracker Packs available daily and family-fun
activities during all school holidays. Stainsby
Mill and Eyam Hall are nearby. **Dogs**: welcome
on leads in park and car park. Assistance dogs
only in gardens.

Access: 🅿️♿🚼🔔🔊💺📷🎵🖼️
Hall 🔊♿🦽 Restaurant 🔊🦽 Garden ➡️🦽
Sat Nav: use S44 5RW. **Parking**: 600-space
car park.

Finding out more: 01246 850430 or
hardwick@nationaltrust.org.uk

Hardwick		M	T	W	T	F	S	S
Hall								
13 Feb–30 Oct*	11–5[1]	·	·	W	T	F	S	S
26 Nov–18 Dec*	11–3[2]	·	·	W	T	F	S	S
Park and restaurant								
Open all year*	9–6	M	T	W	T	F	S	S
Garden and shop								
Open all year*	10–6	M	T	W	T	F	S	S

*Park, garden, restaurant and shop: close at 5, November
to February, or dusk if earlier. Closed 25 December.
[1]Hall also opens Bank Holiday Mondays (April to August).
[2]Only ground and middle floors open at Christmas.

Inside Hardwick, Derbyshire (opposite top),
and the East Court Rose Garden (left) where
Duchess Evelyn, the last lady of Hardwick,
made her mark. Family fun in the garden (below)

Hardwick Estate: Stainsby Mill

Doe Lea, Chesterfield, Derbyshire S44 5RW

🏠 1976

A fully operational Victorian flour mill (above)
giving an insight into the workplace of a
19th-century miller. There has been a mill on
this site for hundreds of years, providing flour
for the local villages and the Hardwick Estate.
Flour is ground regularly showing the cogs and
machinery in action. **Note**: nearest toilets and
refreshments at Hardwick Hall.

Eating and shopping: Stainsby freshly milled
flour for sale. You can learn more about the mill
with a full-colour souvenir guide and pick up
the recipe of the week. Restaurant and gift
shop at nearby Hardwick Hall.

Making the most of your day: why not start
your day at Stainsby Mill, with its children's trail
and activity sheets? Visitors are welcome to
have a go grinding flour on the hand quern.
Dogs: welcome on leads in Hardwick Park.

Access: 📷🖼️🎵📷🖼️ Building 🦽 Grounds 🦽🔊
Parking: limited on-road parking
(not National Trust).

Finding out more: 01246 856522 or
stainsbymill@nationaltrust.org.uk

Hardwick Estate: Stainsby Mill		M	T	W	T	F	S	S
13 Feb–30 Oct*	10–4	·	·	W	T	F	S	S

*Open Bank Holiday Mondays. 28 May to 4 September
open to 5.

Ilam Park, Dovedale and the White Peak

Ilam, Ashbourne, Derbyshire

🏠 🏛 📷 ✿ 🐄 🐴 🛏 ⛺ 1906

The Stepping Stones at Dovedale lead to a riverside footpath through a wildlife and fossil-rich limestone valley dotted with caves and pinnacles. A short walk from Dovedale takes you to Ilam Park, a tranquil parkland nestled beneath steep-sided hills on the bank of the River Manifold. The park features a formal Italian Garden with views across to the rugged backdrop of Thorpe Cloud and Bunster Hill. Short, circular woodland and parkland routes make this a popular choice for families and dog walkers. The thickly wooded Manifold Valley offers a traffic-free cycling route. **Note:** Ilam Hall is let to the Youth Hostel Association.

Eating and shopping: Manifold tea-room at Ilam Park, with uninterrupted views towards Dovedale, serving homemade lunches and cake. Shops at Ilam Park and Dovedale Barn offering postcard-sized walk maps, gifts and information. Café at Wetton Mill (not National Trust) overlooking the River Manifold.

Making the most of your day: school holiday family trails. Clamber and play over the river in Hinkley Hollow. New orchard area developing next to the tea-room. Free weekly guided walks from March to November. **Dogs**: under close control, on leads near livestock and ground-nesting birds.

Access: 🅿 🅳 🚾 📖 🎵 Ilam Park stableyard ♿ 🔲
Ilam Park grounds 🚶 🧗 🚶 ➡ 🔲
Sat Nav: use DE6 2AZ. **Parking**: at Ilam Park 119:132507, also at Dovedale and Wetton Mill, not National Trust (charge including members).

Finding out more: 01335 350503 or peakdistrict@nationaltrust.org.uk

Ilam Park		M	T	W	T	F	S	S
Ilam Park shop and tea-room								
1 Jan–14 Feb	10:30–4*	M	T	W	T	F	S	S
15 Feb–30 Oct	10:30–5*	M	T	W	T	F	S	S
31 Oct–31 Dec	10:30–4*	M	T	W	T	F	S	S
Dovedale mobile barn								
19 Mar–2 Oct	11–5	M	T	W	T	F	S	S

*Shop opens at 11. Tea-room and shop: closed 24 and 25 December. Ilam bunkhouse: open all year (0344 335 1296). Ilam Park Caravan Site: open 27 February to 1 November (01335 350310). Darfar and Redhurst holiday cottages: available to let throughout the year (0344 800 2070). Ilam Hall: available for overnight accommodation via the Youth Hostel Association (01335 350212).

Taking a break at Ilam Park (above), and exploring the garden (below)

Kedleston Hall

near Quarndon, Derby, Derbyshire DE22 5JH

🏠✝🌼🛏🔔🍷 1987

Kedleston is one of the grandest and most perfectly finished houses designed by architect Robert Adam as 'a temple of the arts' and a location for entertainment. Discover the grandeur of this 1760s mansion, which was designed as a show palace with lavish décor, paintings, furniture and sculpture, and lived in over the centuries by the Curzon family. Set in beautiful naturalistic parkland, which blends seamlessly into the surrounding countryside, the 332 hectares (820 acres) are perfect for walks, picnics and spotting wildlife, as well as being home to more than 100 ancient trees. **Note**: medieval All Saints church, containing many family monuments, run by the Churches Conservation Trust.

Eating and shopping: Great Kitchen Restaurant serving hot and cold lunches, cakes and teas. Refreshments available from coffee shop kiosk (peak times only). Gift shop, plant sales and second-hand bookshop.

Making the most of your day: **Indoors** Meet Mrs Garnett, our 18th-century housekeeper. Tours and children's trail. **Outdoors** Five waymarked walks. Talks and tours. Events all year, whatever the weather. **Dogs**: welcome on leads in park and pleasure grounds.

Robert Adam's Kedleston Hall, Derbyshire (above). One of the many special paintings in this 'temple of the arts' (below)

Access: 🅿️ ♿ 🚶 🔶 🖼 🛗 🖥 ⓋⓉ ♿ ⠿ 🅰
Ground floor ♿♿ State floor ♿♿ Grounds ♿ ➡
Sat Nav: follow brown signs.
Parking: 200 yards.

Finding out more: 01332 842191 or kedlestonhall@nationaltrust.org.uk

Kedleston Hall		M	T	W	T	F	S	S
Hall								
27 Feb–30 Oct	12–5*	M	T	W	T	·	S	S
Park and Pleasure Grounds								
1 Jan–12 Feb	10–4	M	T	W	T	F	S	S
13 Feb–30 Oct	10–6	M	T	W	T	F	S	S
31 Oct–31 Dec	10–4	M	T	W	T	F	S	S
Restaurant and shop								
2 Jan–7 Feb	10:30–3:30	·	·	·	·	·	S	S
13 Feb–30 Oct	10:30–5**	M	T	W	T	·	S	S
5 Nov–31 Dec	10:30–3:30	·	·	·	·	·	S	S

*Introductory talk at 11. Hall: last admission 45 minutes before closing (may close early if light level is poor). Hall, restaurant and shop open Good Friday. **Restaurant and shop open Fridays in school holidays. Closed 25 December.

Kinder, Edale and the Dark Peak

near Hope Valley, Derbyshire

🏛 📷 ♿ 🚶 1936

The Dark Peak, from Kinder to the Derwent edges and the Vale of Edale offers exhilarating walks across heather moors, high gritstone edges and windswept tors. Stories and wild nature abound amid the ancient peat bogs and quiet wooded cloughs. You can follow the route of the 1932 Mass Trespass onto Kinder Scout National Nature Reserve, retracing the steps of those early champions of access to wild places. Alternatively a short climb up the 'Shivering Mountain' rewards you with panoramic views from this ancient hilltop fortress of Mam Tor. **Note**: nearest toilets in adjacent villages and at visitor centres at Ladybower Reservoir, Edale and Castleton.

Eating and shopping: Penny Pot in Edale, serving cooked breakfasts, soup, sandwiches and cakes, teas and coffees. Seating and bike racks outside, sofas and log burner inside.

Making the most of your day: guided walks with Rangers, Muck in Days and downloadable walking and cycling routes. **Dogs**: under close control, on leads near livestock and ground-nesting birds.

Wild and rugged Kinder, Edale and the Dark Peak, Derbyshire (above and below)

Access: 📷 ♿ 🐕 🚻 🅿

Sat Nav: use S33 8WA. **Parking**: at Mam Nick car park 110:SK124832. Also at Edale, Castleton, Bowden Bridge, Hayfield, Sett Valley, Hayfield and Upper Derwent Valley, none National Trust (charge including members).

Finding out more: 01433 670368 or peakdistrict@nationaltrust.org.uk

Kinder, Edale and the Dark Peak		M	T	W	T	F	S	S
Penny Pot Café								
1 Jan–13 Mar	10–4					F	S	S
14 Mar–30 Oct	10–4:30	M	T	W	T	F	S	S
30 Apr–25 Sep	8:30–4:30						S	S
4 Nov–31 Dec	10–4					F	S	S

Closed 24, 25 and 26 December, open 27 to 31 December.
Dalehead bunkhouse open all year (0344 335 1296);
Mam Nick car park open all year (SK123832).

Longshaw, Burbage and the Eastern Moors, Derbyshire

Longshaw, Burbage and the Eastern Moors

Longshaw, near Sheffield, Derbyshire

🏛️🏚️🍴✕🛈 1931

A countryside haven on Sheffield's doorstep, Longshaw, Burbage and the Eastern Moors has a network of footpaths and bridleways you can explore within a landscape of skies and silhouettes. Here you'll find long views, with scooping shapes of rocks and hills and gorges where water tumbles through ancient woods and over mossy boulders. A diverse range of wildlife lives peacefully here among abandoned millstones and packhorse routes of the past. The designed landscape around Longshaw Lodge, a former grouse-shooting estate, offers a warm and friendly starting point for your adventure. **Note**: National Trust/RSPB manage Eastern Moors for Peak District National Park Authority/Burbage for Sheffield County Council.

Eating and shopping: Longshaw tea-room serving soup, scones, cakes and dishes using produce plucked straight from the kitchen garden. Shop selling outdoor and wildlife-themed products, maps and guides. Outdoor seats provide views across the valley to Burbage and Higger Tor.

Making the most of your day: woodland walks and natural play. Kitchen garden behind tea-room. Riding on the bridleways. Waymarked walks (map available from shop). Free guided walks (Wednesdays and Sundays). **Dogs**: under close control, on leads near livestock and ground-nesting birds.

Access: 🅿️🚪♿🥾🚻♿ Building 🏠♿
Grounds 🥾🏠➡️♿
Sat Nav: use S11 7TZ (follow brown signs).
Parking: at Woodcroft car park (110: 266800), Wooden Pole and Haywood for Longshaw and at Curbar Gap, Birchen Edge and Shillito Wood for the Eastern Moors. Additional car parks at Surprise View and Burbage, not National Trust (charge including members).

Finding out more: 01433 637904 (Longshaw). 0114 289 1543 (Eastern Moors) or peakdistrict@nationaltrust.org.uk

Longshaw, Burbage, Eastern Moors		M	T	W	T	F	S	S
Tea-room and shop								
1 Jan–14 Feb	10:30–4	M	T	W	T	F	S	S
15 Feb–30 Oct	10:30–5	M	T	W	T	F	S	S
31 Oct–31 Dec	10:30–4	M	T	W	T	F	S	S

Tea-room: last orders 30 minutes before closing. Closed 24 and 25 December. Lodge is not open to the public. White Edge Lodge available as holiday cottage throughout year (0344 800 2070).

Enjoying the breathtaking view at Longshaw

Lyveden

Harley Way, near Oundle,
Northamptonshire PE8 5AT

🏠 ❄ 🎯 ☂ 1922

Tucked away in the heart of the
Northamptonshire countryside lies a
mysterious garden, a remarkable example of
Renaissance design and craftsmanship. Started
by Sir Thomas Tresham in 1595 but never
completed, the garden contains many features
desired by wealthy Elizabethan landowners,
such as a water garden, bizarrely placed on top
of a hill, and an eerie garden lodge covered in
religious symbols – some features of which
remain unexplained to this day. Our audio
guide describes Sir Thomas's dream and how it
all ended in a nightmare for the Tresham family
with their involvement in the Gunpowder Plot.

Eating and shopping: small traditional
Northamptonshire cottage tea-room,
serving homemade cakes and cream teas.
Ice-cream available from visitor reception.
Picnics welcome.

Making the most of your day: free audio
guide. Children's activities available in our
Family Den. Numerous countryside walks.
Dogs: welcome on leads only.

Access: 🅿️♿🚻🚼🧷📷 **Building** 🏠 **Grounds** 🏠
Parking: 100 yards.

Finding out more: 01832 205158 or
lyveden@nationaltrust.org.uk

Lyveden		M	T	W	T	F	S	S
2 Jan–28 Feb	11–4	·	·	·	·	·	S	S
29 Feb–31 Oct	10:30–5	M	T	W	T	F	S	S
5 Nov–31 Dec	11–4	·	·	·	·	·	S	S

Closed 24 and 25 December.

Mysterious Lyveden, Northamptonshire (above and below)

Mr Straw's House

5-7 Blyth Grove, Worksop,
Nottinghamshire S81 0JG

🏠 ❀ 1990

Discover how a grocer's family lived in a
Midlands market town in this extraordinary
home, virtually unchanged since 1923 and full
of treasured possessions and household
objects. Outside, the lovingly tended garden
and orchard include a greenhouse housing
Walter Straw's cacti collection and fruit trees
once used to make preserves. **Note**: to enable
you to enjoy your visit we operate timed
tickets, please book in advance.

Eating and shopping: shop selling jam,
biscuits, plants, souvenirs and gifts.
Coffee area. Picnic benches.

Making the most of your day: changing
exhibitions. Tours and other events
throughout the year.

Access: 🚶 ⣿ 📷 5 Blyth Grove 👤 👥
7 Blyth Grove 👤 👥 Gardens 👤
Parking: on site, in orchard.

Finding out more: 01909 482380 or
mrstrawshouse@nationaltrust.org.uk

Mr Straw's House		M	T	W	T	F	S	S
1 Mar–24 Mar	Tour*		·	T	W	T	F	S	·
26 Mar–5 Nov	Tour*			T	W	T	F	S	·

*Admission by tour only with timed ticket 11 to 5 (please book
in advance). Last tour starts at 4. Closed Good Friday.

The Old Manor

Norbury, Ashbourne, Derbyshire DE6 2ED

🏠 ❀ 🛏 1987

Medieval hall featuring a rare king post,
Tudor door and 17th-century Flemish glass.
Note: parking limited (cars only). Open Fridays,
25 March to 21 October, 11 to 1, and Saturdays,
26 March to 22 October, 1 to 3.

Finding out more: 01283 585337 or
oldmanor@nationaltrust.org.uk

Priest's House,
Easton on the Hill

38 West Street, Easton on the Hill, near
Stamford, Northamptonshire PE9 3LS

🏠 1966

Delightful small late 15th-century building, with
interesting local architecture and museum
exploring Easton on the Hill's industrial past.
Note: open daily all year, 10 to 5. Unmanned.
Access from neighbouring keyholders (details
on property noticeboard).

Finding out more: 01832 205158 or
priestshouse2@nationaltrust.org.uk

Mr Straw's House in Nottinghamshire: 1920s time capsule

Staunton Harold Church

Staunton Harold Estate, Ashby-de-la-Zouch,
Leicestershire LE65 1RW

✚ 1954

One of the few churches built between the
outbreak of the English Civil War and the
Restoration period. **Note**: nearest toilet
500 yards (not National Trust). Parking not
National Trust; Staunton Harold Estate,
charges apply (including members). Open
weekends, 26 March to 30 October and
Wednesday to Sunday, 1 June to 31 August,
1 to 4:30.

Finding out more: 01332 863822 or
stauntonharold@nationaltrust.org.uk

Stoneywell

Whitcroft's Lane, Ulverscroft,
Leicestershire LE67 9QE

🏠 ❄ 2012

Zigzagging from its rocky outcrop, Stoneywell
is the realisation of one man's Arts and Crafts
vision within a family home. Original furniture
and family treasures fill the cottage's quirky
rooms and, outside, every turn conjures
childhood memories of holiday excitement
– one way to the fort, another to the woods
beyond. **Note**: booking essential (including
members), either by phone, email or website.

Eating and shopping: Stables tea-room
(for use by booked visitors only) serving light
lunches, cakes and cream teas. Small range
of Arts and Crafts-inspired gifts and books
available. Picnics welcome in grounds.

Making the most of your day: **Indoors** Guided
house tours all year, and activities and trails for
all the family in the school holidays. **Outdoors**
Games and swing in the garden. Woodland
walks. **Dogs**: assistance dogs only.

Access: 🅿️♿♿♿♿🎧📹♿♿♿
Stables ♿🚻♿ **Cottage** ♿🚻 **Gardens** ♿ ➡️
Sat Nav: use LE67 9QE. **Parking**: for booked
visitors only.

Finding out more: 01530 248040 (Infoline).
01530 248048 (bookings) or
stoneywell@nationaltrust.org.uk

Stoneywell		M	T	W	T	F	S	S
1 Feb–30 Nov	Tour	**M**	**T**	**W**	**T**	**F**	**S**	**S**

Last entry one hour before closing.

Stoneywell, Leicestershire: the realisation of one man's Arts and Crafts vision within a family home

Sudbury Hall and the National Trust Museum of Childhood, Derbyshire (above and below): one visit is never enough

Sudbury Hall and the National Trust Museum of Childhood

Sudbury, Ashbourne, Derbyshire DE6 5HT

🏛 ✿ ▲ ⟟ 1967

There's so much to see and do at Sudbury Hall and the Museum of Childhood. The Hall has one of the most surprising, light and beautiful long galleries in England and is the result of George Vernon's aspirations to create a perfect new home. Get a glimpse of life 'below stairs' in the kitchen and basement, and picture yourself at home in some of the smaller family rooms. The Museum is a place of fun and fascination for all ages. View childhood from the Victorian period to the present day; send your little one up a chimney, play with our hands-on toys and games and join a lesson in the Victorian Schoolroom.

Eating and shopping: tea-room serving light lunches and homemade cakes. Additional refreshments available at peak times. Gift shop, plant sales, sweets and toys.

Making the most of your day: **Indoors** Hands-on toys in the museum. You can see behind the scenes and go to places not normally open to visitors on our themed Hall tours. **Outdoors** Events throughout the year, whatever the weather. Why not take part in a range of family activities during school holidays? Or you could pick up a trail sheet and test your skills in our woodland play area, then discover the wildlife in the Boat House.

Access: 🅿♿♿♿♿♿♿♿♿♿♿♿
Hall 🏠♿ Museum ♿↕♿ Grounds 🏞♿
Parking: 500 yards.

Finding out more: 01283 585337 or
sudburyhall@nationaltrust.org.uk

Sudbury Hall		M	T	W	T	F	S	S
Hall								
13 Feb–30 Oct	1–5*			W	T	F	S	S
Hall tours								
16 Feb–25 Oct	Tour**		T					
Museum, tea-room and shop								
13 Feb–27 Mar	10:30–5¹			W	T	F	S	S
28 Mar–30 Oct	10:30–5¹	M	T	W	T	F	S	S
3 Nov–18 Dec	10:30–4¹				T	F	S	S

*Last admission 45 minutes before closing (Hall may close
early if light level is poor). Open Bank Holidays. **Hall tours
from 11:30. ¹Museum opens at 11.

The laundry at the Museum of Childhood

Tattershall Castle

Sleaford Road, Tattershall,
Lincolnshire LN4 4LR

🏰♿♿♿ 1925

Tattershall Castle proudly rises from the flat
Lincolnshire fens; a survivor of conflict, decay
and restoration. Built of red brick in an era of
stone, this fortified manor is one of the earliest
and finest surviving examples of English
medieval brickwork. A past home to lords,
ladies, soldiers and cows, the castle was built
by the Treasurer of England, Lord Ralph
Cromwell in the 1440s and saved for the nation
by Lord Curzon of Kedleston in 1911. Take the
winding staircase, wander through vast
echoing chambers and walk out onto the
battlements revealing the beauty of the
Lincolnshire countryside. **Note**: access to the
tower is via a spiral staircase only (149 steps).

Eating and shopping: Guardhouse shop
selling hot and cold drinks, wrapped cakes,
sandwiches, crisps, ice-cream, gifts and
souvenirs. Picnics welcome.

Making the most of your day: **Indoors** Free
audio guides for children and adults. **Outdoors**
Events throughout the year, including Easter
Egg fun, medieval re-enactments, open-air
theatre and Christmas market. **Dogs**: welcome
on leads in grounds only.

Access: ♿♿♿♿♿♿ Castle 🏰
Parking: 150 yards.

Finding out more: 01526 342543 or
tattershallcastle@nationaltrust.org.uk

Tattershall Castle		M	T	W	T	F	S	S
13 Feb–30 Oct	11–5	M	T	W	T	F	S	S
5 Nov–11 Dec	11–3						S	S

Last entry one hour before closing. Last audio guides issued
one hour before closing. Some areas of the property may be
temporarily closed for a wedding ceremony.

Winster Market House

Main Street, Winster, Matlock, Derbyshire DE4 2DJ

🏠 1906

An excellent example of its type and the first Derbyshire place acquired by the Trust, at a cost of £50. The Market House became a listed building in 1951. Its origins are in the 16th century, when cheese and cattle fairs featured prominently in the daily life of the area. **Note**: Winster Market House is unstaffed.

Making the most of your day: information room with interpretation panels and a scale model of Winster village. Ilam Park and Dovedale nearby; Longshaw and Eyam Hall are about 17 miles.

Access: 👤

Parking: on street or at small village car parks, not National Trust (charge including members).

Finding out more: 01335 350503 or winstermarkethouse@nationaltrust.org.uk

Winster Market House		M	T	W	T	F	S	S
26 Mar–29 Oct	11–5	M	T	W	T	F	S	S

Tattershall Castle, Lincolnshire (opposite), as seen from across the moat, and its dovecote (above). Winster Market House in Derbyshire (right)

Ulverscroft Nature Reserve

near Copt Oak, Loughborough, Leicestershire

🐾 1945

Part of the ancient forest of Charnwood, Ulverscroft is especially beautiful during the spring – with heathland and woodland habitats. **Note**: assistance dogs only. Sorry no toilet. For Sat Nav use LE67 9QE. Access by permit from Leicestershire and Rutland Wildlife Trust (0116 262 9968), apply several days before visit.

Finding out more: 01332 863822 or ulverscroftnaturereserve@nationaltrust.org.uk

Woolsthorpe Manor, Lincolnshire: Sir Isaac Newton was born in this small stone manor house (above and below)

Woolsthorpe Manor

Water Lane, Woolsthorpe by Colsterworth, near Grantham, Lincolnshire NG33 5PD

🏠 ❖ 1943

A small stone manor house but the birthplace of a great mind – Sir Isaac Newton, world-famous scientist and mathematician whose thinking illuminated his world and continues to influence our lives today. In the plague years of 1665–6 he returned to this farmhouse in rural Lincolnshire, where he used a glass prism in his crucial experiment to split white light into a spectrum of colours, and the fall of an apple inspired his theory of gravity. Today you can still see the famous apple tree and try some of Newton's experiments in the hands-on Science Centre.

Eating and shopping: coffee shop and small shop in ticket office. Second-hand bookshop.

Making the most of your day: **Indoors** Hands-on science and children's activity room. Volunteer-led 'Tales from Woolsthorpe' and science talks. Film. Family events and craft fairs. **Outdoors** Don't miss Isaac's apple tree! **Dogs**: welcome in car park only.

Access: 🅿️ 🅳 🕯️ 🎫 🖼️ ♿
House 🔹 🔹 🔹 🔹 Science Centre 🔹 🔹 🔹
Grounds ➡️ 🔹
Parking: 50 yards.

Finding out more: 01476 860338 or woolsthorpemanor@nationaltrust.org.uk

Woolsthorpe Manor		M	T	W	T	F	S	S
Manor house								
1 Jan–18 Mar*	11–3	M	·	·	·	F	S	S
19 Mar–30 Oct	11–5	M	·	W	T	F	S	S
31 Oct–31 Dec**	11–3	M	·	·	·	F	S	S
Science Discovery Centre and coffee shop								
1 Jan–18 Mar	11–3	M	T	W	T	F	S	S
19 Mar–30 Oct	11–5	M	T	W	T	F	S	S
31 Oct–31 Dec**	11–3	M	T	W	T	F	S	S

Film and grounds open as Science Discovery Centre. Guided tours to manor house November to February 2017. *House open 17 and 18 February. **Closed 24 and 25 December.

The Workhouse, Southwell

Upton Road, Southwell,
Nottinghamshire NG25 0PT

🏠 2002

Walking up the paupers' path towards The Workhouse it is easy to imagine how the Victorian poor might have felt as they sought refuge here. This austere building, the most complete workhouse in existence, was built in 1824 as a place of last resort for the destitute. Its architecture was influenced by prison design and its harsh regime became a blueprint for workhouses throughout the country. The stories of those who lived and worked here in the 1840s help bring the building to life and prompt reflection on how society has tackled poverty through the centuries.

The Workhouse, Southwell, Nottinghamshire: this austere building was a place of last resort for the destitute

Eating and shopping: refreshment room offering hot drinks, cakes and snacks. Shop selling gifts, ice-cream and traditional toys. Picnic benches in the garden.

Making the most of your day: **Indoors** Wide range of events for all, including living history days, storytelling and special tours. Children's trails and hands-on activities. **Outdoors** Re-created Victorian vegetable garden planted with heritage varieties. **Dogs**: assistance dogs only.

Access: 🅿️🐶♿📷🎞️🖥️📺♿♿📷
Building ♿♿♿♿ Grounds ♿➡️♿
Sat Nav: use NG25 0QB. **Parking**: 200 yards.

Finding out more: 01636 817260 or theworkhouse@nationaltrust.org.uk

The Workhouse, Southwell		M	T	W	T	F	S	S
13 Feb–31 Jul	12–5	·	·	W	T	F	S	S
1 Aug–31 Aug	12–5	M	T	W	T	F	S	S
1 Sep–6 Nov	12–5	·	·	W	T	F	S	S

Guided tour of the outside and other buildings at 11 (places limited). House open Bank Holidays from 11. Last admission one hour before closing. Property may close earlier due to light levels.

West Midlands

Croome, Worcestershire

Kinder, Edale and the Dark Peak

Winster Market House

Lyme

Longshaw, Burbage and the Eastern Moors

Eyam Hall and Craft Centre

Chesterfield

Bakewell

Hardwick Estate: Stainsby Mill

Congleton

Hardwick

Mansfield

Little Moreton Hall

Crewe

Biddulph Grange Garden

Wrexham

Erddig

STOKE-ON-TRENT

The Old Manor

Kedleston Hall

Chirk Castle

Downs Banks

Stone

DERBY

Oswestry

Sudbury Hall and the National Trust Museum of Childhood

Calke Abbey

Welshpool

Powis Castle and Garden

Stafford

Shugborough Estate

Stoneywell

Attingham Park Estate: Cronkhill

Shrewsbury

Sunnycroft

Letocetum Roman Baths and Museum

Attingham Park Estate: Town Walls Tower

Attingham Park

Moseley Old Hall

Benthall Hall

Wightwick Manor and Gardens

WOLVERHAMPTON

Tamworth

Carding Mill Valley and the Long Mynd

Morville Hall

Bridgnorth

Wilderhope Manor

Dudmaston

BIRMINGHAM

Birmingham Back to Backs

COVENTRY

Kinver Edge and the Rock Houses

Clent Hills

Knowles Mill

Kidderminster

Packwood House

Baddesley Clinton

Rosedene

Berrington Hall

Hanbury Hall and Gardens

Warwick

Croft Castle and Parkland

Leominster

Wichenford Dovecote

Hawford Dovecote

Coughton Court

Brockhampton Estate

WORCESTER

Kinwarton Dovecote

Charlecote Park

Canons Ashby

Cwmmau Farmhouse

Greyfriars' House and Garden

Stratford upon Avon

Croome

Evesham

Middle Littleton Tithe Barn

Farnborough Hall

The Weir Garden

HEREFORD

The Fleece Inn

Hidcote

Upton House and Gardens

Banbury

Stow

Snowshill Manor and Garden

Chastleton House

Buckingham

Skenfrith Castle

Ashleworth Tithe Barn

Stow-on-the-Wold

Chipping Norton

The Kymin

● **Buildings and/or gardens**

● **Entry points to coast and countryside**

The size of each pin indicates how large a place is and how long you should allow for your visit

🟩 **National Trust land**

Attingham Park, Shropshire: perfect for a full day out

Attingham Park

Atcham, Shrewsbury, Shropshire SY4 4TP

🏠 ❀ 🎣 🍸 1947

Attingham inspires a sense of beauty, space and awe. The imposing entrance, glimpses of the vast mansion (above) against silhouettes of cedars and expansive parkland, epitomise classical design and Italian influence. Its completeness of survival exemplifies the rise and decline, love and neglect of great country house estates. Discovering the Berwick's estate with acres of parkland, miles of walks, the huge organic walled garden, large playfield and welcoming mansion is a full day out. There's so much to see and do at Attingham – whether you're a family looking for activities, both inside and out, or simply in search of a traditional visit to a historic house and parkland. Full of life and locally loved, there's something for everyone all year round.

Eating and shopping: four catering units offer a variety of experiences and styles – the Carriage House Café (open daily), Lady Berwick's waitress-service afternoon tea (bookings accepted), Mansion tea-room and Greedy Pig catering in playfield. Courtyard shopping includes Stables Shop and Grooms' second-hand bookshop.

Making the most of your day: **Indoors** Themed tours. Attingham '1920s Christmas' daily in December. Celebrate ten years of the 'Attingham Re-discovered' project of conservation and restoration. **Outdoors** Young learner cyclists welcome on balance bikes and bikes with stabilisers. Opens 8. Summer late park opening (to 7). Seasonal spectaculars, including winter snowdrops, spring bluebells, summer blossom and autumn tree colour. Event highlights include Snowdrop Evenings, Easter, Hallowe'en and Christmas. Daily family activities during local school holidays. Sporting activities to help you get active, including regular run groups and major events/competitions. Walled Garden and Pleasure Grounds projects continue to transform and restore Attingham. Sunnycroft is nearby. **Dogs**: welcome in grounds on leads (with some identified off-lead areas). Dog walkers' guide available.

Access: 🅿♿♿♿♿⬚🚼👁🅰 Mansion 🚶♿
🔼♿ **Carriage House Café** ♿ **Grounds** ♿➡♿♿
Parking: 25 to 200 yards.

Attingham Park, Shropshire: activities and costumed guides

Finding out more: 01743 708123 (Infoline). 01743 708162 or attingham@nationaltrust.org.uk

Attingham Park		M	T	W	T	F	S	S
Park and playfield								
1 Jan–30 Jun	8–6*	M	T	W	T	F	S	S
1 Jul–4 Sep	8–7	M	T	W	T	F	S	S
5 Sep–31 Dec	8–6*	M	T	W	T	F	S	S
Walled Garden and Carriage House Café†								
Open all year	9–5	M	T	W	T	F	S	S
Mansion								
5 Mar–6 Nov	11–5:30**	M	T	W	T	F	S	S
3 Dec–23 Dec	10:30–4	M	T	W	T	F	S	S
Mansion winter tours								
8 Jan–12 Feb	11–3					F	S	S
26 Feb–28 Feb	11–3					F	S	S
Mansion below-stairs experience and upstairs tours								
13 Feb–21 Feb	11–3:30	M	T	W	T	F	S	S
Lady Berwick's Luncheons and Afternoon Tea								
5 Mar–6 Nov	1–4			W	T	F	S	S
3 Dec–23 Dec	12–3	M	T	W	T	F	S	S

*Park and playfield: January, February, November, December close 5 or dusk if earlier. †Carriage House Café: closes one hour before park. **Mansion: March to November last admission one hour before closing. Mansion tea-room: from 11; 2 January to 12 February and 7 to 27 November weekends only, 13 February to 6 November and 3 December to 2 January 2017 open daily. Greedy Pig playfield catering kiosk: from 11 weekends and daily during school holidays (weather permitting). Stables shops: daily from 10. 24 December: mansion closed; all catering and retail outlets close at 2. Property closed 25 December.

Attingham Park Estate: Cronkhill

near Atcham, Shrewsbury, Shropshire SY5 6JP

🏠♿ 1947

Delightful picturesque Italianate hillside villa designed by Regency architect John Nash, with beautiful views across the Attingham Estate. **Note**: 'Cronkhill Restored' project ongoing. House ground floor, garden and stables open as part of visit. Property contents belong to tenant. Open Friday and Sunday, 6 and 8 May, 22 and 24 July, and 16 and 18 September, 11 to 4.

Finding out more: 01743 708162 or cronkhill@nationaltrust.org.uk

Attingham Park Estate: Town Walls Tower

Shrewsbury, Shropshire SY1 1TN

🏠 1930

This last remaining 14th-century watchtower sits on what were once the medieval fortified, defensive walls of Shrewsbury. **Note**: sorry no toilet or car parking and 40 extremely steep, narrow steps to top floor. Open weekends, 11 and 12 June, 13 and 14 August, 8 and 9 October, 11 to 3.

Finding out more: 01743 708162 or townwallstower@nationaltrust.org.uk

Baddesley Clinton

Rising Lane, Baddesley Clinton, Warwickshire B93 0DQ

🏠✝❁♿🍵 1980

The magic of Baddesley Clinton comes from its secluded, timeless setting deep within its own parkland. From refuge to haven, this atmospheric moated manor house has been a sanctuary since the 15th century. This year discover Baddesley's fascinating late medieval and Tudor history, from hiding persecuted Catholics in its priest's holes to the history of the Ferrers family who lived at Baddesley for more than 500 years. The peaceful gardens include fish pools, walled garden and a lakeside walk, perfect for a tranquil stroll.

Eating and shopping: Barn Restaurant serving hot meals, drinks and snacks and The Stables offering light refreshments. Picnics welcome. Shop selling seasonal gifts, local foods and plants. Second-hand bookshop.

Baddesley Clinton, Warwickshire: its secluded, timeless setting works its magic on everyone, young and old

Making the most of your day: **Indoors** Events, including supper lectures. **Outdoors** Open-air cinema. Family Fun every holiday, as well as Playful Journeys around the estate all year. Welcome talks and garden tours, plus walking trails around the estate and surrounding countryside. Packwood House and Coughton Court are nearby. **Dogs**: welcome on leads in car park and estate public footpaths. Assistance dogs only beyond visitor reception.

Access: ⬚⬚⬚⬚⬚⬚⬚⬚
Building ⬚⬚⬚ **Grounds** ⬚⬚⬚
Parking: 100 yards.

Finding out more: 01564 783294 or
baddesleyclinton@nationaltrust.org.uk

Baddesley Clinton		M	T	W	T	F	S	S
1 Jan–12 Feb[1]	9–4*	M	T	W	T	F	S	S
13 Feb–30 Oct[1]	9–5*	M	T	W	T	F	S	S
31 Oct–31 Dec	9–4*	M	T	W	T	F	S	S

*House: opens 11. Admission to house by timed ticket
(available from reception, not bookable). Closed 24 and
25 December. [1]Parts of the house will be closed from
January to April due to building work.

Moated Baddesley Clinton (above and below), offers a complete escape from the pressures of the 21st century

For information about getting to National Trust places, please see page 3

Benthall Hall, Shropshire: home to the same family for centuries

Benthall Hall

Broseley, Shropshire TF12 5RX

🏠✝❀🌱 1958

Within this fine stone house, discover the history of the Benthall family from the Saxon period to the present day. Outside, the garden includes a beautiful Restoration church, a restored plantsman's garden with pretty crocus displays in spring and autumn, and an old kitchen garden.

Eating and shopping: tea-room serving drinks, cakes and ice-cream.

Making the most of your day: Elizabethan skittle alley. Circular walks through the park and woodland. **Dogs**: in park and woodland only.

Access: 🅿♿🏠♿👜🔊📷🚫
House 🏠🏠 Church 🏠
Parking: 100 yards.

Finding out more: 01952 882159 or benthall@nationaltrust.org.uk

Benthall Hall		M	T	W	T	F	S	S
6 Feb–28 Feb	1–4	·	·	·	·	·	S	S
1 Mar–30 Oct	12:30–5*	·	T	W	·	·	S	S

*House and tea-room: open at 1, March to October. Church: closes at 4 in February; 5, March to October. Tea-room: last orders at 3:30 in February; 4:30, March to October. Open Good Friday and Bank Holiday Mondays. Closes dusk if earlier.

Berrington Hall

near Leominster, Herefordshire HR6 0DW

🏠❀♿🌱🐕🏠☕ 1957

Standing proud and strong, this fine Georgian mansion sits within 'Capability' Brown's final landscape. This year we celebrate the tercentenary of 'Capability' Brown with environmental arts group, Red Earth, who will bring to life the restoration of the park back to Brown's original vision. Designed by Henry Holland and home to the Harley, Rodney and Cawley families, Berrington features jewel-like interiors, a hidden 'below stairs' and hosts a textile exhibition from the Embroiderers Guild. You can experience some of the extremes of the 18th century in the wig and bum shop or explore Brown's final vision, out in the park.

Eating and shopping: shop selling gifts, local products and preserves made from our fruit. Tea-room serving light lunches, afternoon tea and cakes, often using produce from the garden. Second-hand bookshop.

The sweeping staircase at Berrington Hall in Herefordshire

Berrington Hall sits within 'Capability' Brown's fine park

Making the most of your day: **Indoors** Costume collection on view. House quizzes, family activities and dressing-up. Servants' quarters to explore. **Outdoors** Stables and walled garden to discover. Natural play area. Waymarked estate walks. **Dogs**: welcome on leads in parkland and in parts of garden.

Access:
Building **Grounds**
Parking: 30 yards.

Finding out more: 01568 615721 or berrington@nationaltrust.org.uk

Berrington Hall		M	T	W	T	F	S	S
1 Jan–3 Jan	10–4	·	·	·	·	F	S	S
9 Jan–7 Feb	10–4	·	·	·	·	·	S	S
13 Feb–6 Nov	10–5	M	T	W	T	F	S	S
12 Nov–18 Dec	10–4	·	·	·	·	·	S	S
19 Dec–23 Dec	10–4	M	T	W	T	F	·	·
27 Dec–31 Dec	10–4	·	T	W	T	F	S	·

Mansion opens at 11. Last admission one hour before closing.

Biddulph Grange Garden

Grange Road, Biddulph, Staffordshire ST8 7SD

1988

Biddulph Grange Garden is a remarkable survival, a high Victorian horticultural masterpiece and a quirky, playful paradise full of intrigue and surprise. Created by its visionary owner, James Bateman, its design expresses and attempts to reconcile both his religious convictions and his passion for geology, botany and plant collecting. His plant collection comes from all over the world – a visit takes you on a journey from an Italian terrace to an Egyptian pyramid, via a Himalayan glen and Chinese-inspired garden, hidden by tunnels, high hedges and rockwork. The collection includes rhododendrons, dahlias, Wellingtonias and the oldest golden larch in Britain. **Note**: there are 400 steps throughout the garden. The Geological Gallery is open but under restoration.

Eating and shopping: self-service tea-room. Gift shop. Plant centre. Picnic area adjacent to the car park.

Making the most of your day: talks, guided tours, events and children's trails all year. Summer activities. **Dogs**: assistance dogs only in garden.

Biddulph Grange Garden, Staffordshire: the Chinese Temple is one of many quirky delights in this playful paradise

Access: ♿ 🅿 📷 📖 👁 **Garden** 🐾
Parking: 50 yards.

Finding out more: 01782 517999 or biddulphgrange@nationaltrust.org.uk

The intriguing Dahlia Walk at Biddulph Grange Garden

Birmingham Back to Backs in the West Midlands

Birmingham Back to Backs

55-63 Hurst Street/50-54 Inge Street, Birmingham, West Midlands B5 4TE

🏠 ♿ 🍴 2004

An atmospheric glimpse into the extraordinary lives of the ordinary people who crammed into Birmingham's last surviving court of back to backs: 11 houses built, literally, back to back around a communal courtyard. Knowledgeable and engaging guides will take you on a journey in time, from the 1840s through to the 1970s. With fires alight in the grates, and sounds and smells from the past, you will experience an evocative and intimate insight into life and work at the Back to Backs. **Note**: visits by guided tour only (advance booking essential). Eight flights of steep and winding stairs.

Eating and shopping: shop offering a range of Birmingham-based memorabilia and traditional toys and games. 1930s-style sweet shop (not National Trust).

Making the most of your day: year-round events. Ground-floor tour also available if you are unable to manage our steep, winding stairs (booking essential).

Access: [icons] **Building** [icons]
Parking: nearest at Arcadian Centre, Bromsgrove Street (not National Trust).

Finding out more: 0121 666 7671 (booking line). 0121 622 2442 or backtobacks@nationaltrust.org.uk

Birmingham Back to Backs		M	T	W	T	F	S	S
9 Feb–4 Sep	Tour		·	T	W	T	F	S	S
10 Sep–23 Dec	Tour		·	T	W	T	F	S	S

Admission by timed ticket and guided tour only, booking essential. Open Bank Holiday Mondays (but closed next day). During term-time property closed 10 to 1 on Tuesdays, Wednesdays and Thursdays for schools. Last tour times vary in winter. Closed 5 to 9 September.

Simple domestic items bring the Back to Backs to life

Brockhampton Estate

Bringsty, near Bromyard,
Herefordshire WR6 5TB

[icons] 1946

This medieval moated manor house sits at the heart of a 688-hectare (1,700-acre) ancient rural estate. The timber-framed house and romantic chapel ruins lie in unspoilt parkland redesigned in the 19th century. Estate walks run through traditional orchards, working farmland and wild woodlands and offer countryside views and a glimpse into rural Herefordshire life. You can play on the nature trail, spotting wildlife as you climb, balance and build. The manor house, entered through a charming timber-framed gatehouse, is a place to discover the people of Brockhampton, families who lived here and their lives, from 1425 to today.

Eating and shopping: Old Apple Store tea-room serving light lunches, cakes and refreshments. Granary shop near the manor house selling gifts, award-winning local farm produce, sandwiches and refreshments. Second-hand bookshop. Picnics welcome.

Brockhampton Estate in Herefordshire: the romantic moated manor house (below) and a light-filled attic (opposite)

Any questions? Telephone 0344 800 1895 (seven days a week)

Making the most of your day: **Indoors**
Year-round family activities, demonstrations, exhibitions and historical re-enactments.
Outdoors Countryside event days, family trails and games. Natural play trail and geocaching. Waymarked walks and orienteering routes.
Dogs: welcome on leads in grounds, woods and parkland.

Access: [icons]
Building [icons] **Grounds** [icons]
Parking: 100 yards and 1 mile.

Finding out more: 01885 482077 (Infoline).
01885 488099 or
brockhampton@nationaltrust.org.uk

Brockhampton Estate		M	T	W	T	F	S	S
Estate								
Open all year	10–5	M	T	W	T	F	S	S
House, grounds, tea-room and shop*								
2 Jan–14 Feb	11–4	·	·	·	·	·	S	S
15 Feb–30 Oct	11–5	M	T	W	T	F	S	S
5 Nov–31 Dec**	11–4	·	·	·	·	·	S	S

Tea-room opens at 10. *House, grounds and tea-room close 30 minutes before rest of property. **Closed 24 and 25 December.

Carding Mill Valley and the Long Mynd

Church Stretton, Shropshire

[icons] 1965

Once at Carding Mill Valley (above) you are suddenly in the heart of wild countryside. Here families can enjoy playing in the stream and exploring. From the valley, head up to the top of the Long Mynd, with its tranquil surroundings and breathtaking views across Shropshire and beyond.

Eating and shopping: Chalet Pavilion tea-room and roof terrace in Carding Mill Valley serving hot lunches, afternoon teas, drinks and ice-cream. Shop selling gifts, souvenirs, maps and pond nets.

Making the most of your day: family-friendly events all year. Free walks cards available in Carding Mill Valley. **Dogs**: under close control and in sight (livestock/ground-nesting birds).

Access: [icons] **Building** [icon] **Grounds** [icon]
Sat Nav: use SY6 6JG. **Parking**: 50 yards.

Finding out more: 01694 725000 or cardingmill@nationaltrust.org.uk

Carding Mill Valley		M	T	W	T	F	S	S
Tea-room								
1 Jan–12 Feb	10–4	M	T	W	T	F	S	S
13 Feb–30 Oct	10–5	M	T	W	T	F	S	S
31 Oct–31 Dec*	10–4	M	T	W	T	F	S	S
Shop**								
1 Jan	11–4	·	·	·	·	F	·	·
2 Jan–31 Jan	10–4	·	·	·	·	·	S	S
1 Feb–30 Oct	11–5	M	T	W	T	F	S	S
31 Oct–31 Dec	11–4	M	T	W	T	F	S	S

*Tea-room and shop: closed 25 December. **Shop: opens 10 at weekends. Toilets and information hut: open 9 to 7, February half-term to October; 9 to 4:30, November to early February.

266

Charlecote Park

Wellesbourne, Warwick,
Warwickshire CV35 9ER

🏠🍴🎎🛏️♿ 1946

The scene of Shakespeare's reputed poaching exploits, Charlecote Park was already in its middle age by the time Queen Elizabeth I arrived, along the carriage drive through the Gatehouse and on to the welcoming red-brick mansion. Generations of the Lucy family have left their mark on the buildings, gardens and parkland where visitors are intrigued to this day by the family's continuing presence. Charlecote presents a picture of peace and repose, protected by the unnavigable rivers Dene and Avon and by its distinctive cleft-oak paling fences. It is a park where people picnic, play, walk and wander among the Jacob sheep and fallow deer which still roam across the 'Capability' Brown landscape.

Three views of turreted Charlecote Park in Warwickshire. A picture of peace and repose, the house is still home to the Lucy family

Eating and shopping: The Orangery serves a range of meals and light snacks. The Servants' Hall gift shop and Pantry shop sell a range of Charlecote specific and locally sourced produce. Picnics welcome.

Making the most of your day: **Indoors** Hands-on activities bring the Victorian kitchen and outbuildings to life. The house is festively decorated during the extended opening period in December. **Outdoors** Activities throughout the year, including guided park walks, talks, trails and a range of sporting activities. **Dogs**: assistance dogs only.

Access: 🅿️♿🚗🚼🚻🔆📷📹♿🖐️
Building 🏠♿♿ Grounds ♿➡️♿
Parking: 300 yards.

Finding out more: 01789 470277 or charlecotepark@nationaltrust.org.uk

Charlecote Park	M	T	W	T	F	S	S
Tea-room, shop and grounds							
1 Jan–12 Feb*	10:30–4	M	T	W	T	F	S	S
13 Feb–30 Oct**	10:30–5:30	M	T	W	T	F	S	S
31 Oct–31 Dec*	10:30–4	M	T	W	T	F	S	S
House							
13 Feb–25 Mar	11:30–4[1]	M	T		T	F	S	S
26 Mar–30 Oct	11–4:30[1]	M	T		T	F	S	S
5 Nov–18 Dec	11:30–3:30[1]						S	S
'Hidden Charlecote'							
1 Jan–12 Feb*	Tour[2]	M	T	W	T	F	S	S
17 Feb–26 Oct	Tour[2]			W				
31 Oct–31 Dec*	Tour[2]	M	T	W	T	F	S	S

*Whole property closed 27 and 28 January; 24 and 25 December.
**Tea-room and shop close 30 minutes earlier.
[1]House: admission by timed ticket at busy times.
[2]Tours: 12 to 2.

Clent Hills

near Romsley, Worcestershire

🏛️♿ 1959

Set on the edge of Birmingham and the Black Country, this green oasis with panoramic views is the perfect place for a refreshing walk or a picnic on a sunny day. Families can create their own adventures – building dens, hunting for geocaches or simply getting closer to nature. **Note**: nearest facilities at Nimmings Wood entrance.

Eating and shopping: café (not National Trust) at Nimmings Wood car park serving light meals and refreshments.

Making the most of your day: regular guided rambles and family activities. Natural play area and new play trail. **Dogs**: welcome, but please be considerate to other visitors.

Access: 🅿️♿🅰️➡️
Sat Nav: use B62 0NL for Nimmings Wood entrance. **Parking**: at Nimmings Wood; additional parking at Adam's Hill and Walton Hill.

Finding out more: 01562 712822 or clenthills@nationaltrust.org.uk

Clent Hills
Nimmings Wood car park: gates open 8 to 5. Closed 25 December.

Clent Hills, Worcestershire: create your own adventures

Coughton Court

Alcester, Warwickshire B49 5JA

🏛️✝️❄️🔔🍷 1946

Coughton has been home to the Throckmorton family for 600 years. Facing persecution for their Catholic faith, they were willing to risk everything. This year, you can explore their fascinating story and discover a family's ingenuity, resilience and resolve to overcome conflict in all its guises, including the infamous Gunpowder Plot. Coughton is very much a family home with an intimate feel. The Throckmorton family still live here and they created and manage the stunning gardens, including a riverside walk, bog garden and beautiful display of roses in the walled garden.

Eating and shopping: Coughton Kitchen café serving lunch and teas. Drinks and ice-cream available from the Stables Coffee Bar. Coach House shop selling local food and seasonal gifts. Throckmorton family plant sales. Second-hand bookshop.

Making the most of your day: **Indoors** Morning taster tours and welcome talks. Events, including The Daffodil Society National Show and Jigsaw Festival. **Outdoors** Open-air theatre. Countryside walking trails. Woodland walk. Baddesley Clinton and Packwood nearby. **Dogs**: welcome on leads in car park and public footpaths. Assistance dogs only in gardens.

Access: 🅿️🅿️♿♿📷🖼️🎨🎵⠿
House 🔥♿♿ **Grounds** ♿➡️♿
Parking: 150 yards.

Why not share your pictures with us? #nationaltrust

Croft Castle and Parkland

Yarpole, near Leominster,
Herefordshire HR6 9PW

🏠🖼️✝️🏛️❄️♿🐕🛏️🍽️ 1957

This intimate house became the Croft family home before the Domesday Book. There are many compelling 20th-century stories to uncover – this year find out more about the changes at Croft during 1916 and the impact of the war on the family and local parish. Children can experience life on the home front as a wartime child with clothing and memorabilia. Discover how the landscape changed during this period and see the restoration of the wood pasture, then explore the walled garden and parkland to find the Iron Age hill fort and many ancient trees along the way.

Eating and shopping: tea-room serving hot meals, homemade cakes, local beers, ciders and ice-cream. Fresh produce used straight from the garden. Children's and half portions available. Shop selling local gifts, plant sales, home accessories and gardening gifts. Second-hand bookshop. Picnic area.

Making the most of your day: **Indoors** Games, interactive memorabilia and dressing-up. **Outdoors** Family activities, living history, open-air theatre, seasonal events. Natural and castle-inspired play areas. Walks, dog-walking, bird-hide, information barn and orienteering. **Dogs**: welcome, on leads in gardens, parkland and glazed area of tea-room only.

Finding out more: 01789 400777 or coughtoncourt@nationaltrust.org.uk

Coughton Court	M	T	W	T	F	S	S
House, shop and restaurant							
3 Mar–27 Mar	11–5	·	·	·	T	F	S	S
House, shop, restaurant and grounds[1]							
30 Mar–2 Oct	11–5	·	·	W	T	F	S	S
6 Oct–30 Oct	11–5	·	·	·	T	F	S	S
Taster tours[2]							
6 Apr–30 Sep	10:45–11:15	·	·	W	T	F	·

Closed Good Friday, 2 July and 10 September. Open Bank Holiday Mondays. Admission to house and walled garden by timed ticket on weekends and busy days. [1]The walled garden opens at 12. [2]One tour a day focusing on parts of the collection (subject to availability).

Coughton Court, Warwickshire (above and opposite top), and Croft Castle and Parkland, Herefordshire (below)

Sat Nav: use HR6 OBL. **Parking**: 100 yards.

Finding out more: 01568 780246 or
croftcastle@nationaltrust.org.uk

Croft Castle and Parkland		M	T	W	T	F	S	S
Tea-room, garden and parkland								
1 Jan–3 Jan	10–4	·	·	·	·	F	S	S
9 Jan–7 Feb	10–4	·	·	·	·	·	S	S
27 Dec–31 Dec	10–4	·	T	W	T	F	S	·
Castle, tea-room, garden, shop and parkland								
13 Feb–21 Feb	10–4:30	M	T	W	T	F	S	S
27 Feb–30 Oct	10–5	M	T	W	T	F	S	S
5 Nov–18 Dec	10–4	·	·	·	·	·	S	S

Castle opens at 11. Play area: open as parkland.
Shop: opens 11. Tea-room open winter weekends 10 to 4.

Croome

near High Green, Worcester,
Worcestershire WR8 9DW

[icons] 1996

There's more than meets the eye at Croome.
A secret wartime airbase, now a visitor centre,
was once a hub of activity for thousands of
people. Outside is the grandest of English
landscapes, 'Capability' Brown's masterful first
commission, with commanding views over the
Malverns. The parkland, nearly lost but now
restored, is great for walks and adventures with
a surprise around every corner. At the heart of
the park lies Croome Court, once home to the
Earls of Coventry. The 6th Earl was an
18th-century trendsetter, and today Croome
follows his lead using artists and crafts-people
to tell the story of its eclectic past in inventive
ways. Explore four floors of the mansion,
perfect for making new discoveries.

Eating and shopping: 1940s-style restaurant,
Gingkos shop, Gardener's Bothy plant shop
and second-hand bookshop at the visitor
centre. 1940s tea-car serving snacks on busy
days at the play area. Kitty Fisher's Coffee
House serving light lunches in Croome Court's
basement with outdoor service.

Making the most of your day: Indoors
Contemporary exhibitions, including the return
of the collection, the lost Croome tapestries,
Grayson Perry's vibrant tapestries and
celebration of 'Capability' Brown's
tercentenary. All four floors of the house open,
some areas by guided tour. Time Explorers
game for older children around the house.
RAF Defford Museum at the visitor centre.
Outdoors Walled Garden (privately owned with
admission fee towards its restoration) open
days through the year. Regular guided tours of
the park and outer eye-catcher open days. New
family trail around park with special trails every
school holiday. RAF-themed playground and
natural play area close to the visitor centre.
Dogs: welcome on leads. Assistance dogs only
in house, RAF museum, restaurant and shop.

Access: [icons]
House [icons] Park [icons]
Parking: on site.

Finding out more: 01905 371006 or
croome@nationaltrust.org.uk
Croome National Trust Visitor Centre,
near High Green, Severn Stoke,
Worcestershire WR8 9DW

Croome		M	T	W	T	F	S	S
House								
1 Jan–12 Feb*	11–4	M	·	W	T	F	S	S
13 Feb–6 Nov	11–4:30	M	T	W	T	F	S	S
7 Nov–23 Dec*	11–4	M	T	W	T	F	S	S
House**								
26 Dec–31 Dec	Tour	M	T	W	T	F	S	·
Park, restaurant and shop								
1 Jan–12 Feb	10–4	M	T	W	T	F	S	S
13 Feb–6 Nov	10–5	M	T	W	T	F	S	S
7 Nov–23 Dec	10–4	M	T	W	T	F	S	S
26 Dec–31 Dec	10–4	M	T	W	T	F	S	·

*Winter weekdays house open for guided tours only before
1:30. **House open for timed tours only. Park closes
30 minutes later.

**Croome, Worcestershire: the end of an
action-packed day (above), and a
graceful urn, designed by Robert Adam (right)**

Cwmmau Farmhouse

Brilley, Whitney-on-Wye,
Herefordshire HR3 6JP

⌂ ✳ ♨ 🛏 | 1965 |

Sitting deep in the heart of Herefordshire
countryside, this early 17th-century black-and-
white timbered farmhouse has many original
features to explore. **Note**: available as holiday
cottage (0844 800 2070) when not open.
Open Thursday to Sunday, 30 June to 3 July
and 10 to 13 November, 1 to 5.

Finding out more: 01568 780246 or
cwmmaufarmhouse@nationaltrust.org.uk

Downs Banks

near Stone, Staffordshire

♨ | 1950 |

A little wilderness of woodlands and heath,
with easy access walks, in the heart of the
Midlands. **Note**: sorry no toilets. Some
steep paths.

Finding out more: 01889 882825 or
downsbanks@nationaltrust.org.uk

Dudmaston

Quatt, near Bridgnorth, Shropshire WV15 6QN

⌂ ✳ ♨ 🛏 | 1978 |

More than 875 years ago, a Norman knight
chose a spot nestled in the Shropshire
countryside as the perfect place to build a
home, Dudmaston. Wooded parkland and
sweeping gardens provide great walks and
family fun. You can enjoy the woodland
playground, go exploring, or simply find a
tranquil spot and take in the amazing views.
Soak up the family history in the much-loved
and lived-in family rooms, which contrast with
art galleries, created by the last owners, the
Laboucheres, and described as housing 'one
of the most important private modern art
collections in a country house setting'.
Note: the family home of Mr and Mrs Mark
Hamilton-Russell.

Eating and shopping: Orchard tea-room
offering lunch and afternoon tea. Ice-cream
parlour and Apple Store snacks. Second-hand
bookshop. Shop selling local items and gifts.

Making the most of your day: walks maps.
Children's woodland playground. '50 things'
trails. Garden tours. Conservation in action.
Events and family activities programme.
Dogs: welcome on leads in parkland and
orchard only.

For other ways to get involved go to nationaltrust.org.uk/get-involved/volunteer

Access: ⬚⬚⬚⬚⬚⬚⬚⬚
Building ⬚⬚⬚ **Grounds** ⬚➡
Parking: on site or at The Old Sawmill and Hampton Loade.

Finding out more: 01746 780866 or dudmaston@nationaltrust.org.uk

Dudmaston		M	T	W	T	F	S	S
Park, tea-room and shop								
13 Feb–21 Feb**	12–4	·	·	·	·	·	S	S
20 Mar–24 Mar	11:30–5	M	T	W	T	·	·	S
27 Mar–29 Sep	11–5:30	M	T	W	T	·	·	S
2 Oct–31 Oct	11:30–5	M	T	W	T	·	·	S
5 Nov–11 Dec**	11:30–4	·	·	·	·	·	S	S
Galleries								
20 Mar–24 Mar	1–5	M	T	W	T	·	·	S
2 Oct–31 Oct	1–5	M	T	W	T	·	·	S
Hall and galleries								
27 Mar–29 Sep	1–5*	M	T	W	T	·	·	S
Garden and second-hand bookshop								
20 Mar–24 Mar	12–5	M	T	W	T	·	·	S
27 Mar–29 Sep	12–5:30	M	T	W	T	·	·	S
2 Oct–31 Oct	12–5	M	T	W	T	·	·	S

No entry to the car park before opening time.
*House and galleries open at 2 on Sundays.
**Restricted park access – Dingle walks only.

Farnborough Hall

Farnborough, near Banbury,
Warwickshire OX17 1DU

⬚⬚⬚ 1960

Honey-coloured stone house with library and treasures collected during the Grand Tour. Set in landscape gardens with panoramic parkland views. **Note**: occupied and administered by the Holbech family. Open Wednesday and Saturday, 2 April to 28 September, 2:30 to 5:30; also open Sunday and Bank Holiday Monday, 1 and 2 May.

Finding out more: 01295 690002 (Farnborough Hall). 01295 670266 (Upton House) or farnboroughhall@nationaltrust.org.uk

The peaceful lake at Dudmaston, Shropshire (opposite), and a pretty corner of the garden at Greyfriars' House and Garden, Worcestershire (right)

The Fleece Inn

Bretforton, near Evesham,
Worcestershire WR11 7JE

⬚⬚⬚⬚⬚ 1978

Medieval half-timbered longhouse, now a traditional village inn, with barn and orchard. Known for folk music, Morris dancing and asparagus. **Note**: open daily, 10 to 11 (reduced opening 25 December).

Finding out more: 01386 831173 or fleeceinn@nationaltrust.org.uk

Greyfriars' House and Garden

Friar Street, Worcester,
Worcestershire WR1 2LZ

⬚⬚⬚ 1966

Set in the heart of historic Worcester, Greyfriars is a charming timber-framed merchant's house – perfect for getting away from the hustle and bustle. This unique property was rescued by two extraordinary people in the 20th century with a vision to revive this medieval gem and create a peaceful setting.

Eating and shopping: light refreshments served in the walled garden or in Elsie's tea-room (in house) in colder weather. Small retail shop, including plants grown at nearby Hanbury Hall, plus a selection of second-hand books.

Making the most of your day: **Indoors** Themed events throughout the year, including house tours. Children's trails. **Outdoors** Garden games and geocaching. **Dogs**: welcome in garden.

Access: ⬛🏠📷 House 🔥🏠👨‍👩🔥
Parking: none on site. Nearest at Corn Market, King Street and Cathedral Plaza, not National Trust (charge including members).

Finding out more: 01905 23571 or greyfriars@nationaltrust.org.uk

Greyfriars		M	T	W	T	F	S	S
2 Feb–1 Oct*	11–5	·	·	T	W	T	F	S	·
4 Oct–17 Dec*	11–4	·	·	T	W	T	F	S	·

Open Bank Holiday Mondays. *House taster tours available from 11 to 1 (last tour at 12:30), tour places allocated on arrival. Free-flow access from 1.

Hanbury Hall and Gardens

School Road, Hanbury, Droitwich Spa, Worcestershire WR9 7EA

🏛️❄️🛏️🍽️ 1953

A country pad set in the Worcestershire countryside, with an early 18th-century house to discover, views across the Malvern Hills and formal gardens perfect for exploring. Originally a stage-set for summer parties, the house provides a glimpse into the early 18th century. You can see the original wall-paintings by Sir James Thornhill – full of drama, politics and the birth of Georgian life – then relax and play in the gardens with flower meadows, bowls green, walled garden and play areas. To venture further afield, pick up a walks leaflet and find George London's unique Semicircle in the parkland.

Hanbury Hall and Gardens, Worcestershire: the main façade (above), and the formal garden (opposite)

Eating and shopping: Servants' Hall tea-room serving meals made using home-grown produce (where possible) and home-baked cakes and sweet treats. Chambers tea-room serving sandwich lunches and afternoon teas. Stableyard outdoor café (open busy days only). Plants from the walled garden for sale.

Making the most of your day: **Indoors** Art exhibitions and themed weekends. **Outdoors** Regular garden tours and introductory talks. Varied events, play area, concerts and open-air theatre. Free park walks leaflet. **Dogs**: on leads in park and short leads in stableyard. Assistance dogs only in gardens.

Access: 🅿️🐕🚌📷⬛📷📷🚫
Building 🔥🏠♿ Grounds 🔥🏠➡️📷
Parking: 150 yards.

Finding out more: 01527 821214 or hanburyhall@nationaltrust.org.uk

Hanbury Hall and Gardens		M	T	W	T	F	S	S
1 Jan–12 Feb*	Tour	M	T	W	T	F	S	S
13 Feb–30 Oct**	Tour	M	T	W	T	F	S	S
31 Oct–23 Dec†	Tour	M	T	W	T	F	S	S
26 Dec–31 Dec*	Tour	M	T	W	T	F	S	·

*Tours only. **Tours 11 to 1; free-flow 1 to 5. †3 to 23 December, free-flow 11 to 4. Closed 27 and 28 January.

Kinver Edge and the Rock Houses in Staffordshire

Kinver Edge and the Rock Houses

Holy Austin Rock Houses, Compton Road, Kinver, near Stourbridge, Staffordshire DY7 6DL

🏠 🏛 ❀ 🎏 1917

The Holy Austin Rock Houses, inhabited until the 1960s, have no equivalent in the whole of England. Discover how a few extraordinary people carved themselves homes in this imposing sandstone ridge. A walk in the surrounding woodland of Kinver Edge leads to open heath with dramatic views across three counties.

Eating and shopping: tea-room inside restored Rock House serving drinks, cakes and snacks, including our famous rock cakes.

Making the most of your day: **Indoors** Traditional games and range. **Outdoors** Natural play trail. Guided walks and family activities throughout the year. **Dogs**: welcome on leads within grounds of Rock Houses.

Access: 🅿️ 🚻 🖼 🎫 📷 🚐 Building 🦽 Grounds 🦽
Parking: by Warden's Lodge, Comber Road, for the Edge, and Compton Road or Kingsford Lane overflow car park for the Rock Houses.

Hawford Dovecote

Hawford, Worcestershire WR3 7SG

🏠 1973

Picturesque dovecote, which has survived virtually unaltered since the late 16th century, retaining many nesting boxes. **Note**: sorry no toilet or tea-room. Please park carefully to one side of lane. Open daily, dawn to dusk.

Finding out more: 01527 821214 or hawforddovecote@nationaltrust.org.uk

Finding out more: 01384 872553 or kinveredge@nationaltrust.org.uk

Kinver Edge and the Rock Houses		M	T	W	T	F	S	S
Rock Houses								
18 Feb–25 Mar**	11–4*				T	F	S	S
26 Mar–6 Apr	11–4*	M	T	W	T	F	S	S
7 Apr–24 Jul	11–4*				T	F	S	S
25 Jul–4 Sep	11–4*	M	T	W	T	F	S	S
8 Sep–30 Oct**	11–4*				T	F	S	S
5 Nov–11 Dec	11–4*						S	S

*Grounds and tea-room open 10:30 to 4:30. ** Rock Houses, grounds and tea-room open daily during Staffordshire school half-term holidays.

Kinwarton Dovecote

Kinwarton, near Alcester,
Warwickshire B49 6HB

🏠 1958

Rare 14th-century circular dovecote with metre-thick walls, hundreds of nesting holes and original rotating ladder. **Note**: stock may be grazing. Sorry no toilet. Limited parking (not National Trust). Open daily, 5 March to 30 October, 9 to 6.

Finding out more: 01789 400777 or kinwartondovecote@nationaltrust.org.uk

Knowles Mill

Dowles Brook, Bewdley,
Worcestershire DY12 2LX

🏠 1938

Dating from the 18th century, the mill retains much of its machinery, including the frames of an overshot waterwheel. **Note**: Mill Cottage not open to visitors (please respect the resident's privacy). Sorry no toilets or tea-room. No parking at Mill Cottage. Open daily, dawn to dusk.

Finding out more: 01527 821214 or knowlesmill@nationaltrust.org.uk

Letocetum Roman Baths and Museum

Watling Street, Wall, near Lichfield,
Staffordshire WS14 0AW

🏠 🏛 1934

Remains of a once-important Roman staging post and settlement, including *mansio* (Roman inn) and bathhouse. **Note**: in the guardianship of English Heritage. Open-air site accessible March to end of October at reasonable times. Site and Roman finds museum (volunteer-run) open last weekend of month, March to October; Sundays in July and August and Bank Holiday Mondays, 11 to 4.

Finding out more: 0870 333 1181 (English Heritage) or letocetum@nationaltrust.org.uk

Middle Littleton Tithe Barn

Middle Littleton, Evesham,
Worcestershire WR11 8LN

🏠 1975

The largest and finest restored 13th-century tithe barn in the country. **Note**: sorry no toilets. Open daily, 1 April to 31 October, 2 to 5.

Finding out more: 01905 371006 or middlelittleton@nationaltrust.org.uk

Morville Hall

Morville, near Bridgnorth,
Shropshire WV16 5NB

🏠 ✿ ⚑ 1965

Elizabethan gem with a Georgian makeover. Enchanting gardens spill down to the Mor

Brook against the backdrop of Shropshire hills. **Note**: property contents are a mix of items on loan and tenant's own. Open Fridays and Saturdays, 13 and 14 May, 10 and 11 June, 8 and 9 July, 9 and 10 September, 12 to 5.

Finding out more: 01746 780866 (Dudmaston Hall) or morvillehall@nationaltrust.org.uk

Moseley Old Hall

Moseley Old Hall Lane, Fordhouses,
Wolverhampton, Staffordshire WV10 7HY

🏠 🅿️ ♣️ ⬇️ 🔔 1962

This atmospheric farmhouse holds many secrets. Charles II hid here while fleeing for his life after the Battle of Worcester in 1651 – see his hiding place, the bed he slept on and find out how he escaped Cromwell's army. Meanwhile daily life continues, and while a log fire crackles in the grate, the domestic world of the 17th century carries on around you. Outside, protected within the walled garden, are herbs, vegetables, an orchard and a knot garden. Beyond is King's Walk Wood. Part of the Monarch's Way Trail.

Moseley Old Hall in Staffordshire (above and below)

Eating and shopping: tea-room serving light lunches, cakes and scones – baked here throughout the day. Shop selling gifts and plants. Second-hand bookshop.

Making the most of your day: Indoors Guided tours, have-a-go sessions and re-creations of 17th-century life all year. **Outdoors** Children's activities, including two-level tree-house, den-building, rope swings, trails and activity packs. Wightwick Manor nearby. **Dogs**: welcome on leads in garden and grounds.

Access: 🅿️🄳🚻🔆🅰️🏞️📷📹♿
House 🅰️♿ **Garden and woodlands** 🅰️🅰️➡️♿
Parking: on site.

Finding out more: 01902 782808 or moseleyoldhall@nationaltrust.org.uk

Moseley Old Hall		M	T	W	T	F	S	S
House, tea-room and shop								
13 Feb–9 Mar	11–4	M	T	W	·	·	S	S
12 Mar–30 Oct	11–5	M	T	W	·	·	S	S
5 Nov–18 Dec	11–4	·	·	·	·	·	S	S
19 Dec–21 Dec	11–3	M	T	W	·	·	·	·
Tea-room and shop								
1 Jul–30 Sep	11–5	·	·	·	·	F	·	·

Grounds: open as tea-room and shop. House guided tours available from 11:30, self-led entry from 11:45, except Bank Holidays when timed ticket entry is from 11. In February, March, November and December for safety, access to top floor may be limited. Last entry to house one hour before closing.

Packwood House in Warwickshire: the celebrated sculpted yews (above), and a misty view of the house (below)

Packwood House

Packwood Lane, Lapworth, Warwickshire B94 6AT

🏛️✳️🐾🍽️ 1941

Surrounded by beautiful gardens and countryside, Packwood was described by a guest in the 1930s as 'a house to dream of, a garden to dream in'. Lovingly restored at the beginning of the 20th century by Graham Baron Ash, the house has a fascinating architectural history. This year you can discover the detail behind the man, his passion for collecting and his collection. The gardens include brightly coloured, 'mingled style' herbaceous borders, famous sculpted yews and an 18th-century gentleman's kitchen garden.

Eating and shopping: Garden Kitchen café serving hot food, salads, sandwiches and cakes. Shop selling seasonal gifts, local foods and plants, many grown in our own nursery. Picnics welcome by the lakeside and in the picnic area.

Making the most of your day: welcome and garden talks, countryside walking trails and playful woodland Welly Walk. Baddesley Clinton and Coughton Court nearby. Some areas of the gardens may be closed, please call before travelling. **Dogs**: welcome in car park, park footpaths and café terrace. Assistance dogs only in gardens.

Rosedene

Victoria Road, Dodford, near Bromsgrove, Worcestershire B61 9BU

🏠 ♿ 🛏 [1997]

Restored 1840s cottage with an organic garden and orchard, illustrating the mid-19th-century Chartist Movement. **Note**: available to hire as a 'back to basics' holiday cottage. Admission by guided tour (first Sunday of month), 6 March to 4 December (booking essential). Tours at 10, 11:30, 1 and 2:30.

Finding out more: 01527 821214 or rosedene@nationaltrust.org.uk

Access: 🅿️ 🇩 🈳 🔧 📷 ⠿
House 🔾 🏠 ♿ **Grounds** 🔾 🏠 ♿
Parking: 150 yards.

Finding out more: 01564 782024 or packwood@nationaltrust.org.uk

Packwood House		M	T	W	T	F	S	S
House, grounds and gift shop								
13 Feb–24 Jul	11–5	·	T	W	T	F	S	S
25 Jul–4 Sep	11–5	M	T	W	T	F	S	S
6 Sep–30 Oct	11–5	·	T	W	T	F	S	S
Café, shop and park								
1 Jan–12 Feb	9–4	·	T	W	T	F	S	S
13 Feb–24 Jul	9–5	·	T	W	T	F	S	S
25 Jul–4 Sep	9–5	M	T	W	T	F	S	S
6 Sep–30 Oct	9–5	·	T	W	T	F	S	S
1 Nov–31 Dec	9–4	·	T	W	T	F	S	S
House and grounds tours*								
1 Jan–12 Feb	11–3	·	T	W	T	F	S	S
1 Nov–31 Dec	11–3	·	T	W	T	F	S	S

Open Mondays during school holidays (15 February, 21 March and 24 October) and on Bank Holiday Mondays. Admission to the house by timed ticket (not bookable). *Tours run at intervals throughout the day, subject to availability. Closed 24 and 25 December.

Shugborough Estate, Staffordshire: the setting sun bathes the mansion in glorious golden light

Shugborough Estate

Milford, near Stafford, Staffordshire ST17 0XB

🏠 🖼 🍴 ♿ 🛶 👶 🔔 📷 🍽 [1966]

Shugborough is a working, historic estate, featuring a Georgian mansion, working servants' quarters, model farm with rare and native breeds of livestock and walled garden. Home to the Earls of Lichfield, Shugborough is set in 364 hectares (900 acres) of Grade I listed parkland, peppered with unusual monuments. **Note**: entirely operated by Staffordshire County Council. Charge for members for all areas, apart from the house and gardens. Parking charge (including members), refunded on purchase of all-sites ticket.

Eating and shopping: licensed tea-room serving homemade cream teas and meals, including Shugborough's own-recipe sausage and mash and game casserole. Gift shop, ice-cream parlour, old-fashioned sweetshop and craft outlets making and selling handmade goods.

Making the most of your day: **Indoors** Mansion guided tours, 11 to 1. Regular demonstrations of milling, baking and cheese-making. **Outdoors** Events all year, including craft fairs, theatre and family activities. **Dogs**: on leads in formal gardens and main visitor routes.

Access: [icons] Building [icons] Grounds [icons]
Parking: £3 (pay and display, including members). Refunded on purchase of all-sites ticket.

Finding out more: 01889 881388 or shugborough@nationaltrust.org.uk

Shugborough Estate		M	T	W	T	F	S	S
Parkland, gardens, tea-room and shop								
18 Mar–21 Oct	11–5	M	T	W	T	F	S	S
House, servants' quarters, farm and walled garden								
18 Mar–21 Oct	11–5	M		W	T	F	S	S

Access to house by guided tour only 11 to 1.

Sunnycroft

200 Holyhead Road, Wellington, Telford, Shropshire TF1 2DR

[icons] 1999

Hidden down an avenue of towering redwoods is an oasis in the middle of suburbia. Designed to emulate the upper classes, this rare middle-class Victorian survival is a mini estate. Built to last, little was thrown away and the life of a family home envelopes you as you enter. **Note**: arriving by car: use Junction 7 on M54.

Eating and shopping: small Edwardian tea-room. Situated within the house, its doors lead on to the veranda, serving light lunches, cakes, ice-cream and drinks. Picnics welcome on the lawn. Shop selling souvenirs, plants and second-hand books.

Making the most of your day: ideal half-day visit, situated only 20 minutes from Attingham Park. Indoor and outdoor guided tours, children's trails and garden games on offer. Seasonal events, including Edwardian Christmas and handicraft weekend.
Dogs: welcome on leads in grounds only.

Access: [icons] Building [icon] Grounds [icons]
Sat Nav: use TF1 2DP (exit 7 from M54).
Parking: 150 yards. Additional parking in Wrekin Road car park (not National Trust).

Finding out more: 01952 242884 or sunnycroft@nationaltrust.org.uk

Sunnycroft		M	T	W	T	F	S	S
16 Jan–6 Mar	10:30–3						S	S
11 Mar–18 Jul*	10:30–5	M				F	S	S
22 Jul–30 Aug	10:30–5	M	T			F	S	S
2 Sep–31 Oct*	10:30–5	M				F	S	S
5 Nov–4 Dec	10:30–3						S	S
9 Dec–20 Dec	10:30–4	M	T			F	S	S

*Open Tuesday during school holidays. Last admission one hour before closing. Entry by timed tickets with ten-minute introductory talk, then free-flow. Daily guided tours available in main season (not bookable).

Sunnycroft, Shropshire: an Edwardian time capsule

Upton House and Gardens

near Banbury, Warwickshire OX15 6HT

🏠 ❄ 🛏 🔔 🍴 1948

Step back to wartime Britain when Lord and Lady Bearsted moved out and the family-owned merchant bank moved in. Evacuated from London air-raids, the staff set up a typing pool and canteen in the Long Gallery surrounded by Upton's great art collection, with works by Canaletto and Jan Steen and the finest Chelsea porcelain. As the end of the war approaches, discover what happened as the art and the family returned. Outside, the sweeping lawn gives way to tumbling terraces and colourful borders. Relax by the swimming pool, look out for the bog garden and the growing kitchen garden.

Eating and shopping: licensed restaurant serving hot lunches and freshly baked cakes and teas, including gluten-free and vegetarian options. The shop offers gifts, accessories, art books, plants and mementoes of your visit.

Upton House and Gardens, Warwickshire (top)

Making the most of your day: Indoors Changing exhibitions, evocative house tours, cinema tent. **Outdoors** Woodland adventure and games. Wartime Anderson Shelter. Home of National Collection of Asters (flowering in September). Holiday cottages. **Dogs**: assistance dogs only in grounds (other dogs allowed in car park).

Access: 🅿 🅳 ♿ ♿ ♿ ♿ ♿ 🖥 🎵
House and gallery 🚶 ♿ ♿ Grounds 🚶 ♿ ♿
Sat Nav: follow brown signs to car park once you arrive at postcode location.
Parking: 300 yards.

Finding out more: 01295 670266 or uptonhouse@nationaltrust.org.uk

Upton House and Gardens		M	T	W	T	F	S	S
Gardens, restaurant and shop*								
2 Jan–7 Feb	12–4						S	S
13 Feb–30 Oct	11–5	M	T	W		F	S	S
31 Oct–19 Dec	12–4	M				F	S	S
26 Dec–31 Dec	12–4	M	T	W	T	F	S	
House and exhibition**								
2 Jan–7 Feb	12–4						S	S
13 Feb–30 Oct	1–5	M	T	W		F	S	S
31 Oct–19 Dec	12–4	M				F	S	S

Open daily in July and August. *November to March: gardens open by winter walk. 13 February to 30 October: themed tours, 11 to 1, tickets available on arrival (non-bookable). 26 to 31 December: Squash Court Gallery exhibition open. Open 1 January 2017. **Timed tickets operate daily, can be booked online. House opens at 11 on Bank Holiday Mondays.

The Weir Garden

Swainshill, Hereford, Herefordshire HR4 7QF

⌂ ❖ ⚏ 1959

Whatever the season, the natural beauty of this riverside garden is completely captivating. During spring, the ground beneath the ancient trees is carpeted with bulbs; then, in summer, a picnic by the river while watching the wildlife is irresistible. Autumn brings an abundance of seasonal produce in the walled garden. **Note**: sturdy footwear recommended.

Eating and shopping: self-service tea and coffee available. Picnics welcome.

Making the most of your day: events, including walks and talks. Historical secrets to discover, from giant fish to Roman remains. Family trails during school holidays. Brockhampton Estate, Croft Castle and Parkland and Berrington Hall nearby. **Dogs**: assistance dogs only (dogs allowed in car park).

Access: ⚐ Grounds ♿ 🏛
Parking: on site.

Finding out more: 01981 590509 or theweir@nationaltrust.org.uk

The Weir Garden		M	T	W	T	F	S	S
16 Jan–24 Jan	10:30–4	·	·	·	·	·	S	S
30 Jan–6 Nov	10:30–4:30	M	T	W	T	F	S	S
12 Nov–20 Nov	10:30–4	·	·	·	·	·	S	S

Wichenford Dovecote

Wichenford, Worcestershire WR6 6XY

🕊 1965

Small but striking 17th-century half-timbered dovecote at Wichenford Court. **Note**: no access to Wichenford Court (privately owned). Sorry no toilet or tea-room. Please consider local residents when parking. Open every day all year, dawn to dusk.

Finding out more: 01527 821214 or wichenforddovecote@nationaltrust.org.uk

Wightwick Manor and Gardens

Bridgnorth Road, Wolverhampton, West Midlands WV6 8BN

🏠 ❖ 1937

Would you save a house that was only 50 years old? Geoffrey Mander believed his parents' home was worth preserving for the nation to enjoy, giving Wightwick to the National Trust in 1937 and complementing the house's Old English design by filling it with Pre-Raphaelite art and William Morris furnishings. Much-loved by the people of Wolverhampton, the Mander family legacy lives on at Wightwick. The gardens of soft lawns, old yew and fragrant rose offer a place to relax and reflect. Inside, the art, textiles and designs of Rossetti, Morris, De Morgan and their friends are waiting to delight.

Eating and shopping: specialist shop selling William Morris and Arts and Crafts-inspired ranges and plant centre. Tea-room serving light lunches, sandwiches and sweet treats. Garden ticket required to visit shop and tea-room.

Daffodils herald spring at The Weir Garden in Herefordshire. This captivating riverside garden is delightful in every season

Making the most of your day: **Indoors** Events, including specialist talks and tours, throughout the year. **Outdoors** Year-round garden orienteering map, family activities in school holidays. Moseley Old Hall nearby.
Dogs: welcome on leads in garden.

Access: [icons]
Manor [icons] Malthouse [icons] Gardens [icons]
Parking: entrance off A454.

Finding out more: 01902 761400 (Infoline) or wightwickmanor@nationaltrust.org.uk

Wightwick Manor and Gardens		M	T	W	T	F	S	S
House								
1 Jan–12 Feb	12–4	M	·	W	T	F	S	S
13 Feb–30 Jun	12–5	M	·	W	T	F	S	S
1 Jul–31 Aug	12–5	M	T	W	T	F	S	S
1 Sep–30 Oct	12–5	M	·	W	T	F	S	S
31 Oct–31 Dec	12–4	M	·	W	T	F	S	S
Garden, tea-room and shop								
1 Jan–12 Feb	11–4	M	T	W	T	F	· S	S
13 Feb–30 Oct	11–5	M	T	W	T	F	S	S
31 Oct–31 Dec	11–4	M	T	W	T	F	S	S

Last entry to house one hour before closing. Closed 25 and 26 December. A reduced number of rooms will be open January to mid-February and from 27 December.

The beautiful formal garden (top), at Wightwick Manor and Gardens, West Midlands, gives pleasure to many visitors (right)

Wilderhope Manor

Longville, Much Wenlock, Shropshire TF13 6EG

[icons] 1936

Charming Elizabethan manor house with interesting features inside and country walks from the door. **Note**: youth hostel, access may be restricted. Open Sundays, 3 January to 27 March and 2 October to 18 December, 2 to 4; open Wednesdays, 3 April to 25 September, 2 to 4.

Finding out more: 01694 771363 (Hostel Warden YHA) or wilderhope@nationaltrust.org.uk

North West
and the Lakes

Buttermere Valley, Cumbria

North West

Kendal
Sizergh
Fell Foot
Arnside
and Silverdale
Sandscale Haws National
Nature Reserve
Ulverston
Dalton Castle
Barrow-in-Furness
Morecambe
Lancaster
Heysham
Coast
Upper Wharfedale
Malham Tarn Estate
Settle
East Riddlesden Hall
Blackpool
Preston
Gawthorpe Hall
Burnley
Hardcastle Crags
Todmorden
Rufford Old Hall
Southport
Bolton
Rochdale
Marsden Moor Estate
Formby
Wigan
MANCHESTER
Salford
LIVERPOOL
The Beatles' Childhood Homes
The Hardmans' House
Warrington
Sale
Stockport
Kinder, Edale and the Dark Peak
Dunham Massey
Quarry Bank
Lyme
Speke Hall
Tatton Park
Nether Alderley Mill
Hare Hill
Eyam Hall and Craft Centre
Alderley Edge and Cheshire Countryside
Macclesfield
Bakewell
Chester
Little Moreton Hall
Congleton
Crewe
Biddulph Grange Garden
Erddig
Rhyl

Legend

● Buildings and/or gardens

● Entry points to coast and countryside

The size of each pin indicates how large a place is and how long you should allow for your visit

National Trust land

The Lakes

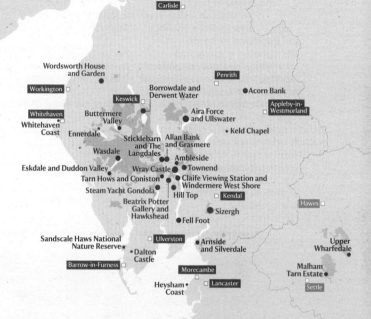

Hadrian's Wall and
Housesteads Fort

Haltwhistle

Allen Banks and
Staward Gorge

Carlisle

Wordsworth House
and Garden

Workington

Penrith

Keswick

Acorn Bank

Borrowdale and
Derwent Water

Whitehaven

Buttermere
Valley

Appleby-in-
Westmorland

Whitehaven
Coast

Aira Force
and Ullswater

Ennerdale

Keld Chapel

Sticklebarn
and The
Langdales

Allan Bank
and Grasmere

Wasdale

Ambleside

Eskdale and Duddon Valley

Wray Castle

Townend

Tarn Hows and Coniston

Claife Viewing Station and
Windermere West Shore

Steam Yacht Gondola

Hill Top

Kendal

Hawes

Beatrix Potter
Gallery and
Hawkshead

Sizergh

Fell Foot

Sandscale Haws National
Nature Reserve

Ulverston

Arnside
and Silverdale

Upper
Wharfedale

Dalton
Castle

Barrow-in-Furness

Morecambe

Malham
Tarn Estate

Heysham
Coast

Lancaster

Settle

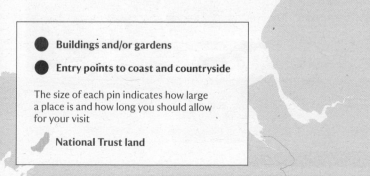

⬤ **Buildings and/or gardens**

⬤ **Entry points to coast and countryside**

The size of each pin indicates how large
a place is and how long you should allow
for your visit

National Trust land

Acorn Bank

Temple Sowerby, near Penrith,
Cumbria CA10 1SP

🏠🖼️✣🚻🛗🖾 1950

At the heart of the Eden Valley, with spectacular views to the Lake District, Acorn Bank is a tranquil haven with a rich and diverse history. The walled gardens shelter a medicinal herb garden and traditional orchards. Woodland walks, famous for springtime daffodils, reveal a half-hidden story of gypsum mining and a working watermill with a medieval past. In the midst of this beautiful estate sits a 17th-century sandstone manor house, once owned by the indomitable author and poet, Dorothy Una Ratcliffe. This unfurnished manor is now partially open to our visitors while under restoration. **Note**: access to fragile grass paths may be restricted after wet weather. Members pay on Apple Day, 9 October (opening arrangements differ on that day, see note in table for details).

Eating and shopping: tea-room serving light lunches, cakes and scones made using produce from the garden and flour from the mill; outside tables in the garden courtyard. Shop selling a selection of gifts, plants and local and national products.

Making the most of your day: watermill machinery operates most weekend afternoons. Wild play area in the woods and secret places for children to discover. Apple Day is a great family day out. **Dogs**: welcome on leads on woodland walks and garden courtyard. Apple Day: assistance dogs only.

Access: 🅿️🔌♿🚻🍼🔲🎧📷 **Watermill** ♿🚶
House ♿🚶🔲 **Grounds** ♿🚶🔲➡️🔲
Parking: large car park.

Finding out more: 017683 61893 or acornbank@nationaltrust.org.uk

Acorn Bank		M	T	W	T	F	S	S
13 Feb–6 Mar*	11–4	·	·	·	·	·	**S**	**S**
12 Mar–30 Oct	10–5*	**M**	·	**W**	**T**	**F**	**S**	**S**
5 Nov–18 Dec	11–4	·	·	·	·	·	**S**	**S**

*Tea-room open 10:30 to 4:30 March to October. Apple Day: Sunday 9 October, 11 to 4:30 (access for event only).

Spotting pond wildlife in the garden at Acorn Bank, Cumbria. This tranquil haven has a rich and diverse history

Aira Force and Ullswater

near Watermillock, Penrith, Cumbria

⚓ 1906

Aira Force is a showcase for the power and beauty of nature, it's a place to escape the ordinary. For 300 years visitors have been drawn here, where rainwater runs from the fells into Aira Beck and thunders in one 65-foot leap over the falls. Yet, Aira Force is much more than an impressive waterfall. A network of trails weave its way from Ullswater lakeshore to Gowbarrow summit, passing towering Himalayan firs, rare red squirrels, woodland glades, picnic spots, and views out across Ullswater. You can start your day in Glenridding and arrive by boat, taking in the sights of Ullswater Valley along the way, then a footpath allows for a stroll back to Glenridding along the lakeshore. **Note**: boat rides on Ullswater operated by Ullswater 'Steamers' (not National Trust).

Water, water everywhere at Aira Force (above), and Ullswater (below), Cumbria

Eating and shopping: tea-room serving light lunches, cakes, ice-cream and hot and cold drinks. Shop selling gifts, ice-cream and souvenirs.

Making the most of your day: *Aira Force Guide* available to buy at the shop for walking trails, points of interest and Rangers' tips. Red squirrel trail and natural play area. Canoe launching at Glencoyne car park. Picnic and pebble skimming at Aira Green. Boat rides with Ullswater 'Steamers'. Wordsworth's daffodils

on Ullswater lakeshore in spring. Footpath from Aira Force to Glenridding. Walks to Gowbarrow summit, the best spot for panoramic views across the Lakeland fells. **Dogs**: under close control (stock grazing).

Access: 🅿️🚻♿🔼🏞 Grounds ♿
Sat Nav: use CA11 0JS for Aira Force; CA11 0NQ for Glencoyne Bay. **Parking**: at Aira Force, Aira Force High Cascades, Aira Force Park Brow and Glencoyne Bay.

Finding out more: 017684 82067 or ullswater@nationaltrust.org.uk

Aira Force and Ullswater		M	T	W	T	F	S	S
Tea-room and shop*								
1 Jan–24 Dec	10–4:30	**M**	**T**	**W**	**T**	**F**	**S**	**S**

*Tea-room: opens at 10:30. Opening times may vary during low season.

Springtime in the woods at Alderley Edge, Cheshire, brings fresh green foliage

Alderley Edge and Cheshire Countryside

Nether Alderley, Macclesfield, Cheshire

🏛️🚣 1946

The dramatic red sandstone escarpment of Alderley Edge has far-reaching views over the Cheshire Plain and towards the Peak District. Numerous paths meander through open pasture, mature pine and beech woodland. The site, designated a Site of Special Scientific Interest for its geology and history of copper mining dating back to the Bronze Age, is also noted for its legend and *The Weirdstone of Brisingamen* novel. For similar countryside experiences, why not visit Bickerton, Bulkeley and Helsby Hills on the Sandstone Ridge, Thurstaston Common on the Wirral, and The Cloud and Mow Cop on the Staffordshire border? **Note**: toilets at Alderley Edge car park only.

Eating and shopping: Alderley Edge: Wizard Tea-room (weekends and some Bank Holidays only) and Wizard Inn (neither National Trust). Ice-cream vendor (when weather is fine). Picnic area close to car park.

Making the most of your day: guided walks provide an insight into the industrial archaeology, geology and legends at Alderley Edge. Waymarked walking routes. Three orienteering courses. Ancient copper mine tours: Derbyshire Caving Club, twice yearly. **Dogs**: under close control. On leads near livestock and ground-nesting birds.

Access: 🅿️♿🚻 Grounds ➡️
Sat Nav: for Alderley Edge use SK10 4UB; for Mow Cop ST7 3PA; for Bickerton SY14 8LN.
Parking: at Alderley Edge, Mow Cop ST7 3PA and Bickerton SY14 8LN (plus roadside elsewhere).

Finding out more: 01625 584412 or alderleyedge@nationaltrust.org.uk

Alderley Edge		M	T	W	T	F	S	S
Alderley Edge car park								
1 Jan–31 Mar	8–5	M	T	W	T	F	S	S
1 Apr–31 May	8–5:30	M	T	W	T	F	S	S
1 Jun–30 Sep	8–6	M	T	W	T	F	S	S
1 Oct–31 Dec	8–5	M	T	W	T	F	S	S

Allan Bank and Grasmere, Cumbria: enjoying the view in comfort

Allan Bank and Grasmere

near Ambleside, Cumbria LA22 9QB

🏛 🎏 ♨ 🖼 1920

Make yourself comfortable in the former home of National Trust founder Canon Rawnsley. Only partially restored and decorated, this isn't a typical National Trust experience. Grasmere's valley unfolds from the picture windows and woodland grounds. Secret hideaways, such as the Victorian viewing tunnel, create an air of mystery. You could have something to eat in the homely kitchen, watch red squirrels as you read by the fire or picnic on the lawn, write on the walls, dig the garden, paint and draw. William Wordsworth was inspired here – and there's even more to discover today. **Note**: disabled parking only on site. Follow directions from Miller Howe Café in centre of village.

Eating and shopping: at Allan Bank light lunches, snacks and tasty cakes are available from the kitchen. Picnics welcome in the gardens. Church Stile shop in Grasmere selling unusual gifts, local books and maps.

Allan Bank, Cumbria: a family picks the perfect spot to rest and take in the scenery

Making the most of your day: **Indoors** Drawing and painting, board games and children's activities. Mountaineering books in the Mountain Heritage Library. **Outdoors** Deckchairs, kitchen garden, woodland trail. Cycle trail along lakeshore (cycle storage at shop). **Dogs**: welcome indoors and out, under control.

Access: 🅿 🗺 📶 ♿ 🅹 Allan Bank 🚶 🏛 🐾
Countryside 🐾
Sat Nav: use LA22 9SW for nearest car park.
Parking: nearest in village, not National Trust (charge including members).

Finding out more: 015394 35143 or allanbank@nationaltrust.org.uk

Allan Bank and Grasmere		M	T	W	T	F	S	S
Allan Bank								
13 Feb–21 Feb	10:30–4	M	T	W	T	F	S	S
26 Feb–13 Mar	10:30–4	·	·	·	·	F	S	S
18 Mar–30 Oct	10–5	M	T	W	T	F	S	S
4 Nov–18 Dec	10:30–4	·	·	·	·	F	S	S
Grasmere gift shop								
2 Jan–7 Feb	11–4	·	·	·	·	·	S	S
13 Feb–30 Oct	10–5	M	T	W	T	F	S	S
4 Nov–16 Dec	11–4	·	·	·	·	F	S	S
17 Dec–31 Dec	10–5	M	T	W	T	F	S	S

Grasmere gift shop: closed 25 and 26 December.

Ambleside

near Windermere, Cumbria

[icons] 1927

Sitting on the northern tip of Lake Windermere, the town of Ambleside is surrounded by countryside. Skelghyll Woods are home to Cumbria's tallest trees. In spring, Stagshaw Gardens bursts into life with displays of azaleas and rhododendrons, and Jenkyn's Field is great for a lakeshore picnic and paddle.

Making the most of your day: Bridge House, Ambleside's smallest building, built on a bridge over a beck. Tall Tree Trail at Skelghyll Woods. Information panels at Ambleside Roman Fort and Stagshaw Gardens. Townend nearby. **Dogs**: welcome under close control (stock grazing).

Access: Bridge House [icons]
Sat Nav: use LA22 0HE for Stagshaw Gardens and Skelghyll Woods; LA22 9AN for Bridge House. **Parking**: at Stagshaw Gardens.

Finding out more: 015394 46402 or ambleside@nationaltrust.org.uk

Ambleside		M	T	W	T	F	S	S
Bridge House								
25 Mar–30 Oct	11:30–4:30	M	T	W	T	F	S	S
Stagshaw Gardens								
Open all year	Dawn–dusk	M	T	W	T	F	S	S

Stagshaw Gardens are at their best April to July.

Vivid blooms at Stagshaw Gardens, Ambleside (below), and the view from Arnside Knott (above), both in Cumbria

Arnside and Silverdale

near Arnside, Cumbria

[icons] 1929

With a wildlife-rich mosaic of limestone grassland, pavement, woodland and meadows this coastal countryside offers fine views over Morecambe Bay and miles of footpaths. Arnside Knott and Eaves Wood are home to butterflies and flowers; Jack Scout's cliffs are perfect for watching the setting sun or migrant birds passing through.

Eating and shopping: variety of small shops, galleries and cafés in and around Arnside and Silverdale villages (not National Trust). Nearest National Trust café at Sizergh.

Making the most of your day: toposcope viewpoint (short uphill from Arnside Knott car park). Silverdale Lots footpath to the cove perfect for strolls. Silverdale village heritage walk. **Dogs**: welcome under control (on leads where stock grazing).

Access: [icon]
Sat Nav: use LA5 0BP for Arnside Knott; LA5 0UG for Eaves Wood (Silverdale), both nearby. **Parking**: at Arnside Knott (signposted from Arnside Promenade) and Eaves Wood, Silverdale. Also in Silverdale village (not National Trust).

Finding out more: 01524 702815 or arnsidesilverdale@nationaltrust.org.uk

The Beatles' Childhood Homes

Woolton and Allerton, Liverpool

🏠 2002

A combined tour to Mendips and 20 Forthlin Road, the childhood homes of John Lennon and Paul McCartney, is your only opportunity to see inside the houses where The Beatles met, composed and rehearsed many of their earliest songs. You can walk through the back door into the kitchen and imagine John's Aunt Mimi cooking him his tea, or stand in the spot where Lennon and McCartney composed 'I Saw Her Standing There'. The custodians take you on a fascinating trip down memory lane in these two atmospheric period houses, so typical of Liverpool life in the 1950s. **Note**: handbags, cameras and recording equipment must be left in secure facilities at both houses. Access to these houses is by National Trust minibus tour only from Liverpool city centre or Speke Hall (charge including members).

Eating and shopping: guidebooks and postcards available at both houses and Speke Hall shop. Speke Hall's Home Farm restaurant serving regional specialities, such as Scouse and Wet Nelly.

The kitchen at John Lennon's childhood home, Mendips

Making the most of your day: departures from convenient pick-up points (city centre and Speke Hall). Our comfortable minibus and easy online booking service allow you to relax, as we take the strain out of visiting.

Access: 🖼️🎨🔲🎵📷 Building ♿
Parking: numerous car parks near collection point (not National Trust) for tours from city centre, or at Speke Hall for tours departing from there.

Finding out more: 0151 427 7231 (booking line) or thebeatleshomes@nationaltrust.org.uk

The Beatles' Childhood Homes	M	T	W	T	F	S	S
2 Mar–29 May	Tour*	·	·	W	T	F	S	S
1 Jun–30 Oct	Tour*	M	T	W	T	F	S	S
2 Nov–27 Nov	Tour*	·	·	W	T	F	S	S

*Admission by guided tour only. Times and pick-up locations vary (please visit website or call for details and tickets).

20 Forthlin Road, Liverpool: Paul McCartney's living room

Beatrix Potter Gallery and Hawkshead

Main Street, Hawkshead, Cumbria LA22 0NS

🏠 1944

Our all-new exhibition for 2016 celebrates the 150th anniversary of the birth of Beatrix Potter and displays original artwork inspired by her love of nature and passion for conserving her treasured Lake District. For a perfect day out, why not follow in Beatrix Potter's footsteps to Hill Top and then spend time outdoors? Hawkshead village is an excellent base for exploring the countryside that inspired Beatrix and many other artists, authors and poets. You can find more about the events and activities taking place to celebrate Beatrix's anniversary throughout 2016, on our website. **Note:** nearest toilet 300 yards in main village car park (not National Trust).

Eating and shopping: small shop in the Gallery selling a variety of Beatrix Potter items and our nearby corner shop stocks lots more local products and gifts. Meals and refreshments available at various pubs and cafés in Hawkshead village (none National Trust).

Making the most of your day: Indoors Original Beatrix Potter artwork on display. **Outdoors** Lots of walking routes around Hawkshead, including to Hill Top, Tarn Hows and Wray Castle, which are all nearby. **Dogs:** assistance dogs only.

Access: 🏢🎨📷📖🖼 **Gallery** 🏛🎫 **Parking:** 300 yards, not National Trust (charge including members).

Finding out more: 015394 36355 (gallery). 015394 36471 (shop) or beatrixpottergallery@nationaltrust.org.uk

Beatrix Potter Gallery/Hawkshead		M	T	W	T	F	S	S
Gallery								
13 Feb–24 Mar	10–3:30	M	T	W	T	·	S	S
26 Mar–26 May	10–4	M	T	W	T	·	S	S
28 May–28 Aug*	10–4	M	T	W	T	F	S	S
29 Aug–30 Oct	10–4	M	T	W	T	·	S	S
Shop								
2 Jan–7 Feb	10–4	·	·	·	·	·	S	S
13 Feb–30 Oct	10–5	M	T	W	T	F	S	S
31 Oct–24 Dec**	10–4	M	T	W	·	·	S	S

*Gallery: open to 5, weekdays, 30 May to 26 August; also open various Fridays throughout year. **Shop: open 22 and 23 December. At busy periods, timed entry system in operation. Hawkshead Courthouse: 26 March to 30 October, access by key from National Trust shop in Hawkshead, no parking facilities.

A new exhibition at the Beatrix Potter Gallery, Cumbria, celebrates the 150th anniversary of Beatrix Potter's birth

Borrowdale and Derwent Water

near Keswick, Cumbria

[icons] 1902

Derwent Water is often called the 'Queen of the Lakes', and as you canoe between the islands with your picnic at the ready it's easy to see why. The boardwalk across the wetlands completes the 10-mile circular lake walk, and the jewel in the crown is Derwent Island House, open to visitors for five special days each year. As Borrowdale winds the 7 miles from Keswick to Seathwaite, there are eight car parks from which you can start your adventure into the fells. Leaflets for iconic routes like Castle Crag and Cat Bells are available in our shop. **Note**: charges apply to members on Force Crag Mine and Derwent Island House open days.

Eating and shopping: Keswick lakeside shop and visitor centre offering local knowledge to help you plan your visit, plus souvenirs, cold drinks and ice-cream. New for this year, our red ice-cream bicycle at Friar's Crag. Selection of tenant-run cafés serving local treats.

A family looks out over Derwent Water from Ashes Wood, Cumbria (above), while visitors explore Force Crag Mine (below)

Making the most of your day: five days a year, you can don a hard-hat for a guided tour of Force Crag Mine processing mill. Windswept and atmospheric, it's a fascinating glimpse into Lakeland's industrial heritage. **Dogs**: under close control at lambing time.

Access: [icons] Derwent Island [icon]
Force Crag Mine [icons] Derwent Water foreshore [icons]
Sat Nav: use CA12 5DJ for Keswick lakeside shop and CA12 5XN for Seatoller (at foot of Honister Pass). **Parking**: at Great Wood, Ashness Bridge, Surprise View, Watendlath, Kettlewell, Bowder Stone, Rosthwaite, Seatoller and Honister Pass.

Finding out more: 01768 774649 or borrowdale@nationaltrust.org.uk

Borrowdale and Derwent Water		M	T	W	T	F	S	S
Shop and information centre								
13 Feb–24 Mar	10–4	M	T	W	T	F	S	S
25 Mar–30 Oct	10–5	M	T	W	T	F	S	S
31 Oct–28 Nov	10–4	M	·	·	·	F	S	S

Shop: open first three weekends in December, 10 to 4.
Visit website for Force Crag Mine and Derwent Island House open days.

Buttermere Valley

near Cockermouth, Cumbria

🍴 🏛 📷 ♿ 🛏 🏕 1935

Whether you start your day at Buttermere, Crummock Water or Loweswater, the Buttermere Valley offers low-level lakeshore walks on accessible footpaths. The high fell ridges around Red Pike and cascading waterfalls make for both seriously impressive backdrops to your holiday snaps and some satisfyingly adventurous ridgeline walking. **Note**: toilets at Buttermere only. For Holmewood bothy bookings please see nationaltrust.org.uk/camping.

Eating and shopping: pubs and cafés in hamlets of Buttermere and Loweswater (none National Trust). Farm in Buttermere selling homemade ice-cream and café serving Butterbeer (neither National Trust).

Buttermere Valley, Cumbria (above and below), offers plenty of space for adventure and discovery

Making the most of your day: Holmewood bothy is a unique place for a camping holiday. In the heart of the woodland and right on Loweswater lakeshore, this is really getting away from it all. **Dogs**: under close control at lambing time.

Access: 🅿 Lakeshore path ➡
Sat Nav: use CA13 9UZ for Buttermere; CA13 0RT for Crummock Water; CA13 0RU for Loweswater. **Parking**: at Honister Pass, Buttermere village, Rannerdale, Cinderdale, Lanthwaite Green, Lanthwaite Wood near Crummock Water and Maggies Bridge at Loweswater.

Finding out more: 01768774649 or buttermere@nationaltrust.org.uk

Claife Viewing Station and Windermere West Shore

near Far Sawrey, Cumbria LA22 0LW

🏛 ♿ 👶 🐕 1962

Why not take to the water on the ferry from Bowness and explore the newly restored Claife Viewing Station and its courtyard, just as early 18th-century tourists to the Lakes did? A new platform in the Viewing Station gives impressive panoramic views of Windermere and the Lakeland fells that have been hidden for years. With 4 miles of lakeshore path towards Wray Castle to explore on bike or on foot, the western shore of Windermere is perfect for a car-free adventure. You can go on to Ambleside, or jump on the Bike Boat and cross the lake to Bowness.

Note: toilets at nearby Ferry House, none at the Viewing Station. Bike Boat (not National Trust) run by Windermere Lake Cruises, summer season only.

Eating and shopping: cosy café in the courtyard open most days at Claife Viewing Station serving tasty homemade cakes and award-winning coffee. Café at Wray Castle also serving cakes, sandwiches, snacks and drinks. Picnics welcome anywhere along the West Shore.

Making the most of your day: why not arrive by boat then stroll up to the Viewing Station to witness fantastic lake views? Lots of events and activities planned throughout 2016. **Dogs**: allowed in countryside, under close control.

Windermere west shore, Cumbria: the path to Claife Viewing Station (above) and the courtyard (below)

Access: Viewing Station 🦽 Café 🚻 🚹
Sat Nav: use LA22 0LP for Ash Landing; LA22 0LR Harrowslack; LA22 0JH Red Nab (all nearby). **Parking**: at Ash Landing and Harrowslack, near Windermere lakeshore, for Claife Viewing Station and at Red Nab.

Finding out more: 015394 41456 or claife@nationaltrust.org.uk

	M	T	W	T	F	S	S
Claife Viewing Station							
Low Wray Campsite							
21 Mar–30 Oct*	M	T	W	T	F	S	S

*For detailed opening times and bookings please visit ntlakescampsites.org.uk

Dalton Castle

Market Place, Dalton-in-Furness, Cumbria LA15 8AX

🏚 1965

Formerly the manorial courthouse of Furness Abbey, this eye-catching 14th-century tower was built to assert the Abbot's authority. **Note**: opened on behalf of the National Trust by the Friends of Dalton Castle. Parking in Dalton town centre (not National Trust). Open Saturdays, 26 March to 24 September, 2 to 5.

Finding out more: 015395 60951 or daltoncastle@nationaltrust.org.uk

Dunham Massey

Altrincham, Cheshire WA14 4SJ

🏠✝🏰❄♟🍴 1976

In 1856 Victorian carriages rolled along the avenues of Dunham's deer-park laden with the family's most treasured possessions. Having suffered the rejection of Cheshire society, Catharine, a former circus performer, and her husband, the 7th Earl, left Dunham and never returned. We take you on Catharine and George Harry's journey to consider what it might be like to leave this home. The newly opened historic stable buildings reveal the comings and goings of the family and their workers, the importance of horses and later the motor car. 'Stitches in Time': from fancy dress to curtains, this display showcases some of our amazing textiles. **Note**: everyone (including members) requires house/garden ticket (and, for house, timed token) – from reception on day.

Eating and shopping: café with indoor and outdoor seating and a large shop selling locally sourced products, food, crafts, and an enticing garden and plant selection, at visitor centre. Stables Restaurant (serving hot lunches) and ice-cream parlour (hours vary).

Making the most of your day: new – the historic stable buildings tell stories of the wider estate. Our herd of fallow deer wander amongst tree-lined avenues in the park. A garden for all seasons awaits: from a large maturing winter garden and a carpet of spring bulbs, to a rose garden full of perfume in summer and an array of vivid autumnal colour. The mill – the oldest building on the estate – celebrates its 400th anniversary. Free guided walks in the garden and deer-park. Events all year round, including open-air theatre and garden parties. Family activities during school holidays. Cycling for under-fives.
Dogs: welcome under close control and on leads in deer-park.

Dunham Massey, Cheshire: seen from the air (below), the full glory of the mansion and parkland becomes clear

Visitors meet one of the gentle fallow deer (opposite)

Ennerdale

Cleator, Cumbria

🏠🏛️♿ 1927

Home of the Wild Ennerdale project with 30 miles of traffic-free tracks and paths – the quiet side of Lakeland. **Note**: sorry no toilet. For Sat Nav use CA23 3AU for Bowness Knott and CA23 3AS for Bleach Green.

Finding out more: 017687 74649 or ennerdale@nationaltrust.org.uk

Eskdale and Duddon Valley

Eskdale, near Ravenglass; Duddon Valley, near Broughton in Furness, Cumbria

✝🏠🏛️♿♿🐾🔭 1926

Eskdale (below) is a valley of contrasts, with upper Eskdale leading to the high mountains, including Scafell, Esk Pike and Bowfell. On the valley floor are meandering riverside and woodland paths. Across high mountain passes lies the Duddon Valley. A diverse landscape with wildflower meadows, woodlands, mountains, hill farms and rivers.

Eating and shopping: pubs at Eskdale Green, Boot and Seathwaite; shops at Eskdale Green, Boot and Ulpha Post Office; café and shop at Dalegarth station (none National Trust).

Access: 🅿️🅿️♿♿♿♿♿🅿️📷♿👓🅿️
House ♿♿♿ Garden and park ♿➡️♿♿
Parking: 200 yards.

Finding out more: 0161 942 3989 (Infoline). 0161 941 1025 or dunhammassey@nationaltrust.org.uk

Dunham Massey		M	T	W	T	F	S	S
House								
27 Feb–30 Oct	11–5*	M	T	W	·	·	S	S
Café and shop								
1 Jan–26 Feb	10–4	M	T	W	T	F	S	S
27 Feb–30 Oct	10–5	M	T	W	T	F	S	S
31 Oct–31 Dec	10–4	M	T	W	T	F	S	S
Garden**								
Open all year	11–5:30	M	T	W	T	F	S	S
Park†								
Open all year	9–5	M	T	W	T	F	S	S
Mill								
27 Feb–30 Oct	12–4	M	T	W	·	·	S	S

*House: last entry one hour before closing, or dusk if earlier. Open Good Friday. **Garden: 1 January to 26 February and 31 October to 31 December closes at 4, or dusk if earlier; extended opening of garden on some summer evenings. †Gates and car park: March to October open to 7:30. White Cottage open on last Sunday of the month, 27 March to 30 October, 2 to 5 (booking essential on 0161 928 0075). Dunham Massey closed 23 November and 25 December (including car park).

Making the most of your day: walks from the La'al Ratty Railway, running through Eskdale (Ravenglass to Dalegarth). Hardknott Roman Fort to explore. Woodland paths in Duddon Valley. Upland walks to Harter Fell and Seathwaite Tarn. **Dogs**: well-behaved dogs welcome. Please follow local and seasonal guidance.

Access: 🦽
Parking: in lay-bys, along roadsides and at some small village car parks (not National Trust).

Finding out more: 019467 23466 or eskdaleandduddon@nationaltrust.org.uk

Note: building works possible later in the year. Launch/slipway facilities available for a wide variety of craft, charges apply (including members).

Eating and shopping: Boathouse Café serving hot and cold drinks, soup and snacks, homemade cakes and pastries. A small selection of children's toys, gifts, maps, picnic rugs and seasonal goods available in the shop. Picnics welcome.

Making the most of your day: seasonal rowing boat hire, April to October (weather permitting). Events. Adventure playground, new Discovery Cottage and easy lake access with 'beach' for paddling. Quiet spots and easy meadow walk. **Dogs**: welcome on leads.

Fell Foot

Newby Bridge, Windermere, Cumbria

🏠♿🍴 1948

Sitting on the southern tip of Lake Windermere with views across the water to the mountains above, this family-friendly park has green lawns sloping down to the lakeshore that are a great place for playing, a picnic or barbecue. It offers the perfect opportunity to get outdoors, stroll along the lakeshore or explore, and is one of the best spots to soak up Windermere in all its beauty. With easy lake access, the park is ideal for paddling, swimming and boating. If you want to take to the water, then boats can be hired from the Boathouse Café.

Fell Foot, Cumbria (above and below): this family-friendly park offers so many activities that you'll be spoilt for choice

Why not share your pictures with us? #nationaltrust

Access: ⓟ ⓓ ⓦ ⓜ ⓐ **Grounds** ⓖ ⓗ
Sat Nav: use LA12 8NN. **Parking:** two large car parks on site.

Finding out more: 015395 31273 or fellfoot@nationaltrust.org.uk

Fell Foot		M	T	W	T	F	S	S
Park								
1 Jan–24 Mar	9–5	M	T	W	T	F	S	S
25 Mar–4 Sep	8–7*	M	T	W	T	F	S	S
5 Sep–31 Dec	9–5	M	T	W	T	F	S	S
Catering and retail facilities								
12 Feb–24 Mar	11–4	M	T	W	T	F	S	S
25 Mar–4 Sep	10–5**	M	T	W	T	F	S	S
5 Sep–30 Oct	11–4	M	T	W	T	F	S	S

*Last admission 6:30. ** Saturdays open from 9. Boat hire available daily, April to October (weather permitting).

Formby

near Formby, Liverpool

🏛🏖🚴🦌 1967

Formby's shifting sands create ever-changing dunes sculpted by the wind and squeezed by surging tides. Sea views over Liverpool Bay to the hills of North Wales can be enjoyed from the wide sandy beaches. Footprint trails 5,000 years old, sometimes reappear as the sea erodes ancient mudflats. Pinewood walks with red squirrels lead to open fields and the Formby Asparagus Trail. Formby is a place for a simple family day out, for healthy exercise and relaxation and a perfect spot for a seaside picnic. **Note:** toilets close at 5:15 in summer, 4 in winter.

Eating and shopping: ice-cream, soft drinks, coffee and confectionery available from mobile vans. A favourite place for picnics. Safe barbecue area is available at the family picnic site.

Making the most of your day: self-guided trails, including the Formby Asparagus Trail and the Asparagus Cycle Trail. Guided walks. Circular and longer walks linked to the Sefton Coastal Path. Orienteering and geocaching. **Dogs:** on a lead on Squirrel Walk and under close control elsewhere (vulnerable wildlife).

Access: ⓟ ⓦ ⓐ ⓑ ⓐ **Grounds** ⓗ ➡
Sat Nav: use L37 1LJ. **Parking:** on site.

Finding out more: 01704 878591 or formby@nationaltrust.org.uk

Formby		M	T	W	T	F	S	S
Car park								
1 Jan–31 Jan	9–4	M	T	W	T	F	S	S
1 Feb–27 Mar	9–4:45	M	T	W	T	F	S	S
28 Mar–25 Sep	9–5:15	M	T	W	T	F	S	S
26 Sep–27 Nov	9–4:45	M	T	W	T	F	S	S
28 Nov–31 Dec	9–4	M	T	W	T	F	S	S

Closed 25 December.

Fun in the sea (above), and a cycling adventure in the pinewoods (below), at Formby, Liverpool

Gawthorpe Hall

Burnley Road, Padiham, near Burnley, Lancashire BB12 8UA

🏠♿ 1972

This imposing house, set in the heart of urban Lancashire, contains fabulously opulent interiors, created by Sir Charles Barry in the 19th century. The Hall displays textiles from the Gawthorpe Textile Collection, including needlework, lace and embroidery, while outside the grounds are popular with dog walkers. **Note**: financed and run in partnership with Lancashire County Council.

Eating and shopping: tea-room serving light snacks.

Making the most of your day: Indoors Guided tours, talks and exhibitions. Events all year, including Victorian Christmas. **Outdoors** Open-air theatre in July and other events, including some for children. **Dogs**: under close control in grounds.

Access: 🅿️♿🚻📷♿📷
Building 🅰️ Grounds 🅰️🅰️🅰️➡️
Parking: 150 yards, narrow access road (passing places).

Finding out more: 01282 771004 or gawthorpehall@nationaltrust.org.uk

Gawthorpe Hall		M	T	W	T	F	S	S
House and tea-room*								
20 Apr–30 Oct	11–5	·	·	**W**	**T**	**F**	**S**	**S**
Grounds								
Open all year	8–7	M	T	W	T	F	S	S

Hall and tea-room open Bank Holidays. *House opens at 12, opening times subject to change. Following last year's maintenance works, please check the website for up-to-date information.

Gawthorpe Hall, Lancashire: Jacobean plasterwork detail

The Hardmans' House

59 Rodney Street, Liverpool, Merseyside L1 9ER

🏠 2003

Behind the imposing Georgian exterior of 59 Rodney Street lies a perfect 1950s time capsule. Uncover the life, work and pastimes of the renowned photographer E. Chambré Hardman and his talented wife Margaret in their glamorous photographic studio and modest home. For your comfort admission by timed tours only. **Note**: admission by guided tour only – booking advised. Entrance on Pilgrim Street at rear of property.

Eating and shopping: shop selling unique photographic prints, postcards, guidebooks and hot drinks. The nearest café (not National Trust) is just a short walk away at the Anglican Cathedral.

The darkroom at The Hardmans' House in Liverpool

Making the most of your day: tours (book your place to avoid disappointment). Family trail. Virtual tour of the house. New temporary exhibition for 2016. Walking trails of Hardman's Liverpool available online.

Access: ☒☒☒☒☒☒☒☒ Building ☒
Parking: none on site. Car parks at Anglican Cathedral and Slater Street, not National Trust (charge including members).

Finding out more: 0151 709 6261 or thehardmanshouse@nationaltrust.org.uk

The Hardmans' House		M	T	W	T	F	S	S
16 Mar–29 Oct	11–3:30	·	·	**W**	**T**	**F**	**S**	·

Admission by timed ticket only, booking advisable (places limited). Open Bank Holiday Mondays.

Hare Hill

Over Alderley, Macclesfield, Cheshire SK10 4PY

✸ ☒ 1978

From spring through to autumn, this woodland garden full of twists and turns and hares and hives awaits to be discovered. At its heart the stunning Walled White Garden blooms in late summer and offers an oasis of peace and calm where you can play, amble around or relax in.

Eating and shopping: external catering at weekends and Bank Holidays only. Hot drinks vending machine within the garden at all other times. Picnics welcome in the garden. Plants for sale. Small second-hand bookstall.

Enjoying a quiet moment at Hare Hill, Cheshire

Playing croquet on the lawn at Hare Hill

Making the most of your day: carved wooden hare trail throughout the garden and bird-spotting in the hide. You can play a game of croquet in the walled garden or enjoy events throughout the season. **Dogs**: assistance dogs only in the garden. On leads and under close control elsewhere.

Access: ☒☒☒ Grounds ☒
Sat Nav: use SK10 4PY to take you 109 yards west of car park. **Parking**: on site.

Finding out more: 01625 584412 or harehill@nationaltrust.org.uk

Hare Hill		M	T	W	T	F	S	S
1 Mar–30 Oct	10–5	·	**T**	**W**	**T**	**F**	**S**	**S**

Open Bank Holiday Mondays. Last admission one hour before closing. Car park: closes at 5. Please note: landscaping work due to start beginning of year – spring opening may be delayed (please check website prior to visit).

Heysham Coast

Heysham, near Morecambe, Lancashire

☒ ☒ ☒ ☒ 1996

A beautiful sandstone walk in coastal grassland and peaceful woodland, leading to a unique ruined Saxon chapel and rock-cut graves. **Note**: nearest facilities in village (not National Trust); park in the main village car park. For Sat Nav use LA3 2RW.

Finding out more: 01524 701178 or heysham@nationaltrust.org.uk

Hill Top

Near Sawrey, Hawkshead, Ambleside,
Cumbria LA22 0LF

🏠 🍴 ❄ 1944

Hill Top is a time capsule of Beatrix Potter's life
and is still full of her favourite things. This year,
with the celebration of the 150th anniversary of
her birth, a visit to her beloved house, the
inspiration for many of her tales, is a 'must'. As
you follow in her footsteps, this small house,
with fragile interiors, excites the senses. Our
website and Facebook page are the best places
to visit for details about what's on. Hill Top can
be very busy and visitors may sometimes have
to wait to enter the house. Beatrix's colourful
garden is always accessible. **Note**: timed-ticket
entry system operating, early sell-outs possible
when particularly busy.

Eating and shopping: neighbouring Sawrey
House Hotel and Tower Bank Arms (neither
National Trust) serving meals, afternoon tea and
refreshments. The Hill Top shop sells an
expansive range of Beatrix Potter books and
collectables, including items exclusive to Hill Top.

Wisteria-clad Hill Top, Cumbria (below), Beatrix Potter's
beloved house. Where better to read her tales (above)?

Making the most of your day: in this special
anniversary year, combine Hill Top with a visit
to nearby Hawkshead and the Beatrix Potter
Gallery, to see a collection of her original
artwork on display. **Dogs**: assistance dogs only.

Access: 🅿 🏞 🖼 ♿ ⦙⦙ ⊘
House 🔣 🔣 Shop 🔣 Garden 🔣 ➡
Parking: limited and for visitors to Hill Top only.

Finding out more: 015394 36269.
015394 36801 (shop) or
hilltop@nationaltrust.org.uk

Hill Top		M	T	W	T	F	S	S
House								
13 Feb–24 Mar	10–3:30	M	T	W	T	·	S	S
26 Mar–26 May	10–4:30	M	T	W	T	·	S	S
28 May–28 Aug*	10–4:30	M	T	W	T	F	S	S
29 Aug–30 Oct	10–4:30	M	T	W	T	·	S	S
Shop and garden								
13 Feb–24 Mar	10–4	M	T	W	T	F	S	S
25 Mar–30 Oct**	10–5	M	T	W	T	F	S	S
31 Oct–23 Dec	10–4	M	T	W	T	F	S	S

*House: open to 5:30, 30 May to 25 August, Monday to
Thursday. **Shop and garden: open to 5:45, 30 May to
25 August, Monday to Thursday. House entry by timed ticket
(places limited). Small car park. Access to garden and shop
free during opening hours. Check website for details of
special openings and advance bookings.

Keld Chapel

Keld Lane, Shap, Cumbria CA10 3NW

✚ | 1918 |

With its rustic stone floor and walls, this 16th-century chapel is thought to have been the chantry for Shap Abbey. **Note**: sorry no facilities. Access daily (for key, see the notice on chapel door). For Sat Nav use CA10 3NW. Open daily, dawn to dusk.

Finding out more: 017683 61893 or keldchapel@nationaltrust.org.uk

Little Moreton Hall

Congleton, Cheshire CW12 4SD

🏠 ✚ 🏛 ✿ | 1938 |

The Cheshire-based Moreton family certainly experienced the highs and lows of life in the 16th century. Throughout the last 500 years this timber-framed hall, surrounded by a moat and set within a small pretty garden, survived the Civil War, spent 250 years tenanted, was in serious danger of falling over and is as intriguing as it is wonky! Colourful Tudor times are brought to life through fantastic guided tours, traditional festivals and celebrations. A rare pre-Reformation chapel, topsy-turvy long gallery and early wallpaper ensure the genuine 'wow' factor is experienced more than once at this iconic Tudor treasure.

Eating and shopping: The Little Tea Room with outdoor orchard seating and Mrs Dale's Pantry serve yummy homemade food produced in the on-site bakery. Ice-cream kiosk (open on sunny days). Large shop in the car park selling gifts, refreshments and local products.

Making the most of your day: **Indoors** Free guided tours. Tudor-themed daily craft activities. Costumes to try on. Exhibitions and family trails. **Outdoors** Theatre in the summer and Yuletide celebrations in December.

Children on the lawn outside the delightfully wonky Little Moreton Hall, Cheshire (above and top)

Dogs: on leads in car park and front lawn only.

Access: 🅿️ 📖 🚪 🛗 🪑 📷 🎦 🎧 👓
Hall 🛗 🪜 🪜 ♿ **Reception** 🪜 ♿
Grounds 🛗 🪜 🪜 ▶
Parking: 100 yards.

Finding out more: 01260 272018 or littlemoretonhall@nationaltrust.org.uk

Little Moreton Hall		M	T	W	T	F	S	S
13 Feb–21 Feb	11–5	M	T	W	T	F	S	S
24 Feb–27 Mar	11–5	·	·	W	T	F	S	S
28 Mar–17 Apr	11–5	M	T	W	T	F	S	S
20 Apr–29 May	11–5	·	·	W	T	F	S	S
30 May–5 Jun	11–5	M	T	W	T	F	S	S
8 Jun–24 Jul	11–5	·	·	W	T	F	S	S
25 Jul–4 Sep	11–5	M	T	W	T	F	S	S
7 Sep–23 Oct	11–5	·	·	W	T	F	S	S
24 Oct–30 Oct	11–5	M	T	W	T	F	S	S
5 Nov–18 Dec	11–4	·	·	·	·	·	S	S

Open Bank Holiday Mondays. Upper floors may close early if light levels are poor.

North West and the Lakes

Lyme, Cheshire: built to impress, the lavish interiors of this imposing mansion hold delights for even the youngest visitor

Lyme

Disley, Stockport, Cheshire SK12 2NR

🏠✝❄♿🏠➡ 1947

Much-loved home of the Legh family for more than 600 years, Lyme sits in 570 hectares (1,400 acres) of parkland, with glorious views across Manchester and the Cheshire Plain. Its lavish interiors reflect the life of a great estate, from its earliest beginnings to its Edwardian 'Golden Era' – the heyday of aristocratic life, with its social whirl of parties, all of which ended with the start of the First World War. You may recognise Lyme as 'Pemberley' from the BBC adaptation of *Pride and Prejudice*, starring Colin Firth, and the 'Big House' in series two of *The Village*. Lyme's ever-changing gardens, with the Reflection Lake, Orangery and Rose Garden, are an ideal place to relax and stroll. **Note**: owned and managed by the National Trust, but partly financed by Stockport Metropolitan Borough Council.

Eating and shopping: restaurant serving light snacks, lunches and desserts. Servants' Hall Tea-Room offers drinks and sweet treats; Timber Yard Café snacks, cakes and drinks. Salting Room Tea Parlour and Garden – full afternoon tea – booking essential. Gift, book and plant shop. Pre-loved bookshop.

Making the most of your day: **Indoors** Activities such as reading in the Library, home to the 15th-century *Lyme Missal* – a rare Caxton prayer book – taking part in Edwardian theatricals in the Long Gallery, dressing-up in Edwardian costumes in the wardrobe department, writing a letter in the Morning Room or visiting Mr Truelove the Butler's rooms 'below stairs'. **Outdoors** Regular Saturday park runs, family orienteering course (changes every month), self-led woodland and moorland walks, adventurous play in Crow Wood Playscape for five- to twelve-year-olds. Sensory play area in garden for under fives. Events, including Easter trails, summer holiday activities, Hallowe'en and Christmas celebrations. **Dogs**: under close control in park; leads near livestock and vehicles; selected days in garden.

Access: 🅿🚗♿🚾🔔📷🎬📺🔊∴🔎
House 🦽♿🚶 Garden 🦽♿🦽➡🚶

The Cage: Elizabethan hunting tower in Lyme's park

Parking: 200 yards.

Finding out more: 01663 762023 or lyme@nationaltrust.org.uk

Lyme		M	T	W	T	F	S	S
House*								
15 Feb–30 Oct	11–5	M	T	·	·	F	S	S
Garden, shop and tea-rooms								
15 Feb–30 Oct	11–5	M	T	W	T	F	S	S
Winter courtyard, shop and tea-room**								
2 Jan–14 Feb	11–3	·	·	·	·	·	S	S
5 Nov–31 Dec	11–3	·	·	·	·	·	S	S
Park†								
1 Jan–29 Mar	8:30–6	M	T	W	T	F	S	S
30 Mar–4 Oct	8–8	M	T	W	T	F	S	S
5 Oct–31 Dec	8:30–6	M	T	W	T	F	S	S
Park: Timber Yard, café and shop								
1 Jan–14 Feb	10–4	M	T	W	T	F	S	S
15 Feb–30 Oct	10–5	M	T	W	T	F	S	S
31 Oct–31 Dec	10–4	M	T	W	T	F	S	S

*Last entry one hour before closing; 25 July to 4 September, also open Thursdays. **Open 1 January. Closed 25 December. †Park gates locked at closing.

Nether Alderley Mill

Congleton Road, Nether Alderley, Macclesfield, Cheshire SK10 4TW

🏚 1950

Concealed under the long sloping roof of this medieval building (below) is a fully restored, working corn mill. Inside, as the waterwheels turn, huge millstones grind the flour. On the guided tours, centuries-old graffiti can be spotted and you can discover more about the life of a miller. **Note**: view by guided tour only. Uneven floor, steep stairs and low ceilings throughout. Limited parking.

Eating and shopping: small range of souvenirs available. Sorry no toilets or food outlets at this property. Nearest National Trust facilities at nearby Alderley Edge.

Access: 🅿 🖥 🚻 Building ♿
Parking: limited.

Finding out more: 01625 527468 or netheralderleymill@nationaltrust.org.uk

Nether Alderley Mill		M	T	W	T	F	S	S
7 Apr–2 Oct	1–4:30	·	·	·	T	·	S	S

Access by guided tour only. Last tour 3:45.

Quarry Bank

Styal, Wilmslow, Cheshire SK9 4LA

🖼️🌸🏚️🔔🍴 1939

When Samuel Greg built Quarry Bank at the beginning of the Industrial Revolution, he founded not only a mill but a whole community. The daily grind of workers is echoed in the Mill with its clattering looms, hissing steam engines and relentless turning of the waterwheel. This contrasts with the quiet pleasures enjoyed by the Gregs in the picturesque garden, where rhododendrons flower by the river. At the Apprentice House, the life of a pauper child is revealed; and visitors can follow the workers' journey home to their cottages in Styal village. In 2016, our major Heritage Lottery-funded project gives the opportunity to witness conservation in action, as the glasshouse and kitchen garden are restored, revealing their compelling stories. **Note**: steep hill with 61 steps from car park.

Quarry Bank, Cheshire (above and below), is one of Britain's greatest industrial heritage sites

Please display your current sticker for free parking

Eating and shopping: shop selling gifts, including fabric and glass cloths produced in the mill. Café serving lunches and afternoon tea. Drinks and snacks available from the Pantry (during busy periods). New café and shop opening in the garden this year. Picnic areas.

Making the most of your day: **Indoors** Series of changing exhibitions throughout the year. Activities for all the family in the school holidays and trails all year round in the Mill. **Outdoors** 2016 is the year we celebrate the Quarry Bank Garden – explore themes including food production, garden design, play and pleasure. Walks leaflets are available for the woods which include both challenging hikes and gentle strolls. The gardens and woods are also great places for children to enjoy some of the '50 things to do before you're 11¾'. **Dogs**: welcome under close control on estate. On leads in garden, Mill Yard and Meadow.

Access: 🅿️♿🔊🦽🏼🎨📺🔦🐾

Building 🏼🏼♿ Grounds ♿➡️📷

Parking: 200 yards (steep hill).

Finding out more: 01625 527468 or quarrybankmill@nationaltrust.org.uk

Quarry Bank		M	T	W	T	F	S	S
Mill, Apprentice House, shop and café								
1 Jan–12 Feb	10:30–3:30	·	·	W	T	F	S	S
13 Feb–30 Oct	10:30–5	M	T	W	T	F	S	S
2 Nov–31 Dec	10:30–4	·	·	W	T	F	S	S
Garden								
13 Feb–30 Oct	10:30–5*	M	T	W	T	F	S	S

Completely closed 4 to 15 January for essential maintenance. Closed 24 and 25 December, open daily 26 December to 1 January 2017. Apprentice House: limited availability, early arrival advised. Popular destination for schools. *Garden closes dusk if earlier.

An ironing lesson in the Apprentice House kitchen

Rufford Old Hall, Lancashire: Shakespeare connections?

Rufford Old Hall

200 Liverpool Road, Rufford, near Ormskirk, Lancashire L40 1SG

🏠❀🏛️ 1936

With 500 years of the Hesketh family history and 80 years of National Trust ownership, Rufford Old Hall has plenty of stories to tell. Its Tudor Great Hall hosted theatrical productions in Shakespeare's time. Did Shakespeare himself spend a short time at Rufford in his youth? And what was the 'moveable' screen used for in the Great Hall? Why not find the answer to these questions yourself and discover Rufford's fascinating past. Victorian-style garden and grounds offering seasonal displays of colours with carpets of bluebells in spring and golden leaves in autumn and views across the Leeds & Liverpool Canal.

Eating and shopping: you can experience local tastes with Lancashire tea in the Victorian tea-room. The shop offers special treats, including Lancashire sauce, Lancashire crisps and plenty of gifts to keep memories of Rufford Old Hall fresh.

Making the most of your day: **Indoors** Daily house talks and seasonal children's trail. Christmas experience with Santa's Grotto. **Outdoors** Guided garden tours. Events, including open-air theatre. Seasonal children's trails and Tudor and Victorian games. **Dogs**: on leads in courtyard and woodland only.

Access: 🅿️ ♿ ⬚ ⬚ ⬚ ⬚ 📷 ⬚ ⬚
Building ⬚ ⬚ ⬚ ⬚ ⬚ **Grounds** ⬚ ⬚ ⬚ ➡️ ⬚
Parking: on site.

Finding out more: 01704 821254 or
ruffordoldhall@nationaltrust.org.uk

Rufford Old Hall		M	T	W	T	F	S	S
13 Feb–21 Feb	11–4	M	T	W	T	F	S	S
22 Feb–20 Mar	11–4	M	T	W	.	.	S	S
21 Mar–3 Apr	11–5	M	T	W	.	.	S	S
4 Apr–24 Apr	11–5	M	T	W	T	F	S	S
25 Apr–29 May	11–5	M	T	W	.	.	S	S
30 May–5 Jun	11–5	M	T	W	T	.	S	S
6 Jun–24 Jul	11–5	M	T	W	.	.	S	S
25 Jul–28 Aug*	11–5	M	T	W	T	F	S	S
29 Aug–23 Oct	11–5	M	T	W	.	.	S	S
24 Oct–6 Nov	11–5	M	T	W	T	F	S	S
12 Nov–18 Dec	11–4	.	.	.	.	.	S	S

Open Good Friday. Car park closes 30 minutes after times
above. Tudor Great Hall occasionally closed until 1 for
weddings. *Property closed on Friday 12 August due to
private event.

Sandscale Haws National Nature Reserve

near Barrow-in-Furness, Cumbria

⬚ ⬚ 1984

Home to natterjack toads, these wild,
grass-covered sand dunes and beach are the
perfect habitat for rare wildlife. **Note**: toilets
(not National Trust). Car park open all year
(height restriction). For Sat Nav use LA14 4QJ.

Finding out more: 01229 462855 or
sandscalehaws@nationaltrust.org.uk

Cyclists and young gardeners at Sizergh, Cumbria

Sizergh

Sizergh, near Kendal, Cumbria LA8 8DZ

🏠 🍴 🏛️ ✳️ ⬚ ⬚ 1950

With more than 750 years of history and
centuries-old portraits sitting alongside
modern family photographs, this medieval
house has been home to the Strickland family.
It is surrounded by rich gardens and a
647-hectare (1,600-acre) estate combining a
newly created wetland, limestone pastures,
orchards and semi-natural woodland, all
inhabited by a rich variety of wildlife, including
the rare hawfinch. There is a limestone rock
garden, where colours change with the
seasons, and its timeless atmosphere makes
this the perfect place to relax. Sizergh has
many tales to tell and it is an unexpected
treasure on the edge of the Lake District.
Note: some opening restrictions apply.
Separate admissions charges may apply for
tours or special events.

Eating and shopping: contemporary licensed
café serving a selection of hot and cold drinks,
meals, snacks and cakes. Shop selling local
products, home accessories, gifts, toys and
plants. Nearby Strickland Arms pub (tenant-run).

Making the most of your day: Indoors
Exhibitions, virtual and guided tours, and
Elizabethan carving of international
significance. **Outdoors** The garden includes the
National Trust's largest limestone rock garden,
four National Collections of Hardy Ferns and a
kitchen garden with bees and hens. The
orchard features over 50 varieties of apple,
some rare and local. A walk through Brigsteer
Wood will take you to a newly created wetland
area and bird hide at Park End Moss. A
bird-feeding station, as well as a network of
footpaths, guided walks and orienteering, are
available in the wider estate. Children can enjoy
a natural play trail and quizzes. **Dogs:** welcome
on estate footpaths (on leads where stock
grazing). House/garden: assistance dogs only.

Access: 🅿️ 🐕 ♿ 🚻 📶 🔍 📺 🎧
Building 🔦 🏚 ♿ Grounds 🚶 ➡️ ♿ ♿
Sat Nav: use LA8 8DZ. **Parking:** 250 yards.

Finding out more: 015395 60951 or
sizergh@nationaltrust.org.uk

Sizergh		M	T	W	T	F	S	S
House*								
6 Mar–30 Oct	12–4	M	T	W	T	·	·	S
Garden, café and shop**								
9 Jan–5 Mar	10–4	M	T	W	T	F	S	S
6 Mar–30 Oct	10–5	M	T	W	T	F	S	S
31 Oct–31 Dec	10–4	M	T	W	T	F	S	S
Estate								
Open all year	9–6†	M	T	W	T	F	S	S

*Guided house tours at 11 and 11:20 (approximately
45 minutes, places limited, £1 per person; tickets to be
collected from reception at least 15 minutes before the tour).
**Parts of garden closed Friday and Saturday in January,
February, November and December. †Closes at 4:30 in winter.
Car park: open 9 to 4:30, 1 January to 6 March and 31 October
to 31 December. Closed 25 December.

The grounds at Sizergh are perfect for
an active day out or quiet reflection

Speke Hall

Speke, Liverpool L24 1XD

🏠 ❋ ♨ ❦ 🛡 ♟ 1944

Speke Hall is a cherished Tudor mansion –
an oasis of beauty, atmosphere and surprise.
Built by the Catholic Norris family during the
unsettled Tudor period, the house has several
hidden security features, including a priest's hole
and eavesdrop. Following years of neglect
(including a spell when it was used as a cowshed),
interiors were revived in a cosy Arts and
Crafts-style during the Victorian push for
improvement. Today you can relax in inviting
gardens and woodland, with seasonal displays of
rhododendrons and bluebells – a tranquil escape
from modern life. The adjacent coastal reserve,
along the shore of the River Mersey, is perfect for
bracing strolls and wildlife walks. Discovering
400 years of history will take a full day.

Eating and shopping: Home Farm Restaurant
serving regional specialities, including Scouse
and Wet Nelly, Stable tea-room offering hot
drinks and homemade cakes. Locally sourced
gifts, as well as plants and books available in
the gift shop.

Making the most of your day: **Indoors**
Costumed guided tours, Victorian billiards to
play. A tricky trail to solve. Hallowe'en, Tudor
and Victorian Christmas events. **Outdoors**
Formal and recently restored kitchen gardens.
The coastal and woodland walks are great to
explore whatever the weather. Why not lose
yourself in the Victorian maze, get stuck into
building a den, climbing, or riding the zip wire
in the woodland play area? Exciting range of
sports activities for all abilities. Easter Egg
hunts, May Day celebrations and open-air
theatre in the summer. **Dogs**: welcome on leads
in the woodland and on signed estate walks.

Access: 🅿 🅿 ♿ 🏫 🔔 📷 🎠 🖥 🎵 ⠿ 🅿
Hall 🔥 ♿ ♿ **Grounds** ♿ ➡ ♿ ♿
Parking: on site.

Surrounded by glorious gardens, magnificent Speke Hall in Liverpool (below and right), is ideal for a family day out

Finding out more: 0151 427 7231 or spekehall@nationaltrust.org.uk

Speke Hall		M	T	W	T	F	S	S
13 Feb–21 Feb	11–4	·	·	**W**	**T**	**F**	**S**	**S**
27 Feb–13 Mar	11–4	·	·	·	·	·	**S**	**S**
16 Mar–24 Jul	11–5	·	·	**W**	**T**	**F**	**S**	**S**
26 Jul–4 Sep	10:30–5	·	**T**	**W**	**T**	**F**	**S**	**S**
7 Sep–30 Oct	11–5	·	·	**W**	**T**	**F**	**S**	**S**
5 Nov–11 Dec	11–4	·	·	·	·	·	**S**	**S**

House: entry before 12:30 by guided tour only (places limited); free-flow access from 12:30. Open Bank Holiday Mondays. Some rooms under cover 13 February to 13 March for conservation reasons. Car park closes 30 minutes after times stated.

Steam Yacht Gondola

Coniston Pier, Lake Road, Coniston, Cumbria LA21 8AN

🖾 🔔 🍽 1980

Rebuilt from the original Victorian Gondola, today's passengers can experience the nostalgia of a cruise once enjoyed by the Victorians. Based on the design of a Venetian *burchiello*, Gondola allows you to watch the steam engine in action and experience a gentle gliding motion in near silence. In the saloons, you can go first class and pretend to be a 'toff', or be an 'oik' in third. Nowadays, we don't segregate you as the Victorians did: the whole boat is worth exploring and the crew love to tell tales about her chequered past and connections to *Swallows and Amazons*.
Note: sailings depart from Coniston Pier (subject to weather conditions). Sorry no toilet on scheduled sailings. Gondola is a historic ship and extremely costly to run. Charge for members, although a small discount is applied on scheduled round-trip cruises.

Eating and shopping: small shop on board selling souvenirs. Bluebird Café (licensed) at Coniston Pier serving local, freshly prepared food. Disembark at Brantwood jetty for Brantwood House gallery and licensed café. Catering available (not National Trust) for private charters. Gift experiences available online.

Steam Yacht Gondola on Coniston, Cumbria. Our cruises offer visitors a day of Victorian nostalgia

Making the most of your day: picnic cruises, 'Engineer for the day' gift experience. Themed events. Downloadable walks available from Gondola's jetties. Joint tickets with partner attractions. Tickets can be bought online in advance. **Dogs**: welcome in outside areas only.

Access: 🅿️ 🚻 ♿ ⛴️ 📷 Gangway ♿ 🦽
Sat Nav: use LA21 8AN. **Parking**: at Coniston Pier, 50 yards, not National Trust (charge including members).

Finding out more: 01539 432733 or sygondola@nationaltrust.org.uk
Booking Office, Low Wray Campsite, Low Wray, Ambleside, Cumbria LA22 0JA

Steam Yacht Gondola		M	T	W	T	F	S	S
Head of Lake cruise								
25 Mar–31 Oct	11–11:45	M	T	W	T	F	·	·
25 Mar–31 Oct	12–12:45	M	T	W	T	F	·	·
25 Mar–31 Oct	1–1:45	M	T	W	T	F	S	S
26 Mar–30 Oct	2:30–3:15	·	·	·	·	·	S	S
26 Mar–30 Oct	3:30–4:15	·	·	·	·	·	S	S
Full Lake cruise								
25 Mar–31 Oct	2:30–4:15	M	T	W	T	F	·	·
Walkers/Full Lake cruise								
26 Mar–30 Oct	11–12:45	·	·	·	·	·	S	S

Visit website for detailed timetable. Piers at Coniston, Monk Coniston and Parkamoor, also Lake Bank and Brantwood (not National Trust). All sailings depart Coniston Pier. Cruises subject to weather conditions.

Sticklebarn and The Langdales

near Ambleside, Cumbria

🍴 🏠 📷 ♿ ⛴️ 🛏️ △ ⛺ 🚩 ⛩️ 1925

Sticklebarn is a traditional pub with panoramic views of the iconic Langdale Pikes. We're running it ourselves to ensure that every penny we make goes back into looking after Langdale Valley. Sticklebarn sits at the heart of miles of walking routes and, with crackling fires, real ales and Lakeland food, there's no better place to unwind after a day on the fells. The ambitious can tackle the major peaks, but it's not all about high-level scrambling. The circular route around Blea Tarn is easily accessible, with views of Little and Great Langdale.

Eating and shopping: pub serving food and drink all day. Outdoor eating on the terrace. Wood-fired pizza oven. Good helpings of hearty Lakeland food, including the irresistible Stickle Toffee Pudding. A range of Cumbrian real ales and our own Sticklebarn Bedrock Gin.

Why not share your pictures with us? #nationaltrust

Making the most of your day: guided ghyll scrambling and rock-climbing. Live music at Sticklebarn. Stay at Great Langdale campsite. New off-road cycle trail from Skelwith Bridge to Sticklebarn. Bike hire at Great Langdale Campsite. **Dogs**: welcome under control.

Access: [icons] **Pub** [icons] **Grounds** [icons]
Sat Nav: use LA22 9JU for Sticklebarn, LA22 9PG for Blea Tarn, LA22 9HP for Elterwater. **Parking**: at Stickle Ghyll, Old Dungeon Ghyll, Blea Tarn and Elterwater village.

Finding out more: 015394 37356 (Sticklebarn) or sticklebarn@nationaltrust.org.uk

Sticklebarn and The Langdales		M	T	W	T	F	S	S
Sticklebarn								
1 Jan–3 Jan	12–11*	.	.	.	.	F	S	S
12 Feb–21 Feb	12–11*	M	T	W	T	F	S	S
22 Feb–24 Mar	12–9	M	T	W	T	F	S	S
25 Mar–30 Oct	12–11*	M	T	W	T	F	S	S
31 Oct–15 Dec	12–6**	M	T	W	T	F	S	S
16 Dec–31 Dec	12–11*	M	T	W	T	F	S	S
Great Langdale Campsite								
Open all year†		M	T	W	T	F	S	S

*Closes 10:30 in the evening on Sundays. **Friday, Saturday and Sunday: open until 9 in the evening. Closed 25 December. †For detailed opening times and bookings please see ntlakescampsites.org.uk

Tarn Hows and Coniston

near Coniston, Cumbria

[icons] 1943

Stunning Tarn Hows offers an accessible circular walk (1¾ miles) through beautiful countryside with majestic mountain views. We have off-road mobility scooters available to hire for less-able visitors. The area around the tarn and Coniston village is a great place to begin your wider Lake District adventure.

Eating and shopping: ice-cream van on site, also selling hot and cold drinks. Numerous catering options nearby, particularly in Coniston and Hawkshead. Picnics welcome.

Making the most of your day: why not theme your day around water and start with a leisurely Steam Yacht Gondola cruise on Coniston Water, then walk through the grounds of Monk Coniston to Tarn Hows? **Dogs**: welcome on leads (stock grazing).

Access: [icons] **Grounds** [icons]
Sat Nav: use LA22 0PP for Tarn Hows or LA21 8DP for Glen Mary (both nearby). **Parking**: on site at Tarn Hows, also at Glen Mary nearby. Parking available in Coniston (not National Trust).

Finding out more: 015394 41456 or tarnhows@nationaltrust.org.uk

Sticklebarn (top) and Great Langdale (above), Cumbria

Tarn Hows, Cumbria: open to all, thanks to accessible paths

Tatton Park

Knutsford, Cheshire WA16 6QN

🏛️🔥❄️🐕🚶🔔🍽️🍷 1960

Set in 400 hectares (1,000 acres) of deer-park, the former Egerton family home is open for you to explore. You're welcome to uncover centuries of history at Tatton's Tudor Old Hall and witness life above and 'below stairs' in the mansion. Why not wander at leisure through glorious gardens and take the children to our working farm? You'll love stopping off in the Stableyard where you can eat, drink, chat, browse and buy from our shops, restaurant and tea-room. There are more than 100 events, ranging from car shows to deer walks, making the perfect day out! **Note**: managed/financed by Cheshire East Council. For tours, RHS show, Christmas and other events supplementary charges may apply (including members). Park car entry charge, £6 (including members).

Eating and shopping: visit the historic Stableyard and enjoy the Stables self-service restaurant and Gardener's Cottage table service tea-room. Speciality shops, including the Housekeeper's Store for the best in local speciality food and drink, gift shop, garden shop and tuck shop.

Making the most of your day: **Indoors** Mansion and Tudor Old Hall. Activities at the farm. Shopping and dining. Many learning activities and events. **Outdoors** Gardens, farm, parkland and adventure playground. Numerous events and learning activities. **Dogs**: on leads at farm and under close control in park only.

The Fernery at Tatton Park, Cheshire (above), and the Japanese Garden (below): two of many delights on offer

Access: 🅿️🚐🚌🛗♿🔦📷📹📱📷
Building ♿🏛️🅿️♿ **Grounds** ♿🏛️➡️🐕
Sat Nav: use WA16 6SG. **Parking**: park car entry charge, £6 (including members).

Finding out more: 01625 374435 (Infoline). 01625 374400 or tatton@cheshireeast.gov.uk tattonpark.org.uk

Tatton Park		M	T	W	T	F	S	S
Parkland, gardens, restaurant and tea-room								
1 Jan–18 Mar*	10–5	·	T	W	T	F	S	S
19 Mar–30 Oct*	10–7	M	T	W	T	F	S	S
1 Nov–31 Dec*	10–5	·	T	W	T	F	S	S
Mansion								
19 Mar–2 Oct	1–5	·	T	W	T	F	S	S
4 Oct–30 Oct	12–4	·	T	W	T	F	S	S
Farm								
2 Jan–13 Mar	11–4	·	·	·	·	·	S	S
19 Mar–30 Oct	12–5	·	T	W	T	F	S	S
5 Nov–31 Dec	11–4	·	·	·	·	·	S	S
Shops								
1 Jan–18 Mar	12–4	·	T	W	T	F	S	S
19 Mar–30 Oct	11–5	M	T	W	T	F	S	S
1 Nov–31 Dec	12–4	·	T	W	T	F	S	S

*Gardens, restaurant, tea-room close one hour earlier. Open Bank Holiday Mondays. Parkland, mansion, farm and garden: last admission one hour before closing. Guided mansion tours at 12, Tuesday to Sunday, 19 March to 2 October (timed ticket, places limited), small charge including members. Old Hall special opening arrangements. Mansion open for Christmas event. Tatton Park closed 25 December.

Townend

Troutbeck, Windermere, Cumbria LA23 1LB

🏛 ❋ 1948

The Brownes of Townend were a simple farming family, but their home and belongings bring to life more than 400 years of extraordinary stories. The farmhouse kitchen has a real fire burning most afternoons and a quirky collection of domestic tools. Throughout the house, intricately carved furniture provides a window into the personality of George Browne. The library contains the family's well-used collection of books, including 45 that are the only remaining copies in the world. Outside, the colourful cottage-style garden is a lovely place to while away some time among the flowers.
Note: closed until the end of July for repairs. Limited access on occasional booked tours (telephone for more information).

Eating and shopping: small selection of souvenirs available. Picnics welcome. Tea-room in Troutbeck village (not National Trust).

Making the most of your day: **Indoors** Guided tours at 11 and 12. 'A Taste of Townend'; food displays every day and living-history cooking demonstrations on Thursdays. Children's trail. **Outdoors** Garden trail for children. Traditional games.

Access: 🅿️ 🚻 🖼 ⬛ 🅰 Building 🚶 Grounds 🚶
Parking: 300 yards.

Finding out more: 015394 32628 or townend@nationaltrust.org.uk

Townend		M	T	W	T	F	S	S
House tours								
23 Jul–30 Oct	11–12*	·	·	W	T	F	S	S
House								
23 Jul–30 Oct	1–5	·	·	W	T	F	S	S

*Entry by guided tour only at 11 and 12 (places limited, first-come, first-served). Open Bank Holiday Mondays. May close early due to poor light.

Become part of the life of a simple farming family on a visit to Townend, Cumbria (above and below)

Wasdale

near Gosforth, Cumbria

✝ 🍴 🏛 ♿ ♿ 🚶 🏠 ⛺ 1920

The birthplace of British mountaineering and it's easy to see why. Wasdale Head lies beneath towering mountains, including England's highest – Scafell Pike. People have lived in the valley since earliest times and the intricate network of walled fields is testimony to the long history of farming in this area. Here too lies England's deepest lake, Wastwater, with the Screes sweeping down from the top of Illgill Head to the lake below, creating ever-changing images on the surface of the water. Towards the southern end of the lake and Nether Wasdale, there are natural woodlands with winding paths. **Note**: limited toilet facilities (we are planning improvements and raising money towards this project).

Stay at Wasdale Campsite, Cumbria (below), and truly immerse yourself in this beautiful wild landscape (above)

Eating and shopping: shop at National Trust campsite in Wasdale. Pub and shop at Wasdale Head and pubs in Nether Wasdale and Santon Bridge (none National Trust).

Making the most of your day: walking and climbing in England's highest mountains. Lakeside, riverbank and woodland rambles. Wild swimming and paddling in Wastwater and rivers. Herdwick sheep graze in fields and on fells. **Dogs**: well-behaved dogs welcome. Please follow local and seasonal guidance.

Access: ♿

Sat Nav: use CA20 1EX. **Parking**: at Lake Head CA20 1EX; Overbeck CA20 1EX (limited space); Nether Wasdale CA20 1ET (limited space).

Finding out more: 019467 26064 or wasdale@nationaltrust.org.uk

	M	T	W	T	F	S	S
Wasdale							
Wasdale Campsite*							
Open all year	**M**	**T**	**W**	**T**	**F**	**S**	**S**

*For detailed opening times and bookings, please visit ntlakescampsites.org.uk

Whitehaven Coast

Whitehaven, Cumbria

🪟 🚂

This post-industrial coastline holds hidden gems with clifftop walks from the Georgian harbour and views to the Isle of Man.
Note: toilet at Haig Pit visitor centre (not National Trust). For Sat Nav use CA28 9BG for Haig Pit and CA28 7LY for Whitehaven Harbour.

Finding out more: 017687 74649 or whitehavencoast@nationaltrust.org.uk

Wordsworth House and Garden, Cumbria: the busy kitchen (top) and relaxing garden (above)

Wordsworth House and Garden

Main Street, Cockermouth, Cumbria CA13 9RX

🏠 ✿ 🔔 🍷 1938

Wordsworth's childhood in this inspiring family home helped turn him into one of the world's best-loved poets. But there's much more to this extraordinary Georgian town house. Costumed servants share the horrible truth about 18th-century life and cellar ghosts tell tales of happiness and heartbreak. Knowledgeable volunteers offer personalised tours, while an audio-guide reveals more of the house's fascinating past. The relaxing garden and cosy café make a perfect ending to a visit. A new exhibition features Beatrix Potter, another lover of landscape, who was inspired by the Lakes and Wordsworth, on the 150th anniversary of her birth.

Eating and shopping: gifts, Wordsworth and local souvenirs. Second-hand books. Café serving light lunches and cakes. Takeaway option available and picnics welcome.

Making the most of your day: **Indoors** New Beatrix Potter exhibition. Talks, harpsichord music, cooking demonstrations and Georgian tastings. Dressing-up, traditional toys and family activities during holidays.

Outdoors Garden tours, heritage chickens and poetry. **Dogs**: on leads in front garden only.

Access: 🅿️ 🐶 🦽 🔊 📷 📺 📱 👓 📷
Building 🦽 ↕ ♿ Grounds 🦽 ♿
Parking: in town centre car parks, none National Trust (charge including members). Please note long-stay car park signposted as coach park, 300 yards, Wakefield Road.

Finding out more: 01900 820884 (Infoline). 01900 824805 or wordsworthhouse@nationaltrust.org.uk

Wordsworth House and Garden		M	T	W	T	F	S	S
House, garden, visitor centre and café								
12 Mar–30 Oct	10:30–5*	M	T	W	T	·	S	S
Visitor centre (shop only)								
2 Nov–23 Dec	10:30–4	·	·	W	T	F	S	·

*Café: open 10:30 to 4:30. House and garden: open at 11; last entry to house one hour before closing (timed tickets may operate on busy days). Open selected Fridays in holidays, please ring for information.

Wray Castle

Low Wray, Ambleside, Cumbria LA22 0JA

🏠 🛏 🚻 🅰 1929

Boarding one of the regular lake cruises from Ambleside allows you to arrive at Wray Castle in style. A gentle walk or cycle here also makes a perfect start to your visit. This unusual and exciting National Trust castle is a place for all the family to explore and enjoy. We don't have any of the original castle contents, so it is more informal and child-friendly. Our Peter Rabbit Adventure is the perfect spot for creative play for our youngest visitors, while older children might like dressing-up or building their own castle. To find out more about the varied history of this fascinating building, why not join one of our regular guided tours? Plus, there's loads to do outdoors. **Note**: car park fills up quickly at peak times. We suggest using alternative transport where possible.

Eating and shopping: café serving hot and cold drinks, cakes, snacks and sandwiches, to eat in or take out. Picnics welcome in the grounds. Gift shop stocking all your castle essentials: wooden swords, fancy dress and archery kits, plus seasonal gifts and souvenirs.

Children adore informal Wray Castle, Cumbria (this page and opposite). From den-building to dressing-up, there is plenty to keep them happy for hours

Making the most of your day: Indoors Guided tours unearth details of the castle's hidden past and help you discover more of this quirky building. Family-friendly activities, including crafts, dressing-up, castle building and games. **Outdoors** Lakeside walks and tree trails, as well as an exciting adventure play area with scramble boards and rope swings. Holiday activities, such as tree-climbing and den-building. Why not stay on the doorstep at Low Wray Campsite – just a short walk away from the castle beside the lake and through woodland? Leave the car at home and walk or cycle here along the lakeshore path from Ferry Nab. **Dogs:** welcome in grounds on leads, assistance dogs only in castle.

Access: 🅿️ 🐕 📱 ♿ 🅿️ 🏠 🎵 ⊘ Castle ♿ 🏠
Parking: limited – fills up quickly at peak times. Not suitable for caravans or campervans.

Finding out more: 015394 33250 or wraycastle@nationaltrust.org.uk

Wray Castle		M	T	W	T	F	S	S
Castle								
13 Feb–21 Feb	10:30–4	M	T	W	T	F	S	S
19 Mar–30 Oct	10–5	M	T	W	T	F	S	S
5 Nov–27 Nov	10:30–4	·	·	·	·	·	S	S
Grounds								
Open all year	Dawn–dusk	M	T	W	T	F	S	S

Additional openings possible.

Additional coastal and countryside car parks in the North West and the Lakes

Borrowdale and Derwent Water			**Glencoyne Bay**	CA11 0NQ	**Windermere West Shore**	
Great Wood	CA12 5UP		High Cascades	CA11 0JY	Red Nab	LA22 0JH
Kettlewell	CA12 5UN		Park Brow	CA11 0JY	Harrowslack	LA22 0LR
Ashness Bridge	CA12 5UN				Ash Landing	LA22 0LP
Surprise View	CA12 5UU		**Wasdale**			
Watendlath	CA12 5UU		Lake Head	CA20 1EX	**Coast**	
Bowderstone	CA12 5XA		Overbeck	CA20 1EX	Sandscale Haws	LA14 4QJ
Rosthwaite	CA12 5XB		Nether Wasdale	CA20 1ET	Arnside Knott	LA5 0BP
Seatoller	CA12 5XN				Eaves Wood	
			The Langdales		(Silverdale)	LA5 0UG
			Blea Tarn	LA22 9PG	Formby	L37 1LJ
Buttermere Valley			Old Dungeon Ghyll	LA22 9JY		
Honister Pass	CA13 9UZ		Stickle Ghyll	LA22 9JU	**Cheshire Countryside**	
Buttermere	CA13 9UZ		Elterwater	LA22 9HP	Alderley Edge	SK10 4UB
Lanthwaite Wood	CA13 0RT				Mow Cop	ST7 3PA
			Coniston		Bickerton	SY14 8LN
Ullswater			Glen Mary	LA21 8DP		
Aira Force	CA11 0JS		Tarn Hows	LA22 0PP		

Yorkshire

Fountains Abbey and Studley Royal Water Garden, North Yorkshire

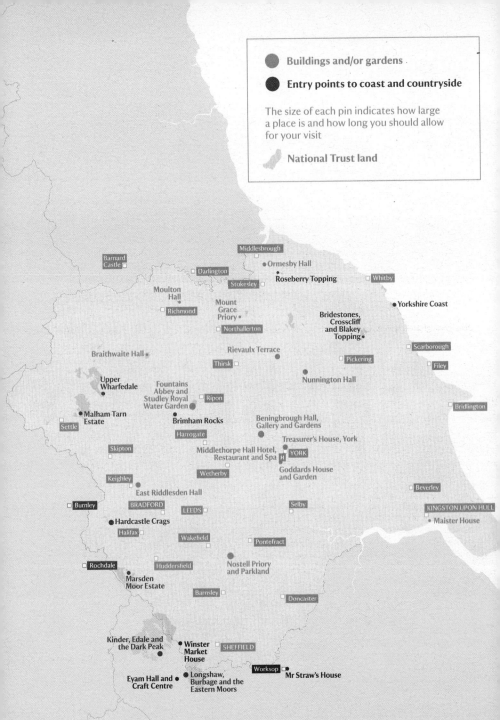

Middlesbrough

Ormesby Hall

Barnard Castle

Darlington

Roseberry Topping

Whitby

Stokesley

Moulton Hall

Richmond

Mount Grace Priory

Northallerton

Yorkshire Coast

Bridestones, Crosscliff and Blakey Topping

Rievaulx Terrace

Thirsk

Pickering

Scarborough

Filey

Braithwaite Hall

Nunnington Hall

Upper Wharfedale

Fountains Abbey and Studley Royal Water Garden

Ripon

Bridlington

Malham Tarn Estate

Brimham Rocks

Settle

Beningbrough Hall, Gallery and Gardens

Harrogate

Skipton

Treasurer's House, York

Middlethorpe Hall Hotel, Restaurant and Spa

YORK

Beverley

Keighley

Wetherby

Goddards House and Garden

Burnley

East Riddlesden Hall

BRADFORD

LEEDS

Selby

KINGSTON UPON HULL

Maister House

Hardcastle Crags

Halifax

Rochdale

Huddersfield

Wakefield

Pontefract

Marsden Moor Estate

Nostell Priory and Parkland

Barnsley

Doncaster

Kinder, Edale and the Dark Peak

Winster Market House

SHEFFIELD

Worksop

Mr Straw's House

Eyam Hall and Craft Centre

Longshaw, Burbage and the Eastern Moors

Beningbrough Hall, Gallery and Gardens, North Yorkshire: cycling lesson in the garden (above), and the magnificent façade

Beningbrough Hall, Gallery and Gardens

Beningbrough, York,
North Yorkshire YO30 1DD

🏛 ❄ 🐾 ♿ ⊤ 1958

As this magnificent house celebrates its 300th anniversary, why not come and discover the stories of its different occupants and their changing fortunes? The architectural grandeur of the rooms is a perfect backdrop for the many important portraits on loan from the National Portrait Gallery, Beningbrough's long-term partner. These portraits feature people who made British history and influenced its culture – many of whom were movers and shakers when the house was built. In the garden, the formal mixed borders contrast with sweeping lawns. There is also a restored walled garden and a play area where children can let off steam. With plenty of garden seats, you can take your time, relax and enjoy the picture-postcard views of the parkland.

Eating and shopping: the Walled Garden restaurant serves morning coffee, afternoon tea and hot lunches, which include freshly picked produce. The shop has an extensive home and garden range. Second-hand books can be found in the Hall library.

nationaltrust.org.uk

Making the most of your day: **Indoors** The hands-on interactive galleries at this award-winning property; Making Faces – 18th-century Style, are perfect for discovering history and portraiture. Sitting for your own virtual digital portrait is a great way to send home a lasting memory. A taste of servant life is found in the Victorian laundry, and the friendly team bring the stories to life in the house. **Outdoors** Got a little more time to spare? Get off the beaten track with year-round parkland walks on riverside paths.
Dogs: welcome on leads in parkland. Assistance dogs only in gardens and buildings.

Access: [icons] Mansion [icons]
[icons] **Stable block** [icons] **Grounds** [icons]
Parking: free, on site.

Finding out more: 01904 472027 or beningbrough@nationaltrust.org.uk

Beningbrough Hall		M	T	W	T	F	S	S
House, gardens, interactive galleries, shop and restaurant								
27 Feb–30 Jun	10:30–5*		T	W	T	F	S	S
1 Jul–31 Aug	10:30–5*	M	T	W	T	F	S	S
1 Sep–30 Oct	10:30–5*		T	W	T	F	S	S
Interactive galleries, gardens, shop and restaurant								
2 Jan–14 Feb	11–3:30**						S	S
16 Feb–21 Feb	11–3:30**		T	W	T	F	S	S
5 Nov–18 Dec	11–3:30**						S	S

*House, interactive galleries and shop open 12. **Interactive galleries open 11:30. Open Bank Holidays and 31 December.

Beningbrough: playtime (above), and a relaxing break (below)

Braithwaite Hall

East Witton, Leyburn, North Yorkshire DL8 4SY

🏠 ♿ 1941

This beautiful 17th-century tenanted farmhouse lies in the heart of Coverdale. **Note**: sorry no toilet. Parts of the Hall are open in June, July and August (by arrangement in advance with the tenant).

Finding out more: 01969 640287 or braithwaitehall@nationaltrust.org.uk

Bridestones, Crosscliff and Blakey Topping

near Pickering, North Yorkshire

⛰ 🚶 1944

Spectacular all year, the Bridestones are a geological wonder – with rock formations, moorland vistas, woodland walks and grassy valleys. **Note**: nearest toilets at Staindale Lake car park. For Sat Nav use YO18 7LR. Dalby Forest drive starting 2½ miles north of Thornton le Dale – toll charges (including members).

Finding out more: 01723 870423 or bridestones@nationaltrust.org.uk

Brimham Rocks

near Summerbridge, Harrogate, North Yorkshire HG3 4DW

⛰ 1970

These rock formations tower over heather moorland, offering panoramic views across Nidderdale. Dating back 320 million years, it is now a haven for climbers and walkers and a natural playground for families to enjoy picnics and nature-spotting. For magical photographs, visit all year and see this landscape through all seasons. **Note**: beware of cliff edges. Nearest toilets 600 yards from car park.

Eating and shopping: shop selling books, gifts and the popular locally made bilberry jam. Hot and cold refreshments and ice-cream available from kiosk. Picnic tables with views of the rocks and seating inside the visitor centre.

Making the most of your day: regular guided walks, events, family activities and climbing days. Visitor centre exhibition space reveals the story of the rocks, conservation work and views to the Vale of York. **Dogs**: welcome on leads.

Access: 🅿️ 🚻 ♿ 🚼 🎫 🔔 🖼 🅿️ 📷 🔄
Building 🔆 ♿ **Grounds** ➡️ ♿
Sat Nav: use HG3 4DW. **Parking**: on site.

Finding out more: 01423 780688 or brimhamrocks@nationaltrust.org.uk

Brimham Rocks		M	T	W	T	F	S	S
Visitor centre, shop and kiosk								
1 Jan–3 Jan	11–4	·	·	·	·	F	S	S
13 Feb–21 Feb	11–5	M	T	W	T	F	S	S
27 Feb–20 Mar	11–5	·	·	·	·	·	S	S
25 Mar–10 Apr	11–5	M	T	W	T	F	S	S
16 Apr–22 May**	11–5	·	·	·	·	·	S	S
28 May–2 Oct	11–5	M	T	W	T	F	S	S
8 Oct–16 Oct	11–5	·	·	·	·	·	S	S
22 Oct–30 Oct	11–5	M	T	W	T	F	S	S
5 Nov–18 Dec**	10:30–4	·	·	·	·	·	S	S

Main gate closes 7, or dusk if earlier. **Also open Bank Holidays, 2 May, 26, 27, 31 December and 1 January 2017.

Arresting shapes at Brimham Rocks, North Yorkshire

East Riddlesden Hall

Bradford Road, Riddlesden, Keighley,
West Yorkshire BD20 5EL

🏠 ✿ ♣ ♠ ⊤ 1934

Step away from the hectic every day and
experience the tranquillity at this small,
friendly house. Home to a wonderful array of
17th-century needlework and original exquisite
plasterwork ceilings created by local craftsmen,
it's brought to life through stories told by
volunteer room guides. The intimate gardens,
with an ever-changing palette of colour,
offer a peaceful space to relax and unwind in.
Children can let off steam in the natural play
areas and get creative in the mud-pie kitchen.
The Hobbit House is waiting to be discovered
and there's no better place to spot wildlife than
at the bird hide.

Eating and shopping: converted bothy, with
shop selling gifts, books, homeware,
gardenware, plants and ice-cream. Assisted
self-service tea-room on first floor serving
sandwiches, jacket potatoes, cakes and drinks.
Accessible table on ground floor. Second-hand
book sale area in the house.

**East Riddlesden Hall, West Yorkshire. The small friendly
house (above), and intimate garden (below)**

Making the most of your day: Indoors Explore
the historic barn and house at your own pace
and enjoy trails, hands-on activities and
dressing-up. **Outdoors** Gardens, bird hide,
herb border, natural playground and children's
Discovery Garden. **Dogs**: welcome on the
lower field. Assistance dogs only in house
and gardens.

Access: 🅿️♿🏠♿🖼️📷📱♿
House, shop and tea-room 🚶♿♿ Gardens ♿♿♿
Parking: 250 yards.

Finding out more: 01535 607075 or
eastriddlesden@nationaltrust.org.uk

East Riddlesden Hall		M	T	W	T	F	S	S
House, shop and tea-room								
13 Feb–21 Feb	10:30–4:30	M	T	W	·	·	S	S
27 Feb–20 Mar	10:30–4:30	·	·	·	·	·	S	S
25 Mar	10:30–4:30	·	·	·	·	F	·	·
21 Mar–30 Oct	10:30–4:30	M	T	W	·	·	S	S
5 Nov–18 Dec*	11–4	·	·	·	·	·	S	S

House: entry may be by guided tour. *Limited access to house
in November and December due to winter conservation work
and low light levels. Tea-room: last entry 15 minutes before
closing. Open Good Friday.

Fountains Abbey and Studley Royal Water Garden, North Yorkshire: this inspiring place, with the atmospheric Abbey ruins, has attracted visitors for centuries

Fountains Abbey and Studley Royal Water Garden

near Ripon, North Yorkshire HG4 3DY

🏛️✝️🏚️✿♨️🛏️🔔☂️ 1983

For centuries people have been drawn to this inspiring place. You'll catch your first glimpse of the atmospheric ruins of Fountains Abbey through the trees as you descend into the valley. Nestled beside the pretty River Skell and framed by cliffs and woodlands, you can lose yourself exploring beneath vaulted ceilings, ancient archways and towering heights. In the Water Garden, classical statues, follies and vistas were all designed to make you catch your breath. Rushing cascades flowing into mirror-like ponds and seasonal wild flowers create surprises around every turn. It's well worth the walk through Serpentine Tunnel to the High Ride for the best views. One of a kind, this special place is now recognised as a World Heritage Site. **Note**: cared for in partnership with English Heritage.

Eating and shopping: restaurant serving fresh homemade food for breakfast, daily specials and Sunday dinner. Light lunches and tasty treats available at Abbey and Studley tea-rooms. Picnics welcome. Large visitor centre shop selling books, homeware, plants and gardenware. Smaller shop by Studley lake.

Making the most of your day: **Indoors** In Porter's Lodge uncover the story of the monks who founded the Abbey and see the mill created by these skilful masters of machinery. Explore the opulent interior of St Mary's church. Step inside the Elizabethan-style Fountains Hall or make it your home from home and stay in one of the holiday apartments. **Outdoors** This summer discover the Water Garden follies, transformed by inventive artists. The hidden herb garden is waiting to be found and riverside paths lead to the deer-park. Free daily guided tours in spring and summer. Family fun activities include den-building, geocaching and a redeveloped playground. **Dogs**: welcome on leads. Fresh water bowls and dog-friendly eating areas outside restaurant and tea-rooms.

nationaltrust.org.uk

Access: [icons]
Fountains Abbey [icons] Fountains Hall [icon]
Water Garden [icons]

Parking: on site at visitor centre (accessible parking at West Gate) and Studley Lakeside (pay and display).

Finding out more: 01765 608888 or fountainsabbey@nationaltrust.org.uk

Fountains Abbey		M	T	W	T	F	S	S
Abbey and Water Garden								
1 Jan–24 Mar*	10–5	M	T	W	T	F	S	S
25 Mar–29 Oct	10–6	M	T	W	T	F	S	S
30 Oct–31 Dec**	10–5	M	T	W	T	·	S	S
Deer-park								
Open all year	6–6	M	T	W	T	F	S	S
Visitor Centre restaurant and shop								
1 Jan–24 Mar*	10–4	M	T	W	T	F	S	S
25 Mar–29 Oct	10–5:30	M	T	W	T	F	S	S
30 Oct–31 Dec**	10–4	M	T	W	T	·	S	S

Last admission one hour before closing. *Closed Fridays in January. **Closed 24 and 25 December. See website or telephone for hall, mill, tea-rooms, Studley Royal shop and St Mary's church opening times.

One of the many Water Garden follies (above), and the Abbey ruins (below), glimpsed across the River Skell

Places may occasionally close for events or bad weather

Goddards House and Garden

27 Tadcaster Road, York,
North Yorkshire YO24 1GG

1984

Nestled on the edge of York racecourse, this former home of the Terry family (think Chocolate Orange) is a warm Arts and Crafts house full of memories. You can sit down, pour yourself a sherry and feel at home, then meander through garden rooms, discovering fragrant borders and hidden corners.

Eating and shopping: lunch served in the Terry's dining-room, with a view of the Arts and Crafts garden from the lavender terrace. Why not treat yourself to a chocolate souvenir to take home?

Making the most of your day: **Indoors** Curl up with a *Terry Times* in the drawing-room. Family trails available. Everyone's welcome to leave their Terry's memories on the typewriter. **Outdoors** Games in the garden.
Dogs: welcome on leads in garden.

Access: **House** **Grounds**
Sat Nav: enter 27 Tadcaster Road, York, not postcode. **Parking**: limited at weekends. On weekdays, car park used by regional office, please use city-centre car parks (1 to 2 miles) or park on nearby Knavesmire Road (off A1036).

Welcoming Goddards House and Garden, North Yorkshire

Finding out more: 01904 771930 or goddards@nationaltrust.org.uk

Goddards		M	T	W	T	F	S	S
2 Mar–30 Oct	10:30–5	·	·	W	T	F	S	S
18 Nov–18 Dec	10:30–4	·	·	·	·	F	S	S

Open spring and summer Bank Holiday Mondays.

Hardcastle Crags

near Hebden Bridge, West Yorkshire

1950

A gem in the South Pennines, this beautiful valley has miles of footpaths through woodlands rich in wildlife. Roe deer make it their home, the drumming of woodpeckers carries across the valley and northern hairy wood ants build their impressive nests. Seasonal colours are stunning, with carpets of bluebells in spring and golden leaves in autumn. Waymarked paths follow Hebden Water or climb the valley sides along old packhorse routes. Gibson Mill, a former cotton mill and Entertainment Emporium, offers the chance for refreshment and at the same time to explore what it really means to be 'off the grid'. **Note**: steep paths and rough terrain.

Eating and shopping: Weaving Shed Café serving sandwiches, soup, cakes and ice-cream. Shop selling books, gifts, cards and sweets.

Hardcastle Crags in West Yorkshire: it really is possible to 'get off the grid' in this South Pennine wilderness

Making the most of your day: **Indoors**
Dressing-up in period costume at Gibson Mill.
Outdoors Variety of trails with downloadable
options, plus guided walks and seasonal
events. **Dogs**: under close control at all times.

Access: [icons]
Building [icons] Grounds [icons]
Sat Nav: for Midgehole car park use HX7 7AA;
Clough Hole car park HX7 7AZ. **Parking**: at
Midgehole car park, 1 mile to Gibson Mill, or
Clough Hole car park, ¾ mile (steep walk).

Finding out more: 01422 844518 (weekdays).
01422 846236 (weekends) or
hardcastlecrags@nationaltrust.org.uk

Hardcastle Crags		M	T	W	T	F	S	S
Gibson Mill and Weaving Shed Café								
2 Jan–27 Mar	11–3	.	.	.	.	.	S	S
28 Mar–30 Oct*	11–4	M	T	W	T	F	S	S
5 Nov–18 Dec	11–3	.	.	.	.	.	S	S

*Gibson Mill: closed Fridays, 28 March to 30 October.

Maister House

160 High Street, Hull, East Yorkshire HU1 1NL

[icon] 1966

A merchant family's tale of fortune and tragedy
is intertwined with the intriguing history of
Maister House. **Note**: staircase and entrance
hall only on show. Sorry no toilet. Open
weekdays, 1 January to 30 December, 10 to 4.

Finding out more: 01723 870423 or
maisterhouse@nationaltrust.org.uk

Malham Tarn Estate

Waterhouses, Settle, North Yorkshire

[icons] 1946

High up in the Dales, with views across rolling
fields, limestone pavements and the tarn, the
peacefulness of this National Nature Reserve
makes it perfect for enjoying the great
outdoors. With walking and cycle routes and a
'Tramper' available to hire, go for a stroll, picnic
or family adventure. **Note**: nearest toilet at
Malham National Park car park or Orchid
House exhibition.

Eating and shopping: tea-rooms, pubs
and facilities in Malham village
(none National Trust).

Exploring the Malham Tarn Estate, North Yorkshire

Why not share your pictures with us? #nationaltrust

Making the most of your day: guided walks, events, outdoor activities. Accessible boardwalk through reserve. Cycle trails around the tarn. Family events during holidays. Orchid House exhibition. Walking routes for all abilities, tramper available to hire. **Dogs**: welcome on leads (livestock roaming).

Access: Town Head Barn [icon] Grounds [icons] **Sat Nav**: use BD24 9PT. **Parking**: off-road at Waterhouses and at Watersinks car park, south side of Malham Tarn.

Finding out more: 01729 830416 or malhamtarn@nationaltrust.org.uk

Marsden Moor Estate

Marsden, Huddersfield, West Yorkshire

[icons] 1955

The landscape and history of Marsden Moor, within the South Pennines and Peak District National Park, will bring out the explorer in you. Pule Hill and Buckstones offer breathtaking views, and there are miles of footpaths and bridleways to enjoy, while spotting the wildlife which inhabits this internationally important habitat. **Note**: sorry no toilet.

Eating and shopping: tea-rooms, restaurants and shops in Marsden village (none National Trust).

Marsden Moor Estate, West Yorkshire: remote and wild, with breathtaking views and an internationally important habitat

Making the most of your day: events, family activities and guided walks all year. Walking routes available (OS map required) from Estate Office exhibition room. Why not visit the 'Framing the Landscape' artwork and Stanza Stone? **Dogs**: welcome on leads.

Access: Exhibition Room [icon] Grounds [icon] **Sat Nav**: use HD7 6DH for Marsden village. **Parking**: at Marsden village (not National Trust), Buckstones and Wessenden Head.

Finding out more: 01484 847016 or marsdenmoor@nationaltrust.org.uk

Marsden Moor Estate		M	T	W	T	F	S	S
Exhibition Centre								
Open all year	9–5	M	T	W	T	F	S	S
Closed 25 December.								

Middlethorpe Hall Hotel, Restaurant and Spa

Bishopthorpe Road, York, North Yorkshire YO23 2GB

[icons] 2008

William and Mary house, built in 1699, set in eight hectares (20 acres) of manicured gardens and parkland. **Note**: access is for paying guests of the hotel, including for luncheon, afternoon tea and dinner. Children over the age of six welcome.

Finding out more: 01904 641241. 01904 620176 (fax) or info@middlethorpe.com middlethorpe.com

Moulton Hall

Moulton, Richmond,
North Yorkshire DL10 6QH

🏠 1966

Elegant 17th-century tenanted manor house
with a beautiful carved staircase. **Note**: sorry
no toilet. Visit by arrangement in advance
with the tenant.

Finding out more: 01325 377227 or
moultonhall@nationaltrust.org.uk

Mount Grace Priory

Staddle Bridge, Northallerton,
North Yorkshire DL6 3JG

✝ 1953

Discover how medieval Carthusian monks
lived. Explore priory ruins, garden and
Arts and Crafts-style manor house rooms.
Note: operated by English Heritage; members
free, except on event days. Contact English
Heritage for opening times.

Finding out more: 01609 883494 or
mountgracepriory@nationaltrust.org.uk

The elegant Top Hall at Nostell Priory, West Yorkshire

Nostell Priory and Parkland

Doncaster Road, Nostell, near Wakefield,
West Yorkshire WF4 1QE

🏠 ✝ ❀ ♨ ⬛ ⊤ 1954

Home to the Winn family for more than 350
years, Nostell is a window into a world of
splendour. The grand interiors, designed by
Robert Adam, contain a world-renowned
collection of Chippendale furniture, with many
pieces in their original setting. Children can
enjoy finding the mouse in the 18th-century
doll's-house, dressing-up in the Servants' Hall
and joining in family activities. While exploring
the 121-hectare (300-acre) estate, you can take
in the colours and scents of the rose, kitchen
and menagerie gardens and spot wildlife as you
wind your way along lakeside paths. Follow the
parkland trails to discover woodland and
wildflower meadows, with the Carriageway and
Hardwick Beck paths providing all-weather
tracks to run, walk, cycle and scoot.

Eating and shopping: Courtyard Café serving
hot food and refreshments. Bite to Eat kiosk
offering snacks and drinks at peak times. Shop
selling gifts, souvenirs and plants. Picnics
welcome in the park and gardens.

Making the most of your day: **Indoors**
Year-round events, including family activities
five days a week during school holidays, craft
fairs and talks. Regular tours of the house and
stables, 'Upstairs Downstairs' tour of the attics
and cellars. Family house guide, dressing-up
and costumed characters on selected days.
Special opening in December, when the house
is decorated for Christmas. **Outdoors**
Geocaching, den-building, children's outdoor
play area. Guided parkland and church walks.
Regular running, walking and cycling groups,
all-weather track in Obelisk Park. **Dogs**: under
close control at all times. Assistance dogs
only in gardens.

Access: 🅿️♿🚐♿🐾♿📷♿👶👁️📖
House ♿🔼♿ Grounds ♿♿➡️♿
Parking: 650 yards.

Finding out more: 01924 863892 or
nostellpriory@nationaltrust.org.uk

Nostell Priory and Parkland		M	T	W	T	F	S	S
House*								
27 Feb–30 Oct	1–5			W	T	F	S	S
3 Dec–18 Dec	10–4						S	S
Gardens, shop and tea-room**								
1 Jan–26 Feb	10–4	M	T	W	T	F	S	S
27 Feb–30 Oct	10–5	M	T	W	T	F	S	S
31 Oct–31 Dec	10–4	M	T	W	T	F	S	S
Parkland†								
Open all year	7–7	M	T	W	T	F	S	S

*House: open 11 to 12 for guided tours (places limited and allocated on arrival). Last admission to house 45 minutes before closing. **Gardens: last admission 30 minutes before closing. Rose Garden: may close for private functions. †Parkland: closes dusk if earlier. Closed 25 December.

The lake at Nostell Priory and Parkland (above), and enjoying the excellent cycling routes (right)

Nunnington Hall

Nunnington, near York,
North Yorkshire YO62 5UY

🏠 ❀ 1953

Whatever the weather, whatever the season, a trip to Nunnington Hall offers a perfect day out for all the family. This welcoming and friendly home, with its enchanting house and beautiful gardens, is within easy reach of York and Scarborough. You can learn about the Fife family, owners of the Hall in the 1920s and, if you're brave enough, hear the Hall's ghostly tales! In spring, the beautiful wildflower meadows in the organic gardens bloom. In summer, the lawn is perfect for relaxing, or you could picnic by the meandering River Rye. In autumn the orchards are bountiful with produce.

Nunnington Hall, North Yorkshire: a family favourite

Eating and shopping: licensed waitress-service tea-rooms within atmospheric historic rooms. Outdoor self-service kiosk during peak times with seating next to the river. Picnics welcome – tables are situated around the grounds. Shop selling a wide range of National Trust favourites and local ranges.

Making the most of your day: **Indoors** Family fun activities, 1920s games, dressing-up, activity room, art exhibitions, seasonal events, trails, theatre, concerts and Father Christmas. **Outdoors** Tepee-glade, mud-pie kitchen, bird-spotting, quoits, pooh-sticks, giant chess, croquet. **Dogs**: welcome on leads in the garden.

Access: 🅿♿🚻 **Building** 🏛♿ **Grounds** ♿ **Parking**: on site.

Finding out more: 01439 748283 or nunningtonhall@nationaltrust.org.uk

Nunnington Hall		M	T	W	T	F	S	S
13 Feb–21 Feb	11–5	M	T	W	T	F	S	S
23 Feb–27 Mar	11–5	·	T	W	T	F	S	S
6 Sep–23 Oct	11–5	·	T	W	T	F	S	S
24 Oct–30 Oct	11–4	M	T	W	T	F	S	S
5 Nov–11 Dec	11–4	·	·	·	·	·	S	S
House, tea-room and garden*								
28 Mar–10 Apr	11–5	M	T	W	T	F	S	S
12 Apr–31 Jul	11–5	·	T	W	T	F	S	S
1 Aug–4 Sep	11–5	M	T	W	T	F	S	S

Open Bank Holiday Mondays. *Tea-room and garden open at 10:30.

The kitchen at Ormesby Hall, Redcar & Cleveland

Ormesby Hall

Ladgate Lane, Ormesby, near Middlesbrough, Redcar & Cleveland TS3 0SR

🏠❄️♿🔔⛺ 1962

Once home to the Pennyman family, the spirit of this Georgian home remains true to the kind couple who lived here last, Colonel Jim and his arts-loving wife Ruth, with the intriguing legacy of Jim's ancestor 'Wicked' Sir James. The garden is relaxing with walks around the wider estate.

Eating and shopping: cold drinks and snacks available. A more varied offer, including hot drinks, is available on Bank Holidays and during the school summer holidays.

Making the most of your day: the model railway exhibition on the first floor is fun for all ages. A relaxing lounge area gives families the chance to play games, and includes a children's activity room. **Dogs**: welcome on leads in the parkland.

Access: 🅿️♿♿🔖🎧📷🎬♿🅿️
Building 🅰️♿ Grounds ➡️♿
Parking: on site.

Finding out more: 01642 324188 or ormesbyhall@nationaltrust.org.uk
Church Lane, Ormesby, Middlesbrough TS7 9AS

Ormesby Hall		M	T	W	T	F	S	S
6 Mar–1 Nov	10–5	**M**	**T**	·	·	·	·	**S**

Additionally open for Model Railway Weekends.

Rievaulx Terrace

Rievaulx, Helmsley, North Yorkshire YO62 5LJ

🏠❄️♿ 1972

Created by the Duncombe family and finished *circa* 1757, Rievaulx Terrace was designed primarily for promenading and dining in style. It maintains this unique feeling of grandeur and tranquillity today. The woods are a perfect start to your visit, giving tantalising glimpses of the terrace and the views beyond, as well as opportunities to enjoy nature and wildlife. When you leave the woods and walk down the terrace, spectacular views of Rievaulx Abbey and the valley beyond are revealed through man-made vistas. Finally you will find the Ionic Temple, where the family dined under the magnificent painted ceiling. **Note**: no access to Rievaulx Abbey (English Heritage).

Eating and shopping: ice-cream, cold drinks and sweet snacks available. Picnics welcome. Shop selling gifts and souvenirs.

Gracious Rievaulx Terrace, North Yorkshire

Making the most of your day: natural play and den-building areas for children, rope swing, balance beam, log-scotch, quoits, stepping stones and our tranquil sky glade. Ionic Temple open regularly. Family trails and activities (school holidays). **Dogs**: welcome on leads.

Access: 🅿️♿🏠🔄🎵 Visitor centre ♿
Temples 🔄 Grounds ♿➡️🔄♿
Parking: 100 yards.

Finding out more: 01439 798340 (summer). 01439 748283 (winter) or rievaulxterrace@nationaltrust.org.uk

Rievaulx Terrace		M	T	W	T	F	S	S
13 Feb–25 Mar	10–4	M	T	W	T	F	S	S
26 Mar–4 Sep	10–5	M	T	W	T	F	S	S
5 Sep–30 Oct	10–4	M	T	W	T	F	S	S

Last admission one hour before closing or dusk if earlier.

Rievaulx Terrace: grandeur and tranquillity

Roseberry Topping

near Newton-under-Roseberry, North Yorkshire

🏛️🧺🌳 1985

Affectionately known as 'Yorkshire's Matterhorn', layers of geological history have shaped this iconic hill. Stunning views, woodland walks and wildlife. **Note**: nearest parking at Newton-under-Roseberry – also the location of the toilets – not National Trust (charge including members). For Sat Nav use TS9 6QR.

Finding out more: 01723 870423 or roseberrytopping@nationaltrust.org.uk

Treasurer's House, York

Minster Yard, York, North Yorkshire YO1 7JL

🏛️❄️🛏️🍴 1930

Tucked behind York Minster, this hidden gem has gone through many transformations, from a 'bug-ridden slum' to an Edwardian gentleman's town house. In 1897, Frank Green (the grandson of a wealthy industrialist) bought Treasurer's House and created a lavish show home, grand enough to impress Edward VII during his visit. Frank built a large collection of fine antiques, art and furniture. Interestingly, this was the first house ever given to the National Trust complete with its collection. The award-winning garden is an oasis of calm, so relax and enjoy unrivalled views of the Minster.

Eating and shopping: Below Stairs Café (licensed), enjoyed by locals and visitors alike, offers table service, morning coffee, lunch and afternoon tea. Around the corner, on Goodramgate, is the Trust's large high-street shop which sells a broad selection of gifts and stylish souvenirs.

Making the most of your day: why not take a hard-hat tour to the cellar to revisit the site of Treasurer's most famous ghost story? Family trails and dressing-up available during school holidays. **Dogs**: welcome on a lead, in the garden.

Access: 🅳 🎞 🖥 🔊 ⦂ 📷
House 🅻 🅳 🍴 Garden 🅻
Parking: nearest at Lord Mayor's Walk. Park and ride from city outskirts recommended.

Finding out more: 01904 624247 or treasurershouse@nationaltrust.org.uk

Treasurer's House		M	T	W	T	F	S	S
1 Mar–31 Oct	11–4:30	M	T	W	T	F	S	S
10 Nov–18 Dec	11–4:30	·	·	·	T	F	S	S

Tucked away behind York Minster, Treasurer's House, York (left), is a hidden gem. The award-winning garden (above) is an oasis of calm in the city

Upper Wharfedale, North Yorkshire: unrivalled views

Upper Wharfedale

near Buckden, North Yorkshire

🅿️♿️♿️ 1989

This Dales landscape with fields of sheep and cows, the wildflower meadows in early summer and characteristic dry-stone walls and barns, is a wonderful place to relax and enjoy the great outdoors. Explore the river and woodland valleys by foot or by bike.

Eating and shopping: village tea-rooms, shops, pubs and farm shops (not National Trust).

Making the most of your day: guided walks, events, workshops and activities. Family events during school holidays. Exhibition at Town Head Barn in Buckden. **Dogs**: welcome on leads due to livestock.

Access: 🅿️♿️ Town Head Barn ♿️ Grounds ➡️

Yorkshire Coast: views, drama, walks and cycling

Sat Nav: use BD23 5JA. **Parking**: in Kettlewell and Buckden, pay and display, not National Trust (charge including members).

Finding out more: 01729 830416 or upperwharfedale@nationaltrust.org.uk

Yorkshire Coast

near Ravenscar, North Yorkshire

🏛️♿️🚋🚩🅿️ 1976

The coastline from Saltburn to Filey is breathtakingly dramatic, with sea views, clifftop walks, cycling routes and sandy bays with excellent rock-pooling and fossil-hunting. Ravenscar Visitor Centre will give you lots of ideas and there's also a coastal exhibition at the Old Coastguard Station, Robin Hood's Bay.

Eating and shopping: Old Coastguard Station shops selling gifts, books, maps and toys.

Making the most of your day: **Indoors** Exhibitions at the Old Coastguard Station. **Outdoors** Family events, geocaching, wildlife activities and guided walks. **Dogs**: welcome on lead at most events. Assistance dogs only in Old Coastguard Station.

Access: ♿️♿️♿️♿️ Visitor centre ♿️ Grounds ♿️ Sat Nav: for Ravenscar use YO13 0NE. **Parking**: on roadside at Ravenscar. Pay and display at Saltburn, Runswick Bay and Robin Hood's Bay, not National Trust (charge including members).

Finding out more: 01723 870423 or yorkshirecoast@nationaltrust.org.uk

Yorkshire Coast		M	T	W	T	F	S	S
Old Coastguard Station								
1 Jan–3 Jan	10–4	·	·	·	·	F	S	S
9 Jan–7 Feb	10–4	·	·	·	·	·	S	S
13 Feb–21 Feb	10–4	M	T	W	T	F	S	S
27 Feb–13 Mar	10–4	·	·	·	·	·	S	S
19 Mar–6 Nov	10–5	M	T	W	T	F	S	S
12 Nov–11 Dec	10–4	·	·	·	·	·	S	S
17 Dec–22 Dec	10–4	M	T	W	T	·	S	S
28 Dec–31 Dec	10–4	·	·	W	T	F	S	·
Ravenscar Visitor Centre								
19 Mar–6 Nov	10–4:30	M	T	W	T	F	S	S

North East

Northumberland Coast, Northumberland

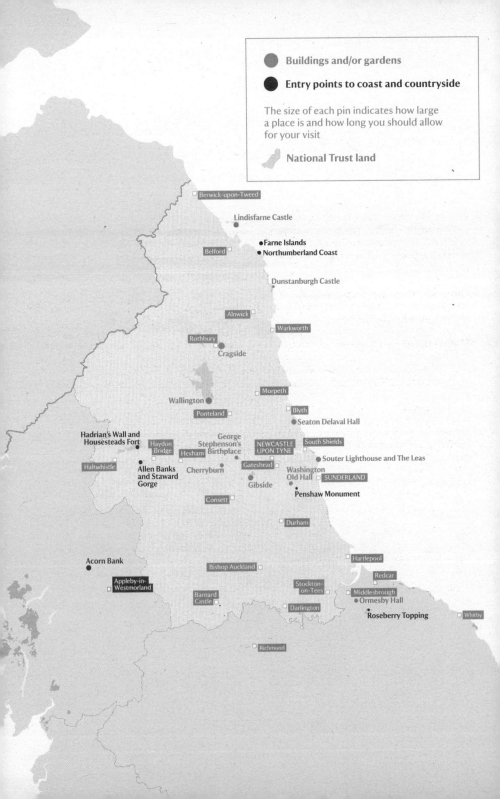

Buildings and/or gardens

Entry points to coast and countryside

The size of each pin indicates how large
a place is and how long you should allow
for your visit

National Trust land

Berwick-upon-Tweed

Lindisfarne Castle

Farne Islands
Northumberland Coast

Belford

Dunstanburgh Castle

Alnwick

Warkworth

Rothbury
Cragside

Morpeth

Wallington
Ponteland

Blyth
Seaton Delaval Hall

Hadrian's Wall and
Housesteads Fort

Haydon
Bridge

George
Stephenson's
Birthplace

NEWCASTLE
UPON TYNE

South Shields

Hexham

Souter Lighthouse and The Leas

Haltwhistle

Allen Banks
and Staward
Gorge

Cherryburn

Gateshead

Washington
Old Hall

SUNDERLAND

Gibside

Penshaw Monument

Consett

Durham

Acorn Bank

Appleby-in-
Westmorland

Bishop Auckland

Hartlepool

Redcar

Barnard
Castle

Stockton-
on-Tees

Middlesbrough
Ormesby Hall

Darlington

Roseberry Topping

Whitby

Richmond

Allen Banks and Staward Gorge

near Ridley Hall, Bardon Mill, Hexham,
Northumberland NE47 7BP

🏠 🏛 👥 👤 1942

With its deep gorge, created by the River Allen
and the largest area of ancient semi-natural
woodland in Northumberland, this 250-hectare
(617-acre) site provides the perfect excuse for
an adventure. There are many miles of
waymarked walks and the ornamental woods
are home to a fantastic array of wildlife.

Eating and shopping: picnics welcome at the
numerous beauty spots – in the woodland and
kitchen garden or by the river.

Making the most of your day: events and
downloadable trails. Victorian suspension
bridge, medieval pele-tower and reconstructed
Victorian summerhouse. **Dogs**: welcome under
close control.

Access: 🏛 Grounds 🦽
Sat Nav: post code directs to Ridley Hall –
turn left at Ridley Hall gates for Allen Banks
car park. **Parking**: at Allen Banks.

Finding out more: 01434 321888 or
allenbanks@nationaltrust.org.uk

Allen Banks and Staward Gorge	
Car park open dawn to dusk.	

Allen Banks and Staward Gorge, Northumberland

Cherryburn

Station Bank, Mickley, Stocksfield,
Northumberland NE43 7DD

🏠 🛏 ❀ 👤 🍽 1991

This unassuming Northumbrian farmstead
(above) is the birthplace of famous artist and
naturalist Thomas Bewick. Set in a tranquil
garden with views across the picturesque Tyne
Valley, you can enjoy the natural world that
inspired his work, explore the museum with
Bewick's pioneering wood engravings and meet
the friendly farm animals.

Eating and shopping: gift shop offering
books and a selection of original Bewick prints
hot off the historic presses. House offers
snacks, hot and cold drinks and ice-cream.
Farmyard picnic area.

Making the most of your day: **Indoors** Regular
printing demonstrations, museum and
original birthplace. **Outdoors** Family trail,
mini-adventure play area and school holiday
activities following in young Tom's footsteps.
Paddock walk and farmyard with seasonal
animals. **Dogs**: welcome on short leads in
garden and grounds (animals in farmyard).

Access: 🅿 🅿 💺 🚻 🛗 📷 🏛 ⚫ 🚫
Birthplace 🦽 🦽 🦽 **Café and museum** 🦽 🦽 🚻
Grounds 🦽 🦽 🦽 ➡
Sat Nav: use NE43 7DD. **Parking**: 100 yards.

Finding out more: 01661 843276 or
cherryburn@nationaltrust.org.uk

Cherryburn		M	T	W	T	F	S	S
13 Feb–30 Oct	Tour	**M**	**T**	**W**	**T**	**F**	**S**	**S**

Cragside

Rothbury, Morpeth, Northumberland NE65 7PX

Cragside, Northumberland (above and opposite): a wonder of the Victorian age, this was the most technologically advanced home of its time

Trip the light fantastic to the home where modern living began. Lord and Lady Armstrong used their wealth, art and science in an ingenious way. Cragside was the first house in the world to be lit by hydroelectricity, making it a wonder of the Victorian age. What began as a modest country retreat became the most technologically advanced home of its time. Cleverly including every home comfort imaginable, the house evolved into an Arts and Crafts masterpiece. Outside, their passion for landscaping and gardening was equally ambitious, engineering the landscape and experimenting with plants on a spectacular scale. Combining rocky crags, tumbling water, placid lakes, towering North American conifers and great drifts of rhododendrons, creating changing scenes in the landscape.
Note: challenging terrain and distances (stout footwear essential).

Eating and shopping: tea-room serving hot meals, sandwiches, hand-crafted sweet treats and afternoon tea. Kiosks at the visitor centre, house and play area offering drinks, snacks and ice-cream. Shop selling souvenirs, gifts, local food, crafts and a selection of plants.

Making the most of your day: Indoors The Armstrong's vast collection of British art and furniture sits alongside items of scientific curiosity and engineering innovation. Victorian baking demonstrations using the original range on Wednesdays, and family activities, special exhibitions and events throughout the year.
Outdoors Six-mile estate drive through rugged woodland. A vast network of paths, including lakeside trails and walks for all abilities – from family strolls to challenging hikes. Idyllic formal garden with seasonal planting and views across Northumberland. Regular guided walks and tours. Fantasy landscape, including a rhododendron labyrinth and adventure play area. Free shuttle bus between key features.
Dogs: welcome on leads outdoors.

Access:
House **Visitor centre** **Estate**
Parking: nine car parks on estate.

Finding out more: 01669 620333 or cragside@nationaltrust.org.uk

Cragside		M	T	W	T	F	S	S
House								
13 Feb–30 Oct*	11–5		T	W	T	F	S	S
15 Feb–21 Feb*	11–5	M	T	W	T	F	S	S
28 Mar–9 Apr*	11–5	M	T	W	T	F	S	S
2 May–8 May*	11–5	M	T	W	T	F	S	S
30 May–5 Jun*	11–5	M	T	W	T	F	S	S
25 Jul–4 Sep*	11–5	M	T	W	T	F	S	S
24 Oct–30 Oct*	11–5	M	T	W	T	F	S	S
Gardens and woodland								
13 Feb–30 Oct**	10–6		T	W	T	F	S	S
4 Nov–18 Dec**	11–4					F	S	S

*House: last entry one hour before closing; entry is controlled (queueing at busy times). **Gardens and woodland: open 10 to 6 on Mondays when house open, during local school holidays and Bank Holidays. Last admission at the gate is 4 (3 in winter). Last entry to estate drive is 5:30.

Dunstanburgh Castle

Craster, Alnwick, Northumberland NE66 3TT

[icon] [icon] 1961

Iconic castle ruin occupying a dramatic position with spectacular views of the Northumberland coastline – one-mile walk from Craster. **Note**: managed by English Heritage. National Trust members admitted free. Sorry no toilets. Parking at Craster, pay and display, not National Trust (charge including members). Contact English Heritage for opening times.

Finding out more: 01665 576231 or dunstanburghcastle@nationaltrust.org.uk

Farne Islands, Northumberland (above and below)

Farne Islands

Northumberland

[icon] [icon] [icon] 1925

One of the UK's best wildlife spectacles. An exhilarating boat trip to the islands gives an unparalleled peek into the world of 23 nesting seabird species, including thousands of puffins, Arctic terns and guillemots. In autumn, visit the grey seal colony, where over 1,000 pups are born each year. **Note**: basic toilet facilities on Inner Farne only. Bring a hat – nesting terns will divebomb! Access by boat from Seahouses – separate charge applies (including members).

Eating and shopping: shop in Seahouses selling a range of gifts and local produce. Some souvenirs also available on the islands.

Making the most of your day: St Cuthbert's chapel, with vibrant stained glass, and Victorian lighthouse. Visitor centre. Easy-access boardwalk. Seasonal tours and events. Lindisfarne Castle and Northumberland Coast nearby. **Dogs**: not allowed (including assistance dogs) due to very sensitive nature of the colony.

Access: [icon] Grounds [icon]
Sat Nav: use NE68 7RQ. **Parking**: in Seahouses, not National Trust (charge including members).

Finding out more: 01665 721099. 01289 389244 (Lindisfarne Castle) or farneislands@nationaltrust.org.uk

Farne Islands		M	T	W	T	F	S	S
Inner Farne Island								
1 Apr–30 Apr	10:30–5:30	M	T	W	T	F	S	S
1 May–31 Jul	1:30–5:30	M	T	W	T	F	S	S
1 Aug–30 Oct	10:30–5:30	M	T	W	T	F	S	S
Staple Island								
1 May–31 Jul	10:30–1:30	M	T	W	T	F	S	S

Landings only on Inner Farne and Staple Islands. Seahouses information centre and shop open all year, 10 to 5.

George Stephenson's Birthplace

near Wylam, Northumberland NE41 8DS

🏠 ✳ ⚓ 1949

Beside Wylam's historic Waggonway on the idyllic banks of the River Tyne, this simple cottage (above) was railway pioneer George Stephenson's birthplace. The costumed guides bring to life the story and challenges of a mining family living in one room, whose engineering legacy still lives on today.

Eating and shopping: tea-room serving light snacks and homemade cakes, with garden seating.

Making the most of your day: **Indoors** Tiny room decorated exactly as in 1781, the year of Stephenson's birth. **Outdoors** You can stroll or cycle along the route of one of the world's first steam railways. **Dogs**: welcome on leads in garden.

Access: 🅿️ 👨‍🦽 🎫 ♿ :: 🔊
Birthplace 🔩 Café 🔩 Garden 🔩
Parking: in village, then ½ mile along Wylam Waggonway.

Finding out more: 01661 843276 or georgestephensons@nationaltrust.org.uk

George Stephenson's Birthplace		M	T	W	T	F	S	S
Cottage, tea-room and tea-garden								
13 Feb–30 Oct	Tour	·	·	·	T	F	S	S
Tea-room and tea-garden								
2 Jan–7 Feb	11–3	·	·	·	·	·	S	S
5 Nov–18 Dec	11–3	·	·	·	·	·	S	S
Open Bank Holiday Mondays.								

Gibside

near Rowlands Gill, Gateshead, Tyne & Wear NE16 6BG

➕ 🚻 📷 ✳ 🐕 🧺 ⛺ 🔔 🍴 1974

You can enjoy a welcome escape from the stresses of modern life by exploring Gibside, following trails which meander through woodland and gardens and offer views across the Derwent Valley. There are fascinating historic buildings and ruins to discover and you might even spot some of the wonderful wildlife, such as red kites and roe deer. You can also find out about wealthy heiress Mary Eleanor Bowes, her dramatic love-life and her gardening passion. This historic landscape is in the process of being restored to its former glory, a rare example of a designed landscape from the 18th century. **Note**: work to the Walled Garden continues.

Eating and shopping: Gibside café. Carriage House coffee shop and Renwick's second-hand books at the Stables. Kiosk at adventure play area (weekends and holidays). Gibside shop selling plants and gifts. Friday and Saturday evening pub and beer garden. Twice-monthly market.

Gibside, Tyne & Wear: perfect antidote to modern stress

Making the most of your day: **Indoors** Palladian chapel with unique three-tier pulpit. Gibside story and wildlife interpretation at the Stables. **Outdoors** Walled Garden and wider estate to explore. Walks and family-friendly events. Adventure play areas. **Dogs**: welcome on leads. Assistance dogs only in Strawberry Castle Adventure play area.

Access: Chapel Stables Garden
Parking: 382 yards from café and shop (uphill walkway).

Finding out more: 01207 541820 or gibside@nationaltrust.org.uk

Gibside		M	T	W	T	F	S	S
Landscape gardens, woodlands, café and shop*								
1 Jan–28 Feb	10–4	M	T	W	T	F	S	S
29 Feb–30 Oct	10–6**	M	T	W	T	F	S	S
31 Oct–31 Dec	10–4	M	T	W	T	F	S	S
Beer garden and pub*								
Open all year	6–9	·	·	·	·	F	S	·
Chapel								
2 Jan–28 Feb	10–4	·	·	·	·	·	S	S
29 Feb–30 Oct	10–5	M	T	W	T	F	S	S
5 Nov–31 Dec	10–4	·	·	·	·	·	S	S

*Estate: closed 24 and 25 December. Pub and beer garden: closed 25 December. Last entry: winter 3:30, summer 4:30.
**Café and shop close at 5.

Gibside: a gentle pace of life

Hadrian's Wall and Housesteads Fort

near Bardon Mill, Hexham, Northumberland NE47 6NN

1930

You can enjoy breathtaking views (above) at one of the Roman Empire's best-maintained outposts in northern Europe. Here, you can walk in the footsteps of Romans and Reivers across 110 miles of World Heritage Site, where the wall and fort provide a real insight into a Roman soldier's life. **Note**: fort owned by National Trust, managed by English Heritage. ½ mile uphill from visitor centre.

Eating and shopping: visitor centre offering sandwiches and snacks, ice-cream and drinks. Shop selling books, cards, gifts, souvenirs and plants. Picnics welcome.

Making the most of your day: **Indoors** Museum (not National Trust) with dressing-up clothes and video presentation. **Outdoors** Play area. Why not walk along the wall to Milecastle 37 and Sycamore Gap? Cottages for rent. **Dogs**: welcome on leads.

Access: Visitor centre Museum
Parking: at Housesteads, Steel Rigg and Cawfields, not National Trust (charge including members).

Finding out more: 01434 344525 or housesteads@nationaltrust.org.uk

Hadrian's Wall and Housesteads Fort
Open daily (limited opening over Christmas and New Year).

Lindisfarne Castle

Holy Island, Berwick-upon-Tweed,
Northumberland TD15 2SH

[icons] 1944

Location is the thing at Lindisfarne Castle. A former fort, converted into a holiday home, the castle is a beautiful blend of old and relatively new. Edward Hudson, seeking a quiet retreat from London, fell in love with the castle and undertook the conversion alongside renowned architect Sir Edwin Lutyens; this romantic castle is full of the intimate spaces typical of Lutyens' work. Outside, the upper battery offers panoramic views across the coast, including the Farne Islands. There are shoreline walks, the unexpected grandeur of the lime kilns and the summer-flowering garden, designed by Gertrude Jekyll, waiting to be explored. **Note**: some rooms closed due to conservation project. Toilets limited. Island accessed via tidal causeway.

Eating and shopping: souvenirs, coffee machine, water, snacks and ice-cream available. National Trust shop in village.

Making the most of your day: regular events and family trails. Kites and binoculars available to borrow. Occasional seal-spotting from the upper battery and rock-pooling events.
Dogs: welcome on leads. Assistance dogs only in castle.

Romantic Lindisfarne Castle, Northumberland (above and below): beautiful blend of old and relatively new, full of intimate spaces

Access: [icons] Castle [icons] Grounds [icon]
Parking: at main island car park, 1 mile, not National Trust (charge including members). Private transfer available most days.

Finding out more: 01289 389244 or lindisfarne@nationaltrust.org.uk

Lindisfarne Castle		M	T	W	T	F	S	S
Castle*								
13 Feb–30 Oct	10–3		T	W	T	F	S	S
13 Feb–30 Oct	12–5		T	W	T	F	S	S
1 Aug–31 Aug	10–3	M	T	W	T	F	S	S
1 Aug–31 Aug	12–5	M	T	W	T	F	S	S
Garden								
Open every day all year								

*Opening times vary due to tides, either 10 to 3 or 12 to 5. Check times before visiting. Open Bank Holiday Mondays. Some additional Monday openings throughout season and some weekend openings in winter.

Northumberland Coast: white sand and blue skies

Northumberland Coast

Northumberland

🛏️ 🏛️ ⚡ 🛏️ 1935

From Lindisfarne to Druridge Bay, you'll find wide open skies above white sands and blue seas. This unspoilt coastline is rich in pretty fishing villages, wildlife and deserted beaches, with excellent rock pools. Look out for seals, dolphins, wading shorebirds and nesting terns at Long Nanny. **Note**: public car parks only (charge including members).

Eating and shopping: shops on Holy Island and Seahouses. Cafés, pubs and shops in coastal towns and villages (none National Trust).

Making the most of your day: little tern nesting colony at Long Nanny (June to August), access from High Newton. Events, including guided walks, '50 things' and wildlife spotting. Farne Islands, Dunstanburgh Castle, Lindisfarne Castle nearby. **Dogs**: welcome, some local restrictions may apply.

Access: 🔥
Sat Nav: for Low Newton use NE66 3EH; Druridge Bay NE61 5EG; St Aidans' Dunes NE68 7SH. **Parking**: limited at Druridge Bay. Also at Holy Island, Seahouses, Beadnell, Newton by the Sea and Craster, none National Trust (charge including members).

Finding out more: 01289 389244 or northumberlandcoast@nationaltrust.org.uk

Penshaw Monument

near Penshaw, Tyne & Wear

🏛️ 🏛️ ⚡ 1939

Enjoy walks and magnificent views from this 70-foot high tribute to the 1st Earl of Durham. An iconic Wearside landmark. **Note**: sorry no toilets. For Sat Nav use DH4 7NJ. Open daily; tours to top of monument on Saturdays, Sundays and Bank Holidays, 25 March to 25 September.

Finding out more: 01207 541820 or penshaw.monument@nationaltrust.org.uk

Seaton Delaval Hall

The Avenue, Seaton Sluice, Northumberland NE26 4QR

🏛️ ❄️ ⚡ 2009

It may have been one of architect Sir John Vanbrugh's smallest country houses, but it was home to the larger-than-life Delaval family. The Hall still bears the scars of the fierce fires which almost condemned it to ruin 200 years ago. You will enter a world where an extraordinary lifestyle was acted out in the most colourful way. Great theatre and drama can still be found in the house, gardens and surrounding landscape, which have served as the stage for an incredible tale of changing fortunes. The story of Seaton's survival is as dramatic as any theatrical production.

Eating and shopping: café serving hot and cold drinks, snacks and sweet treats throughout the year. In fine weather, ice-cream, coffee and tea are served from the summerhouse. Shop selling souvenirs, gifts and plants, located in the ticket hut.

Vanbrugh's Seaton Delaval Hall, Northumberland (opposite, inside and out): the stage for an incredible tale of changing fortunes

Why not share your pictures with us? #nationaltrust

Making the most of your day: Indoors

Vanbrugh's architecture, with remarkable 18th-century stables. Great Hall with fire-damaged interior and original statues.

Outdoors Beautiful gardens, woodland walks and coastal landscape. Events and activities.

Dogs: welcome on leads outdoors.

Access: 🅿️ 🚻 🔄 📷 🎵 Hall ♿
Stables 🔄 **Grounds** ➡️
Parking: 500 yards.

Finding out more: 0191 237 9100 or seatondelavalhall@nationaltrust.org.uk

Seaton Delaval Hall		M	T	W	T	F	S	S
Central hall, stables and gardens								
2 Jan–21 Feb	11–3	·	·	·	·	·	S	S
27 Feb–23 Oct	11–5	M	·	·	T	F	S	S
28 Mar–10 Apr	11–5	M	T	W	T	F	S	S
30 May–5 Jun	11–5	M	T	W	T	F	S	S
25 Jul–4 Sep	11–5	M	T	W	T	F	S	S
24 Oct–30 Oct	11–5	M	T	W	T	F	S	S
5 Nov–24 Dec	11–3	·	·	·	·	·	S	S
West wing								
27 Feb–30 Oct	11–5*	M	·	·	T	F	S	S

*West wing: open daily in main school holidays, as for central hall, stables and gardens. Last admission 45 minutes before closing.

Souter Lighthouse and The Leas

Coast Road, Whitburn, Sunderland, Tyne & Wear SR6 7NH

1990

Scale the heights to the top of a lighthouse which was truly modern for its time – the first purpose-built to be lit by electricity. While you catch your breath, you can gaze straight out to sea, north to the Cheviot Hills and south to Roseberry Topping. The Leas is dotted with wildflower meadows with bee orchids, perennial flax, yellow rattle and red clover hidden among the coastal grassland. A saunter through Whitburn Coastal Park is great for bird-spotting and the local nature reserve provides water and rest for birds making their way across the sea and along the coast.

Eating and shopping: Lighthouse Café serving light lunches, soup, cakes and refreshments. Local dishes Panacklety and Singin' Hinnies are a must-try. The Treasure Chest shop stocks coastal gifts.

Souter Lighthouse and The Leas, Tyne & Wear: the lighthouse (below), is set on a stunning coastline (above)

For other ways to get involved go to nationaltrust.org.uk/get-involved/volunteer

Making the most of your day: events and family activities, including rock-pool rambles, bug hunting and birdwatching. Pirate days and holiday crafts. Car boot sales. Outdoor play area. Foghorn demonstrations, talking telescope and wildlife garden. **Dogs**: all welcome on leads outdoors.

Access: 🅿 🅓 ♿ 🔆 🔊 📷 ♿
Building ♿ 🅱 **Grounds** ♿ ♿ 🅱
Parking: on site.

Finding out more: 0191 529 3161 or souter@nationaltrust.org.uk

Souter Lighthouse and The Leas		M	T	W	T	F	S	S
13 Feb–30 Oct	11–5	M	T	W	T	F	S	S
31 Oct–27 Nov	11–4	M	T	W	T	F	S	S
3 Dec–18 Dec	11–4						S	S

Wallington

Cambo, near Morpeth,
Northumberland NE61 4AR

🏠 ✿ ♿ 1941

Gifted to you by Sir Charles Philips Trevelyan, Socialist MP and 'illogical Englishman', Wallington has something for everyone. Set within an 18th-century landscape, the house is surrounded by a huge working estate and over 20 miles of walks. The West Wood is full of wildlife and wild play spaces, the East Wood is home to towering trees and the Walled Garden is bursting with colour, whatever the season. Further afield, you can take a circular walk to Broomhouse Farm or enjoy a stroll by the river. At the heart of the estate, the Trevelyan's informal home is full of treasured collections – make yourself at home in the impressive rooms and find out about this unconventional family.

Eating and shopping: Clocktower Café serving brunch, lunch and afternoon tea. Takeaway refreshments available from the new Clocktower Kiosk and the Walled Garden Kiosk (seasonal). Wide range of gifts and souvenirs for sale in our shops and plant centre.

Wallington, Northumberland: something for everyone

Making the most of your day: **Indoors** Soak up the atmosphere in the Trevelyan's home – discover Northumberland's history in the Pre-Raphaelite paintings around the Central Hall, warm up next to the AGA in the kitchen or relax on the sofas in the Drawing Room. Tours and activities, including conservation in action, cookery demonstrations and Christmas events in December. **Outdoors** Smell the heady fragrance in the Edwardian conservatory in the Walled Garden. Activities to celebrate the 300th anniversary of 'Capability' Brown during the summer, including tours of Rothley Lake. Wildlife hide, adventure playground, play train and fort. Regular guided walks and family activities during school holidays.
Dogs: welcome on leads outdoors and on all walks.

Wallington: while the house (right), is full of treasured collections, the grounds and gardens (above and top), offer just as much to intrigue and delight visitors of all ages

Access: 🅿♿🚻♿🐕📷📶📱

House ♿♿💺🔊 Grounds ♿♿♿➡️👓🔊

Parking: on site.

Finding out more: 01670 773600 or wallington@nationaltrust.org.uk

Wallington		M	T	W	T	F	S	S
Walled garden, woodland and estate*								
Open all year	10–6	M	T	W	T	F	S	S
House								
13 Feb–30 Oct	12–5	M	T	W	T	F	S	S
Shops and café								
1 Jan–12 Feb	10:30–4:30	M	T	W	T	F	S	S
13 Feb–30 Oct	10:30–5:30	M	T	W	T	F	S	S
31 Oct–23 Dec	10:30–4:30	M	T	W	T	F	S	S
27 Dec–31 Dec	10:30–4:30		T	W	T	F	S	

Woodland and estate: closes dusk if earlier.
*Walled garden: closes 7 in summer; 4 in winter.
Last orders in café 30 minutes before closing.

Washington Old Hall

The Avenue, Washington Village,
Washington, Tyne & Wear NE38 7LE

🏠 ❄ 🔔 🍸 1956

The name Washington is very important in
world history. Did you know that the capital of
the USA would not bear this name, if it wasn't
for this little gem in North East England?
A warm and friendly welcome awaits at this
historic house and tranquil garden.

Making the most of your day: **Indoors** Group
tours. Christmas crafts fayre. Santa visits.
Outdoors Fourth of July Independence Day
ceremony. School holiday nature
investigations. Open-air theatre by Pantaloons.
Dogs: welcome on leads in garden only.

Access: 🅿 ♿ 🚻 📷 🎧 🚶 ⊘
Building 🔼🔽 Grounds 🔼🔽 ➡
Parking: on site (additional unrestricted
parking on The Avenue).

Finding out more: 0191 416 6879 or
washingtonoldhall@nationaltrust.org.uk

Washington Old Hall		M	T	W	T	F	S	S
26 Mar–31 Oct*	10–5	M	T	W	·	·	S	S
10 Dec–22 Dec	12–7	M	T	W	T	F	S	S

*Open daily during local school holidays and half-terms.
Closed for weddings: 14 and 28 May, 3 and 25 June, 23 July,
6 and 12 August, 1 and 8 October.

Washington Old Hall, Tyne & Wear: the tranquil garden

Wales

Dinefwr, Carmarthenshire

Cemlyn and the
North Anglesey Coast
Holyhead

Llandudno
Conwy
Bodysgallen
Hall Hotel,
Restaurant
and Spa
Rhyl

LIVERPOOL
The Hardmans' House
The Beatles'
Childhood
Homes
Speke Hall

Langefni
Bangor
Aberconwy
House
Conwy Suspension Bridge

Plas Newydd
House and Gardens
Penrhyn
Castle
Bodnant Garden

Chester

Caernarfon
Segontium
Carneddau
and Glyderau
Ogwen Cottage

Hafod
y Llan
Ty Mawr Wybrnant

Wrexham

Craflwyn and
Beddgelert

Erddig

Porthdinllaen

Criccieth

Chirk Castle

Porthmadog

Oswestry

Plas yn
Rhiw
Llanbedrog
Beach

Porthor

Shrewsbury

Porth Meudwy
Abersoch
Porth
y Swnt

Dolmelynllyn
Estate

Attingham Park

Dolgellau

Welshpool
Powis Castle
and Garden

Carding Mill
Valley and the
Shropshire Hills

Machynlleth

Newtown

Aberystwyth

Llandrindod
Wells

Croft Castle
and Parkland

Llanerchaeron

The Weir Garden

Mwnt
Penbryn

Builth Wells

HEREFORD

Cardigan

Cilgerran Castle

Dolaucothi
Estate
Woodland
Dolaucothi Gold Mines

Skenfrith
Castle

St David's Visitor
Centre and Shop

Cwmdu

Brecon

The Kymin

Paxton's
Tower
Dinefwr

Brecon
Beacons

Carmarthen

Martin's
Haven

Colby
Woodland
Garden

Henrhyd Falls

Merthyr
Tydfil

Marloes Sands
and Mere
Pembroke
Tudor Merchant's
House
Llanelli
Aberdulais Tin Works
and Waterfall

Chepstow

Stackpole
Swansea
Neath
Port Talbot
Newport

Stackpole Outdoor
Learning Centre

Rhossili and
South Gower Coast
Pennard, Pwll Du
and Bishopston Valley

Bridgend

Tredegar House

CARDIFF

Dyffryn
Gardens

Aberconwy House

Castle Street, Conwy LL32 8AY

🏠 1934

This is the only medieval merchant's house in Conwy to have survived the turbulent history of the walled town over seven centuries. Furnished rooms and helpful volunteers bring different periods in its history alive. **Note**: nearest toilets 50 yards. Steps to all parts of property.

Eating and shopping: gift shop.

Making the most of your day: Easter events. Father Christmas will be visiting in December. **Dogs**: assistance dogs only.

Access: 🔲🎧 Building 🦽
Parking: none on site.

Finding out more: 01492 592246 or aberconwyhouse@nationaltrust.org.uk

Aberconwy House		M	T	W	T	F	S	S
House								
27 Feb–31 Oct	11–5	M	T	W	T	F	S	S
3 Dec–18 Dec	11–5	·	·	·	·	·	S	S
Shop								
1 Jan–1 Mar	11–5		T	W	T	F	S	S
2 Mar–31 Dec	10–5	M	T	W	T	F	S	S

House and shop closed 25 December.

Aberconwy House, Conwy: medieval merchant's home

Mae'r wybodaeth sydd yn y llawlyfr hwn am feddiannau'r Ymddiriedolaeth Genedlaethol yng Nghymru ar gael yn Gymraeg o Swyddfa'r Ymddiriedolaeth Genedlaethol, Tŷ Tredegar, Casnewydd, NP10 8YW, neu drwy e-bostio wa.customerenquiries@nationaltrust.org.uk

Aberdulais Tin Works and Waterfall, Neath Port Talbot

Aberdulais Tin Works and Waterfall

Aberdulais, Neath, Neath Port Talbot SA10 8EU

🏠🏛️👪☕ 1980

If you like archaeology, you'll love some of the secrets that have been uncovered here at Aberdulais – one of Britain's oldest tin works. As you wander through the site, you'll find yourself at the very heart of the earliest industry in Britain. You'll also discover how Aberdulais played its part in shaping the world as we know it today. If you think you've seen Aberdulais before, think again – we've made new discoveries and we're dying to share them with you. We aim to enthral and fascinate all ages… Whoever thought history could be so much fun? **Note**: waterwheel and turbine subject to water levels and conservation work.

Eating and shopping: Old School House tea-room serving light lunches, soup, cakes and refreshments. Gift shop and second-hand bookshop.

Making the most of your day: various activities throughout the year, including Conservation in Action and handling collections. Family Tin Detectives packs, Victorian costumes, archaeology days and guided tours. **Dogs**: welcome on leads and inside buildings. Assistance dogs only in Old School House tea-room.

Access: ▣▣▣▣▣▣▣
Stable and Tin Exhibition ▣▣▣
Turbine House ▣▣▣▣▣
Grounds ▣▣▣▣▣
Sat Nav: follow brown signs. **Parking**: 50 yards.

Finding out more: 01639 636674 or aberdulais@nationaltrust.org.uk

Aberdulais		M	T	W	T	F	S	S
2 Jan–14 Feb	11–4	.	.	.	.	.	S	S
15 Feb–21 Feb	11–4	M	T	W	T	F	S	S
27 Feb–20 Mar	11–4	M	T	W	T	F	S	S
21 Mar–4 Sep	10:30–5	M	T	W	T	F	S	S
5 Sep–30 Oct	11–4	M	T	W	T	F	S	S
4 Nov–18 Dec	11–4	.	.	.	.	F	S	S

Tea-room opening times vary from main property.

Activity at Aberdulais Tin Works and Waterfall

Bodnant Garden

Tal-y-Cafn, near Colwyn Bay, Conwy LL28 5RE

▣ ▣ ▣ 1949

In the foothills of Snowdonia this 32-hectare (80-acre) garden features scenery, plant collections and horticultural styles from formal to pastoral and wild to exotic. One family's vision, the garden was established in 1874 by Victorian entrepreneur Henry Pochin, who transformed the landscape with rare trees and shrubs from around the world. You can enjoy Italianate terraces with roses, herbaceous beds and parterres, shaded shrub borders and the drama of The Dell, with its waterfalls and towering conifers. Every season brings new delights – magnolias and rhododendrons in spring, roses and water lilies in summer, rich leaf colour in autumn and frosted landscapes in winter. New areas to explore include the Winter Garden, Old Park meadow, Yew Dell and the Far End.

Eating and shopping: two tea-rooms as well as two open-air refreshment kiosks. Picnic areas. Shop and neighbouring garden centre and craft units (not National Trust).

Making the most of your day: events all year, including monthly guided walks with a gardener, family trails and holiday activities for children. **Dogs**: welcome daily January, February, November, December. May to August, Wednesday evenings (5 to 8).

Access: ⛽🚻♿🚼📷🔔 **Grounds** ♿➡♿
Parking: 150 yards.

Finding out more: 01492 650460 or bodnantgarden@nationaltrust.org.uk

Bodnant Garden			M	T	W	T	F	S	S
1 Jan–29 Feb	10–4		M	T	W	T	F	S	S
1 Mar–31 Oct	10–5		M	T	W	T	F	S	S
1 Nov–23 Dec	10–4		M	T	W	T	F	S	S
27 Dec–31 Dec	10–4		·	T	W	T	F	S	·

Garden open until 8 on Wednesdays from May to August.

From formal to pastoral and wild to exotic, there is something for everyone at Bodnant Garden, Conwy (top, left and below)

The romantic gardens at Bodysgallen Hall, Conwy

Bodysgallen Hall Hotel, Restaurant and Spa

The Royal Welsh Way, Llandudno,
Conwy LL30 1RS

🏠❄️♿📠🔔♨️🍽️ 2008

This Grade I listed 17th-century house, set
within 89 hectares (220 acres) of parkland, has
the most spectacular views towards Conwy
Castle and Snowdonia. The romantic gardens,
which have won awards for their restoration,
include a rare parterre filled with sweet-
smelling herbs, as well as several follies,
cascade, walled garden and formal rose
gardens. Beyond, the hotel's parkland
offers miles of stunning walks and views to the
coastline. **Note**: access is for paying guests of
the hotel, including for luncheon, afternoon tea
and dinner, and the Spa. Children over the age
of six welcome.

Finding out more: 01492 584466.
01492 582519 (fax) or info@bodysgallen.com
bodysgallen.com

Brecon Beacons

Powys

🏠🏛️♿ 1936

The Brecon Beacons, Sugarloaf and Skirrid
have captivated visitors for hundreds of years
with their soaring mountain peaks and tranquil
valleys. With lush farmland, ancient moorland
and southern Britain's highest mountain,
Pen y Fan, they are perfect for hill-walking and
exploring hidden streams and woodlands.
By contrast, Clytha Estate is a great place to
have a picnic or take a short walk, meandering
through parkland with views of Clytha House
and Castle. In the heart of Wales you can
discover the vast, remote moorlands of
Abergwesyn Commons or ramble over the
Begwns with their panoramic views of the
Brecon Beacons. **Note**: only toilets at
Pont ar Daf car park in the Brecon Beacons.

Making the most of your day: family activities
throughout the year, including Wild
Wednesdays at the Sugarloaf in the summer
holidays. Bunkhouse near Pen y Fan. Why not
visit The Kymin? **Dogs**: welcome on leads.

Access: 🚶

Sat Nav: use LD3 8NL. **Parking:** main car park at Pont ar Daf, off A470; alternatives not all National Trust.

Finding out more: 01874 625515 or brecon@nationaltrust.org.uk

Brecon Beacons, Powys (above and below)

Snowy Carneddau and Glyderau, Gwynedd

Carneddau and Glyderau

Nant Ffrancon, Bethesda, Gwynedd

🏨 🐾 1951

This 8,498-hectare (21,000-acre) mountainous area includes Cwm Idwal Nature Reserve, renowned for its geology and Arctic-Alpine plants, such as the rare Snowdon lily. There are eight tenanted upland farms here and nine peaks over 3,000 feet, including the famous Tryfan, where Edmund Hilary trained for his ascent of Everest. The area is home to a variety of wildlife, including otters, feral ponies and rare birds such as dotterel and peregrine. The 60 miles of footpaths attract 500,000 walkers each year, while the bleak, photogenic landscapes have proved popular with artists. **Note:** mountainous and difficult terrain – please come well equipped and check the weather. Charges apply in the National Park car parks.

Eating and shopping: facilities at Ogwen visitor centre, including food kiosk (not National Trust) and a warden centre run in partnership with Snowdonia National Park and Natural Resources Wales.

Making the most of your day: easy walk to Cwm Idwal allows visitors to enjoy Snowdonia at its most dramatic and follow in the footsteps of Charles Darwin, who 'discovered' glaciation here. **Dogs**: on a lead at all times.

Access: 👤
Sat Nav: use LL57 3LZ. **Parking**: at Ogwen Lake (not National Trust).

Finding out more: 01248 600954 or carneddau@nationaltrust.org.uk

Peaks at Carneddau and Glyderau

Cemlyn and the North Anglesey Coast

Cemaes Bay, Anglesey

✝ 🏚 🏛 📷 ⚄ 🚂 🛏 🛌 1971

Ruggedly beautiful, the north coast of Anglesey has a unique coastline of rocks, small bays and headlands and is a delight for walkers. Cemlyn is recognised for its National Nature Reserve and is a designated Area of Outstanding Natural Beauty and home to the rare spotted rock rose. Renowned for its breeding colonies of Sandwich, common and Arctic terns, Cemlyn Bay is a hive of seabird activity in spring and summer. Headland paths offer dramatic land and seascapes during autumn and winter. The brackish lagoon is separated from the sea by a remarkable shingle ridge. **Note**: nearest toilets in Cemaes Bay, 3 miles (not National Trust).

Why not share your pictures with us? #nationaltrust

Cemlyn and the North Anglesey Coast, Anglesey: ruggedly beautiful, the coast is home to rare flora and fauna

Making the most of your day: numerous footpaths and downloadable walks to help you explore. Events, including pram walks and walking festival. Summer fair at Swtan, a restored whitewashed cottage nearby (LL65 4EU). **Dogs**: welcome under control near livestock.

Access:
Sat Nav: use LL67 0DY. **Parking**: at Bryn Aber car park, Cemlyn.

Finding out more: 01248 714795 or cemlyn@nationaltrust.org.uk

Chirk Castle, Wrexham: where history comes to life

Chirk Castle

Chirk, Wrexham LL14 5AF

1981

Completed in 1310, Chirk is the last Welsh castle from the reign of Edward I still lived in today. Features from its 700 years include the medieval tower and dungeon, 17th-century Long Gallery, grand 18th-century state apartments, servants' hall and historic laundry. The refurbished east wing depicts the life of Lord Howard de Walden during the 1930s. The award-winning gardens contain clipped yews, herbaceous borders, shrub and rock gardens. A terrace with far-reaching views looks out over the Cheshire and Shropshire plains, while the parkland provides a habitat for rare invertebrates and wild flowers, and contains many mature trees.

Eating and shopping: tea-room serving hot and cold food, drinks and cakes. Seasonal kiosk at Home Farm selling hot and cold drinks and snacks. Gift shops with plant sales and second-hand books.

Making the most of your day: Indoors You can explore the medieval fortress and dungeon, Myddelton family home, servants' rooms and Victorian laundry. **Outdoors** There are the award-winning gardens and 194-hectare (480-acre) estate to discover. **Dogs**: welcome on leads. Assistance dogs only in formal gardens and Pleasure Ground wood.

Access: [icons]
State rooms [icons] **Adam Tower** [icons]
Gardens [icons]
Parking: at Home Farm by ticket office, then 200 yards (via steep hill) to castle.

Finding out more: 01691 777701 or chirkcastle@nationaltrust.org.uk

Chirk Castle		M	T	W	T	F	S	S
Estate								
Open all year*	7–7	M	T	W	T	F	S	S
Garden, tower, shops and tea-rooms								
30 Jan–31 Mar	10–4	M	T	W	T	F	S	S
1 Apr–30 Sep	10–5	M	T	W	T	F	S	S
1 Oct–30 Oct	10–4	M	T	W	T	F	S	S
5 Nov–27 Nov	10–4						S	S
3 Dec–23 Dec	10–4	M	T	W	T	F	S	S
State rooms								
30 Jan–21 Feb†	12–4						S	S
27 Feb–31 Mar**	12–4	M	T	W	T	F	S	S
1 Apr–30 Sep**	12–5	M	T	W	T	F	S	S
1 Oct–30 Oct**	12–4	M	T	W	T	F	S	S
5 Nov–27 Nov†	12–4						S	S
3 Dec–23 Dec	11–4	M	T	W	T	F	S	S

*Estate open to 9, June to August. **Guided State Room tours 11:15 and 11:30 (places limited). †Guided tour only, timed tickets available on the day (places limited).

Chirk Castle: straight from a children's storybook

Cilgerran Castle

near Cardigan, Pembrokeshire SA43 2SF

[icon] 1938

13th-century castle overlooking the Teifi Gorge – the perfect location to repel attackers. Walk the walls and admire the stunning views. **Note**: in the guardianship of Cadw – Welsh Government's historic environment service. Dogs on leads allowed. Open daily, 2 January to 31 March, 10 to 4; 1 April to 31 October, 10 to 5; 1 November to 31 December, 10 to 4 (closed 24 to 26 December).

Finding out more: 01239 621339 or cilgerrancastle@nationaltrust.org.uk

Colby Woodland Garden

near Amroth, Pembrokeshire SA67 8PP

[icons] 1980

A short walk from the beach, this hidden wooded valley, with its secret garden and industrial past, is a place for play. There are fallen trees to climb, rope swings and playful surprises everywhere. Spring brings bluebells, camellias, rhododendrons and azaleas, while the walled garden gives year-round colour, peace and seclusion. There are woodland walks, meandering streams and ponds with stepping stones and log bridges in the wildflower

meadow, and the whole valley teems with wildlife. Fun learning activities and exploration packs are available, and there are picnic and campfire spots in the meadow and free games to borrow. **Note**: house not open.

Eating and shopping: shop, plant sales and second-hand books. Bothy tea-room (concession). Gallery selling Pembrokeshire arts and crafts. Picnics welcome.

Making the most of your day: rope swings, den-building, pond-dipping, camp fires, duck racing, activity sheets, exploration packs, dam building and games equipment. Virtual tour and film. Easter trails, wildlife events and holiday activities. **Dogs**: under control in estate woodlands. On leads in garden and meadow.

Access: 🅿️🅿️♿🅦🅒🔔🔍📷🔆📷
Grounds 🦽➡️♿
Parking: 50 yards.

Finding out more: 01834 811885 or colby@nationaltrust.org.uk

Colby Woodland Garden		M	T	W	T	F	S	S
Woodland, walled gardens and bothy exhibition								
2 Jan–12 Feb	10–3	M	T	W	T	F	S	S
31 Oct–23 Dec	10–3	M	T	W	T	F	S	S
Woodland, walled gardens, shop and bothy exhibition								
13 Feb–30 Oct	10–5	M	T	W	T	F	S	S
Gallery and tea-room								
19 Mar–30 Oct	10–4:30	M	T	W	T	F	S	S

Car park open as woodland and walled gardens. Closed 1 January, 24 to 31 December.

Colby Woodland Garden, Pembrokeshire (opposite and below): a place to play

Conwy Suspension Bridge

Conwy LL32 8LD

🏠 ♿ 1965

Designed in the 1820s by Thomas Telford, this graceful bridge (above) with its beautifully restored tiny toll-keeper's house has stunning views over the Conwy Estuary. Kept open by a husband and wife at a time when trade and travel brought Conwy to life, it never closed, whatever the weather. **Note**: sorry, no toilet.

Eating and shopping: why not bring a picnic to enjoy on the grassed area?

Making the most of your day: superb views of the river and castle. **Dogs**: allowed.

Access: Building 🦽 Grounds 🦽
Parking: none on site.

Finding out more: 01492 573282 or conwybridge@nationaltrust.org.uk

Conwy Suspension Bridge
Open 27 February to 31 October. Toll House opening times available at Aberconwy House (01492 592246).

Craflwyn and Beddgelert

near Beddgelert, Gwynedd

🏛🏚 1994

The 81-hectare (200-acre) Craflwyn Estate is set in the heart of beautiful Snowdonia, within a landscape steeped in history and legend. There is a network of paths and woodland walks to explore and tumbling waterfalls to discover. At Craflwyn you can learn about the Princes of Gwynedd before venturing up to nearby Dinas Emrys, the legendary birthplace of Wales's national emblem, the red dragon. Within a couple of miles of Craflwyn, there are great walks for all abilities, from a village stroll at pretty Beddgelert to the rugged Fisherman's Path down the spectacular Aberglaslyn Pass. **Note**: Craflwyn Hall is run and managed by HF Holidays (surrounding land open to the public).

Eating and shopping: picnics welcome at Craflwyn. Local crafts on offer in Tŷ Isaf shop in Beddgelert. The village also has a selection of restaurants, cafés, taverns and hotels (not National Trust).

Making the most of your day: you can learn the story of Prince Llywelyn's faithful hound by visiting Gelert's Grave. Children's adventure packs, maps and guides available from Tŷ Isaf shop. Guided walks and events. **Dogs**: welcome under control near livestock.

Access: 🦽
Sat Nav: use LL55 4NG. **Parking**: in Craflwyn.

Finding out more: 01766 510120 or craflwyn@nationaltrust.org.uk

Craflwyn and Beddgelert, Gwynedd (above and below), lies at the heart of beautiful Snowdonia

Why not share your pictures with us? #nationaltrust

Cwmdu

Llandeilo, Carmarthenshire

⊞ 🍴 ♿ 1991

Georgian terrace with pub, post office, chapel and vestry. Representing a rural Welsh village of the past. **Note**: pub and shop run by community. For Sat Nav use SA19 7DY.

Finding out more: 01558 685088 or cwmdu@nationaltrust.org.uk

Dinefwr

Llandeilo, Carmarthenshire SA19 6RT

🏛 🖼 ✠ 🏰 🔊 ❀ ♿ 🚲 🐕 📷 🍴 1990

A place of legends and folklore, Dinefwr's long history has featured power, glory, downfall and loss. There is even a direct link with the past through our iconic White Park cattle, which have been kept here for 1,000 years. Walks lead through ancient woods, with gnarled veteran trees, and you can seek the inhabitants of the Bogwood and Mill Pond and walk in the footsteps of medieval princes – viewing 'your kingdom' from the castle on the hill. After exploring the tranquil countryside, you can continue your adventure in atmospheric Newton House, discovering the many changes the years have wrought. **Note**: Dinefwr Castle is owned by the Wildlife Trust and is in the guardianship of Cadw.

Eating and shopping: Billiard Tea-room, fully licensed. Castle Walk Café serving a simple offer to parkland walkers, dogs welcome. Inner Courtyard with a gift shop and plant sales. Pre-loved bookshop. China Passage art gallery showcasing local artwork for sale.

Making the most of your day: **Indoors** Daily 'hidden house' tours. **Outdoors** Seasonal tours of parkland National Nature Reserve. Tractor trailer tours of estate and White Park cattle (summer). School holiday and family activities. Holiday cottages. **Dogs**: welcome in outer park on leads (cattle/sheep grazing). Not permitted in the deer-park.

Access: 🅿 🚗 📖 🚶 🔊 📷 🚲 🔍
Newton House 🚶 🔊 ⬆ 🍴 ♿
Castle 🚶 🚶 Parkland 🚶 🚶 ➡
Sat Nav: enter Dinefwr. **Parking**: 50 yards.

Finding out more: 01558 824512 or dinefwr@nationaltrust.org.uk

Dinefwr		M	T	W	T	F	S	S
Parkland, boardwalk and deer-park								
1 Jan–27 Mar	10–4*	M	T	W	T	F	S	S
28 Mar–30 Oct	10–6*	M	T	W	T	F	S	S
31 Oct–31 Dec	10–4*	M	T	W	T	F	S	S
Newton House, grounds, café and shop								
2 Jan–27 Mar	11–4**	·	·	·	·	F	S	S
28 Mar–30 Oct	11–6**	M	T	W	T	F	S	S
4 Nov–18 Dec	11–4**	·	·	·	·	F	S	S
19 Dec–31 Dec	11–4**	M	T	W	T	F	S	S

*Boardwalk and deer-park close one hour earlier. Last admission to Newton House one hour before closing.
**Billiard Tea-room last orders 30 minutes after last house admission. Cadw manages Dinefwr Castle and may alter opening times. Property closed 24 and 25 December; open other Bank Holidays.

Dinefwr, Carmarthenshire: a history of power, glory, downfall and loss

Dolaucothi Estate Woodland

near Pumsaint, Llanwrda, Carmarthenshire

[icons] 1944

Hours of woodland walks and a multi-user trail with route information in Dolaucothi Gold Mine welcome centre; plenty to discover. **Note**: for Sat Nav use SA19 8US.

Finding out more: 01558 650809 or dolaucothi@nationaltrust.org.uk

Dolaucothi Gold Mines

Pumsaint, Llanwrda, Carmarthenshire SA19 8US

[icons] 1941

Not your average National Trust visit, this hidden gem reveals the story of the quest for gold more than 2,000 years ago. You too can try your luck by panning for gold, and anything you find you keep. Or you can venture on an overground tour of the Roman archaeology, go underground to experience the harsh conditions of Victorian times and listen to what 1930s miners had to say in their very own words about their final efforts to search for gold. Why not join us for the ultimate adventure and discover centuries of stories in just one day? **Note**: steep slopes, stout enclosed footwear essential. Minimum height, no carried children/pushchairs on underground tours. Caravan park on site; pitch charges (including members).

Eating and shopping: tea-room (concession) offering light refreshments. Shop specialising in Welsh gold jewellery (also available online) and gifts. Dolaucothi Arms (tenant-run) offering food and accommodation. Picnic tables in the mine yard.

Dolaucothi Gold Mines, Carmarthenshire: discovering the quest for gold

Making the most of your day: **Indoors** Underground guided tours throughout day. 1930s machinery sheds. **Outdoors** Overground self-guided audio tour of Roman workings. Children's trails. Walks around woodland estate. **Dogs**: welcome on leads in mine yard not on underground tours.

Access: [icons] Tea-rooms [icon] Machinery sheds [icon] Mine yard [icon] [icon]
Parking: on site; overflow car park opposite main entrance.

Finding out more: 01558 650809 or dolaucothi@nationaltrust.org.uk

Dolaucothi Gold Mines		M	T	W	T	F	S	S
Gold mines, gift shop and tea-room								
18 Mar–30 Jun	11–5	M	T	W	T	F	S	S
1 Jul–31 Aug	10–6	M	T	W	T	F	S	S
1 Sep–30 Oct	11–5	M	T	W	T	F	S	S
Caravan site								
17 Mar–30 Oct	Dawn–dusk	M	T	W	T	F	S	S
Estate and walks								
Open all year		M	T	W	T	F	S	S
Dolaucothi Arms*								
1 Jan–20 Mar	4–11		T	W	T	F	S	S
22 Mar–30 Oct	12–11		T	W	T	F	S	S
1 Nov–31 Dec	4–11		T	W	T	F	S	S

Gold Mines peak season: Victorian tour 11, 12, 1, 1:30, 2:30, 3 and 4:30; Roman tour 12:30, 2 and 3:30. Off-peak season: Victorian tour 11:30, 12:30, 2:30 and 3:30; Roman tour 12:30. *Tuesdays, 5 to 11; Saturdays, 12 to 11; Sundays, 12 to 8. Open Bank Holidays, but closed on Tuesdays following a Bank Holiday Monday.

Underground at Dolaucothi Gold Mines (above), and Dolmelynllyn Estate, Gwynedd (below)

Making the most of your day: estate walks leaflet guides visitors around the more interesting parts of the estate, such as Rhaeadr Ddu waterfall, Cefn Coch gold mines and the wildlife-rich oak woodlands. **Dogs**: welcome on leads.

Access: 🔲
Sat Nav: use LL40 2TF. **Parking**: on site.

Finding out more: 01341 440238 or dolmelynllyn@nationaltrust.org.uk

Dolmelynllyn Estate

near Dolgellau, Gwynedd

🔲🔲🔲 1936

Dolmelynllyn Estate covers 696 hectares (1,719 acres) and comprises two tenanted farms, with the remaining woodland managed by the Trust. Dolmelynllyn Hall is Grade II listed, with well-preserved formal gardens, walled kitchen garden, Britain's largest bee-bole wall, ornamental lake and parkland.
Note: Dolmelynllyn Hall is a privately run hotel, not a pay-to-enter property.

Eating and shopping: two National Trust-owned but tenanted hotels on the estate offering refreshments and light meals. Picnic site.

Dyffryn Gardens

St Nicholas, Vale of Glamorgan CF5 6SU

🏠 ✿ 2012

A garden for all seasons, celebrated for its botanical collection, among the best in Wales. Meandering through the gardens, you will discover intimate garden rooms, formal lawns, and an extensive arboretum. The reinstated glasshouse in the kitchen garden houses an impressive collection of rare cacti and orchids. Designed by the eminent landscape architect Thomas Mawson, the gardens are the early 20th-century vision of Reginald Cory. Dyffryn House stands at the heart of the garden. This Grade II* listed house is built as a gallery from which to view the landscape. Partially restored, the house is used as a blank canvas to interpret the gardens and Cory family history.

Eating and shopping: tea-room serving kitchen garden produce, including an edible-flower menu in the summer and hearty soups in the autumn. Shop selling plants and gifts.

Autumn at Dyffryn Gardens, Glamorgan

Visitors explore the gardens (above), which surround this partially restored house (opposite)

Making the most of your day: network of garden rooms and champion trees in the arboretum to discover. Family events and play area. Tredegar House nearby. **Dogs**: welcome on short leads.

Access: 🅿️ ♿ 🚻 House ♿ 🛗
Grounds ♿ 🦽 ➡️ 🚻 ♿
Sat Nav: use CF5 6ST. **Parking**: on site.

Finding out more: 02920 593328 or dyffryn@nationaltrust.org.uk

Dyffryn Gardens		M	T	W	T	F	S	S
Gardens, tea-room and shop								
1 Jan–28 Feb	10–4	M	T	W	T	F	S	S
29 Feb–20 Mar	10–5	M	T	W	T	F	S	S
21 Mar–25 Sep	10–6	M	T	W	T	F	S	S
26 Sep–30 Oct	10–5	M	T	W	T	F	S	S
31 Oct–31 Dec*	10–4	M	T	W	T	F	S	S
House								
1 Jan–28 Feb	12–3				T	F	S	S
3 Mar–20 Mar	12–4				T	F	S	S
21 Mar–25 Sep	12–4	M	T	W	T	F	S	S
29 Sep–30 Oct	12–4				T	F	S	S
3 Nov–31 Dec*	12–3				T	F	S	S

Last admission one hour before closing. Tea-room: last orders 30 minutes before closing. *Closed 25 and 26 December.

Erddig

Wrexham LL13 0YT

🏠 ✝ 🏛 ❄ ♨ | 1973 |

Erddig tells the 250-year story of a gentry family's relationship with its servants. A large collection of servants' portraits and carefully preserved rooms capture their lives in the early 20th century. Upstairs is a treasure trove of fine furniture, textiles and wallpapers, while outdoors you can explore the 18th-century formal garden with grand lawns, avenues of pleached limes and a Victorian parterre. The 486-hectare (1,200-acre) landscape pleasure-park, designed by William Emes, is a haven of peace and natural beauty, perfect for riverside picnics. Discover the 'cup and saucer' or explore the remains of a Norman motte-and-bailey castle.

Eating and shopping: second-hand bookshop and gift shop selling crafts, sweet treats and plants. Restaurant serving light lunches, cakes and cream teas. Café and tea-garden offering Welsh ingredients, including Erddig apples, herbs, honey and cider. Picnics welcome.

Making the most of your day: **Indoors** Themed tours. Christmas event. You are welcome to play the piano. **Outdoors** Open-air theatre, Easter trail and Christmas programme. Orienteering and walking maps. Wolf's Den natural play area. **Dogs**: welcome in country park.

Access: 🅿️ 📷 🖾 🚻 🖼 🍴 🆚 ♿ 🔄
Building 🔅 🔆 Grounds 🔅 🔆 🅿️
Sat Nav: do not use, follow brown signs.
Parking: on site, 200 yards from ticket office.

Finding out more: 01978 355314 or erddig@nationaltrust.org.uk

Erddig		M	T	W	T	F	S	S
House								
1 Feb–11 Mar†	11:30–2:30	M	T	W	T	F	S	S
12 Mar–30 Oct	12:30–3:30	M	T	W	T	F	S	S
31 Oct–31 Dec*	11:30–2:30	M	T	W	T	F	S	S
Garden, natural play area, restaurant and shop								
1 Jan–24 Mar	11–4	M	T	W	T	F	S	S
25 Mar–30 Oct††	10–5	M	T	W	T	F	S	S
31 Oct–31 Dec	11–4	M	T	W	T	F	S	S

†Limited house opening for fireside chats and selected highlight tours. *Ground-floor servants' quarters only.
††23 July to 27 August: open to 9 on Saturday.
Closed 25 December. Timed tickets operate on Bank Holidays and during busy periods.

Fun and relaxation at Erddig, Wrexham (below and bottom)

Any questions? Telephone 0344 800 1895 (seven days a week)

Hafod y Llan

near Beddgelert, Gwynedd

[icons] 1998

Hafod y Llan, in the beautiful Nantgwynant Valley, is the largest farm run by the National Trust, part of which is designated a National Nature Reserve and a Site of Special Scientific Interest. It extends from the valley floor to the summit of Snowdon and visitors are free to wander the many paths which cross this unique landscape. **Note**: as this is a working farm, access to the farmyard is by foot only.

Hafod y Llan, Gwynedd (above and below): a working farm

Eating and shopping: refreshments available at nearby Caffi Gwynant (not National Trust).

Making the most of your day: network of paths cross Hafod y Llan, including the Watkin Path leading to the summit of Snowdon. **Dogs**: welcome on leads.

Access: [icon]
Sat Nav: use LL55 4NQ. **Parking**: on farm for campsite only. Car park near farm entrance (not National Trust).

Finding out more: 01766 890473 or hafodyllan@nationaltrust.org.uk

Henrhyd Falls

Coelbren, Powys

[icon] 1947

The highest waterfall in south Wales, Henrhyd Falls plunges down into a wooded gorge – a haven for damp-loving wildlife. A pleasant walk takes you to the falls and down the Nant Llech Valley, passing an old landslide and disused watermill. **Note**: sorry no toilet. Steep descent to waterfall.

Making the most of your day: downloadable walk available on website. National Trust and Geopark archaeological walk leaflet available locally. Why not visit nearby Brecon Beacons and Aberdulais Tin Works and Waterfall? **Dogs**: welcome on leads.

Access: [icon]
Sat Nav: use SA10 9PH.
Parking: adjoining property.

Finding out more: 01874 625515 or henrhydfalls@nationaltrust.org.uk

Henrhyd Falls, Powys, plunges into a wooded gorge

The view from The Kymin, Monmouthshire

Llanbedrog Beach

Llanbedrog, Gwynedd

🏛 2000

Best known for its colourful beach huts, this wonderful stretch of sand has been enjoyed by generations. Its sheltered waters, fantastic views over Cardigan Bay and adjacent wooded and craggy landscape make this a real gem of Llŷn. **Note**: toilet (not National Trust).

Eating and shopping: shops and cafés at Llanbedrog and at nearby Pwllheli and Abersoch (not National Trust).

Making the most of your day: events during summer months. Children's adventure packs, maps and guides available at car park welcome cabin. Beach huts available to hire. **Dogs**: welcome.

Access: 🦽
Sat Nav: use LL53 7TT. **Parking**: on site.

Finding out more: 01758 760469 or llanbedrog@nationaltrust.org.uk

The Kymin

Monmouth, Monmouthshire NP25 3SF

🏠 ♿ 🔔 🍴 1902

Lord Nelson and Lady Hamilton were delighted with this Georgian banqueting house and Naval Temple when they visited in 1802. The Kymin is still a great spot from which to enjoy panoramic views of the Brecon Beacons and Wye Valley. The woods and pleasure grounds are also perfect for picnics.

Eating and shopping: refreshments and snacks available (when Round House open). Picnics welcome.

Making the most of your day: self-guided walks, including bluebell walks in spring. Garden games available to hire (when Round House open). Special events throughout the year. **Dogs**: welcome in house and grounds.

Access: 🅿 🅳 ♿ Round House 🦽 ♿
Naval Temple ♿ Grounds ➡
Parking: limited.

Finding out more: 01600 719241 or kymin@nationaltrust.org.uk

Llanbedrog Beach, Gwynedd (bottom), and beach huts

The Kymin		M	T	W	T	F	S	S
Round House								
26 Mar–31 Oct	11–4	M	·	·	·	·	S	S
Grounds								
Open all year	7–9	M	T	W	T	F	S	S

Open Good Friday. Car park open during daylight hours only.

Llanerchaeron

Ciliau Aeron, near Aberaeron,
Ceredigion SA48 8DG

🏠 🔧 ❀ 🛏 👜 🔔 ☂ 1989

Totally self-sufficient 18th-century Welsh minor gentry estate. The villa, designed in the 1790s, is the most complete example of the early work of John Nash. It has its own service courtyard with dairy, laundry, brewery and salting house, giving a full 'upstairs, downstairs' experience. The walled kitchen gardens, pleasure grounds, ornamental lake and parkland offer peaceful walks, while the Home Farm complex has an impressive range of traditional, atmospheric outbuildings. A working farm, there are Welsh Black cattle, Llanwenog sheep and rare Welsh pigs as well as chickens, geese and doves. Woodland walks available.

Eating and shopping: café serving light meals and cakes (not National Trust). Picnic site. Fresh garden produce and plants, farm meat, local crafts, art, gifts and books for sale. Second-hand bookshop.

Making the most of your day: activities during local school holidays, including crafts, gardening, nature activities and self-led trails. Special events days. Cycle hire. **Dogs**: welcome on the woodland walks and in the parkland on leads.

Llanerchaeron, Ceredigion (top), and the farmyard (right)

Access: 🅿 🔧 🚻 👜 🔊 🎞 📷 ⓥⓣ 🔊 📍
Visitor building 🚶 ♿ Villa 🚶 🚶 ♿
Grounds 🚶 ➡ ♿
Parking: 50 yards.

Finding out more: 01545 570200 or
llanerchaeron@nationaltrust.org.uk

Llanerchaeron		M	T	W	T	F	S	S
Entire property								
13 Feb–21 Feb	11:30–3:30	M	T	W	T	F	S	S
19 Mar–31 Oct*	10:30–5:30	M	T	W	T	F	S	S
Farm, garden, woodland walks and shop only								
2 Jan–7 Feb	11:30–3:30						S	S
22 Feb–18 Mar	11:30–3:30	M	T	W	T	F	S	S
1 Nov–31 Dec**	11:30–3:30	M	T	W	T	F	S	S
Christmas Fair								
3 Dec–4 Dec	11–4						S	S

Last admission one hour before closing. *Villa opens 11:30.
**Closed 24 to 26 December. Geler Jones Rural Life Collection open 19 March to 1 November, Wednesday and Friday, 12 to 4. Parkland and woodland walks open daily.

Marloes Sands and Mere

Marloes, Pembrokeshire

🏛️🏖️♿ 1941

If you want to relax, then this long sandy beach is the perfect spot to laze. If you are feeling a bit more active, there are interesting rock formations and rock pools to discover, or you could explore the inland mere, with its abundant birdlife. **Note**: nearest toilets by Runwayskiln farm, alongside track from the car park to Marloes Mere.

Eating and shopping: information point at Martin's Haven. Shop, café and pub in nearby Marloes village (not National Trust).

Making the most of your day: for rock-pooling, birdwatching and getting closer to nature why not pick up a nature discovery Tracker Pack (available from the car park)? **Dogs**: welcome under close control.

Access: 🚻♿🦽➡️
Sat Nav: use SA62 3BH. **Parking**: on site.

Finding out more: 01348 837860 or marloessands@nationaltrust.org.uk

Martin's Haven

near Marloes, Pembrokeshire

🏛️🏖️♿🏕️ 1981

The gateway to Skomer Island and a fabulously wild headland with fine panoramic views of St Bride's Bay. For a really varied and exciting day, why not combine spotting marine wildlife with discovering traces of ancient settlements? **Note**: nearest toilets by the slipway.

Eating and shopping: information point at Martin's Haven. Shop, café and pub in nearby Marloes village (not National Trust).

Making the most of your day: nature discovery Tracker Packs, available from car park, for rock-pooling, birdwatching and getting closer to nature. **Dogs**: welcome under close control.

Access: 🚻♿➡️
Sat Nav: use SA62 3BJ. **Parking**: on site.

Finding out more: 01348 837860 or martinshaven@nationaltrust.org.uk

Mwnt

near Cardigan, Ceredigion

➕♿🏖️ 1963

Beautiful secluded bay with a sandy beach – perfect for spotting dolphins, seals and other amazing wildlife. Small café and shop. **Note**: steep steps to beach. For Sat Nav use SA43 1QF.

Finding out more: 01545 570200 or mwnt@nationaltrust.org.uk

Marloes Sands and Mere, Pembrokeshire (left), is the perfect beach for playing games or simply relaxing. If you fancy being even more active, then there are many rock pools to explore

Making the most of your day: Indoors Visit the nearby information centre to learn more about Cwm Idwal. **Outdoors** Range of rock-climbing and mountain walking routes available in addition to a National Cycle Network. **Dogs**: allowed on leads only.

Access: ♿
Sat Nav: use LL57 3LZ. **Parking**: at Ogwen Lake (not National Trust).

Finding out more: 01248 605739 or ogwen@nationaltrust.org.uk

Ogwen Cottage

Open Easter, Whitsun, summer holidays and Bank Holidays (excluding 1 January, 25 and 26 December), 8 to 4, as well as additional busy periods (if Rangers' work programme allows).

Ogwen Cottage, Gwynedd: walkers' information point

Ogwen Cottage

Nant Ffrancon, Bethesda, Gwynedd LL57 3LZ

♿ 2014

Ogwen Cottage is a newly acquired countryside hub for the Carneddau and Glyderau Ranger team. It serves as an information point for walkers exploring nearby Cwm Idwal, Tryfan, Y Glyderau and Carneddau. We'll also be providing outdoor learning experiences in partnership with the Outward Bound Trust. **Note**: open Easter, Whitsun, summer holidays and Bank Holidays (excluding 1 January, 25 and 26 December), 8 to 4.

Eating and shopping: small retail outlet on site and food kiosk within walking distance at the visitor centre (not National Trust).

Paxton's Tower

Llanarthne, near Dryslwyn, Carmarthenshire

🏛️♿ 1965

Known as 'Golwg y Byd' (Eye of the World), Paxton's is said to give a view of seven counties. **Note**: sorry no toilet. Nearest National Trust facilities at Dinefwr in Llandeilo. For Sat Nav use SA32 8HX.

Finding out more: 01558 823902 or paxtonstower@nationaltrust.org.uk

Penbryn

near Sarnau, Cardigan, Ceredigion

♿🚠 1967

One of Ceredigion's best-kept secrets, this beautifully secluded sandy cove lies down leafy lanes, edged with flower-covered banks. **Note**: café (open daily) serving a wide selection of snacks and drinks. For Sat Nav use SA44 6QL.

Finding out more: 01545 570200 or penbryn@nationaltrust.org.uk

Pennard, Pwll Du and Bishopston Valley

near Southgate, Swansea

🏛️🏖️⛰️ 1954

Spectacular cliffs, caves where mammoth remains have been found, rare birds, an underground river, bat roosts, silver-lead mining, ancient woodland, smuggling and limestone quarrying are just a few of the wonders of this area. There are also numerous archaeological features and two important caves – Bacon Hole and Minchin Hole. **Note**: due to dangerous rip tides, swimming in Three Cliffs Bay is not advised.

Eating and shopping: coffee shop, village stores, tea-rooms and a pub in Pennard (none National Trust). Picnics welcome.

Making the most of your day: Pennard provides a great starting point for a variety of walks, on which you can enjoy wild flowers and spot rare birds, such as choughs and Dartford warblers. **Dogs**: welcome, but please be aware livestock graze freely across Pennard Burrows.

Access: ♿
Sat Nav: use SA3 2DH. **Parking**: at Southgate car park.

Finding out more: 01792 390636 or pennard@nationaltrust.org.uk

Spectacular Pennard Cliffs, Swansea (above and below left)

Penrhyn Castle

Bangor, Gwynedd LL57 4HT

🏛️🖼️✚❀🐾☕ 1951

Open the door and step inside where the Pennant family and their famous guests dined and played in opulent fashion. You can't help but be taken aback by the vast luxurious rooms, Gothic stairways and fine art on display. Hear tales of star-crossed lovers, sugar and slate fortunes and delve 'below stairs' into the Victorian kitchens. The extensive grounds are perfect for exploring and enjoying spectacular views of Snowdonia and the North Wales coast. Little explorers can climb trees, make dens and run wild in the adventure playground. There's something for everyone at Penrhyn, just expect the unexpected.

Eating and shopping: light meals and homemade cakes available in our coffee shop; hot food and lunches in the tea-room. Gift shop in the heart of the castle. New Stables shop and second-hand bookshop.

Why not share your pictures with us? #nationaltrust

Making the most of your day: Indoors You can take a behind-the-scenes tour and climb aboard an engine in the Railway Museum. **Outdoors** Explore the medieval church ruins and find peace in the walled garden. **Dogs**: welcome on leads in grounds. Assistance dogs only in the castle and walled garden.

Access: 🅿️🐕♿🎫♿🚻📷🏛️🔨♿📷 🔊
Castle ♿♿♿ Stable block ♿♿ Grounds ♿♿
Parking: 500 yards.

Finding out more: 01248 353084 or penrhyncastle@nationaltrust.org.uk
Penrhyn Castle, Bangor, Gwynedd LL57 4HT

Penrhyn Castle		M	T	W	T	F	S	S
Castle, shop, tea-room and Victorian kitchens								
13 Feb–26 Feb*	12–3**	M	T	W	T	F	S	S
27 Feb–6 Nov	12–5**	M	T	W	T	F	S	S
Garden, parkland and Railway Museum								
13 Feb–26 Feb	11–3	M	T	W	T	F	S	S
27 Feb–6 Nov	11–5	M	T	W	T	F	S	S
7 Nov–31 Dec	12–3	M	T	W	T	F	S	S
1 Jan–12 Feb	12–3	M	T	W	T	F	S	S
Coffee shop and stable shop								
27 Feb–6 Nov†	12–4	·	·	·	T	F	S	S

*Ground floor only – by guided tour. **Tea-room and shop: open at 11. †Coffee shop and stable shop: open all week during school holidays. Castle taster tours offered whenever possible. Selected areas of the castle open for winter weekend and guided tours. Closed 25 December.

Penrhyn Castle, Gwynedd: a classic castle, full of treasures

Eating and shopping: visitor centre gift shop, Old Dairy tea-room serving hot food, sandwiches and cakes. Mansion coffee shop serving sandwiches and cakes, second-hand bookshop and specialist gift shop. Local ice-cream served from the sun room.

Making the most of your day: Indoors Find out more about family life with a taster tour. Outdoors Walks and talks with the gardeners, a full events calendar, including traditional summer fair and regular farmers' market. Dogs: welcome on short leads in designated woodland areas.

Access: ⓟ🅳♿🚻👨‍🦽🦼💺💻☐⊡🅰
Building 🔼♿🅛 Grounds ♿ ➡
Parking: 400 yards from main entrance.

Finding out more: 01248 714795 or plasnewydd@nationaltrust.org.uk

Plas Newydd		M	T	W	T	F	S	S
House*								
13 Feb–21 Feb	11–3:30	M	T	W	T	F	S	S
27 Feb–6 Mar	11–3:30	·	·	·	·	·	S	S
12 Mar–6 Nov	11–4:30	M	T	W	T	F	S	S
17 Dec–30 Dec	11–2:30	M	T	W	T	F	S	S
Garden, shop and tea-room								
2 Jan–7 Feb	11–4	·	·	·	·	·	S	S
13 Feb–21 Feb	11–4	M	T	W	T	F	S	S
27 Feb–6 Mar	11–4	·	·	·	·	·	S	S
12 Mar–6 Nov	10:30–5:30	M	T	W	T	F	S	S
7 Nov–31 Dec	11–3	M	T	W	T	F	S	S

*Entry by timed ticket. Whole property closed 25, 26 and 31 December. Rhododendron garden at its best April to June.

Majestic Plas Newydd House and Gardens, Anglesey (above and below right)

Plas Newydd House and Gardens

Llanfairpwll, Anglesey LL61 6DQ

🏠🏛❄🏊⛰🌲🌳 1976

The ancestral home of the Marquess of Anglesey sits majestically on the shores of the Menai Strait, enjoying breathtaking views of Snowdonia. The surrounding gardens are great for exploring and include an Australasian arboretum, Italianate terrace garden and extensive woodland walks. There's plenty for little explorers too, including a hand-built tree house, nine-hole Frisbee™ golf course, and adventure playground – you might even meet one of the resident red squirrels! The house is home to a Waterloo-inspired military museum, works of art, regular exhibitions and, at its heart, Rex Whistler's famous 58-foot fantasy landscape mural.

Entry is still possible at most places up to 30 minutes before closing

Plas yn Rhiw

Rhiw, Pwllheli, Gwynedd LL53 8AB

1952

The house was rescued from neglect and lovingly restored by the three Keating sisters, who bought it in 1938. The views from the grounds and gardens across Cardigan Bay are among the most spectacular in Britain. The house is 16th-century with Georgian additions, and the garden contains many beautiful flowering trees and shrubs, with beds framed by box hedges and grass paths. It's stunning whatever the season.

Eating and shopping: tea-room serving a selection of fresh sandwiches, soup, cakes and drinks; picnics also available to take out. Shop selling gifts, plants, books and prints of Honora Keating's landscapes. Cold drinks and ice-cream also available in the shop.

Making the most of your day: **Indoors** Virtual tour available on iPad and guided tours available by arrangement. **Outdoors** Woodland walks and a native-apple orchard. Holiday cottages within walking distance. **Dogs**: on woodland walk below shop only (on leads).

Access:
Building **Grounds**
Parking: 100 yards (narrow lanes).

Finding out more: 01758 780219 or plasynrhiw@nationaltrust.org.uk

Plas yn Rhiw		M	T	W	T	F	S	S
17 Mar–28 Mar*	12–5	**M**	·	·	**T**	**F**	**S**	**S**
29 Mar–13 Apr*	12–5	**M**	**T**	**W**	**T**	**F**	**S**	**S**
14 Apr–23 May*	12–5	**M**	·	·	**T**	**F**	**S**	**S**
25 May–18 Jul*	12–5	**M**	·	**W**	**T**	**F**	**S**	**S**
19 Jul–12 Sep*	12–5	**M**	**T**	**W**	**T**	**F**	**S**	**S**
15 Sep–26 Sep*	12–5	**M**	·	·	**T**	**F**	**S**	**S**
29 Sep–23 Oct**	12–4	·	·	·	**T**	**F**	**S**	**S**
24 Oct–30 Oct**	12–4	**M**	**T**	**W**	**T**	**F**	**S**	**S**

January and February: garden and snowdrop wood open occasional weekends. *Tea-room: open as property, but 11 to 4:30. **Tea-room open as property, but from 11 to 3:30.

Corner of one of the Keating sisters' bedroom (below), at Plas yn Rhiw, Gwynedd, and the 16th-century house (above)

Porth Meudwy, Gwynedd: sheltered cove

Porth y Swnt

Henfaes, Aberdaron, Pwllheli,
Gwynedd LL53 8BE

🏠🎨🛏️ 2010

This exciting interpretation centre, at the heart of the beautiful fishing village of Aberdaron, shines a light on Llŷn's unique culture, heritage and environment. You can experience Bardsey Island's retired lighthouse optic up close, follow in the footsteps of pilgrims for a journey across the Sound in the video pod, catch up on what Llŷn's Rangers are up to and form your reflective thoughts in the Sea of Words. If you want to stay longer, our Henfaes holiday apartments are also in the centre of the village.

Eating and shopping: gift shop in visitor centre; cafés, pubs and convenience stores in village (not National Trust).

Making the most of your day: **Indoors** Audio guide, children's scrapbooks, events during school holidays. **Outdoors** Walks and access to the Wales Coast Path. Adventure packs, beach fun days, seafood festival, guided walks and cycle rides. **Dogs**: beach access restricted during summer.

Porth Meudwy

near Aberdaron, Gwynedd

🎨 1990

Nowhere expresses the essence of the area better than this sheltered cove on the wild and rocky coastline west of Aberdaron. It was from here that the pilgrims set out to Ynys Enlli (Bardsey Island). Today fishermen still bring the daily catch in to the cove. **Note**: sorry no toilet.

Eating and shopping: in Aberdaron village (not National Trust).

Making the most of your day: the Wales Coast Path – a birdwatchers' paradise – runs dramatically along the clifftop. **Dogs**: welcome.

Access: 🏷️
Sat Nav: use LL53 8DA. **Parking**: ½ mile.

Finding out more: 01758 760469 or porthmeudwy@nationaltrust.org.uk

Porth y Swnt, Gwynedd: this interpretation centre (below and opposite top), shines a light on local heritage

An old fishing village perched on the end of a thin ribbon of land stretching into the Irish Sea, with its clear sheltered waters lapping against stout stone houses, Porthdinllaen really is a jewel. You can watch fishermen bring in the daily catch while relaxing with a drink at the Tŷ Coch Inn. **Note**: nearest toilet in village (not National Trust). Steps from car park down to beach.

Eating and shopping: refreshments available at Tŷ Coch Inn (not National Trust).

Making the most of your day: events during summer for all the family. Wonderful walking on the coastal path – maps and guides available at car park welcome cabin. Find out about village history at 'Caban Gruff'. **Dogs**: welcome.

Access: ⊞ ⓖ
Sat Nav: use LL53 6DA. **Parking**: on site for beach; 1 mile from village.

Finding out more: 01758 760469 or porthdinllaen@nationaltrust.org.uk

Access: ⓟ ⓦⓒ ⓑ 🅰 Car park ⓑ ⓑ
Parking: on site.

Finding out more: 01758 703810 or porthyswnt@nationaltrust.org.uk

Porth y Swnt		M	T	W	T	F	S	S
2 Jan–31 Mar	10–4	M	T	W	T	F	S	S
1 Apr–30 Jun	10–5	M	T	W	T	F	S	S
1 Jul–31 Aug	10–6	M	T	W	T	F	S	S
1 Sep–30 Sep	10–5	M	T	W	T	F	S	S
1 Oct–31 Dec	10–4	M	T	W	T	F	S	S

Closed 1 January, 25 and 26 December.

Two views of the pretty fishing village of Porthdinllaen, Gwynedd

Porthdinllaen

Morfa Nefyn, Gwynedd

⬜ 1994

Porthor

Aberdaron, Gwynedd

[🏛] [1981]

This wonderful beach is famous for its 'whistling sands' and glistening waters. If the joys of sandcastles and sunbathing are not enough for you, then why not have a go at surfing? The sea here is perfect. In addition, the Wales Coast Path runs in both directions from the car park. **Note**: nearest toilet in car park.

Eating and shopping: beachside café and shop offering everything from lunch to sun cream (not National Trust).

Making the most of your day: famous beach and glorious clifftop coast path to explore. Children's adventure pack available from car park. **Dogs**: seasonal restrictions on beach apply from 1 April to 30 September.

Access: [🚻] [♿]
Sat Nav: use LL53 8LG. **Parking**: on site.

Finding out more: 01758 760469 or porthor@nationaltrust.org.uk

The perfect sea and 'whistling sands' make Porthor, Gwynedd (above and below), the most irresistible beach

Powis Castle and Garden

Welshpool, Powys SY21 8RF

🏰 ✳ ⌂ ▲ ⌶ 1952

The Herbert family spent more than 400 years transforming a medieval fortress into the comfortable family home you see today. Furnished with sumptuous fabrics and exquisite works of art from around the world, the interior reflects the Elizabethan to Edwardian periods. The UK's largest private collection of Indian treasures is housed in the Clive Museum. From weaponry to a gold bejewelled tiger's head, the collection is unique. The world-renowned gardens are an eclectic mix of Italianate terraces filled with herbaceous borders, a formal garden with clipped yews and a woodland area which boasts a number of champion trees.

Eating and shopping: restaurant (licensed) and garden coffee shop. Gift shop and plant sales.

Making the most of your day: **Indoors** Themed tours and daily introductory talks about the castle. Family fun trails. **Outdoors** Talks on the garden every day. Children's activities during school holidays and family trails. **Dogs**: assistance dogs only.

Powis Castle and Garden, Powys (above and right)

Access: 🅿 🅳 ♿ 🚻 🧷 📷 🎨 🖥 VT ⠿
Building 🔢 **Grounds** 🔢 🔢 ➡ ♿
Sat Nav: postcode misdirects, enter Powis Castle. **Parking**: on site.

Finding out more: 01938 551944 (Infoline). 01938 551929 or powiscastle@nationaltrust.org.uk

Powis Castle and Garden		M	T	W	T	F	S	S
Castle, Clive Museum and garden*								
2 Jan–14 Feb**	11–4						S	S
15 Feb–27 Mar	11–4	M	T	W	T	F	S	S
28 Mar–30 Sep	11–5	M	T	W	T	F	S	S
1 Oct–23 Dec**	11–4	M	T	W	T	F	S	S
Restaurant and shop								
2 Jan–14 Feb¹	11–4						S	S
15 Feb–27 Mar	10–4†	M	T	W	T	F	S	S
28 Mar–30 Sep††	10–5†	M	T	W	T	F	S	S
1 Oct–31 Dec††	10–4†	M	T	W	T	F	S	S

*Garden: open from 10 until 31 December; 28 March to 30 September, open to 6. **Reduced number of state rooms open. ¹Restaurant opens 10. †Shop opens at 11. ††Garden coffee shop open (opening times vary); garden shop open until 24 December. Limited catering offer in January and February. Gardens, shop and restaurant open 1 January, 11 to 4. Closed 25 December.

Rhossili, Swansea: all the ingredients for a perfect holiday

Finding out more: 01792 390707 or
rhossili@nationaltrust.org.uk

Rhossili and Gower		M	T	W	T	F	S	S
Shop								
2 Jan–12 Feb	10:30–4	·	T	W	T	F	S	S
13 Feb–24 Mar	10:30–4	M	T	W	T	F	S	S
25 Mar–29 Apr	10:30–4:30	M	T	W	T	F	S	S
30 Apr–4 Sep	10–5*	M	T	W	T	F	S	S
5 Sep–30 Oct	10:30–4:30	M	T	W	T	F	S	S
31 Oct–23 Dec	10:30–4	M	T	W	T	F	S	S
27 Dec–30 Dec	10:30–4	·	T	W	T	F	·	·

Car park open 9 to 6. Visitor Centre closes 15 minutes before
shop. *August: shop open until 6 at weekends.

Rhossili and South Gower Coast

Coastguard Cottages, Rhossili, Gower,
Swansea SA3 1PR

🏕️🏛️⛰️🏖️🧭 1933

Perched on the clifftop overlooking the
spectacular Rhossili Bay (Britain's best beach:
Trip Advisor Travellers' Choice Awards 2013
and 2014), Rhossili Shop and Visitor Centre
offers everything you need to enjoy beautiful
Gower, from local information and advice,
to tempting treats and gifts to remember
your day. **Note**: Worm's Head island access
restricted March to August. Very steep steps
and slope to beach.

Eating and shopping: self-service
refreshments and Swansea's famous
Joe's ice-cream available all year.

Making the most of your day: visitor
information and advice on tides, local beaches,
access, facilities and walks available. Free
family geocaching trails (booking essential at
peak times). **Dogs**: welcome (on leads near
livestock please). Beach is dog-friendly all year.

Access: 🅿️♿🚻🏷️📷📷
Visitor Centre ♿ Grounds ♿ ▶
Parking: large pay and display car park at
end of village. Suitable for motorhomes
(no overnight stays).

St David's Visitor Centre and Shop

Captain's House, High Street, St David's,
Pembrokeshire SA62 6SD

🏖️🏛️ 1974

Overlooking the Celtic Old Cross in the centre
of St David's, Wales's smallest historic city, the
visitor centre and well-stocked shop is open all
year. For a complete guide to the National
Trust in Pembrokeshire, visitors can take a tour
of our special places, beaches and walks using
interactive technology. **Note**: sorry no toilet.

Eating and shopping: books, cards, maps,
wide range of gifts and local produce.
Walks leaflets available.

The view from St David's Head, Pembrokeshire

Making the most of your day: guided walks, evening talks and events. St David's Head, Porth Clais, Solva and Abereiddi nearby.

Access: Building 🔥
Parking: none on site.

Finding out more: 01437 720385 or stdavidsshop@nationaltrust.org.uk

St David's Visitor Centre		M	T	W	T	F	S	S
2 Jan–21 Mar	10–4	M	T	W	T	F	S	
22 Mar–31 Dec	9–5*	M	T	W	T	F	S	S

*Closes 4 on Sundays. Closed 1 January, 25 to 27 December.

Segontium

Caernarfon, Gwynedd

🏛 1937

Fort built to defend the Roman Empire against rebellious tribes. **Note**: in the guardianship of Cadw – Welsh Government's historic environment service. Museum not National Trust. For Sat Nav use LL55 2LN. For details of opening arrangements, please contact Cadw (01443 336105).

Finding out more: 01443 336000 or segontium@nationaltrust.org.uk

Skenfrith Castle

Skenfrith, near Abergavenny, Monmouthshire NP7 8UH

🏛 1936

Remains of early 13th-century castle, built beside the River Monnow to command one of the main routes from England. **Note**: in the guardianship of Cadw – Welsh Government's historic environment service. Open every day all year.

Finding out more: 01874 625515 or skenfrithcastle@nationaltrust.org.uk

Stackpole

near Pembroke, Pembrokeshire

🏛 1976

A former grand estate stretching down to some of the most beautiful coastline in the world, including Broadhaven South, Barafundle and Stackpole Quay. Today Bosherston Lakes, famous for their superb display of lilies, and the dramatic cliffs of Stackpole Head are a National Nature Reserve. The former site of the grand Stackpole Court and nearby Lodge Park Woods give the historical background to this magnificent estate and reveal the story behind the designed landscape.

Eating and shopping: The Boathouse at Stackpole Quay is a popular attraction, offering ready-made picnics for the beach, homemade cakes and scones or local Pembrokeshire ice-cream – perfect after a long walk.

Stackpole, Pembrokeshire (above and below)

Making the most of your day: guided kayak and coasteering sessions allow you to explore the coast from the water. Family events, from '50 things' to wild camping with Rangers. Stay at the Outdoor Learning Centre. **Dogs**: under close control on the estate.

Access: 🅿️🚐♿️📷 Building 🏛️ Grounds 🏛️➡️
Sat Nav: for Stackpole Quay use SA71 5LS; Broadhaven South SA71 5DZ; Bosherston Lakes SA71 5DR. **Parking**: at Stackpole Quay, Broadhaven South, Bosherston Lakes and Stackpole Court.

Finding out more: 01646 661359 or stackpole@nationaltrust.org.uk

Stackpole		M	T	W	T	F	S	S
Boathouse tea-room								
13 Feb–21 Feb	11–3:30	M	T	W	T	F	S	S
27 Feb–13 Mar	11–3:30	·	·	·	·	·	S	S
19 Mar–3 Apr	11–4	M	T	W	T	F	S	S
4 Apr–30 Oct	10–5	M	T	W	T	F	S	S
5 Nov–11 Dec	11–3:30	·	·	·	·	·	S	S
17 Dec–30 Dec*	11–3:30	M	T	W	T	F	S	S
Estate								
Open all year	Dawn–dusk	M	T	W	T	F	S	S

*Boathouse tea-room closed 24 and 25 December.

There is so much to discover at Stackpole

Stackpole Outdoor Learning Centre

Old Home Farm Yard, Stackpole, near Pembroke, Pembrokeshire SA71 5DQ

🏠🏛️♿️🛏️🍴👜🔔🍸 1976

Located in the heart of the Stackpole Estate, our eco award-winning centre provides residents with easy access to Bosherston Lakes, Stackpole Quay and award-winning beaches – including Barafundle and Broadhaven South – as well as the historic site of Stackpole Court. The recently refurbished centre can house up to 140 guests and offers flexible accommodation with modern facilities, including a theatre, meeting and classroom space. It is ideal for groups, corporate clients, celebrations, family holidays and couples' getaways. We also offer special interest breaks, covering subjects as wide-ranging as photography, health, well-being and wildlife identification. **Note**: contact the centre for activity programmes, prices and availability.

Picnic at Tredegar House, Newport

Eating and shopping: self-catering or chef-catered options. Meals provided by an experienced inhouse National Trust catering team. Full entertainment licence for events with bar. Residents' barbecue area. Shop and information hub.

Making the most of your day: events, including rock-pool rambles, wild camping, guided walks, open-air theatre and concerts. Hire one of our bikes to explore the area or join our kayaking or coasteering guided tours! **Dogs**: assistance dogs only.

Access: 🅿️ 🚻 🚻 🛗 🚮 📷
Sat Nav: do not use, instead follow brown signs. **Parking**: free for guests.

Finding out more: 01646 661425 (reception). 01646 661359 (estate office) or stackpoleoutdoorlearning@nationaltrust.org.uk

Stackpole Outdoor Centre	Open every day all year

Please contact the centre for more information on residential group bookings, courses and activities.

Stackpole Outdoor Learning Centre, Pembrokeshire (top)

Tredegar House

Newport NP10 8YW

🏛️ ❀ 🏊 🔔 2012

For centuries, the flamboyant Morgan family called this Grade I listed 17th-century Restoration mansion their home. With tales of giant birds' nests, riotous parties, dark arts, war heroism and animal menageries – the Morgan's was certainly no ordinary household. You can hear about the lives of their servants and connect with the hands-on spaces that served the family. Enjoy lakeside walks and an avenue of ancient oak trees within the 36-hectare (90-acre) parkland, then meander through the formal walled gardens and explore the impressive Grade I listed stables. An oasis hidden a stone's throw from the industrial setting of Newport. **Note**: roadworks likely to cause delays. Trialling new ways of opening. Roof project early spring.

Eating and shopping: tea-room serving light lunches, homemade cakes and hot drinks. Cosy gift shop selling souvenirs, books, gifts and plants.

Making the most of your day: Indoors Introductory talks. Family trails and hands-on activities. Yearly programme of things to do. Traditional Christmas experience. **Outdoors** Lakeside walks, formal gardens and seasonal garden talks. Dyffryn Gardens nearby. **Dogs**: welcome in the parkland, formal gardens and tea-room (homemade dog treats a menu staple).

Access: ⓟ 🔧 🔧 🔧 ⌨ ♿ House 🔧
Reception ⓑ Grounds 🔧 🔧
Parking: on site.

Finding out more: 01633 815880 or tredegar@nationaltrust.org.uk

Tredegar House		M	T	W	T	F	S	S
House and garden†								
13 Feb–20 Mar*	11–4	M	T	W	T	F	S	S
21 Mar–30 Oct**	11–5	M	T	W	T	F	S	S
26 Nov–18 Dec	11–5	·	·	·	·	·	S	S
Tea-room and shop								
9 Jan–7 Feb	10–4	·	·	·	·	·	S	S
13 Feb–20 Mar	10–4	M	T	W	T	F	S	S
21 Mar–30 Oct	10–5	M	T	W	T	F	S	S
2 Nov–16 Dec	11–3	·	·	W	T	F	S	S
26 Nov–18 Dec	10–5	·	·	·	··	·	S	S
Park								
Open all year	Dawn–dusk	M	T	W	T	F	S	S

†Garden: opens 10:30. House: last entry one hour before closing. *House: access to some areas by tour only. **House: fully open. Due to extensive road works, please check website for opening arrangements before visiting.

Flamboyant Tredegar House, Newport

Tudor Merchant's House, Pembrokeshire

Tudor Merchant's House

Quay Hill, Tenby, Pembrokeshire SA70 7BX

🏠 | 1937 |

Over 500 years ago when Tenby was a busy trading port, a merchant built this three-storey house to live in and trade from. Today, this unaltered house and shop have been furnished with exquisitely carved replicas and brightly coloured wall-hangings which re-create the atmosphere of life in Tudor Tenby.
Note: sorry no toilet.

Eating and shopping: shop range includes specially made Tudor-style pottery (design based on finds at the house), pewterware, horn cups, glass, beeswax candles and books about the Tudors.

Making the most of your day: Tudor Family Fortunes game, superstitions scrolls, lay the high table, costumes to try on and replica toys. Easter, Hallowe'en and Tudor-themed family events. Colby Woodland Garden and Stackpole nearby. **Dogs**: assistance dogs only.

Access: ♿ Building 🏠
Parking: very limited on-street parking. Several pay-and-display car parks, not National Trust (charge including members).

Finding out more: 01834 842279 or tudormerchantshouse@nationaltrust.org.uk

Tudor Merchant's House		M	T	W	T	F	S	S
13 Feb–21 Feb	11–3	M	T	W	T	F	S	S
27 Feb–20 Mar	11–3	·	·	·	·	·	S	S
21 Mar–17 Jul	11–5	M	·	W	T	F	S	S
18 Jul–4 Sep	11–5*	M	T	W	T	F	S	S
5 Sep–30 Oct	11–5**	M	·	W	T	F	S	S
5 Nov–31 Dec	11–3	·	·	·	·	·	S	S

Open Tuesday in Bank Holiday weeks, 11 to 5. *Tuesday and Wednesday: open until 6:15 for costumed guided tours.
**Closed Tuesday, except for 25 October.
Closed 25 December.

Tŷ Mawr Wybrnant

Penmachno, Betws-y-Coed, Conwy LL25 0HJ

🏚️♿ 1951

Hidden in the beautiful Conwy Valley, this traditional upland farmhouse was the birthplace of Bishop William Morgan, who first translated the Bible into Welsh. This is one of the most important houses in the history of the Welsh language. Two copies of William Morgan's original Bible are on display. **Note**: access via narrow track.

Eating and shopping: picnics welcome.

Making the most of your day: **Indoors** Introductory talks and exhibition room. Virtual tours available. **Outdoors** Tudor kitchen garden, woodland walks and two animal puzzle trails. **Dogs**: under close control.

Access: 🅿️♿📷♿ Building 🏠♿ Grounds 🏠
Sat Nav: no access from A470.
Parking: 500 yards.

Finding out more: 01690 760213 or tymawrwybrnant@nationaltrust.org.uk

Tŷ Mawr Wybrnant		M	T	W	T	F	S	S
17 Mar–30 Sep	12–5	·	·	·	T	F	S	S
1 Oct–6 Nov	12–4	·	·	·	T	F	S	S

Open Bank Holiday Mondays.

Tŷ Mawr Wybrnant, Conwy: a traditional upland farmhouse

Additional coastal and countryside car parks in Wales

Ceredigion
Mwnt — SA43 1PS
Penbryn — SA44 6QL

Llŷn Peninsula
Uwchmynydd — LL53 8DD

Pembrokeshire
Broadhaven — SA71 5DR
Bosherston — SA71 5DW
Porthclais — SA62 6RR

Snowdonia
Cregennan — LL39 1LX
Nantmor — LL55 4YG

Northern Ireland

Mount Stewart, County Down

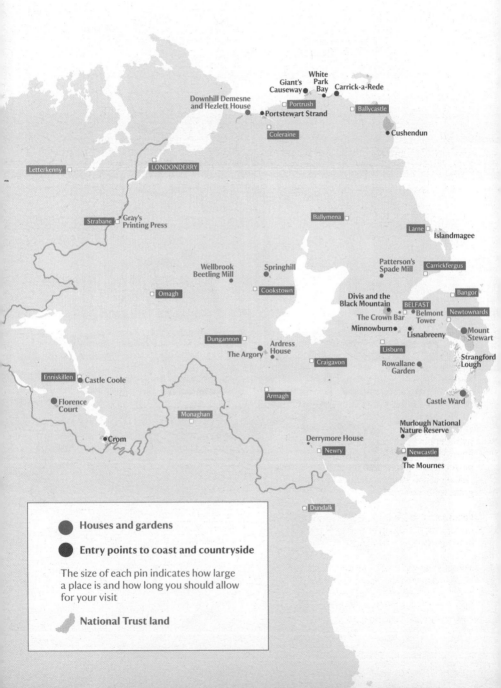

Giant's Causeway
White Park Bay
Carrick-a-Rede
Downhill Demesne and Hezlett House
Portrush
Portstewart Strand
Ballycastle
Cushendun
Coleraine
Letterkenny
LONDONDERRY
Gray's Printing Press
Strabane
Ballymena
Larne
Islandmagee
Wellbrook Beetling Mill
Springhill
Patterson's Spade Mill
Carrickfergus
Omagh
Cookstown
Divis and the Black Mountain
Bangor
BELFAST
The Crown Bar
Belmont Tower
Newtownards
Dungannon
Minnowburn
Lisnabreeny
Mount Stewart
The Argory
Ardress House
Lisburn
Strangford Lough
Enniskillen
Castle Coole
Craigavon
Rowallane Garden
Florence Court
Armagh
Castle Ward
Monaghan
Crom
Murlough National Nature Reserve
Derrymore House
Newry
Newcastle
The Mournes
Dundalk

● Houses and gardens

● Entry points to coast and countryside

The size of each pin indicates how large a place is and how long you should allow for your visit

🔶 National Trust land

Feeding the resident chickens in the cobbled farmyard at Ardress House, County Armagh

Ardress House

64 Ardress Road, Annaghmore, Portadown, County Armagh BT62 1SQ

🏠 🔊 ❄️ 🎣 1959

Nestling in 40 hectares (100 acres) of rolling countryside, this 17th-century farmhouse is an elegant example of 18th-century remodelling, with detailed plasterwork and fine Georgian interiors. The cobbled farmyard is the perfect spot for children to feed the resident chickens, and the nearby apple orchards are great for exploring.

Eating and shopping: takeaway hot and cold drinks and ice-cream available. Picnics welcome in the garden or woodlands.

Making the most of your day: miniature Shetland ponies, donkeys, Soay sheep, geese and chickens. Children's play area and original farmyard, including dairy, smithy and threshing barn. **Dogs**: on leads in garden only.

Access: 🦽 Building 🔾 ♿ Grounds 🗺️ ➡️
Parking: 10 yards.

Finding out more: 028 8778 4753 or ardress@nationaltrust.org.uk

Ardress House		M	T	W	T	F	S	S
Farmyard and house								
13 Feb–16 Feb	12–5	M	T	.	.	.	S	S
12 Mar–20 Mar	1–6	.	.	.	.	.	S	S
25 Mar–3 Apr	1–6	M	T	W	T	F	S	S
9 Apr–26 Jun	1–6	.	.	.	.	.	S	S
1 Jul–29 Aug	1–6	M	.	.	T	F	S	S
3 Sep–25 Sep	1–6	.	.	.	.	.	S	S
2 Oct–30 Oct	12–5	.	.	.	.	.	.	S
Lady's Mile Walk								
Open all year	Dawn–dusk	M	T	W	T	F	S	S

House: admission by guided tour, last tour one hour before closing. Open Bank Holiday Mondays and all other public holidays in Northern Ireland. Closed 25 and 26 December and 1 January.

The Argory

144 Derrycaw Road, Moy, Dungannon,
County Armagh BT71 6NA

🏚️❄️🐾🔔⛟ 1979

This Irish gentry house can trace more than
190 years of history. Built in the 1820s for the
MacGeough Bond family, the house and
surrounding riverside estate came into
existence due to a quirky stipulation in a will.
The interior of this understated and intimate
house still evokes the eclectic tastes and
interests of the family. The rose garden, with its
unusual sundial, pleasure gardens and wooded
riverside walks along the River Blackwater are
ideal for exploring.

Eating and shopping: Courtyard Coffee Shop
serving home-baked scones, sandwiches,
paninis and cakes. Gift shop offering a wide
range of products: jewellery, books and items
for the home and garden. Bookshop with
second-hand books for all tastes and interests.
Picnics welcome.

The Argory, County Armagh: the gracious staircase (above), and understated façade (below). Hide and seek fun (opposite)

Why not share your pictures with us? #nationaltrust

Belmont Tower

82 Belmont Church Road, Belfast,
County Down BT4 3FG

🏠 🍴 2013

For more than 100 years this prominent
Gothic-style late-Victorian building (below)
buzzed to the sound of children playing and
learning in its former life as Belmont Primary
School. Today this inspirational space has
been restored and adapted to offer classes,
conference facilities, coffee shop, gift shop
and C. S. Lewis exhibition.

Eating and shopping: freshly prepared food
and delicious scones at Belmont Tower Café.
Gift shop on the ground floor including some
local art and crafts.

Making the most of your day: Indoors Guided
tours. Children's interactive room and events.
Easter Egg hunts, Country Fair, Santa's
Grotto. **Outdoors** Variety of walks and trails.
Children's play area with zip line. Snowdrop
walks (February). **Dogs**: on leads in grounds
and garden.

Access: 🅿️♿ 🚻 📷 👓 Grounds ♿ ➡️
Parking: 100 yards.

Finding out more: 028 8778 4753 or
argory@nationaltrust.org.uk

Making the most of your day: community
groups, such as Belfast Historical Society, baby
sensory and wine-making. Exhibition on the life
of C. S. Lewis. **Dogs**: assistance dogs only.

Access: ♿ 👁️ 🎵 ♿ 🔁
Parking: on site and on street at Belmont Road
and Belmont Church Road.

Finding out more: 028 9065 3338 or
belmonttower@nationaltrust.org.uk

Belmont Tower		M	T	W	T	F	S	S
Open all year	9–4*	**M**	**T**	**W**	**T**	**F**		·

*Saturdays and July: closes 3. Open evenings and other times
for booked classes and events. Closed 1 January, 25 to
28 March, 12 and 13 July, 25 and 26 December.

The Argory		M	T	W	T	F	S	S
Courtyard café and shop								
6 Feb–28 Feb	12–5	·	·	·	·	·	S	S
15 Feb–16 Feb	12–5	**M**	**T**	·	·	·	·	·
House, courtyard café and shop								
12 Mar–20 Mar	12–5	·	·	·	**T**	**F**	S	S
21 Mar–3 Apr	12–5	**M**	**T**	**W**	**T**	**F**	S	·S
7 Apr–29 May	12–5	·	·	·	**T**	**F**	S	S
1 Jun–30 Jun	12–5	·	·	**W**	**T**	**F**	S	S
1 Jul–31 Aug	12–5	**M**	**T**	**W**	**T**	**F**	S	S
1 Sep–30 Sep	12–5	·	·	·	**T**	**F**	S	S
1 Oct–30 Oct	12–4	·	·	·	·	·	S	S
24 Oct–28 Oct	12–4	**M**	**T**	**W**	**T**	**F**	·	·
Grounds								
Open all year	10–5	**M**	**T**	**W**	**T**	**F**	S	S

House: admission by guided tour, last tour one hour before
closing. Open Bank Holiday Mondays and all other public
holidays in Northern Ireland. Closed 1 January and 25 and
26 December.

Carrick-a-Rede

Ballintoy, County Antrim BT54 6LS

📧 ⛰ 1967

Connected to the cliffs by a rope bridge (right) across the Atlantic Ocean, this rocky island is the ultimate clifftop experience. Jutting out from the rugged North Antrim Coast Road, the 30-metre-deep and 20-metre-wide chasm separating Carrick-a-Rede from the mainland is traversed by an amazing rope bridge that was traditionally erected by salmon fishermen. If you are bold enough to make the crossing, you will be rewarded by unique geology and wildlife, and enjoy uninterrupted vistas across the seas of Moyle to Rathlin Island and far beyond to the Scottish islands. Carrick-a-Rede offers clifftop birdwatching and windswept coastal scenery. **Note**: number crossing bridge at any one time restricted. Open weather permitting. Entrance 119a Whitepark Road.

Eating and shopping: Weighbridge tea-room and gift shop offering hot food, snacks, sweets, gifts and souvenirs.

Making the most of your day: coastal path – part of the Causeway Coast Way from Portstewart to Ballycastle and the Ulster Way. Birdwatching and coastal scenery. Unique flora and fauna. Guided tours (by prior arrangement). **Dogs**: on leads (not permitted to cross bridge).

Access: 🅿 🚻 ♿ 📷 ⓟ Grounds 🚶 ♿ ➡
Parking: on site.

Finding out more: 028 2076 9839 or carrickarede@nationaltrust.org.uk

Carrick-a-Rede		M	T	W	T	F	S	S
Bridge								
1 Jan–28 Feb	9:30–3:30	M	T	W	T	F	S	S
29 Feb–20 Mar	9:30–6	M	T	W	T	F	S	S
21 Mar–3 Apr	9:30–7	M	T	W	T	F	S	S
4 Apr–29 May	9:30–6	M	T	W	T	F	S	S
30 May–4 Sep	9:30–7	M	T	W	T	F	S	S
5 Sep–30 Oct	9:30–6	M	T	W	T	F	S	S
31 Oct–31 Dec	9:30–3:30	M	T	W	T	F	S	S

Last entry to bridge 45 minutes before closing. Car park and North Antrim coastal path open all year. Bridge open weather permitting. Closed 24 to 26 December.

Castle Coole

Enniskillen, County Fermanagh BT74 6JY

🏠👥🔔🍽 1951

Glimpse what 18th-century life was like in the stately home of the Earls of Belmore through the story of the people who lived and worked here. Widely recognised as one of the finest Neo-classical houses in Ireland, Castle Coole sits grandly in wooded parklands that change with the seasons and are ideal for family walks. Showcasing the fine architectural design of James Wyatt and opulent Regency interiors, guided tours also reveal life 'below stairs' in the suite of servants' rooms and quarters. Located on the edge of Enniskillen, the estate affords sweeping views from the shores of Lough Coole.

Eating and shopping: Tallow House tea-room. Gift shop selling souvenirs and second-hand bookshop (volunteer-run).

The 18th century comes to life at Castle Coole in County Fermanagh (above and top right)

Making the most of your day: **Indoors** Events throughout the year. 'Upstairs downstairs' guided tours of the mansion. Enjoy the cosy Tallow House tea-room **Outdoors** Events, including Easter Sunday treasure hunts. Trails and walks. **Dogs**: under control.

Access: 🅿♿♿🏞📖🔍
Building 🏛🏛🏛 Grounds 🏛➡
Parking: 150 yards.

Finding out more: 028 6632 2690 or castlecoole@nationaltrust.org.uk

Castle Coole		M	T	W	T	F	S	S
Grounds								
1 Jan–29 Feb	10–4	M	T	W	T	F	S	S
1 Mar–1 Nov	10–7	M	T	W	T	F	S	S
2 Nov–31 Dec	10–4	M	T	W	T	F	S	S
House, tea-room and shop								
12 Mar–20 Mar	11–5	·	·	·	T	·	S	S
25 Mar–3 Apr	11–5	M	T	W	T	F	S	S
9 Apr–30 Apr	11–5	·	·	·	·	·	S	S
1 May–30 May	11–5	M	·	W	T	F	S	S
1 Jun–31 Aug	11–5	M	T	W	T	F	S	S
1 Sep–30 Sep	11–5	M	·	W	T	F	S	S

House: admission by guided tour, last tour one hour before closing. Open Bank Holiday Mondays and all other public holidays in Northern Ireland.

Castle Ward

Strangford, Downpatrick,
County Down BT30 7LS

🏠🏛️🗄️🌿♿️🚶🚲🛶📷🔔🍴 1953

High on a hillside, with views across the tranquil waters of Strangford Lough, the distinctly different styles of Gothic and classical collide at Castle Ward. This eccentric 18th-century mansion within a 332-hectare (820-acre) walled demesne is one of the most peculiar architectural compromises between two people. The former home of the Viscounts Bangor, guided tours reveal the history of the different façades. In the Farmyard Craft Village and gardens you can browse and stroll among handmade pottery, flowers and subtropical plants, while the extensive grounds are criss-crossed by a 21-mile network of family-friendly multi-use trails. The impressive laundry, tack room, children's Victorian play centre and adventure playground provide further opportunities to explore the demesne.
Note: 1 March to 30 November visitor access to livestock grazing areas may be restricted.

Eating and shopping: Stableyard tea-room. Gift shop selling local produce and souvenirs. Second-hand bookshop.

Making the most of your day: **Indoors** Guided house tours. **Outdoors** Network of multi-use trails. Bicycles for hire. Farmyard with animals. Victorian play centre, adventure playground. Tracker Packs and children's activities. Events, including Easter Fair, Pumpkinfest, Jazz in the Grounds and Santa's House. Iconic filming locations – Winterfell from *Game of Thrones*. Caravan park and pods available for hire.
Dogs: on leads in grounds only (livestock grazing areas out of bounds).

Access: 🅿️♿️🧎♿️🚻♿️🎧🖼️♿️👓
Building 🦽♿️🔼 Grounds 🦽♿️➡️
Sat Nav: use BT30 7BA and follow brown signs.
Parking: on site.

Eccentric Castle Ward in County Down
(above and below), is wonderfully family-friendly

Castle Ward		M	T	W	T	F	S	S
Parkland, woodland and garden								
1 Jan–28 Feb	10–4	M	T	W	T	F	S	S
29 Feb–3 Apr	10–6	M	T	W	T	F	S	S
4 Apr–11 Sep	10–8	M	T	W	T	F	S	S
12 Sep–31 Dec	10–6	M	T	W	T	F	S	S
House, laundry and pastimes centre								
5 Mar–20 Mar	12–5	·	·	·	·	·	S	S
23 Mar–3 Apr	12–5	M	T	W	T	F	S	S
6 Apr–26 Jun	12–5	·	·	W	T	F	S	S
27 Jun–4 Sep	12–5	M	T	W	T	F	S	S
7 Sep–30 Oct	12–5	·	·	W	T	F	S	S
Stableyard tea-room, shop and second-hand bookshop								
2 Jan–20 Mar	12–4	·	·	·	·	·	S	S
23 Mar–3 Apr	11–5	M	T	W	T	F	S	S
6 Apr–26 Jun	11–5	·	·	W	T	F	S	S
27 Jun–4 Sep	11–5	M	T	W	T	F	S	S
7 Sep–22 Dec	12–5	·	·	W	T	F	S	S

House: last admission one hour before closing. Timed tickets apply to guided house tours. Open Bank Holiday Mondays and all other public holidays in Northern Ireland. Tea-room, shop and second-hand bookshop: also open 15 to 19 February, 12 to 4; 9 to 11 March, 16 to 18 March and 24 to 25 October, 12 to 5. Corn mill operates Sundays, Easter to September, 2 to 5. Closed 25 and 26 December.

The Gothic Boudoir at Castle Ward (below), and tranquil Crom in County Fermanagh (above right)

Crom

Upper Lough Erne, Newtownbutler, County Fermanagh BT92 8AJ

[icons] 1987

Home to islands, ancient woodland and historical ruins, this 810-hectare (2,000-acre) demesne sits in a tranquil landscape on the peaceful southern shores of Upper Lough Erne. One of Ireland's most important conservation areas, it has many rare species and is great for relaxing walks, cycling and boat trips. **Note**: 19th-century castle not open to public.

Eating and shopping: afternoon tea, gifts and souvenirs available in visitor centre. Convenience goods and outdoor clothing also for sale.

Making the most of your day: historic castle ruins. Cot trips (Bank Holiday Mondays). Holiday cottages, campsite and glamping pods. Boat hire. **Dogs**: under control.

Access: [icons] Building [icons] Grounds [icons] Parking: 100 yards.

Finding out more: 028 6773 8118 or crom@nationaltrust.org.uk

Crom		M	T	W	T	F	S	S
Grounds								
12 Mar–31 May	10–6	M	T	W	T	F	S	S
1 Jun–31 Aug	10–7	M	T	W	T	F	S	S
1 Sep–1 Nov	10–6	M	T	W	T	F	S	S
Visitor centre								
12 Mar–30 Sep	11–5	M	T	W	T	F	S	S
1 Oct–30 Oct	11–5	·	·	·	·	·	S	S

Open Bank Holiday Mondays and all other public holidays in Northern Ireland. Last admission one hour before closing. Tea-room open as visitor centre (closed October).

The Crown Bar

46 Great Victoria Street, Belfast,
County Antrim BT2 7BA

[icons] 1978

Belfast's most famous pub remains one of the finest examples of a high-Victorian gin palace complete with period features. **Note**: run by Mitchells & Butlers. Open Monday to Saturday, 11:30 to 11; Sunday, 12:30 to 10 (telephone to check public and Bank Holiday openings).

Finding out more: 028 9024 3187 or info@crownbar.com

Cushendun

County Antrim

[icons] 1954

Nestled at the mouth of the River Dun (Brown River) at the foot of Glendun, Cushendun is a very charming historic village steeped in character and folklore. The surrounding hills are a patchwork of farms, small fields, hedgerows and traditional stone walls. Sheltered harbour and beautiful beach. Views of Scotland.

Pretty little Cushendun, County Antrim (above and below)

Eating and shopping: Corner House tea-room in the village offers great coffee, delicious home-baked scones, sweet treats and a tasty hot food menu using fresh local produce. Pub and restaurant facilities also available in the village.

Making the most of your day: discover the local wildlife on a circular walking trail. Explore the grounds of historic Glenmona House. River fishing, sea angling, boating, horse-riding and golfing facilities nearby.

Access: [icon]
Sat Nav: use BT44 0PH. **Parking**: car park adjacent to Corner House tea-room and at Glenmona House.

Finding out more: 028 2176 1560 (Corner House tea-rooom). 028 2073 3320 (North Coast Office) or cushendun@nationaltrust.org.uk

Derrymore House

Bessbrook, Newry, County Armagh BT35 7EF

[icons] 1953

Resting peacefully in a landscape demesne, this 18th-century thatched cottage is rich in history and a great place for walks. **Note**: sorry no toilet. Grounds open all year. Treaty Room open 2 and 30 May, 12 and 13 July, 29 August, 2 to 5:30.

Finding out more: 028 8778 4753 or derrymore@nationaltrust.org.uk

Divis and the Black Mountain

Hannahstown, near Belfast, County Antrim

🏛🚻♿ 2004

Sitting in the heart of the Belfast Hills, this 809-hectare (2,000-acre) mosaic of upland heath (below) and blanket bog is a great place for a wild countryside experience. There are four walking trails to explore, affording panoramic views across Belfast and a wealth of flora, fauna and archaeological remains to discover. **Note**: cattle roam freely during summer months. Mountain environment and weather conditions can change rapidly.

Eating and shopping: tea, coffee and light refreshments available in The Barn (seasonal opening).

Making the most of your day: guided walks on biodiversity and archaeology. **Dogs**: welcome, but please note cattle roam freely during summer.

Access: 🅿♿🅿♿🚻 Visitor centre 🅿 Mountain 🅿 **Sat Nav**: use BT17 0NG. **Parking**: on Divis Road, opposite Divis Mountain gates.

Finding out more: 028 9082 5434 or divis@nationaltrust.org.uk

Downhill Demesne and Hezlett House

Mussenden Road, Castlerock, County Londonderry BT51 4RP

🏠🏛🚻♿♿🚗🔔🍴 1949

Mussenden Temple, Downhill Demesne, County Londonderry

The sheltered gardens, cliff-edge landmark and striking ruins of a grand headland mansion bear testament to the eccentricity of the Earl Bishop who once made this 18th-century demesne his home. Mussenden Temple, perched atop sheer cliffs, offers panoramic views of the famous Antrim coastline and is a great place for walking and kite-flying. Nearby at Hezlett House, life in a rural 17th-century cottage is told through the people who once lived there. One of the oldest thatched cottages left standing in Northern Ireland, it boasts a rare cruck frame and houses the Downhill Marble Collection.

The atmospheric ruins of Downhill House (top), and looking down on a perfect beach at Downhill Demesne

Eating and shopping: tea and coffee facilities at Hezlett House. Picnics welcome in gardens.

Making the most of your day: Indoors Christmas at Hezlett House. Guided tours on request (booking essential). **Outdoors** Numerous events throughout year, including Easter Egg hunts and Kite Festival. Brand new outdoor Bishop's Play Trail. **Dogs**: on leads only.

Access: [icons] **Building** [icon] **Grounds** [icon]
Parking: at Lion's Gate.

Finding out more: 028 7084 8728 or downhilldemesne@nationaltrust.org.uk Hezlett House, 107 Sea Road, Castlerock, County Londonderry BT51 4TW

Downhill and Hezlett		M	T	W	T	F	S	S
Downhill Demesne grounds								
Open all year	Dawn–dusk	M	T	W	T	F	S	S
Hezlett House and facilities								
12 Mar–4 Sep	10–5	M	T	W	T	F	S	S
10 Sep–25 Sep	10–5	·	·	·	·	·	S	S

Open Bank Holiday Mondays and all other public holidays in Northern Ireland. Hezlett House and facilities closed 24, 25 and 26 December.

Florence Court

Enniskillen, County Fermanagh BT92 1DB

[icons] 1954

Surrounded by lush parkland and thick woodland with Benaughlin mountain rising in the background, Florence Court enjoys a majestic countryside setting in West Fermanagh. There is something for everyone to enjoy at this extensive and welcoming place. On a guided tour of the Georgian mansion you can hear stories about the Cole family and their staff, who lived here for over 250 years. Outdoors take a gentle walk or long cycle along 10 miles of trails in the adjoining forest park and see fascinating industrial heritage features, including the water-powered sawmill and blacksmith's forge. The gardens are home to the mother of all Irish yew trees, as well as the kitchen garden which is being restored to its 1930s character.

Eating and shopping: Stables tea-room. Coach House gift shop.

Making the most of your day: events throughout year. Children's Tracker Packs. **Dogs**: on leads in garden and grounds only.

Access: [icons]
Building [icons] **Grounds** [icons]
Parking: 500 yards.

Florence Court, County Fermanagh: the Georgian mansion (opposite top), and discovering the grounds and gardens (below and opposite bottom)

Finding out more: 028 6634 8249 or
florencecourt@nationaltrust.org.uk

Florence Court		M	T	W	T	F	S	S
Gardens and park								
1 Jan–29 Feb	10–4	M	T	W	T	F	S	S
1 Mar–1 Nov	10–7	M	T	W	T	F	S	S
2 Nov–31 Dec	10–4	M	T	W	T	F	S	S
House, tea-room and shop								
12 Mar–20 Mar	11–5	·	·	·	T	·	S	S
25 Mar–3 Apr	11–5	M	T	W	T	F	S	S
9 Apr–30 Apr	11–5	·	·	·	·	·	S	S
1 May–31 May	11–5	M	T	W	T	·	S	S
1 Jun–31 Aug	11–5	M	T	W	T	F	S	S
1 Sep–29 Sep	11–5	M	T	W	T	·	S	S
1 Oct–30 Oct	11–5	·	·	·	·	·	S	S

House: admission by guided tour, last tour one hour before
closing. Open Bank Holiday Mondays and all other public
holidays in Northern Ireland. Open Irish Bank Holiday,
31 October. Grounds closed 25 December.

Giant's Causeway

44 Causeway Road, Bushmills,
County Antrim BT57 8SU

Follow in the legendary footsteps of giants at Northern Ireland's iconic World Heritage Site. The famous basalt columns of the Causeway landscape, left by volcanic eruptions 60 million years ago, are home to more than Finn McCool. Its nooks and crannies are dotted with dainty sea campion, and defensive fulmars protect their cliff nests. Windswept walking trails wind through this Area of Outstanding Natural Beauty, with an all-accessible walk at Runkerry Head and more challenging terrain along the Causeway Coast Way. The interactive exhibition and innovative audio-guides unlock the secrets of the landscape and regale visitors with legends of giants.

Eating and shopping: light lunches and snacks available in Visitor Centre. Lunch and evening meals in the Causeway Hotel. Gift shop.

Making the most of your day: **Indoors** Interactive exhibition brings the stories of the Causeway to life. **Outdoors** Audio-guides (nine languages) reveal the landscape's secrets. Walking trails for all abilities. Guided tours. Family fun events. **Dogs**: on leads only.

Access:
Visitor Centre **Causeway Hotel**
Grounds
Parking: on site and park and ride in Bushmills village.

Finding out more: 028 2073 1855 or giantscauseway@nationaltrust.org.uk

Giant's Causeway		M	T	W	T	F	S	S
Stones and coastal path								
Open all year	Dawn–dusk	M	T	W	T	F	S	S
Visitor Centre								
1 Jan–29 Feb	9–5	M	T	W	T	F	S	S
1 Mar–31 Mar	9–6	M	T	W	T	F	S	S
1 Apr–30 Sep	9–7	M	T	W	T	F	S	S
1 Oct–31 Oct	9–6	M	T	W	T	F	S	S
1 Nov–31 Dec	9–5	M	T	W	T	F	S	S

Last admission to Visitor Centre one hour before closing. Closed 24 to 26 December.

There are about 40,000 astonishing black basalt columns at Giant's Causeway in County Antrim (above and below)

Gray's Printing Press

49 Main Street, Strabane,
County Tyrone BT82 8AU

🏠 1966

The indelible story of printing is told behind
this Georgian shop front in Strabane, once
reputed as Ireland's printing capital.
Note: open 26 March, 11 June, 2 July,
10 September and 29 October, 12 to 3
(times subject to change).

Finding out more: 028 7084 8728 or
grays@nationaltrust.org.uk

Islandmagee

near Larne, County Antrim

🏛 🏠 💧 ⚓ 🚶 1996

Once the site of smuggling and home to an
ancient monastery, Islandmagee peninsula's
coastline is steeped in history. An Area of
Special Scientific Interest, it has some of
Northern Ireland's largest colonies of cliff-
nesting seabirds and offers views of the
famous Antrim coast. **Note**: paths uneven
and steep in places.

Islandmagee, County Antrim: steeped in history

Eating and shopping: Earl's café in Mullaghboy
village serving food, tea and coffee and The
Rinkha in Ballystrudder village offering
famous ice-cream (neither National Trust).
Picnics welcome.

Making the most of your day: coastal walks
and yearly guided walk at Portmuck.
Dogs: on leads only.

Access: Portmuck and Skernaghan ♿
Sat Nav: use BT40 3TP. **Parking**: at Portmuck
and Skernaghan Point (not National Trust).

Finding out more: 028 9064 7787 or
islandmagee@nationaltrust.org.uk

Lisnabreeny

near Belfast, County Down

🏠 🏛 💧 ❄ ⚓ 1938

The path through this easily overlooked haven
(above) on the edge of Belfast climbs along a
tumbling stream through a wooded glen and
across rolling farmland to emerge at a hilltop
rath at the summit of the Castlereagh Hills.
This picturesque setting affords sweeping views
across the city and beyond. **Note**: sorry no
toilet. Uneven paths and steep steps.

Making the most of your day: viewpoint and
Second World War memorial commemorating
US servicemen who died in Northern Ireland.
Walks through glen, woodlands and ancient rath.
Yearly guided walk. **Dogs**: welcome on leads.

Access: Glen ♿
Sat Nav: use BT8 6SA. **Parking**: on Lisnabreeny
Road (no parking on Manse Road).

Finding out more: 028 9064 7787 or
lisnabreeny@nationaltrust.org.uk

Having fun on the water at Minnowburn, County Down

Mount Stewart

Portaferry Road, Newtownards,
County Down BT22 2AD

🏠 ✳️ ⚱️ 🍵 1976

Voted one of the world's top ten gardens, Mount Stewart reflects a rich tapestry of design and planting artistry bearing the hallmark of its creator. Edith, Lady Londonderry's passion for bold planting schemes, coupled with the mild climate of Strangford Lough, means rare and tender plants from across the globe thrive in this celebrated garden, with the formal gardens exuding a distinct character and appeal. Explore the exquisite house, recently restored to glory. Experience a changing offer that is filled with fascinating stories about the Londonderry family, a world-class collection of paintings and many other internationally significant items. Discover a family home where art, history, politics and gardening go hand in hand.

Eating and shopping: locally sourced gifts sold in our shop. Garden shop selling a range of gardening items and plants specially propagated from our world-class garden. Tea-room with a range of homemade food and many products made from local produce.

Minnowburn

near Belfast, County Down

🏛️ 🚴 ✳️ 💪 🚶 ⚱️ 1952

Just a few miles from Belfast city centre yet in the heart of the country, this 52-hectare (128-acre) naturally mixed countryside is a paradox all of its own. Nestled in the heart of the Lagan Valley Regional Park, it has riverside, meadow and woodland walks and is rich in wildlife. **Note**: sorry no toilet. Trails are uneven and steep in places.

Eating and shopping: Piccolo Mondo van (not National Trust) serves food, tea and coffee in car park at weekends. Lock Keeper's Inn (not National Trust) serving food, tea and coffee, ¾ mile along riverside path. Picnic tables in Terrace Hill garden.

Making the most of your day: guided walks, including heritage, history and woodlands. Waymarked walks, including the Giant's Ring Trail. Sculpture trail. Riverside and pond walks. Terrace Hill Garden. **Dogs**: on leads only.

Access: 🦽
Sat Nav: use BT8 8LD. **Parking**: on site.

Finding out more: 028 9064 7787 or minnowburn@nationaltrust.org.uk

Mount Stewart, County Down:
the breathtaking Central Hall

Dogs: welcome on short leads in all areas.

Access: ⬚⬚⬚⬚⬚⬚⬚⬚
Building ⬚⬚⬚ Grounds ⬚⬚➡⬚⬚
Parking: 200 yards.

Finding out more: 028 4278 8387 or
mountstewart@nationaltrust.org.uk

Mount Stewart		M	T	W	T	F	S	S
Formal and lakeside gardens, tea-room and shop								
1 Jan–4 Mar	10–4*	M	T	W	T	F	S	S
5 Mar–30 Oct	10–5	M	T	W	T	F	S	S
31 Oct–31 Dec	10–4*	M	T	W	T	F	S	S
House								
2 Jan–13 Mar	11–3	·	·	·	·	·	S	S
14 Mar–30 Oct	11–5	M	T	W	T	F	S	S
5 Nov–31 Dec	11–3	·	·	·	·	·	S	S
Temple of the Winds								
6 Mar–30 Oct	2–5	·	·	·	·	·	·	S

*Tea-room and shop: close at 5 weekends, Bank Holidays
and public holidays. House: admission by free-flow
(guided tours on selected days); October open times
may change (check website for details). Open Bank Holiday
Mondays and all other public holidays in Northern Ireland.
House, formal and lakeside gardens, tea-room and
shop closed 25 and 26 December.

Making the most of your day: **Indoors** You can
explore the recently restored family home and
discover a wealth of new treasures. Seasonal
events and continuing conservation in action.
Outdoors Why not stroll around the walled
garden, discover interesting new walks and join
a garden tour? Don't miss the lakeside walk,
where the colours and smells vary from season
to season. In the formal gardens look out for
the creation of a 14-foot-high Irish yew topiary
statue depicting a Fomorian – a half-human,
half-demon associated with Strangford Lough.

**The celebrated and artistic garden at
Mount Stewart (above and below), has been
voted one of the top ten in the world**

The Mournes

near Newcastle, County Down

🏛🏊🚶 1992

These famous wildlife-rich mountains (below) are criss-crossed by well-marked coastal and mountain paths. Great for exploring, the National Trust-maintained paths stretch from the shore into the heart of the Mournes, offering views over Dundrum Bay, stretching to the Isle of Man on a clear day.

Eating and shopping: picnics welcome. Nearest shops, restaurants and cafés in Newcastle (none National Trust).

Making the most of your day: outstanding views from Bloody Bridge. Coastal path to St Mary's Chapel ruins. Birdwatching. **Dogs**: welcome under control.

Access: 🦽
Sat Nav: use BT33 0EU for Slieve Donard and BT33 0LA for Bloody Bridge. **Parking**: for Slieve Donard, park in Newcastle; for Bloody Bridge, park on A2.

Finding out more: 028 4375 1467 or mournes@nationaltrust.org.uk

Murlough National Nature Reserve

near Dundrum, County Down

🏛🏊🚶🐾 1967

Home to seals, Neolithic sites and Ireland's first nature reserve, Murlough (above) is one of the most extensive examples of dune landscape in Ireland. A network of paths and boardwalks through these ancient dunes, woodland and heath makes it ideal for relaxed walks and spotting a wonderland of wildlife. **Note**: limited toilet facilities.

Eating and shopping: beach café (seasonal opening, not National Trust). Picnics welcome on beach or in car park.

Making the most of your day: self-guided nature walk and series of guided walks. Volunteer events and family activities throughout year. **Dogs**: welcome on leads, restrictions apply when ground-nesting birds breeding or cattle grazing.

Access: 🅿 Grounds 🦽
Sat Nav: use BT33 0NQ. **Parking**: on site.

Finding out more: 028 4375 1467 or murlough@nationaltrust.org.uk

Murlough		M	T	W	T	F	S	S
Nature reserve								
Open all year		M	T	W	T	F	S	S
Facilities								
12 Mar–20 Mar	10–6						S	S
25 Mar–3 Apr	10–6	M	T	W	T	F	S	S
9 Apr–29 May	10–6						S	S
30 May–4 Sep	10–6	M	T	W	T	F	S	S
10 Sep–2 Oct	10–6						S	S

Open Bank Holiday Mondays and all other public holidays in Northern Ireland.

Why not share your pictures with us? #nationaltrust

Patterson's Spade Mill

751 Antrim Road, Templepatrick,
County Antrim BT39 0AP

🏠🏛♿🔔☕ 1991

Travel back in time and witness history literally
forged in steel at the last working water-driven
spade mill in daily use in the British Isles. Dig
up the history and culture of the humble spade
and visit bygone life fashioning steel into
spades during the industrial era.

Eating and shopping: handcrafted spades on
sale and made to specification. Tea and coffee
available from drinks machine.

Making the most of your day: guided tours
and demonstrations for all the family.
Dogs: on leads only.

Access: 🅿🅳♿🚼 Building ♿🅱 Grounds ♿
Parking: 50 yards.

Finding out more: 028 9443 3619 or
pattersons@nationaltrust.org.uk

Patterson's Spade Mill		M	T	W	T	F	S	S
25 Mar–3 Apr	12–4	M	T	W	T	F	S	S
9 Apr–29 May	12–4	.	.	.	.	.	S	S
30 May–28 Aug	12–4	M	T	W	.	.	S	S
3 Sep–25 Sep	12–4	.	.	.	.	.	S	S

Admission by guided tour, last tour one hour before closing.
Open Bank Holiday Mondays and all other public holidays in
Northern Ireland from 25 March to 25 September.

The forge at Patterson's Spade Mill in County Antrim

The dunes at Portstewart Strand, County Londonderry

Portstewart Strand

Portstewart, County Londonderry

🏛♿📏🔔☕ 1981

Sweeping along the edge of the north coast,
this 2-mile stretch of golden sand is one of
Northern Ireland's finest beaches and affords
uninterrupted views of the coastline. It's an
ideal place for lazy picnics, surfing and long
walks into the wildlife-rich sand dunes.

Eating and shopping: award-winning Harry's
Shack with great new catering offer. Mobile
beach retail and information service.

Making the most of your day: waymarked
nature trail. Barmouth Estuary bird hide. Events
during peak season. **Dogs**: on leads only.

Access: 🅿♿♿♿ Café ♿ Beach ♿▶
Sat Nav: use BT55 7PG. **Parking**: on beach.

Finding out more: 028 7083 6396 or
portstewart@nationaltrust.org.uk

Portstewart Strand		M	T	W	T	F	S	S
Beach								
Open all year	Dawn–dusk	M	T	W	T	F	S	S
Facilities								
14 Mar–1 May	10–7	M	T	W	T	F	S	S
2 May–28 Aug	10–8	M	T	W	T	F	S	S
29 Aug–11 Sep	10–6	M	T	W	T	F	S	S

Barrier to beach closes one hour after facilities close.
Open Bank Holiday Mondays and all other public holidays in
Northern Ireland. Facilities: may open at other times or close
earlier (weather dependent); closed 24 to 26 December.

Rowallane Garden

Saintfield, County Down BT24 7LH

[✤][♠][T][1956]

Carved into the County Down drumlin landscape since the mid-1860s, this inspirational 21-hectare (52-acre) garden is 'a world apart'. The passion and shared vision of the Reverend John Moore, and later his nephew Hugh Armytage Moore, created a garden where you can leave the outside world behind and immerse yourself in nature's beauty. The formal and informal garden spaces are home to magical features mingled with native and exotic plants, such as drifts of rare rhododendrons. It is a great place for a leisurely walk or just to relax on a seat and soak up the atmosphere.

Eating and shopping: garden café with views across the gardens. Café shop selling Rowallane Garden soap, honey and pottery, alongside other gift items. Second-hand bookshop. Pottery providing unique Rowallane Garden items and garden pots.

Two views of inspirational Rowallane Garden in County Down: 'a world apart'

Making the most of your day: events, including spring and autumn plant fair, Ghosts and Gourds and Yuletide market. Children's activity sheets. **Dogs**: on leads in garden only.

Access: [P♿][♿wc][♿!!][♨] Grounds [♿][♿]
Parking: on site.

Finding out more: 028 9751 0131 or rowallane@nationaltrust.org.uk

Rowallane Garden		M	T	W	T	F	S	S
Garden								
1 Jan–29 Feb	10–4	M	T	W	T	F	S	S
1 Mar–30 Apr	10–6	M	T	W	T	F	S	S
1 May–31 Aug	10–8	M	T	W	T	F	S	S
1 Sep–31 Oct	10–6	M	T	W	T	F	S	S
1 Nov–31 Dec	10–4	M	T	W	T	F	S	S
Café								
2 Jan–28 Feb	11–3:30	·	·	·	·	·	S	S
3 Mar–27 Mar	11–4	·	·	·	T	F	S	S
28 Mar–3 Apr	11–4	M	T	W	T	F	S	S
6 Apr–30 Apr	11–4	·	·	W	T	F	S	S
1 May–30 Aug	11–5	M	T	W	T	F	S	S
31 Aug–23 Oct	11–4	·	·	W	T	F	S	S
24 Oct–30 Oct	11–4	M	T	W	T	F	S	S
5 Nov–31 Dec	11–3:30	·	·	·	·	·	S	S

Open Bank Holiday Mondays and all other public holidays in Northern Ireland. Closed 25 and 26 December.

Springhill

20 Springhill Road, Moneymore, Magherafelt,
County Londonderry BT45 7NQ

🏠✣♨🔺🔺🍷 1957

Hundreds of years ago the Lenox-Conyngham family chose this bucolic spot to build their home and, after ten generations, this 17th-century plantation house is still regarded as 'one of the prettiest houses in Ulster'. The welcoming family home they created is brought to life on enlightening guided tours of its portraits, furniture and decorative arts. The old laundry houses Springhill's celebrated costume collection of 18th- to 20th-century pieces that capture its enthralling past. There is a visitor centre, a natural play trail and short walks around the estate that are perfect for a leisurely stroll.

Eating and shopping: takeaway drinks, snacks and ice-cream available from the visitor centre. Tea-room serving homemade scones and cakes. Retail area with a range of items for the home and garden. Bookshop with second-hand books for all tastes and interests.

Making the most of your day: **Indoors** Guided tours. Costume exhibition. **Outdoors** Walks and children's natural play trail. Events, including Easter Egg fun and country fairs. **Dogs**: on leads in grounds only.

The tower at Springhill, County Londonderry (above), and the house (below): a welcoming family home

Access: 🅿♿🚽📷📖🎵∴ Building ♿♿
Parking: 50 yards.

Finding out more: 028 8674 8210 or springhill@nationaltrust.org.uk

Springhill		M	T	W	T	F	S	S
Visitor centre								
6 Feb–28 Feb	12–5						S	S
15 Feb–16 Feb	12–5	M	T					
Visitor centre, house and costume collection								
12 Mar–20 Mar	12–5						S	S
21 Mar–3 Apr	12–5	M	T	W	T	F	S	S
9 Apr–30 Apr	12–5						S	S
1 May–29 May	12–5					F	S	S
2 Jun–30 Jun	12–5				T	F	S	S
1 Jul–31 Aug	12–5	M	T	W	T	F	S	S
3 Sep–25 Sep	12–5						S	S
2 Oct–30 Oct	12–4							S
24 Oct–28 Oct	12–4	M	T	W	T	F		
Grounds								
Open all year	10–5	M	T	W	T	F	S	S

House: admission by guided tour, last tour one hour before closing. Open Bank Holiday Mondays and all other public holidays in Northern Ireland. Closed 1 January; 25 and 26 December. Visitor centre has refreshment area and shop. Servants' Hall tea-room also open at weekends when visitor centre is open.

Strangford Lough

County Down

🏛️ ♿ 🏞️ 🚶 1969

The tidal treasures of Britain's largest sea lough and one of Europe's key wildlife habitats await discovery. This delicately balanced landscape is rich in natural and built heritage. Northern Ireland's first Marine Conservation Zone and the winter home for up to 90 per cent of the world's light-bellied brent geese.

Eating and shopping: nearest tea-room and shop at Mount Stewart and Castle Ward. Also numerous restaurants serving dishes made from local produce, including meat produced on the surrounding land and seafood from the lough, and arts and crafts shops (none National Trust).

Making the most of your day: birdwatching (some of the best in UK), rock-pooling and geocaching. Red squirrels and seals to spot. Canoe and cycle trail.

Access: 🦽
Sat Nav: use BT22 1RG. **Parking**: small car park at Ballyquintin or parking around Lough (not all National Trust).

Finding out more: 028 4278 7769 or strangford@nationaltrust.org.uk

Strangford Lough, County Down (above and below): Britain's largest sea lough and one of Europe's key wildlife habitats

Wellbrook Beetling Mill

20 Wellbrook Road, Corkhill, Cookstown, County Tyrone BT80 9RY

🖼️🛈 1968

You can step back in time and discover how yarn was spun at Northern Ireland's last working water-powered linen beetling mill (above). Hands-on demonstrations reveal the importance of the linen industry in 19th-century Ireland. The glen is ideal for relaxing walks and perfect for a picnic by the Ballinderry River.

Eating and shopping: small cottage shop. Picnic tables near river.

Making the most of your day: **Indoors** Tours of the mill, covering history and linen-making processes. **Outdoors** Walks up to the head-race. **Dogs**: on leads in grounds only.

Access: 🅿️🚻♿🖼️ Building ♿🪜 Grounds ♿🪜
Parking: 10 yards.

Finding out more: 028 8675 1735 or wellbrook@nationaltrust.org.uk

Wellbrook Beetling Mill		M	T	W	T	F	S	S
12 Mar–25 Sep	2–5						S	S

Admission by guided tour. Last entry one hour before closing. Open Bank Holiday Mondays and all other public holidays in Northern Ireland. Closed 1 January, 25 and 26 December.

White Park Bay

near Ballintoy, County Antrim

🖼️🏖️🐾 1939

Embraced by ancient dunes, Neolithic settlements and passage tombs, this arc of white sand nestles between two headlands on the North Antrim coast. Home to a range of rich habitats for a myriad of wildlife, its secluded location makes it ideal for quiet relaxation and peaceful walks.

Eating and shopping: shops, restaurants and cafés in nearby towns (not National Trust). Picnics welcome.

Making the most of your day: part of the Causeway Coast Way and the Ulster Way.

Access: 🅿️
Sat Nav: use BT54 6NH. **Parking**: on site.

Finding out more: 028 2073 3320 or whiteparkbay@nationaltrust.org.uk

White Park Bay, County Antrim, is an arc of white sand

National Trust Holidays

We're all about helping people get closer to special places. Stay at a cosy cottage on a coastal path, a campsite where you sleep under the stars, or look after the great outdoors on a working holiday. Whatever you're into, here's your chance to get even closer to the places we care for. And you'll be helping look after them too.

Find out more about our cottages, bunkhouses, campsites and working holidays.

nationaltrustholidays.org.uk

Themed index

Activities

Adventure playgrounds/ play areas

nationaltrust.org.uk

Film and television

Industrial heritage

Quick stop

Easily accessible from major roads, the following are perfect places to break your journey.

Alphabetical index